THE ONE YEAR®
DEVOS *for* TEEN GIRLS

THE ONE YEAR®
DEVOS *for* TEEN GIRLS

DANNAH GRESH *and* SUZY WEIBEL

Tyndale House Publishers, Inc.
Carol Stream, Illinois

Visit Tyndale online at www.tyndale.com.

TYNDALE, Tyndale's quill logo, *The One Year,* and *One Year* are registered trademarks of Tyndale House Publishers, Inc. The One Year logo is a trademark of Tyndale House Publishers, Inc.

The One Year Devos for Teen Girls

Copyright © 2013 by Dannah Gresh. All rights reserved.

Cover photo copyright © Michael Flippo/iStockphoto. All rights reserved.

Interior footprints copyright © Leontura/iStockphoto. All rights reserved.

Designed by Jacqueline L. Nuñez

Published in association with literary agent Mike Keil, 3040 Americus Dr., Thompson's Station, TN 37179.

Unless otherwise indicated, all Scripture quotations are taken from the *Holy Bible*, New Living Translation, copyright © 1996, 2004, 2007 by Tyndale House Foundation. Used by permission of Tyndale House Publishers, Inc., Carol Stream, Illinois 60188. All rights reserved.

Scripture quotations marked NIV are taken from the Holy Bible, *New International Version,*® NIV.® Copyright © 1973, 1978, 1984, 2011 by Biblica, Inc.™ Used by permission of Zondervan. All rights reserved worldwide. www.zondervan.com. (Some quotations may be from the previous edition of the NIV, copyright © 1984.)

Scripture quotations marked ESV are taken from *The Holy Bible*, English Standard Version® (ESV®), copyright © 2001 by Crossway, a publishing ministry of Good News Publishers. Used by permission. All rights reserved.

Scripture quotations marked *The Message* are taken from *The Message* by Eugene H. Peterson, copyright © 1993, 1994, 1995, 1996, 2000, 2001, 2002. Used by permission of NavPress Publishing Group. All rights reserved.

Scripture quotations marked NASB are taken from the New American Standard Bible,® copyright © 1960, 1962, 1963, 1968, 1971, 1972, 1973, 1975, 1977, 1995 by The Lockman Foundation. Used by permission.

ISBN 978-1-4143-7159-7

Printed in the United States of America

20   19   18   17   16   15
 8   7   6   5   4   3

Introduction

Well, girls, here we go! It's going to take you a full year to do these devotions, and it's taken us about a full year to put them together for you. That's an even exchange!

We set out to tackle your top concerns. The first thing we did, as a matter of fact, was send out an e-mail to one hundred college girls we know personally and ask them this question: *When you were in high school, what were the top ten topics you wish someone had challenged you with?* The girls were a great help to us, and we salute them!

This devotional is not set up chronologically. In other words, you can begin your journey any day of the year. To get the most out of it, we recommend you do a couple of things. First, be diligent and purposeful. Keep at it for the full year, setting aside a specific time each day to tackle your devotional—the earlier in the day, the better. Second, be sure to work on each day's action step. These will put muscle behind what your mind encounters. James 1:22 says we must not merely listen to what God's Word says. That would be like reading each day's devotion and leaving it at that. We must also do what the Word says, and that is the purpose of these action steps. If you complete them, you are fulfilling James's command that we are not only hearers of the Word, but doers as well.

Each month tackles a different issue you come face-to-face with as a follower of Christ. Every week or so we'll switch angles and get a fresh view of the topic we are tackling. Are you ready to be stretched? If you're not exhausted and exhilarated at the end of this year, then we haven't done our job. But the race is up to you. Persevere. Stick with it. It will be an uphill battle at times, and you will grow weary . . . but run in such a way as to win this race!

On your mark. (The crowd roars.) Get set. (A hush falls.) Go!

We're running this one with you,

Dannah and Suzy

What Does God Want from Me This Year?

O people, the LORD has told you what is good, and this is what he requires of you: to do what is right, to love mercy, and to walk humbly with your God. MICAH 6:8

It's a brand-new year.

Clean slate.

Let's see if we can start the year by figuring out what God wants.

Are you supposed to date that boy? Get a job? Go on that missions trip this summer? Think of something you really want to do, and let's filter it through the Word of God.

The good news is that God keeps things pretty simple for us. We tend to complicate things as human beings, thinking we need to know exactly what God wants us to do.

God is our Father. He loves us, so he keeps it simple. What does he want from us? It's right there in the Bible verse at the top of the page. Choose what you will, but follow these three precepts from Micah 6. If anything you want to choose violates even one of those three commands, then you are outside of God's will. Simple.

1. *"Do what is right."* Do only what is good for everyone. We are not to harm others, be it emotionally, physically, or even while joking. So whatever you might choose, be certain that no one is harmed.
2. *"Love mercy."* Since you have been forgiven a great deal, you should show the same measure of forgiveness to others. That's what mercy is: showing compassion or kindness even when the other person doesn't deserve it.
3. *"Walk humbly with your God."* This means we understand God's plan is better than ours. He is God, and we are not, so he gets the final say in all matters. Dating a nonbeliever? Not debatable. Dressing immodestly? Not an option. Being part of a church? It's essential—no ifs, ands, or buts. To not follow God's precepts is to vainly challenge his lordship.

So, that question you had about what to do. What's the answer?

 Use Micah 6:8 to make all your decisions this year. Memorize the verse, and invite God to bring it to your mind often.

JANUARY 2
Notice Someone

Pure and genuine religion in the sight of God the Father means caring for orphans and widows in their distress and refusing to let the world corrupt you. JAMES 1:27

Today, I (Dannah) noticed someone.

She was a sweet older lady sitting on a park bench, and for some reason God drew me to her like a magnet. I didn't know why, but I was supposed to make a beeline for her.

I did.

After awkwardly talking about our nails, I told her I thought God wanted me to encourage her with hope. She began to weep. She was, in fact, a believer in Jesus but was really discouraged. She had just been asking him if he saw her.

He did. And I got to tell her so.

How often do I walk by people in need and ignore them? How often do you?

Our verse for today is God's simple instructions. He tells us what true religion looks like (the word the writer James uses for *religion* refers to the outward practice of religion observable to others—how we act). Again God keeps things simple for us. Through James, God is saying, "I want you to take care of the downtrodden, and I want you to avoid the pitfalls of this world. That's what it looks like to love me and to follow me." It's no easy thing to meet the needs of other people. People have a lot of needs! Would we even have any time for a job or sports or to get our homework done if we were constantly dropping everything for someone in need? Probably not. But we can keep our eyes and hearts open to find the person (or people) God wants each of us specifically to help. God has a way of showing us when we ask him to!

The other way we show God we love him is by avoiding the corruption of this world . . . and that's not easy either. Cheating, lying, tricking our teachers or parents or friends, stealing, violating any law, escaping our responsibilities. . . . The list of how this world's corruption can be tempting goes on and on. But the bottom line is that we're called to avoid those pitfalls. It's simple, but not easy. That's how God rolls. And that's why we need to stay close to God to receive the help we need to show genuine religion.

 **STEP** Take the first step: notice someone in need.

BIG ACTION STEP: Do something about it.
DG

JANUARY 3
Meet with Me

Before daybreak the next morning, Jesus got up and went out to an isolated place to pray. Later Simon and the others went out to find him. When they found him, they said, "Everyone is looking for you."
MARK 1:35-37

God wants to hang out with you. Seriously. Just like you can't wait to hang out with your friends? God wants to hang out with you.

One of my favorite books is *My Heart—Christ's Home* by Robert Boyd Munger. The lead character (meant to be "everyman"—you and me) invites Jesus into his heart and asks him to make a home for himself there. Jesus asks for a tour of the man's home and heart, but the man suddenly wants to clean up before Jesus can sneak a peek. In his home, the man has embarrassing magazines, food that tastes like greed and selfishness, an unused workshop, and things rotting in the closet.

But the living room is cozy and inviting, and Jesus immediately expresses a liking for the space. He offers an invitation—every morning he will be waiting for the man in an overstuffed chair by the fireplace. This chance to meet one-on-one with Jesus every day is thrilling—and for a time the two meet daily. But slowly the pressures of the man's schedule begin to crowd out the time he has available to meet with his houseguest. One day while rushing out the door, the man catches sight of Jesus sitting quietly by the fireplace. Sheepishly the man enters the room and apologizes, realizing Jesus has not missed even a single day waiting for him. And then Jesus utters a profound line: "You have forgotten that this hour means something to me also."

Have you, like I sometimes do, begun to believe you are the only one who benefits from meeting with God? We get so "busy" with life that we don't even realize that God is missing that time with us like we are missing that time with him.

Here's the fix. Jesus prayed *early*, according to today's verse. The early morning is the ideal time to meet with God—before phones ring, friends text, or bacon starts sizzling. Go peek in that living room right now. I know you'll find him waiting. Every morning. He is there.

 **Action STEP** Make it a goal to get up earlier to do these devos and read the Scriptures included . . . all year long.

Help Someone

Even the Son of Man came not to be served but to serve others and to give his life as a ransom for many. MATTHEW 20:28

> *"Everybody can be great . . . because anybody can serve. . . . You only need a heart full of grace. A soul generated by love."*
> MARTIN LUTHER KING JR.

Consider some of these amazing studies of human behavior as it relates to serving others. The results are stunning:

- Cornell University discovered from a test field of hundreds of retiree volunteers that fewer health problems were reported than from retirees who do not volunteer.
- Over a course of nine years, Dr. Larry Scherwitz at University of California–San Francisco found that men who frequently used the words *I, me, my,* and *mine* were far more likely to suffer heart attacks. Those words themselves are not dangerous, but they are indicative that the subject feels isolated from other people and thus focuses on himself more.
- Dr. David McClelland from Harvard took saliva samples from students before and after having them watch a film featuring Mother Teresa caring for orphans in Calcutta, India. After the film, students registered a tremendous increase in salivary immunoglobulin A, an antibody designed to protect the human immune system. Just thinking about doing good makes us healthier!

We are created in the image of the living God—created to draw life by giving life to others. Thank God this world is bigger than you and me, right? There are places to go and things to do . . . and life to be gained.

 Sign up to volunteer somewhere. Take a friend with you—someone who needs an immunity boost!

JANUARY 5

Go against the Flow

Don't copy the behavior and customs of this world, but let God transform you into a new person by changing the way you think. Then you will learn to know God's will for you, which is good and pleasing and perfect.
ROMANS 12:2

Crowds are unbelievably influential. Pontius Pilate was swayed when crowds demanded the thief Barabbas be released and Jesus crucified. Even recently, crowd hysteria allowed one group of protesters on Wall Street to gain enough influence that "Occupy" groups cropped up in over eighty-two countries. Of course, not everyone knew just what the group was occupying. One protester, when asked, said, "Everyone, let's just sit here and wait for nothing to happen, so that eventually something happens."

Public opinion is not always sensible. Miley Cyrus's nineteenth birthday party landed on YouTube, with Miley making a comment about smoking "too much *#! weed." One site conducted a poll: Do you think Miley Cyrus gets unfairly criticized? Of the site visitors who responded, 81 percent said, "Yes! It's unfair!" Thirteen percent said, "No, she's a role model and should act as such." This left 6 percent of the population undecided. The poll is neither scientific nor is the website very respectable, but the statistics were telling nonetheless. People simply do not have much of a foundation on which to build opinions.

Paul urges us in Romans to gain a foundation. There are two places we can build. We can build on this world, but we already know from both Jesus' parable about the wise and foolish builders (see Matthew 7:24-29) and the story of the three little pigs that if we build on a firm foundation we will have much greater success. The foundation for our opinions and decisions must be formed by every word that proceeds from the mouth of God. Our minds will then be transformed so we not only know *what* God says, but we are also *aligned with* his thoughts. His will and his passions become our own when we are made a new creation!

Will the crowd always be wrong? Not likely. But chances are if "everyone is doing it," "it" deserves prayer and a second look. Better cross crowd mentality off the list of good decision-making tools!

 **Action STEP** Think about an area of your life where you stand alone in a decision or an opinion. Avoid being confrontational or prideful—in fact, you may even want to keep your opinion to yourself. Be sure it is based on biblical truth rather than a desire to be different from everyone else.

Get out of Your Comfort Zone

"Why is the LORD taking us to this country only to have us die in battle? Our wives and our little ones will be carried off as plunder! Wouldn't it be better for us to return to Egypt? . . . Let's choose a new leader and go back to Egypt!" NUMBERS 14:3-4

Extroverts are people who are fueled by spending time and interacting with others. Introverts are drained by stimulation and need more alone time for their batteries to recharge. Dannah and I are both introverts. I have a distinct strategy at parties. I head for the quietest corner of the room and hang out with whoever joins me. My husband, Jonathan, however, is a true extrovert and flat out works the room. If you have been at a party with Jonathan, you know he was there! I am learning to be much more intentional in social situations, thanks to Jonathan's influence. I don't want to miss out on any God appointments!

Yes, God has a strategy too. His plan is to keep us on our toes so we can do all of the amazing things he has prepared for us. Though he provides plenty of time for recharging, his plan does not include letting us get too comfortable. Why? When we settle into comfort zones our growth is stunted. God uses trials and challenges to conform us more into his image. But, if we're not careful, when we face challenges, we can end up like the Israelites in today's Scripture.

When God led his people out of Israel they discovered that they had left one challenge (slavery) for another (homelessness). Disobedience had landed them in both predicaments, but God loved them and promised them a rescue with great honor at the end of the road. They should have known they could trust God. He had already done some pretty miraculous things to keep his promise.

In today's Scripture, God was leading the Israelites via the long route to the Promised Land. In their stubbornness, they couldn't see it. "We should just go back to Egypt!" they kept crying. I'm sure you know the rest of the story—instead of accomplishing the purposes God had planned for them, most Israelites died homeless and dispirited in the desert.

 Make a "bucket list" today of three risks you would like to take for God before leaving high school—three ways you can leave your comfort zone—and begin to look for ways to fulfill that list!
SW

Stake Out Your True Real Estate

When you believed in Christ, he identified you as his own by giving you the Holy Spirit, whom he promised long ago. The Spirit is God's guarantee that he will give us the inheritance he promised and that he has purchased us to be his own people. EPHESIANS 1:13-14

One day you will be ready to complete one of the most exciting transactions of your life—purchasing a house. When you go to buy that house, one of the first things you will do is make your first payment toward the house. You will write a check for $1,000 or $2,000 as Earnest Money. This is a cash promise that you will keep your part of the deal. If you back out on the sale, you'll lose the money. The check is not held until the sale is finished, either. It is cashed! You "own" rights to the house, although you don't get to occupy it right away.

Now think about how buying a home is similar to God's redemption of you. God built you, but before he could occupy his own home, another tenant (sin) did a number on you! You were no longer quite the showpiece he designed, stained now by selfishness and its consequences, but God had a plan. He bought you back.

Look how Paul parallels this in Ephesians 1:13: "When you believed in Christ, he identified you as his own by giving you the Holy Spirit." The Holy Spirit is God's earnest money, a promise paid and cashed in advance! Though we are still in these old bodies, the Holy Spirit lives within us, and he is already in the process of fixing us up, because we already belong to him.

You have been purchased. A deposit has been made as a mark of God's intentions to honor his contract, and the deposit has already been paid in full. Today's passage in Ephesians says a lot of things have been done in advance for you. You were raised with Jesus (see Ephesians 2:5-6), so you already have new life. There is a spot with your name on it right next to the throne of God, so you are already part of God's family. You truly are owned, loved, provided for.

Action **STEP** If you have professed Christ as your Savior, take some time to meditate on this powerful truth: *I am already dead to sin, living a new life, and have been given my inheritance in heaven.* If you have not taken the big step, ask yourself why not. Talk to a Christian you trust about any doubts or concerns you may have.

JANUARY 8
Pray like This

[Jesus said,] "Pray like this. . . ." MATTHEW 6:9

One of the most amazing indictments ever pronounced against me was the day my friend Danae leaned back against the passenger seat of my car and sighed, "I just wish I had someone to pray with who really knew *how* to pray."

For a while I was indignant. How dare she! She didn't think I knew how to pray? But then a couple of years went by, and I began to see it was true. I didn't know the first thing about prayer. What a realization to wake up to, but trust me: it is life giving when we realize our limitations. Rather than remain quiet in times of group prayer, as I had been doing, I resolved to learn how to pray.

Yes, prayer is something we can literally practice and improve. There are some rules governing prayer, but there's a lot of freedom as well. In teaching his disciples to pray, Jesus pointed out a couple of distinct prayer faux pas.

First, he pointed out that praying in public with the intention of showing off isn't his preferred method. He'd rather invite you to a private conversation. This calls for humility in your prayer life. He says it like this:

> When you pray, go away by yourself, shut the door behind you, and pray to your Father in private. Then your Father, who sees everything, will reward you. (Matthew 6:6)

Next, Jesus explained that we don't have to say the same thing over and over again. Of course, we do tend to drone on and on about our needs, but that's not necessary. Our all-powerful King doesn't really need instruction on handling our needs.

> When you pray, don't babble on and on . . . for your Father knows exactly what you need even before you ask him! (Matthew 6:7-8)

 Take a few moments to ask God to be the teacher. Are you willing to be the student? Are you ready to learn how to pray?
SW

Start Every Prayer with Adoration

Pray like this: Our Father in heaven, may your name be kept holy. May your Kingdom come soon. May your will be done on earth, as it is in heaven. Give us today the food we need, and forgive us our sins, as we have forgiven those who sin against us. And don't let us yield to temptation, but rescue us from the evil one. MATTHEW 6:9-13

The Lord's Prayer, as this passage is called, is familiar to most people. It has been recited in church services for centuries. But do we truly understand the words we recite? If so, then we understand the important elements of prayer, which are easily described by a simple acronym:

ACTS: **A**doration, **C**onfession, **T**hanksgiving, and **S**upplication

Every time we pray we should begin with a heart of adoration and worship, continue with confessing our sins, thank God for his many blessings, and conclude by asking him to have favor on our requests. As you reread the Lord's Prayer, you will notice all four of the ACTS elements can be found within. But let's just focus on adoration today.

Before we even get to adoration, notice that Jesus reveals to us the proper recipient of our prayer—our Father. That must bring up as many different pictures of "dad" as there are readers of this devotion! But Jesus' intent is clear. We are not praying to a condemning judge, a shrewd businessman, or even a benevolent dictator. We are praying to the one responsible for our being; he is gentle and kind and always wants the best for us.

Once we have the title down, Jesus teaches us to begin by lavishing God with adoration. After all, if we are going to benefit from the extreme riches of his grace, his unmatched power, and the freedom with which he gives good gifts to us, shouldn't we pretty much be in awe of his ability to do so?

This is the King of the universe. He spoke the world into existence. Nothing is too difficult for him. He brings princes and rulers to their knees in submission. The wind and the waves obey him. And he is your Father. Unbelievable!

 Go to one of your favorite places, whether it is a breathtaking outdoor vista or the comfiest chair on the face of the planet, and offer words of adoration to your heavenly Father! Don't worry about the other elements of prayer yet. Simply tell God how amazing he is.

Always Confess Your Sins

Confess your sins to each other and pray for each other so that you may be healed. The earnest prayer of a righteous person has great power and produces wonderful results. JAMES 5:16

I can't bear keeping my mistakes a secret. My mom says the epitome of this trait showed up when I was five years old. The world was a much safer place back then, and I was allowed to have the run of my rather large neighborhood. The only rule was this: I was not allowed to set even one foot past the stop sign separating the neighborhood from a busy highway.

True to human nature, as soon as I was told not to do something, I was going to consider it an invitation. What would happen if I put one foot three inches in front of the stop sign? Nothing. Crickets. No lightning bolt from the heavens. And yet I *was* struck with a crippling guilt. I had done the one thing I was forbidden to do. I returned home in tears, collapsed into my mom's arms, and confessed my sin.

Confession is the second element of prayer. To confess means literally to *agree* with God, particularly that our sins have impacted our relationship with him. The wages of sin is death (see Romans 6:23)—if *I'm* not going to die, someone else had to. There was a debt to be paid, and it impacted God severely to make the payment. This is why Jesus reminds us to pray, "Forgive us our debts" (Matthew 6:12, NIV). It is in essence a statement of, "I agree you paid my debt."

Confession also sets us back in right relationship. I didn't need to tell my mom about the stop sign. She loved me regardless. I told her because I was tortured without the confession. I had broken her trust and my guilt was going to be a wall between us. Boy, does the wall ever come tumbling down when we humble ourselves and take responsibility for what we've done! It's a big part of the healing James mentions in today's verse.

 Taking a position of humility, either kneeling or lying on the ground, confess your sins to God. Agree your choices have put up a wall between you, but get ready for the sweet, sweet sound of the wall coming down and for the joy of restored fellowship with your Father! SW

Make Every Day Thanksgiving

Yes, they knew God, but they wouldn't worship him as God or even give him thanks. And they began to think up foolish ideas of what God was like. As a result, their minds became dark and confused. ROMANS 1:21

Have you noticed the more sophisticated a nation is, the more it tends toward spiritual confusion? After all, when one is so wise, how can she fall for a truth so simple?

Ancient Egypt had a résumé that should automatically qualify for a Nobel Prize. Sophisticated systems of writing, medicine, agriculture, construction, and mathematics led Egypt to become a world power. Yet the ancient Egyptians were not satisfied with one God. They created by their own imaginations over one hundred gods and goddesses to worship.

Classical Greece is credited with the birth of Western civilization. Its heritage includes Plato, Socrates, and Aristotle. The main gods in Greece were actually science, literature, philosophy, and art, though a complex mythology of gods and goddesses was also developed.

The Roman Empire is known for military and political prowess, giving the world Machiavelli and Julius Caesar. At one time the Roman Empire constituted half of the known world. By the time Rome was at the top, there was a common belief every person had a spark of the divine within. Humanity was no longer having to search outside of one's self to find an object of worship.

This downward spiral is very common, and it can be found in the study of most prodigals. It begins with knowledge of God, but a refusal to glorify him as such. We begin to come to him as my songwriter friend Jessica Witmer says, "ho hum, twiddling our thumbs." It's a short jump from the ho-hum platform to the one where we stop saying thank you to God for the hundreds of mercies he showers on us every day. And once we stop breathing thank-yous to the one who has given us the mercy of that breath to begin with, it's yet another short jump to futile and foolish hearts. Let's not end up like the Egyptians, Grecians, and Romans. (I don't think we'd look that good in those tunics, anyway.) Let's make every day Thanksgiving.

 Check out this "poster" that has been going around on Facebook: "Dear God, I wanna take a minute, not to ask for anything from you, but simply to say thank you for all that I have." Do this!

It's Okay to Ask for Some Things

Give us today our daily bread. MATTHEW 6:11, NIV

Where do you go when you need something? Do you turn to your friends? To your family? To the bank or the old credit card for a loan? Jesus invites us to ask God for what we need.

Give us today our daily bread. These six little words provide so many lessons in prayer! First, there is the first word *give*, written in imperative form—a *demand*. Hold up! Is this the boldness with which Jesus teaches us to approach our heavenly Father? You bet.

And *give* ends up being an operative word in this teaching:

> If you sinful people know how to *give* good gifts to your children, how much more will your heavenly Father *give* good gifts to those who ask him. (Matthew 7:11, emphasis added)

Though he has "raised" us to be industrious, it's good to have an awareness that every gift we have has been *given* to us by Dad.

Take note what we are to ask for. A better car? That A on the test? Jesus chose his words carefully. Bread is not a fancy food. It is flour and water, maybe a little bit of yeast—about as basic as it gets. Very few things honestly constitute needs. Food enough to live, clothing to cover our bodies, and shelter. . . . Those are needs.

Jesus next addresses how often to ask and how much to ask for. Each new day we should seek God with this request. God, today I need *this* day's supplies. Ever watch the show *Extreme Couponing*? The first time I saw the show I couldn't determine if the coupon queen was being interviewed in some massive store or if she was in . . . her basement? Really? She had enough deodorant for six years and enough toothbrushes to last until she was eighty! Do we need more than enough? God wants us to come to him every day to ask for exactly what we need because this keeps us close to him. It keeps us dependent on the right guy!

 Sit down and determine on paper your daily *needs*. See if you can come up with three realistic and measurable changes you can make in order to stop chasing after *more* than what you really need.

Here's What
Your Prayers Will Do

Pray in the Spirit at all times and on every occasion. Stay alert and be persistent in your prayers for all believers everywhere. EPHESIANS 6:18

If we pray little, it is probably because we do not really believe that prayer accomplishes much at all. Author and teacher Wayne A. Grudem said that. Hits ya between the eyes, doesn't it?

This portion of Ephesians comes right after Paul has taught the church about the full armor of God. Notice every single piece of God's armor is defensive . . . except for the Word of God, which is the sword. And the Word of God is what we use to pray. Nothing you can say or utter could ever be as powerful as the words contained between the leather-bound covers of your Bible!

Every moment of every day is perfect for prayer. We tend to think of prayer as something done in groups or aloud, but the few seconds your head pokes into your locker to grab books? That's a perfect time to whisper a prayer. When you step to the free-throw line, up to the plate, or onto the gymnastics mat, what better time to ask in one breath for God to be glorified? Prayer is not a meeting. It's kind of a lifestyle.

Paul also says to pray on every occasion. Prayers typically tend to fall into two categories: we pray because things are falling apart, or we pray because things are going well. Which side do you think you lean toward? Paul reminds us to pray when circumstances touch every possible spectrum of our lives— whether God has given or taken away, when we are well and when we are hurting. Every occasion invites prayer.

What exactly does prayer do? Prayer is not for God's benefit. We cannot tell him anything he doesn't know, nor can we instruct him. But prayer has a powerful effect. It stirs the compassionate heart of a God who loves us. It draws us intimately together. It helps us to see the world through God's eyes and unleashes his unmatched power. Prayer is the engine that drives any good thing we might hope to accomplish in our lives. There is one thing we must learn, and that is the discipline of prayer!

 **Action STEP** Talk to God about everything and at all times today.

Pray for Even "That" Person

You have heard the law that says, "Love your neighbor" and hate your enemy. But I say, love your enemies! Pray for those who persecute you! In that way, you will be acting as true children of your Father in heaven. For he gives his sunlight to both the evil and the good, and he sends rain on the just and the unjust alike. MATTHEW 5:43-45

I have a broken friendship. I've tried to reconcile, and I've even tried to wait it out. She just doesn't like me anymore. Time has only served to enable bitterness to rear its ugly head, and I find myself being competitive, if only in my heart. One who once was a friend is now an enemy. Got any relationships in your life like that?

Jesus says the prescription is prayer. I'm supposed to pray for this person. His language on this one is pretty clear. And it's coming directly from his mouth.

This is one of those situations where Jesus is painting a picture for us of how we might truly become different from the rest of the world. Most of us want to know our faith is not empty. We want to know that "accepting Christ" means our lives would show outward signs that something tremendous and authentic has happened to us. It doesn't get much more radical than praying for people who legitimately despise us!

There will always be people who do not like you. The root of the problem isn't even mentioned in Jesus' command; you'll notice his command is to pray *for* those who persecute us. Jesus didn't say, "Get to the root of the problem and fix it and then you will be like your Father in heaven." He didn't say, "If you can figure out *why* she is so mean, you will then know how to pray about this situation."

His command is simply to pray for those who hate us and who persecute us. The promise is we will be made more like Jesus when we do so, and we will have proof he has made us new creations—our "old selves" never would have done this! But there's another unspoken result of praying for our enemies: we somehow change in the process. That root of bitterness is removed from the softened soil of our hearts, and before we know it, we find ourselves actually cheering for the "bad guy" to become a good guy!

 Pray today, all day, for an "enemy." Be sure you are not praying for solutions to the problem but simply prayers of blessing for his or her life.
DG

Do I Have to Go to Church to Be a Christian?

Let us not neglect our meeting together, as some people do, but encourage one another, especially now that the day of his return is drawing near. HEBREWS 10:25

It's not uncommon for Christians to go through a time of wondering why church attendance is such a big deal. Well, attending church is big enough for God to include this passage in Hebrews right in the middle of warning the church not to give in to complacency. Why? Because God knows comfort is downright desirable. But comfort can also be deadly!

Today's Bible verse calls us to meet as a church. Spending time with other believers is a tremendous advantage. When we feel alone in our principles, we suffer. When surrounded by others who share our goals, who are willing even to share our struggles, we have a strength we could never have on our own. How sad would it be to have no one willing to pray with you, no one you could confess your secrets to, and no one you could call for safe advice? It doesn't take long after leaving the church to find oneself in that very situation.

Another important reason for meeting is to avoid apostasy, which at its root simply means to abandon the faith. You want to make a piece of steel sharp and effective for its work? Rub it against another piece of steel. Likewise, if we are not in contact with other Christians we become dull and lose our usefulness (see Proverbs 27:17). It's not a principle worth testing—the results are proven, and they are the same every time. There simply is no way to remove oneself from fellowship with other believers and remain effective as a follower of Christ.

 *Action* **STEP**

1. *If church seems "boring"* . . . sing during worship and take notes during the sermon. Do this for one month and see if things feel different.
2. *If church seems "fake"* . . . resolve to answer truthfully every time someone at church asks, "How are you doing?" Will this be you leading by example?
3. *If church seems "irrelevant"* . . . journal each week on the sermon topic. Begin with, "What am I going to do about this?"
4. *If church seems "inconvenient"* . . . turn it into your only Sunday activity!

JANUARY 16

Is There a Place for Me at Church?

Don't let anyone think less of you because you are young. Be an example to all believers in what you say, in the way you live, in your love, your faith, and your purity. Until I get there, focus on reading the Scriptures to the church, encouraging the believers, and teaching them. 1 TIMOTHY 4:12-13

Last year, a group of high school students came to my husband and me to talk to us about where they fit in at church.

"We want to be part of the church," the students said. "We want to be integrated into everything. No offense, but not all of us are necessarily wired to be babysitters, and that's what we automatically get assigned to do whenever there is a church event."

We helped them take their spiritual gifting test and talked through how they might fit in. One student stepped up big time to find his place. Caleb has a gift of prayer. He began to bless the church by setting up each week, praying over empty seats before adults arrived and for kids as he set up the children's area. When there were planning meetings and prayer meetings, he was the only teenager to show up. He asked for assignments and was faithful to complete them.

When Paul tells Timothy, "Don't let anyone think less of you because you are young," he is telling Timothy that there should be nothing in his character that causes people to look down upon youth. True, there should be no cause to dismiss teens because of their age, but neither should Timothy or Caleb give the church cause to dismiss teens due to their behavior.

Why does Caleb want to hang out with all of the old fogies of the church? He wants to make a difference. He knows he is uniquely gifted, and he figures since there's no magic age for serving, why not start now? And he knows his best shot at becoming the man he wants to be is surrounding himself with such godly men now. Caleb hasn't been singled out by church leadership. He has simply made himself available. He shows up. He says, "What can I do?" or "I'll take care of that." He's seventeen, and he acts like it. But he's also a man, and he acts like it. Well done, Caleb.

 Attend an open planning meeting or service project at your church. Be prepared to volunteer time and work hard to complete what you sign up for.
SW

JANUARY 17

Do I Really Have to Rest on the Seventh Day?

Jesus said to them, "The Sabbath was made to meet the needs of people, and not people to meet the requirements of the Sabbath. So the Son of Man is Lord, even over the Sabbath!" MARK 2:27-28

If your family is like mine, you don't get much time to kick up your feet and breathe. Drama class. Tennis lessons. Homework. Babysitting. Youth group. Fund-raisers. Horseback riding. Bible study. My attitude has always been that if I took a day to rest, things would fall apart. Then my pastor preached a message on the Sabbath. One of the reasons he said we should take a day to rest is to tell our spirits that we don't run the world. God does. Ouch! That hurt a little.

Our family now mandates a Sunday Sabbath rest until five o'clock in the afternoon. No TVs. No iPods. No computers. There's a lot of napping and a lot of game playing. Nothing serious. Do you know what has fallen apart? Nothing. Nada. We were created to rest. If we weren't, it probably wouldn't have been placed in the Ten Commandments and then reaffirmed in the New Testament. (Have you ever heard that those are not God's Ten Suggestions?)

Now here's the problem: while the Sabbath was created for our good, there is still a *commandment* that we take a day off and set it apart from the rest of the week (see Exodus 20:8-10). We, the church, are failing miserably at this! It's not uncommon to see kids come to church in their softball or soccer uniforms because they have to leave early for a tournament. Sunday is known as "homework day" universally, because Monday is the first day of the school week! Students put in the bulk of their work hours on weekends. And somehow in the shuffle, the Sabbath gets lost.

The Sabbath was made for us. To rest and reflect on all we have to be thankful for? Indeed. But also made for us by a Dad who knows how prone we are to forget . . . and to wander. If our faith is a living thing, doesn't it follow that it requires to be fed, to be rested, and to receive our most tender care?

Take a real Sabbath this week. No work. No school stuff. Afterward, Facebook us and tell us what kind of impact it has on your week. We bet it'll refuel you so well you'll be more productive all week long. DG

I Keep Getting Asked to Do Things at Church That I Don't Like

Since I, your Lord and Teacher, have washed your feet, you ought to wash each other's feet. I have given you an example to follow. Do as I have done to you. JOHN 13:14-15

My friend Bill has an odd hobby. He "crashes" Hollywood parties. He has a knack for getting into private events and having his photograph taken with movie stars. One of his prized possessions is a picture with Meryl Streep on the red carpet at the Oscars. Bill says he merely asked Ms. Streep if he could escort her down the red carpet and she agreed. Wow.

Like Bill, most people are drawn to the glamour of fame like moths to a porch light! As I've traveled around the country with Secret Keeper Girl, our ministry to tween girls, I've noticed something. It takes us about twelve hours to set up, run, and tear down a show. Mathematically, since we need about twenty-five people working nonstop to accomplish this, the typical show requires about three hundred man-hours! How many of these hours are spent onstage? Two and a half.

Here's the interesting part—after nearly every show, someone asks how to get a job as a cast member. Only *one* person has ever asked if there was any way she could be hired as a crew member!

There's nothing wrong with dreaming God would give you a platform one day as an artist, a speaker, an actor, a dancer, or an athlete. But if we take our cues from the King of kings—the one who was with God from the beginning—what do we find him doing? (Hint: Check out the potentially smelly verse above!)

No matter how important God enables your voice to become one day, an example has been set for you by the one who wasn't too important to wash feet. It's not the most glamorous job, but he promises you will be blessed if you serve.

 Use an online concordance to put together a list of three additional verses that point to serving others as a way of life, and copy them onto note cards. Carry the cards with you this week to remind you of the importance of serving.

Good Morning, Miss Ambassador

We are Christ's ambassadors; God is making his appeal through us.
We speak for Christ when we plead, "Come back to God!"
2 CORINTHIANS 5:20

Over twelve million. That's how many people have seen the viral YouTube video "United Breaks Guitars." Quickie review: United Airlines passenger Dave Carroll's guitar was reportedly tossed around recklessly and broken during handling. Dave wanted the airline to pay for the damage. They initially refused. So, he wrote a little ditty and it went viral.

This refusal cost the airline a $180-million stock plunge from bad PR. That could have bought Mr. Carroll fifty-one thousand guitars! If the employees (read: ambassadors) of United had treated Dave Carroll better, it might have looked different. Maybe they could have treated his guitar with care to begin with. Maybe those who had the authority to pay for it could have. Then he might have written a tune that made United look heroic!

We are Christ's ambassadors. We represent him. Just tonight on Facebook we noticed that a guy who comments on Christian culture had posted something about a church running a tasteless Easter campaign. The Easter invite depicted a roadkill rabbit and the spilled contents of an Easter basket. The card read, "Bunnies stay dead. Jesus didn't." This guy is followed by thousands of people who proceeded to besiege the church's Facebook page with harsh and spiteful disapprovals of the card—people from all over the world *who don't know a single person at the church!*

We have to be twice as careful these days as ambassadors. Within seconds, one indiscretion, one unkind word or stupid decision could be broadcast to the world. And we *are* his ambassadors. An ambassador represents the interests of her home nation (heaven) in a foreign land (earth). God is making an appeal to the world through us. What will that appeal look and sound like after the world sorts through the photo albums and videos of our lives? One thing is clear from Paul's directives: the appeal made through you and me should look like heaven.

 Oh, go ahead! Get on YouTube and look up "United Breaks Guitars." But first, give yourself a grade on your ambassadorship. What could you do to improve?

Who's Walking with You?

These older women must train the younger women to love their husbands and their children, to live wisely and be pure, to work in their homes, to do good, and to be submissive to their husbands. Then they will not bring shame on the word of God. TITUS 2:4-5

I marvel that the animals born on my farm know how to be exactly what they are. Llamas. Goats. Chickens. Within an hour of birth, the llamas are up and looking for mama's milk. Our little goat Mayzie has only ever had a bottle, but she bends at the knees as if she were drinking from mama. The chicks start scratching for bugs within a day after birth . . . and they aren't even able to eat bugs yet!

Then there are humans. We don't know how to eat, clean ourselves, or even sleep through the night unless taught. God created us with the need to be trained. He loves when we submit ourselves to a relationship where we can learn how to be what he's created us to be. He even spells out in Titus that we should learn to be wives and mothers from older women.

The goal of mentorship is not to find good advice givers. The goal of mentorship is to learn by imitation. The ultimate objective is maturity so the mentee is prepared to become a mentor herself. These goals are best achieved by finding an older woman who looks like the woman you dream of becoming one day. Ask her how she became that woman, then listen and imitate as if your life depended on it! Here are some good things to do as you walk through life together:

1. Read the Bible together. A baby must be fed, but an older person can feed herself. A mentor helps you arrive at the place where you can feed yourself from God's truth.
2. Learn accountability. Nothing will hold your feet to the fire like an older, trusted woman asking you on a regular basis if you are living a life of integrity and protecting your purity.
3. Pray. Mentoring means someone is praying for you, but also teaching you how to pray.
4. Serve together. The disciples got to watch Jesus at work for two years. Finally, he gave them the green light to work alongside him.

 *Action* STEP Make your short list—the names of three women you would like to imitate in Christ. Seek God in prayer as to which woman he would have you approach for a mentoring relationship.
DG

A Modern Woman of God

We keep on praying for you, asking our God to enable you to live a life worthy of his call. 2 THESSALONIANS 1:11

You husbands must give honor to your wives. Treat your wife with understanding as you live together. She may be weaker than you are, but she is your equal partner in God's gift of new life. Treat her as you should so your prayers will not be hindered. 1 PETER 3:7

As a girl I wanted to do mostly nontraditional jobs: a marine biologist or a Navy Seal. In my tweens I wondered if I could be a professional baseball player. I really hated being told I was "good for a girl" and often set out to prove I was good, period.

This made it difficult to swallow Peter's label for women: a "weaker partner"? It's too easy for me to think God means "inferior." But this is one of those situations where we are in trouble if we do not study God's Word. Peter refers to a comparative physical weakness here, and he is right. To this day I maintain an excellent glove and an arm strong enough to play third base on competitive coed softball teams. But I will never be able to pull in some of the line drives other third base*men* can get. I can't jump that high. I am not the physical specimen men are. Peter isn't saying women are inferior, but less physically strong.

He then goes on to reconcile men and women as equal partners in Christ. "She is your equal partner in God's gift of new life" (1 Peter 3:7). Eventually I came to realize the chip on my shoulder had little to do with gender. I was struggling with the desire to be important, and any reference to limitations on my part simply rubbed me the wrong way. With some horror, I realized these were the very things the angel Lucifer struggled with!

Here is what I believe God wants from the modern godly woman: freedom in Christ to manage, lead, create, and win. Yet I am called to live in submission to Jesus as the head of everything, and with the same respect to my husband as the head of our household. I am called to imitate God's goodness so that God may be glorified. Jesus gets the honor and the glory. His name gets the praise. He may raise me up. He may subject me to humility. Jesus is the creator, owner, and sustainer of all. It's not about gender. It's about Jesus.

 Practice deflecting all praise to Jesus today, especially if you are feeling unnoticed, disregarded, or dismissed. SW

JANUARY 22
The Bible at a Glance

The word of God is alive and powerful. It is sharper than the sharpest two-edged sword, cutting between soul and spirit, between joint and marrow. It exposes our innermost thoughts and desires. HEBREWS 4:12

How much do you know about the number one bestselling book of all time? It has been translated into more than two thousand languages; more than six billion copies have been sold. No book has ever come close to experiencing the same marketing success. The majority of books published will never sell more than one thousand copies. J. K. Rowling's Harry Potter series has sold about 400 million copies. That series is seven books, and is still 600 *million* shy of one billion . . . no competition.

This bestselling book, the Bible, was written over six thousand years ago, long before the printing press was invented. The Bible took 1,500 years to write and has over forty different authors. There are more original (hand-copied) versions of the Bible in existence than any other manuscript. For example, we have over five thousand handwritten (Greek) copies of the New Testament. Only thirty-seven handwritten copies of Aristotle's works still exist.

Consider how the Bible was copied. Jewish scribes had to look at what they were copying not one word at a time, not one letter at a time, but one *stroke* at a time! Between each letter, the scribe had to place a measuring rod the width of one human hair to assure no two letters would bleed together.

There is one more convincing attribute belonging to the Bible alone: more people have died due to translating and distributing the Bible than any other book in the history of literacy. Many laid their lives on the line so you and I could have affordable copies in our own languages. Foremost was William Tyndale, after whom the publishing house of this book was named. Tyndale was burned at the stake in 1536 for daring to provide God's Word to the common man in his own language—English. Only for a conviction of truth, alive and powerful, a sword that cuts man to his very soul, would a man be willing to suffer such a death.

How many Bibles does your family own? Do an inventory. Take some time to thank God for the privilege of having his Word so readily available to you! And don't forget to read the world's all-time bestselling book!

The Circle of the Earth

God sits above the circle of the earth. The people below seem like grasshoppers to him! He spreads out the heavens like a curtain and makes his tent from them. ISAIAH 40:22

You've probably heard of a guy named Copernicus. He was a scientist whose brilliant mind caused him to believe the sun was the center of our universe. At the time, people were just self-absorbed enough to think the earth must certainly be the center. His theory—called heliocentrism—created a great deal of controversy in the church. His book supporting the theory wasn't published until he was almost dead. (In fact, rumor says he first held a copy of it and then died the same day.) But scientists who followed him suffered gravely for believing in his theory. One of them was Galileo. Heard of him? He spent his entire life under house arrest after stating he believed the sun was the center of the universe. The church believed him to be heretical—in conflict with Christian doctrine.

Another big "heretical" thought was that the earth was round. Men were actually burned at the stake by the church for saying the globe might be . . . well, globular!

Here's the deal: the church is fallible. It is made up of men and women who get things wrong.

But the Bible is the infallible Word of God.

When men and women were being burned at the stake by church leaders who falsely believed the earth was flat, these words testified on behalf of the victims: "God sits above the circle of the earth."

Two thousand years before groundbreaking scientists declared the earth round and the sun the center of the universe, the Scriptures spoke of it. Incidentally, this was such a profound thought to one of our first astronauts that he is said to have surrendered his life to Christ on his first mission when he saw the earth as a circle.

The Scriptures can be trusted. While the men and women who teach from Scripture can fail, God's Word does not.

 Google "Copernicus heliocentricity." Check out the cool images that he drew and believed in when no one else did.

The Earth Is My Witness

You will hear of wars and threats of wars, but don't panic. Yes, these things must take place, but the end won't follow immediately. Nation will go to war against nation, and kingdom against kingdom. There will be famines and earthquakes in many parts of the world. MATTHEW 24:6-7

Dannah and I live in an area of the country not exactly prone to natural disaster. In fact, the lack of earthquakes, floods, hurricanes, etc., is one of the reasons our region earned the moniker "Happy Valley." We were pretty surprised, then, to experience our first earthquake not long ago. I found it odd that my Bernese mountain dog, afraid of his own shadow, seemed unaware of the movement, which made me doubt myself. I immediately checked Facebook, our most instantaneous and reliable news source. Sure enough, I had just survived my first earthquake.

Many evangelical Christians attribute natural disasters to Jesus' prophetic words found in three of the four Gospels. An increase in natural disasters means an increase in birth pains. Jesus is returning soon. Other people, mostly those with non-faith or science backgrounds, attribute the increase in natural disasters to global warming. There is room, biblically, for both to be true. Jesus says these things must take place. Revelation says at the opening of the seventh seal a third of all the earth's land and sea population and a third of the earth's vegetation will pass away. Environmental woes certainly could contribute to such a promise. These things must happen.

The earth is testifying to us. Every time things take a turn for the "worse," we are one step closer to Jesus' return and the arrival of his Kingdom. Have you ever watched *Extreme Makeover: Home Edition*? At the beginning of each show the lucky family's old home is razed to the ground. It is dusty, noisy, messy, destructive . . . and sometimes emotional for the family as they watch all of their memories come crashing to the ground. But the old home has to come down if the new one is to be built. This old house of ours has been compromised—pests have moved in, the wood is rotting, and the windows and walls don't keep out the cold any longer. God is building us a new home with materials that will never rot or fade away. And every strike of the bulldozer is one step closer to the "move that bus!" moment.

 **STEP** Read God's promises for your future home here— Revelation 21.

JANUARY 25

Now You See Me, Now You See Jesus

"Lord," exclaimed Ananias, "I've heard many people talk about the terrible things this man has done to the believers in Jerusalem! . . ." But the Lord said, "Go, for Saul is my chosen instrument to take my message to the Gentiles and to kings, as well as to the people of Israel." ACTS 9:13-15

I once saw a miracle happen to a young man in our youth group. Jason was having brushes with the law, and his music choices were becoming more violent and crude. At a New Year's youth group event the kids were filling out resolutions. Jason was not working on his, and when I challenged him to complete it, he informed me he didn't need one. "I'll probably be dead by this time next year," he said. But God had other plans. Jason was miraculously driven to his knees on the floor of his closet one night. Alone with God, he surrendered.

It happened to actor Kirk Cameron, too. Kirk was made famous at a young age thanks to his heartthrob role on the sitcom *Growing Pains*. He had everything he could possibly want, except the girl he had his eye on. He went to church to impress her dad, heard the gospel for the first time, and pondered it for a month. Finally, sitting alone in his car on the shoulder of a busy freeway, he realized if he were to get in a car wreck and die that very day, he would not enter heaven. Cameron surrendered his life to Jesus right there in the driver's seat of his sports car.

Maybe you know Gene "Malice" Thornton from the hip-hop band Clipse? He grew up in church, but strayed from his faith—doing what he wanted to do and what everyone else was doing became his drug. Rebirth led Malice to a name change. He goes by No Malice now. The rhyme maker who once produced cocaine-laced lyrics infuses his life with open praises to his creator these days.

Acts chapter 9 begins by informing us that Paul (Saul) was eager to kill Jesus' followers. How is it, less than one year later, this man had the most powerful ministry in the history of the church? Jesus changes lives. Perhaps there is no greater evidence for the truth of God's Word than a life completely and radically changed.

 As a tribute to your Savior, write a blog or make a video explaining how Jesus has changed your life. SW

They Will Know

Jesus told [the man whom he had healed from blindness], "I entered this world to render judgment—to give sight to the blind and to show those who think they see that they are blind." Some Pharisees who were standing nearby heard him and asked, "Are you saying we're blind?" "If you were blind, you wouldn't be guilty," Jesus replied. "But you remain guilty because you claim you can see." JOHN 9:39-41

Brian was a junior in high school when he made his first trip to Haiti. He and our other young missionaries came from strong, middle-class families with a lot of good fashion sense, nice hair, and big smiles. . . . That was the week they all, especially Brian, figured out how useless all of their merits were. On the final day Brian received a hug from a little guy who then handed him a thin, threadbare bag filled with marbles. Brian was seventeen years old. He didn't play marbles, though it was the boy's favorite game. Actually, it was the boy's *only* game. I remember Brian holding those marbles up before the church on his return and recounting the story. He was unable to keep it together, and the rest of the team had to hold him as he wept.

How is it that those who have so little can express the greatest joy and give the most freely? Maybe it has something to do with what Jesus said: "Where your treasure is, there your heart will be also" (Matthew 6:21, NIV; Luke 12:34, NIV). When author Kelsey Timmerman heard of Jesus' love from the pulpits of million-dollar churches in his home state of Indiana, he was unmoved. But he says when he went to the slums of Nairobi, he prayed for the first time ever. The stories from the slum didn't surprise Timmerman. He had seen the pictures. It was the *faith* of the people that rocked his world.

Jesus chose this Scripture, of all things, to read when he stood in the Temple in Jerusalem: "The Spirit of the Sovereign LORD is upon me, for the LORD has anointed me to bring good news to the poor. He has sent me to comfort the brokenhearted and to proclaim that captives will be released and prisoners will be freed" (Isaiah 61:1). When the poor and the oppressed meet Jesus, they have no doubt what they have found is real. They remember their chains, and no amount of thanks is too much. Oh, that we could see so clearly!

 Ask God to show you how your blessings may be keeping you from seeing clearly the one who blesses.

How Could They Know?

When I look at the night sky and see the work of your fingers—the moon and the stars you set in place—what are mere mortals that you should think about them, human beings that you should care for them? . . . You gave them charge of everything you made, putting all things under their authority . . . the birds in the sky, the fish in the sea, and everything that swims the ocean currents. PSALM 8:3-4, 6, 8

You've seen *Finding Nemo* and remember Crush, the "surfer dude" turtle and his little son Squirt, right? He got Marlin to Sydney just a little bit faster by teaching him to take the East Australian Current, which by the way "totally" exists. As Crush would say, "Righteous!"

After seeing that movie, children the world over grow up assuming there are currents and mountains and valleys in the ocean. But until recently, scientists believed the bottom of the ocean was probably just a sandy disc and would have never guessed there were actual "highways" that turtles and fish could use to follow their dinner!

But God knew. And he's planted a love for his Word in a lot of scientists, including Matthew Maury. In the 1800s Maury was an officer in the US Navy. He loved and believed the Bible. One day he was reading Psalm 8. He was amazed verse 8 spoke of the fish and all creatures swimming in the "paths of the seas." (In the version above the word *current* is used.) Believing his Bible, Maury was determined to find these pathways no one knew existed. He found there were in fact many paths, or currents, which were like rivers flowing through the sea. Maury wrote the first book on oceanography and became known as the "pathfinder of the seas."

The funny thing is, the words inspiring his search were written more than three thousand years earlier by King David, who probably never even saw the ocean. But God inspired him to write in truth about what exists in the depths.

The Bible spoke of the valleys and mountains of the sea thousands of years before scientists discovered them. Indeed, our Bible is the inspired Word of God.

 **Action STEP** Okay, this one's fun. Get on YouTube and search for "Do you have your exit buddy?" for a fun look at the East Australian Current. Then maybe get smart and Google "East Australian Current" to check it out.

What's in It for Me?

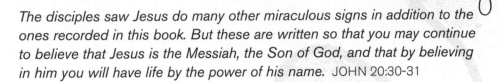

The disciples saw Jesus do many other miraculous signs in addition to the ones recorded in this book. But these are written so that you may continue to believe that Jesus is the Messiah, the Son of God, and that by believing in him you will have life by the power of his name. JOHN 20:30-31

Not every book is for every reader, which explains why the average book only sells one thousand copies. What does the Bible offer that causes billions of people to read it? Here is a short list of what you might be able to do when you read it:

1. *Meet God*: If ever you would want to know what the God of the universe thinks, what he wants from you, why he created you, what he plans to do . . . this is a book written just for you.
2. *Be taught*: Most books offer the opinions of the author or other experts. The Bible is an instruction manual, not an op-ed piece.
3. *Take warning*: There is right, and then there is wrong. The Bible shines a light on the difference between the two and enables you to walk on a path that is safe.
4. *Fix it*: Your life is full of error. So is mine. But it's nothing that can't be corrected. The Bible is the definitive volume on making such adjustments so we no longer miss the target.
5. *Follow*: "There is a path before each person that seems right, but it ends in death" (Proverbs 14:12). The Bible illuminates the only path that will lead, in the end, to life.
6. *Get ready*: You don't know at what moment God will call you, either to work with him here on earth or to your eternal home. The Bible is a gymnasium for your soul, preparing you to be mature and training you (like an athlete) in righteousness.
7. *Meet You*: Who am I? This may be the underlying philosophical question of the ages. Well, the moment you find out who he is, you find out who you are.

There is no end to the good the Bible is able to work in our lives if only we will *read* it! It's not a good luck charm, though. Only if we read *and* do what it says will we reap the benefits.

 *Action* **STEP** Get in the habit of reading your Bible every day. What is your plan to develop this habit?

Good Pain

God loved the world so much that he gave his one and only Son, so that everyone who believes in him will not perish but have eternal life. God sent his Son into the world not to judge the world, but to save the world through him. JOHN 3:16-17

Elisabeth Elliot wrote the bestselling book *Passion and Purity* about her pursuit of a godly man whom she later submitted to with honor. Their love story ended tragically. Jim was speared to death as he and four others attempted to make contact with an unreached Auca tribe in Ecuador. Elisabeth was able later to bridge the gap and lived for two years with the same people who had killed her husband, seeing a majority of them become brothers and sisters in Christ.

Shortly after writing *Passion and Purity* Elliot was a guest speaker at Wheaton College, her alma mater and my school at the time. I was thoroughly and grievously *un*impressed. I had my own problems, consumed by a relationship in danger of going down the toilet. Instead of spending a week learning from one of the most amazing women God has ever raised up in his church, I drowned in self-pity and concentrated on my own small-minded questions. Maybe you've had questions like these before:

Why would God allow his five missionaries to be slaughtered in Ecuador? Why didn't he protect people on 9/11?

How could he stand by and not stop droughts, tornadoes, and tsunamis?

Author C. S. Lewis, in his book *The Problem of Pain,* said pain is "God's megaphone to rouse a deaf world." Is it possible that unless we come face-to-face with not only our own pain and disappointments, but also the horrors of evil and destruction, we remain deaf and unmoving? Then pain *would* be good, or useful, to us.

Losing her husband moved Elisabeth to love the Aucas in a way she did not before. In her grief, she came to know God's love in such a way it gave voice to her trademark quote: "'You are loved with an everlasting love'—that's what the Bible says—'and underneath are the everlasting arms.'" Through her own grief, she'd come to know that God holds us when we fall to tragedy. The experience "roused" her heart to move. She became instrumental in bringing God's love to a people who'd never known it.

 **STEP** Is something bad happening in your life right now? Fall into his everlasting arms today.

Good War

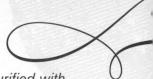

According to the law of Moses, nearly everything was purified with blood. For without the shedding of blood, there is no forgiveness.
HEBREWS 9:22

There may not be a stranger gift to receive from your parents than a will, but that's exactly what Rachael and Marie received as a gift from me and their dad in the middle of a church youth retreat. The youth pastor had sent letters to parents asking for a "gift of significance and meaning without much cost involved." Jonathan and I thought this was a moving gesture—the girls just thought it was creepy. After all, the will details what the girls will receive *after* their parents are dead. Even though it is painful to think about, death actually brings about new laws, new promises, new life.

And in the same way, war brings about change. The Bible talks plenty about war. In the Old Testament, we see Israel led continually into war by her various kings, yet no war would be necessary if not for sin. Israel was rebellious, and part of God's dealing with her was showing her what she could expect from a life without his blessing. Conversely, some of her greatest military victories were pronouncements of what his favor looks like. God is dealing with a broken and rebellious world that will not settle for peace.

Honest questions are derived from war. If the American Revolution had not happened, would we still be loyal to England? If there had been no conflict over states' rights and the freeing of slaves, would we have ever seen our first African American president? If America had not drawn a line in the sand after 9/11, how many more homeland attacks would America have endured? These are honest questions.

None are as poignant as this question: If Jesus had not died on the cross as a payment for our sins, waging war on sin's consequences, would you stand justified before God today?

In order for Rachael and Marie to fully receive the assets of their parents, Mom and Dad must first die. That's how a will works. Yes, war is ugly. Death, however, brings new life, new laws, and new promises. At the very least we need to recognize the sacrifices made for us by those who have been willing to shed their blood.

Pray for those who are at war today. Be sure to thank Jesus for the gift of his shed blood, his promise of your inheritance.
SW

JANUARY 31
Good Boundaries

They are darkened in their understanding and separated from the life of God because of the ignorance that is in them due to the hardening of their hearts. Having lost all sensitivity, they have given themselves over to sensuality so as to indulge in every kind of impurity, and they are full of greed. EPHESIANS 4:18-19, NIV

It just happened again. A seventeen-year-old student walked into the cafeteria of his high school and opened fire on random victims. By the time he was brought before a judge, three of his victims had died. As is often the case, neighbors say he was a normal boy who played outside with his sister and was helpful and polite to neighbors. Why are kids killing kids? How is it possible a person would become so embittered and dark he could pull the trigger of a gun for the sick pleasure of taking out random victims?

Behavior specialists identify disorders such as oppositional defiance or conduct disorder to explain why kids are capable of hurting others. They suggest maybe these kids have dysfunctional neurotransmitters that do not allow the aggressor to be restricted in his bad behavior. Experts point to parental drug use, marital problems, and violence in the home as red flags, yet they are unable to explain why only a percentage of kids who have dysfunctional families act out with any kind of violence.

The Bible offers its own answer . . . one we feel is superior to the ones psychologists are giving. The Bible says people who are left to seek their own way, their own pleasures, and who are indulged at every turn of their narcissistic yearnings will "lose all sensitivity." This literally means they lose the ability to fear consequences for their behaviors. For years our culture has been obsessed with enhancing self-esteem, but we've done so at the price of failing to realize the number one thing breeding confidence in kids is growing up with boundaries. Hearing no is good! On the other hand, when we allow people to indulge in whatever they please with no restrictions, they grow to become people who will stop at nothing.

The fact is, some evil comes into this world because we have not obeyed God's boundaries for our lives. It's time we start.

 **Action STEP** Practice observing boundaries today, no matter how small. Say no to that Little Debbie snack you really want. Turn off Facebook a little earlier. Bite your tongue when you feel like talking back to your mom. Learn to love boundaries as they construct a lovely you!

FEBRUARY 1
Near-Death Revival

The end of the world is coming soon. Therefore, be earnest and disciplined in your prayers. Most important of all, continue to show deep love for each other, for love covers a multitude of sins. Cheerfully share your home with those who need a meal or a place to stay. 1 PETER 4:7-9

In the spring of 2003, Aron Ralston went into the Arizona desert for what he thought to be some simple rock climbing. Because the danger level was minimal, he broke the cardinal rule of climbers. He did not tell anyone where he would be. An eight-hundred-pound boulder fell on his hand, trapping him to a rock wall. He was toast. For four grueling days he rationed the little bit of water he had and made a video journal.

In his videos, Ralston regretted his selfish approach to life. He confessed busyness kept him from answering family phone calls. He mourned allowing a girlfriend to drift away due to inattentiveness. He thought of the wife he had not even met yet and the son he would one day raise. He didn't want it to end like this. On the fourth day, he decided he wanted to live, and to live differently, so he pulled out his dull pocketknife and began the terrifying two-day process of cutting off his arm below the elbow.

Today Ralston is selflessly married and has the son he dreamed of when pinned by that boulder. He spends his life much differently now, even returning phone calls to his mom! His near-death experience brought revival to his life.

What if you had six days to reflect on your life? What thoughts would be recorded on your video journal? What would you say to your parents? To your friends? What dreams are you ready to chase? To be honest, we are all in such a situation. We have no promise of tomorrow, and the New Testament is a constant reminder to be ready for Jesus' return.

Peter says one thing should be done above all others, and that is to show love. Tragedies are often a reminder to our souls. What have we taken for granted? We neglect the things dearest to us, assuming they will always be around. Thank God for the times we are permitted to glimpse a future without this love and a chance to right our course!

 **Action STEP** What would you regret/long for if it seemed your life were ending today? Maybe, since you're still around, you could set a couple of things straight.

FEBRUARY 2

Disaster on the Increase

Nation will go to war against nation, and kingdom against kingdom. There will be great earthquakes, and there will be famines and plagues in many lands, and there will be terrifying things and great miraculous signs from heaven. LUKE 21:10-11

Every time we experience a natural disaster or massive tragedy in our world, people wonder if it is a sign from God. People want to know if God is raining judgment on his people through earthquakes, tsunamis, floods, tragedies like the 9/11 attacks, etc.

I think it's important to note that while we don't know why certain things like earthquakes and floods happen, sometimes tragedies like 9/11 are a direct result of sin. A group of terrorists set out with rebellious, hate-filled hearts to commit heinous acts of murder. These kinds of things are bound to happen, but they don't necessarily mean the victims are being punished. These acts were introduced by sin, they will increase as the end draws near, and *they will cease only when Jesus returns to reign.*

When Luke says, "Nation will go to war against nation," in the verse printed above, he parallels other passages speaking of Jesus' return. The things we are seeing now foretell of Jesus' return and are a direct result of sin's grip on this world. You and I rarely see with our eyes the battle being waged between God and the spirits of darkness; what we see are the desperate attempts of the enemy trying to win as many to his side as possible before he meets his final destiny. And we see a patient, loving God who does not want anyone to be destroyed. His desire is for people to repent. So he waits. He bides his time. He loves and calls us to love. He offers freedom and waits to see who will receive it. He is not too late or moving too slowly. He is God—holy, just, and right.

 **Action STEP** Are you ready for Jesus' return? Are you helping others to be ready?

FEBRUARY 3
Run to Me

The name of the LORD is a strong fortress; the godly run to him and are safe. PROVERBS 18:10

I had dreamed for years of being on Broadway and had spent countless hours chasing my dream. It seemed the train was finally on the right track when I earned a full scholarship for a master's degree in acting. Broadway, here I come! God let me know quickly he had other plans for me. I had been on campus only a week when I met the man who was to become the love of my life.

The train began derailing when I explained I would be leaving the program to marry. Part of my final grade that first year was to audition for a theater company on the East Coast. "We know you can't perform this summer, but you have to audition for a grade." But then I was on the callback list. "It's still part of your grade," my professors assured me. Next thing I knew I possessed not only an invitation to join the company, but I had been cast in some of the juiciest lead roles ever. This was a dream come true! The timing could not have been more disastrous.

I immediately tried to call the wife of my director and mentor at Wheaton College. She would know what to do. June had been through the marriage and theater thing. The phone line was dead . . . as a doornail. Not even a dial tone. I fought for a tone for over twenty minutes, finally conceding I had *nowhere to run but to God*. By the time I was calmed and steadied by the truest love of my life, Jesus, wouldn't you know the dial tone was back? June was then simply able to confirm for me I had indeed heard from God and he would walk with me as I walked away from this dream and into God's plan.

I wonder if sometimes things happen simply so God can remind us to run to his arms. We get distracted and try to run other places, but God wants us to run first to him. He is the truest friend we will ever have, and the surest place to find answers.

 Practice going to God first in the little things but especially in the big ones!
SW

FEBRUARY 4

No Pain, No Gain

When troubles come your way, consider it an opportunity for great joy. For you know that when your faith is tested, your endurance has a chance to grow. JAMES 1:2-3

It's called resistance, and muscles cannot grow without it. The term *resistance* in weight training refers to anything pushing against our muscles, which then causes them to contract. Resistance could come from the weight of a barbell, a training partner, or something as organic as paving stones or containers of water. These masses, pushing against our muscles, cause the muscles to strain and contract in resistance.

When you work out using resistance training, the initial result is *damage* to your muscles. Small rips and tears occur (catabolism), which are ideally met by a period of rest and inactivity during which your body can respond with its God-programmed repair system. Anabolism is the process through which your body naturally repairs the rips and tears, simultaneously producing muscle growth.

God makes the most of every opportunity to remind us in this life that we will have troubles. The word James uses in today's verse for troubles typically refers to troubles from *outside* an individual. In your faith you will meet with resistance of many kinds, causing you to press into the weight.

James promises the result of outside resistance to our faith will be growth. Pain is inevitable as we go through spiritual catabolism—it's not pleasant to be ridiculed, shunned, or maligned. Anyone who tells you they can go through that without some emotional rip and tear is not being truthful. But it is possible, even in the midst of breakdown, to experience joy; joy is your promise and inheritance. Sometimes there is a hint of the healing even in the midst of the pain.

Years ago, resistance training was natural. The lifestyle of farming, home-steading, and providing the basic necessities of food and shelter saw to it. Today, we live in a culture engineered for inactivity. Without supplementing our lives with some resistance training, our health is in danger. Spiritually, we have become engineered for inactivity as well. Most American Christians would be stunned to face persecution of any sort. The fact remains: without resistance, you cannot grow. It kind of makes you think, doesn't it?

 *Action* **STEP** Hit a gym and get some muscle rip 'n' tear going. As you heal in the days following, ask God to provide your faith with the same opportunity.

But It Feels So Good!

I run with purpose in every step. I am not just shadowboxing. I discipline my body like an athlete, training it to do what it should. Otherwise, I fear that after preaching to others I myself might be disqualified.
1 CORINTHIANS 9:26-27

I don't think there's anything better than a cozy bed mussed up and warmed by a night of sleep. Lots of heavy blankets and one puffy comforter on top is just the right recipe to make me push "snooze" repeatedly.

When I was growing up, there was a popular idiom: If it feels good, do it! It probably wouldn't take much for you to be convinced this is bad advice, but we both know sometimes we live by it. When it comes to my bed, I certainly do.

The heart of the matter lies in Paul's description of the athlete in 1 Corinthians 9. When we run a race, we train to win. The prize may be a trophy or a ribbon. In Paul's day it was a crown of greens or a wreath fitting over the victor's head. This crown had the shelf life of a dozen roses. Alive when given, it would soon wilt.

The prize we as Christians run for is eternal. There are little secondary "prizes" we can collect along the way, but they are not lasting. In fact, many things that feel so good in the temporal are deceptive. They not only wilt and fade, but they take a piece of our souls with them. Sexual sin, alcohol abuse, and casual hookups—all of these leave scars of immense proportion. Even sleeping in can do long-term harm. Getting up early to read the Word of God trains the heart for truth each day, preventing us from falling into those other forms of "pleasure."

I'm in a new season of trying to rise early to be with the Lord. In fact, as I write my new book, I'm taking a ten-day challenge to discipline myself by getting up at four thirty in the morning to be with the Lord! Radical? Not really. I'm just trying to beat my body into submission. I want the eternal reward.

 How does God want you to discipline your body? Maybe he wants you to set the alarm for six o'clock or to start exercising so you have more energy to serve him. Set a goal and begin to train your soul for spiritual victory.
DG

FEBRUARY 6

The Frog in the Kettle

Don't be fooled . . . for "bad company corrupts good character." Think carefully about what is right, and stop sinning. 1 CORINTHIANS 15:33-34

Ever consider the difference between a warm-blooded creature and a cold-blooded one? Warm-blooded creatures need to keep inside body temperatures at a steady level. If cold, they will burn energy to warm up. If hot, the body will cool itself by sweating. Cold-blooded creatures simply assume the temperature of their surroundings. Frogs are cold blooded.

A legendary frog experiment teaches us something about ourselves. A frog was placed in a kettle of boiling water. Immediately recognizing the vast difference between his blood temperature and the water, the little guy jumped out of the kettle before he could be scalded. He was next placed in a kettle of water at room temperature. He happily swam about as the temperature of the water was raised one degree at a time. Because he was created to assume the temperature of his surroundings, the frog eventually boiled, never aware he was in danger!

Humans are warm blooded, but our spiritual side has cold-blooded tendencies. If you were to step today into the vilest of situations where every law in God's Word was brazenly ignored, you would jump out. This happened to Megan when she attended her first college party. She had been looking forward to newfound college freedom, unaware of how little she had seen of the seedy underside of life. She left within thirty minutes, her eyes and ears scalded by things she had never imagined.

Consider the kettle. If you were to begin a friendship with this same group of people in a "cooler" atmosphere, you may not feel yourself being cooked. And eventually you might be able to attend a party like the one Megan dropped in on and experience little to no shock because you got used to things little by little. Paul was quoting a Greek play when he said, "Bad company corrupts good character." The church was beginning to embrace bad theology from teachers they were listening to. Slowly these teachers were leading the church away from the truth of the gospel.

Who are you listening to? What's the temperature of the water you are swimming in? These are good questions to consider; no one is immune from the plague of the frog in the kettle.

 **Action STEP**   Ask a mentor, parent, or adult leader to provide a brutally honest evaluation of your three closest associations. Good company or bad?

FEBRUARY 7

Relatively Speaking

Jesus told them, "My message is not my own; it comes from God who sent me. Anyone who wants to do the will of God will know whether my teaching is from God or is merely my own. Those who speak for themselves want glory only for themselves, but a person who seeks to honor the one who sent him speaks truth, not lies." JOHN 7:16-18

I still have this vague memory of the morning after junior prom. My friend's mom had valiantly stayed up all night with us. Somehow we managed to get on a controversial topic over breakfast, and I remember my friend's mom saying, "Yeah, well that's her truth. It's not my truth." I remember wondering how people could have two different truths. Turns out they can't.

My friend's mom embraced *relativism*. It's a nice notion, believing that everyone can have his or her own set of truths. It just isn't biblical. Relativism shouldn't be confused with statements such as "Beauty is in the eye of the beholder." You and I may look at photos of five models and pick two different girls as the most beautiful. Neither of us is wrong; we just each operated under a different truth. Little *t*. When "truth" begins with a lowercase *t*, we are talking subjectivity, or opinions.

When "Truth" begins with a capital *T*, we are dealing in nonnegotiables, not based on opinion. Jesus is God. There is no other way to heaven. That is Truth. Just as the sky is blue because there is a standard of color, Jesus is God because there is a standard of God written in his book of Truth.

When we come to a nonnegotiable, there are only three options. Let's say person A and person B disagree. Person A says Jesus is the only way to heaven. Person B says there are many ways to heaven.

1. If person A is right, person B is entirely wrong.
2. If person B is right, person A is entirely wrong.

I hope you can see there is absolutely no way for both to be correct. They cannot both have their own Truth. They are in direct opposition to each other.

Even Jesus didn't make up his own Truths! He said that his message was not his own. It was his Father's. He conformed to the standard of Truth written in the Scriptures of the Old Testament. You and I must find our Truth in the Bible too.

 Can you go a whole day without speaking one opinion, only Truth? Opinion is not necessarily bad. It is just imperative that we learn to tell the difference!
SW

FEBRUARY 8
Why Hell Matters

"My thoughts are nothing like your thoughts," says the LORD. *"And my ways are far beyond anything you could imagine. For just as the heavens are higher than the earth, so my ways are higher than your ways and my thoughts higher than your thoughts."* ISAIAH 55:8-9

The year 2011 was a firestorm for Christians, revolving around the issue of heaven and hell. One influential pastor wrote a book subtitled *A Book About Heaven, Hell, and the Fate of Every Person Who Ever Lived.* The gospel, he says in the book, is widely perceived as teaching that God will send every person who does not believe in Jesus to hell. What kind of God is this? he asks. And, how could we ever love or trust such a God? How could this ever be good news?

A second influential pastor responded with a book subtitled *What God Said about Eternity, and the Things We've Made Up.* His book acknowledges that although it may *feel* good to believe a loving God would not send billions of people to hell, God's Word still says those whose names are not written in the Lamb's Book of Life will be thrown into the lake of fire (see Revelation 20:15). The book of 1 John says if you have Jesus, you have life and if you don't . . . you don't. This doesn't stop us from reading God's Word and saying, "Really, God? Did you really just say that? I wouldn't say that."

God's ways are not our ways. His thoughts are not our thoughts. He is the potter, and we are the clay (see Isaiah 45:9; 64:8). Imagine the pride of one lump of clay explaining to another lump of clay what the potter is like. Any time we say something like, "I could never believe in a God who . . ." we are putting God's actions in submission to our own reasoning. If he does something we don't understand, must the fault rest with him? *Isn't it possible God actually has a higher and more perfected sense of justice than we have?*

God does not want anyone to perish. He has more grace in one little finger than you or I possess combined. None of this negates the fact he is a holy God. He does not *send* anyone to hell; we jump in that lake of our own free will when refusing to receive his invitation and provision (Jesus) for reconciliation. No matter how good it might feel to be inclusive, we have to stick to what the potter says.

 *Action* STEP Admit to God in prayer that *all* of your ways are in submission to his. Ask God to help you live each day according to his truth.

FEBRUARY 9
Authentic or Copycat?

Examine yourselves to see if your faith is genuine. Test yourselves. Surely you know that Jesus Christ is among you; if not, you have failed the test of genuine faith. 2 CORINTHIANS 13:5

About six years ago I began to be the kind of person who pays cash for things. As a cash user, it's hard to justify ninety dollars for a pair of shoes. Still, I saved and spent ninety dollars on my first pair of TOMS, fur lined boots so warm I use them for winter rides on my scooter. I knew when I bought those shoes, somewhere in the world a child who needed shoes was going to receive a free pair. I felt good about that.

I'll support, and even pay a little extra for, products made by a company attempting to do some genuine good in the world. I'll staunchly defend them to their detractors. *Hey—they are doing something. What are you doing other than complaining?*

Several years into TOMS' campaign to put shoes on disadvantaged kids, another company decided to get in on the action. Make no mistake—TOMS is a for-profit company funding its own nonprofit charity. It has grown into a huge company thanks to excellent designers and a well-defined mission statement. Big companies make big money—that's what they do. It was no surprise other shoe companies wanted to imitate the TOMS model; what surprised TOMS was the fact that a big, established shoe company publicly aligned themselves with nearly identical shoe designs, a similar four-letter name, and a commercial saying they were "proud to join companies like TOMS" . . . without ever contacting TOMS! That big shoe company was relentlessly hounded with accusations of profiteering, meaning the public assumed this shoe company wanted a free ride on the good name of TOMS. It just didn't ring authentic.

Paul encouraged the church at Corinth to examine their lives at the end of his second letter. How about you? Are you truly obedient to God? Is there fruit in your life? Do you love other people? Have you misused God's Word? Are you real? It's good to serve and to be a champion for the defenseless . . . but only if it's the 24-7 you. We have to live what we say we believe. The copycats are all too easy to spot.

 Research the website of an inspiring ministry. Why did they start? What do they do? Who are they aligned with? Who are their detractors?

FEBRUARY 10

Attending the Church of Pastor Sheets

It's not important who does the planting, or who does the watering. What's important is that God makes the seed grow. The one who plants and the one who waters work together with the same purpose. And both will be rewarded for their own hard work. For we are . . . God's workers. And you are God's field. You are God's building. 1 CORINTHIANS 3:7-9

Statistics say five out of every six people who grew up Protestant are leaving the church in their twenties. They aren't skipping—they've quit attending. Some might admit they attend the "church of Pastor Sheets." (As in bedsheets!)

As a church we've kind of shot ourselves in the foot. At one point we decided too many young people found church irrelevant. The music wasn't up to date, the sermons were dry, liturgy was too old fashioned, so we spent millions upon millions of dollars spicing things up. We bought lights and sound equipment, installed coffee bars and large play areas for children. Now, wouldn't you know it, there is a mass exodus of twentysomethings because they are saying they want an authentic serving body that spends more on missions and issues of justice than on a big ministry center. They want to sing hymns, and they would like a little bit of honor and liturgy in their services.

Here's the thing: we (you and I included) need to be certain of just what "church" is. Paul addresses the issue with a farming metaphor. Some of us are planters (missionaries, evangelists, artists). We cast the seed and pray it takes root in good soil. Some are caretakers (pastors, teachers, liberators). We fight weeds, prop up weaker plants, and provide daily sustenance. When we work together, along with God as he causes growth, church happens. If the work of the church flourishes, one party alone was responsible—God. If he is left out of the picture, nothing grows to begin with. It's as simple as that.

This is something no one can walk away from as a follower. While it doesn't require a building to cast seed and water plants, the church is the system God ordained. We work under him, with him, and for him. He is the boss. When he says keep meeting together, we should submit to his authority. It's not for the doughnuts and coffee, the great music, or the new friends we meet. It's for Christ and his Kingdom.

 *Action* **STEP** Give Pastor Sheets the boot. Make a covenant with God to put his body, the church, at the top of your priority list. Become a lifetime colaborer.

Playing God

"You won't die!" the serpent replied to the woman. "God knows that your eyes will be opened as soon as you eat it, and you will be like God, knowing both good and evil." GENESIS 3:4-5

From the beginning I could see Joey (not his real name) was not going to make it in my classroom. Joey was one of those kids who would turn right if you said turn left. He stood when he should be sitting, sang when he should be quiet . . . and was ridiculously charming. The world was his oyster, as they say. Joey had one major issue, and it played out to be his downfall. He didn't want to do what authorities asked him to do. One day midway through his eighth grade year, I asked him why he couldn't pull it together and behave. He shrugged. "I know right from wrong. I'm just going to do what I want to do." Two days later he was expelled.

This is Satan's game, and he is so good at getting us to play along! God had been straight with Adam and Eve—if you eat from this tree the consequence will be death. Satan played on a trait in Eve we all share. "Eating that fruit will make you just like God," Satan told her, "and he can't handle anyone being just like him." Satan's game: make them want to be God. When we buck authority, we are playing the role of God in our own lives. That's sin.

I'm not sure people talk about sin anymore. I have tried to talk about sin with a few girls at Joey's old school. Here are some of the responses I've gotten: I have been un-friended on Facebook. I have been told, "You don't know me. You don't know my heart." I have been lied to in an effort to cover up sin. I have been told my standards are too high.

I'm not trying to be a killjoy. Sin is a big deal because it leads to death. That's why God sets up guidelines for living and people in authority to help us live inside those guidelines. He loves us and wants us to be safe. There is no safety, no wisdom, quite like allowing God to be God. Trust me.

 Identify one area where you have been bucking authority. Surrender.

BIG ACTION STEP: Ask forgiveness from the authority you have been challenging and inform him or her of your intended change.
SW

Blurring the Truth

They traded the truth about God for a lie. So they worshiped and served the things God created instead of the Creator himself, who is worthy of eternal praise! Amen. ROMANS 1:25

Bobby Montoya was born distinctly male. By the time he was seven Bobby was a *Girl* Scout. You heard right. After much pressure from his mother, the Girl Scouts of America accepted him into a Colorado troop because he "identified" as a girl. Stop right there! It's possible a boy can be attracted to a boy. It's possible a boy can like pink and frills. It's possible a boy can prefer Barbie dolls to Matchbox cars. But it is not possible for a boy to *be* a girl.

As discussed on February 7, truth conforms to a standard or an original. We know the sky is blue because there exists a color chart upon which we base color. We know Alaska is north because there exists an axis upon which we judge direction. And we know a boy is a boy because there exists a set of biological standards by which to discern male from female.

We live in a society that blurs the truth all the time. This stems from a worldview known as *monism*, declaring everything is equal, unified, and one. There is no distinction between male and female. No distinction between a Creator and the created. No distinction between religions. Everything is one. A leading thinker in the movement, Carl Jung, even warned we must beware of thinking of good and evil as opposites.

Dr. Peter Jones recently coined the phrase "two-ism" to describe a Christian worldview in response to all this "unity." Two-ism declares God is a Creator who is distinctly separate from creation. God defines truth.

one-ism

Some things are worth fighting for, truth being one of them. Conformity to a standard or an original matters simply because truth is ultimately determined by God. (In fact, Jesus is the Way, the Truth, and the Life. If he *is* truth, we must protect it.) The apostle Paul says God gives up on a society that exchanges God's truth for a lie. In the following days' devotions, we'll be encouraging you to fight . . . but fight fair!

two-ism

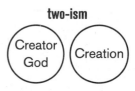

 **STEP** Google "Bobby Montoya" and check out the story for yourself. Think through the issue.

FEBRUARY 13

Our Creator Is "In" and "Above"

O LORD, our Lord, your majestic name fills the earth! Your glory is higher than the heavens. PSALM 8:1

Suzy and I both live in State College, Pennsylvania, which is home of the Penn State Nittany Lions. It is said that if you live here, your blood runs blue to match the school's colors. For the record, Suzy's is pretty blue while Dannah isn't much of a sports fanatic. Both of us had a moment where our blood froze when it was announced our team's beloved coach of almost fifty years had died suddenly. Turns out it was a lie.

Coach Paterno *was* fighting for his life in a hospital bed, having been diagnosed with cancer just weeks earlier, but he was not dead. Death would come soon, but for now someone had taken a piece of truth—he was close to death—and turned it into a lie. Lies almost always begin with a thread of truth.

We believe that the currently pervasive lie of monism (see yesterday's devotional) started with a thread of truth. Take a peek at Psalm 8:1. God is *in* all the earth. He "fills" everything. He has written his name into all of creation . . . into you and me. If we stopped there, it would be easy to adopt a worldview much like the beautiful blue characters of the movie *Avatar* who feel spiritually connected to a god who is in everything; they worship by worshiping creation. This would be an incomplete picture of the true God.

God has set his glory "higher" than the heavens. He is *above* us. This means he is distinct from creation. His essential being transcends the world we see and experience.* You cannot define God without this critical part of his mysterious character. He is your creator, distinct and outside of you.

The fact that he is above but can also be *in* us means he loves us. He thinks of you and yearns for you and pursues you. It is sad that so many cheat themselves out of experiencing the intense yearning and pursuit of God's love by believing God dwells *only* in us. If he is not first above us, we miss the love story of Creation.**

 Read Psalm 8. Consider this thought: "What am I that he thinks of me?" (see Psalm 8:4). Think all day today about the fact he *thinks* about you!

---

* See also Psalm 113:4; 57:5; Isaiah 40:22; John 1:1.
**This devotion was inspired by a message delivered by Dr. Peter Jones at truthXchange, February 2012.

FEBRUARY 14
Of Robots, Monkeys, and Mice

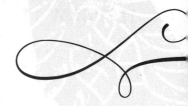

We destroy every proud obstacle that keeps people from knowing God.
We capture their rebellious thoughts and teach them to obey Christ.
2 CORINTHIANS 10:5

Did you know that somewhere in a lab right now there are scientists trying to decide whether to mix human DNA with DNA of monkeys and mice? In another lab there are scientists seeking to develop the technology to make a human robot, complete with emotions. Crazy? Yes. Impossible? No.

There are many benefits to these studies. Imagine how a lung cancer patient could have a digital lung implanted to save his or her life. Someone at imminent risk of a heart attack could receive a robotic heart. What if we could plant human DNA into monkeys and mice to discover a cure for cancer? These are all good and noble purposes.

The study of improving humans and eliminating aging is called *trans-humanism*. The goal is to transcend the unfortunate human tendency to die. The trouble with this science is many of its champions treat it as a sort of religion, the goal of immortality always on their minds. It is our modern-day tower of Babel. Is this something you think Christians should weigh in on? (Check out Genesis 11:1-9 if you don't know about the tower of Babel.)

God's Word says we're supposed to take everything captive as it rises up against the truth of God. While this can be about unhealthy personal thoughts, it can be argued that we also have a responsibility to address cultural thoughts, opinions, and ideas that rise up against God. It is reasonable to hope a lung cancer patient could be saved with a digital lung. That is a good thing. But it becomes an assault on God and his ordered world to think we can become immortal, and that has to be addressed.

We're kind of glad we write books for teens and are not the theologians called to tackle the science of transhumanism. But we're also glad there are scientists out there following Jesus and taking unholy thoughts captive for the Kingdom of God.

 Consider this seemingly impossible question Christian theologians debate: What would happen if the science to mix a human and a monkey worked? Would we have a being that is half monkey and half human one day? If we did, would that half human need salvation?

"He Loved Me Then!"

God showed his great love for us by sending Christ to die for us while we were still sinners. ROMANS 5:8

I believe the church is sometimes without love when we address the issue of homosexuality. I grieve for those I counsel who have to fight to feel loved by the body of Christ. Damon was one of those.

Damon had been the head of his school's Gay-Straight Alliance. At the time, he was a practicing homosexual. Since then, he'd surrendered to Jesus and found freedom in living according to God's plan for sexuality. But he was still burdened.

He recounted for me many GSA rallies and meetings fueled with the message "Christians don't love us" and "the God of Christians doesn't love us." This was easy to believe considering the encounters many alliance members had with Christians. Damon asked me if it would be okay to go back to his GSA and simply tell them he'd discovered that God does love him.

Yes! Oh yes!

God brought to my mind the solid truth that he loved both Damon and me before we loved God. He loved us while we were yet sinners. I also remembered a girl I'd sat next to on a plane whose lesbian mother had been shot in the leg by a Christian. Learning I was a Christian, she physically recoiled and said, "Christians hate us." It shocked me! I told her any true Christian would love her since God is love. The look on her face told me she didn't believe me. But as I kept talking to her, I saw the wall come down, and we had a great conversation about God. I was able to love her without agreeing with the sin of homosexuality. It is possible. I yearn for Christians to respond in love to those struggling with same-sex attraction, the aftermath of abortion, teen pregnancy, and other sins we often "fight" over.

 Do you know someone struggling with homosexuality, lying, abortion, pornography, overeating, or hatred? Ask God how you can tell and show that person today that he loves him or her.
DG

Holy Rebellion

Jesus said to them, "Give back to Caesar what is Caesar's and to God what is God's." And they were amazed at him. MARK 12:17, NIV

Corrie ten Boom, her sister Betsie, and their father were simple people living above their storefront shop when the social question of the century arose. The Nazi regime, with white supremacists who wanted to kill off "less superior" forms of life, including Jews, was in full drive. At first, it seemed the Jewish people were merely losing rights and being relocated to new neighborhoods. They were really being sent to concentration camps where they were worked to death, incinerated, or shot. The ten Booms disobeyed their government by hiding Jews in their home until they were caught in 1944 and sent to a concentration camp themselves.

Jesus was once asked about a controversial social issue: taxes. A much crueler and more deceptive tax process was in play back in the day, and Jesus' enemies wanted to put him in a tough position. So, they asked him if he thought people should pay taxes. He knew it was a trap. His answer? "Give back to Caesar what is Caesar's and to God what is God's." He knew money was not and is not an eternal resource. It was a part of this temporary earth system. It wasn't really "his." Therefore, he didn't fight the corruption of the tax system.

In most cases, God simply wants us to submit to the governing authorities he allows to be in place over us. But there are drastic times when he calls us to gently, humbly, quietly act in holy rebellion.

The lives of people are eternal resources. They are "his." The ten Boom family knew this. They stood against their government at the risk of their own lives. It's important to note they did so with tremendous humility and love for those committing the hate crimes. What power of God's Spirit was in them to love their enemies!

Being a holy rebel according to God's rules requires tremendous discernment and love. But don't expect a lot of accolades from the world along the way! Corrie's father and Betsie both died in those camps.

 *Action* **STEP** Identify one woman you completely admire. Ask her, What social issue do you believe may be an area where we must disagree with our government to give to God what belongs to him?

Political Polarity

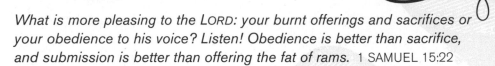

*What is more pleasing to the LORD: your burnt offerings and sacrifices or
your obedience to his voice? Listen! Obedience is better than sacrifice,
and submission is better than offering the fat of rams.* 1 SAMUEL 15:22

Have you noticed Americans generally don't fall into two distinct political
categories any longer? It's no longer merely Republicans and Democrats,
elephants and donkeys. Why does it even matter? Because whether you
are staunchly in one polarized corner or the other, whether you are a
bystander or cynical, chances are you will vote at some point. It's the
right thing to do.

Despite the division of American politics into nine observed categories
ranging from staunch conservative to the disengaged (not interested), there is
great polarity raging between conservative and liberal. David Sedaris, a liberal
essayist, explains the situation well. A friend he trusted said something com-
plimentary about former Republican presidential candidate Sarah Palin, and
Sedaris admitted he did not want to listen to the kind sentiments. He wanted
to hear she had been mean and snarky—an ugly woman like the stereotype he
housed in his polarized mind-set. This was an honorable admission, as he also
said he knew he had to listen to the good with the bad.

Jesus claimed no political affiliations. Though he was supportive of honor-
ing systems put into place by law or rule ("Give to Caesar what belongs to
Caesar," Matthew 22:21), he did not assert power at any time via political arenas even though the setting was ripe for him to do so. We are firmly convinced
Jesus is neither a Republican nor a Democrat. His is a Kingdom, not a democracy. Whatever government can do to enable the will of God to be done on
earth as it is in heaven is good. Whatever it may do to grieve the heart of God
or go against his will is not good. Our government, let's face it, does both. The
answer is not *in* politics, policies, or pundits (experts in the political arena). No
law passed by man, no economic proposal, no green initiative will ever please
God like our obedience to him.

 Is it possible to be an educated voter *and* refuse to
enter the political war? Ask your friends, your parents,
and your youth leaders what they think.

Looking Back

Don't you realize that those who do wrong will not inherit the Kingdom of God? Don't fool yourselves. Those who indulge in sexual sin, or who worship idols, or commit adultery, or are male prostitutes, or practice homosexuality, or are thieves, or greedy people, or drunkards, or are abusive, or cheat people—none of these will inherit the Kingdom of God. Some of you were once like that. But you were cleansed; you were made holy; you were made right with God by calling on the name of the Lord Jesus Christ and by the Spirit of our God. 1 CORINTHIANS 6:9-11

I didn't live a holy life in high school. It looked like I did, but in the dark I was sinful. Between teaching Sunday school and witnessing for Jesus in poverty-stricken neighborhoods, I was having sex with my Christian boyfriend. It was the great heartache of my life. I hated my sin but could not stop. I was "indulging in sexual sin." That's me up there in 1 Corinthians 6!

I never told anyone. Why?

Because back then the church did a lot of foolish things to people whose sin showed up in 1 Corinthians 6. We kicked pregnant girls out of the church. We voted against AIDS research. We were silent when gay kids and abortionists were murdered. We denied the problem of pornography though it was in our midst.

To be clear, the sins listed above are harmful and devastating and should not be tolerated. But I wish that someone somewhere could have stood up and told me that they'd sinned like I had. That they had once been living 1 Corinthians 6 but God had changed them. This would have been better than casting such harsh judgment that I kept my sin and lifestyle a secret.

It doesn't matter what our sin—sexual, idolatrous, adulterous, perverted, dishonest, greedy, self-medicating, abusive—Paul uses the word *tauta*, or "monster," to describe our condition before Jesus came in and changed us. Why would God suddenly become like us and become tolerant of monstrous behavior? He won't. But he even loves those who have a sinful lifestyle. And we can change our monstrous behavior toward those who have not yet been justified by faith. We can love, defend, deliver, and protect, all the while knowing something has to shake down in their lives, or they are lost.

 **Action STEP** Ask God to give you an authentic broken heart for those who are living apart from him. Ask him for his heart. And get ready to be rocked.
DG

Religious Persecution

[Jesus said,] "If the world hates you, remember that it hated me first. The world would love you as one of its own if you belonged to it, but you are no longer part of the world. I chose you to come out of the world, so it hates you." JOHN 15:18-19

James and John were two of Jesus' closest disciples. They were called the "sons of thunder" for their zeal in following Christ. They gave even their lives. *Foxe's Book of Martyrs* reports, "When this James . . . was brought to the tribunal seat [for being a Christian], he that brought him [John] and was the cause of his trouble, seeing him to be condemned and that he should suffer death, was in such sort moved therewith in heart and conscience that as he went to the execution he confessed himself also, of his own accord, to be a Christian. And so were they led forth together." James kissed him. They were both beheaded.

Martyrdom is still a reality in most of the Christian world . . . more than 170,000 Christians die for their faith per year. Could martyrdom ever visit the shores of a free nation such as America?

Jesus seems to be readying us for the inevitable. The day will come when protections are set aside and zeal for something else will take center stage. It is a struggle to imagine this could happen in what we call a "Western nation," typically allowing more freedoms than "Eastern rule" nations (such as China or Russia). Recently, however, wearing of the traditional Muslim head covering, the burka, was banned in public places in France. Women who appear in public wearing a burka can be fined the equivalent of US$200. Men who force women to wear a burka can face huge fines in the $40,000 range as well as imprisonment. While these are examples of bans on Muslim dress in a Western country, could Christianity be next?

Well, consider that a 2012 ruling from our own White House started a firestorm by attempting to require religious employers to pay for abortion and contraceptive services for employees, regardless of the employer's stated tenets of faith. Such challenges to religious freedom are not outside the realm of either God's will or his ability to care for us. Because freedom of religion is a godly principle, it will be challenged on that basis alone. Expect it. But don't fear it.

 Stand up against injustices everywhere. Do so with love, gentleness, kindness, and knowledge derived from having educated yourself well. But know you will meet opposition.

Easy Come, Easy Go

[God] ensures that orphans and widows receive justice. He shows love to the foreigners living among you and gives them food and clothing. So you, too, must show love to foreigners, for you yourselves were once foreigners in the land of Egypt. DEUTERONOMY 10:18-19

Our Pure Freedom ministry team recently journeyed into Canada. It's scary crossing an international border. The "welcome center" smells a little like suspicion, and it feels a bit more like *detention*. Complying 100 percent with international rules, we still felt like total criminals when the guy with a gun poked his head in and began asking questions about where we had been and what we were up to. This is the border between two *free* countries!

Our brothers and sisters in North Korea are not free. They may not cross into independent South Korea. If they do leave without permission, they are returned to imprisonment, forced labor, or execution. China is no place to flee to—the Chinese government routinely returns exiles to North Korea. China claims to be returning refugees based on international law and "humanitarian principles." It's hard, isn't it, to reconcile imprisonment and death with the concept of "humanitarianism"? The one bright spot in all this is *your* generation—young Chinese are beginning to speak boldly, insisting an alliance with North Korea is damaging China's international reputation.

From the moment Adam and Eve left the Garden, God has kept his people wanderers, perhaps as a reminder of their true home. We could begin to believe this is it . . . home. We belong here. This land belongs to us. And then, it's not long before we begin mistreating the foreigner and the alien. Instead, maybe we should look at those who are "foreigners" or "aliens" as an opportunity for us to show hospitality. By helping them, we have a chance to show the same hospitality shown to Moses, Daniel, Abraham, and Jesus—all of whom were in need of kindness when far from home.

God does not see it as a burden to show compassion to oppressed and displaced people. He loves them. It is his honor to love them, bless them, and promise them a home. It is *our* honor to be his coworkers in this endeavor.

 **Action STEP** One day you will have a home you will be free to open to a stranger. Begin preparing your heart now by praying for and learning about refugees from North Korea and other oppressed countries.

FEBRUARY 21
Free to Be Criticized

A gentle answer deflects anger, but harsh words make tempers flare.
The tongue of the wise makes knowledge appealing, but the mouth
of a fool belches out foolishness. PROVERBS 15:1-2

I miss seeing Simon Cowell on *American Idol.* Trust me, it's not his spirit of humiliation—um, constructive criticism—I'm missing. I think Simon helped contestants in a way current judges are not willing to. Simon said the difficult things, but things that were also truth. *Could* current judges say the hard things? I love their spirit of encouragement, but perhaps the kids on the show would have a more accurate picture of their potential if they heard the truth.

Are you and I free enough to receive criticism? British prime minister Winston Churchill once said, "Criticism may not be agreeable, but it is necessary. It fulfills the same function as pain in the human body. It calls attention to an unhealthy state of things." If we receive feedback with even a hint of defensiveness, we are in danger of missing out on a chance to grow.

Here are some ideas to help you graciously receive criticism and benefit from the wisdom of people kind enough to be truthful.

1. Avoid giving explanations for why you did things the way you did them unless you are asked directly. Verbal defense clearly communicates to critics that their input is incorrect and therefore unvalued. Instead, make knowledge appealing, as today's verse in Proverbs says.
2. Restate the criticism in your own words and thank your critics for sharing their opinion. You may choose to disregard their advice later, but for now they know you have listened. Your sincere thankfulness (a gentle answer) insures good will.
3. Ask yourself, "Is there a valid point in this critique?" One thing my family hates to see on *American Idol* is a contestant arguing with industry insiders about professional advice others would be paying thousands of dollars to receive. Talk about a mouth belching out foolishness!
4. Don't take it personally. When possible, engage in conversation with your critics. They likely have some truth for you to chew on!

 God has equipped you to do amazing things, but everything takes practice. Find a way to ask—that's right—*ask* for constructive criticism today. Get ready to learn, and be set free!
SW

FEBRUARY 22

Whatever Happened to Nineveh?

[The Lord said,] "Should I not have concern for the great city of Nineveh, in which there are more than a hundred and twenty thousand people who cannot tell their right hand from their left?" JONAH 4:11, NIV

Iraq has been in the news a lot recently, and by recently I mean most of your lifetime. So what's the deal with this infamous little country, roughly the size of California and home to over thirty-two million people?

Iraq has quite the history. Scripture describes the Garden of Eden as being located at the point where the Tigris River meets the Euphrates. Archaeological digs and Bible history pinpoint the Garden's likely locale in modern-day Iraq. Nineveh, the great capital city of the Assyrian Empire, was also located in Iraq. If you recall from *Veggie Tales* viewings, Nineveh caused the prophet Jonah a great deal of trouble. Jonah was told to go to Nineveh and insist the people repent, but Jonah, like most Israelites, hated the Assyrians. Assyria had relentlessly attacked Israel, plundering her cities and taking God's people into captivity. Jonah could hardly believe God would want to show mercy to the people who had committed such atrocities. But rescue Nineveh God did. After using three days in the belly of a big fish to convince Jonah he meant business, God used the reluctant prophet to lead an entirely wicked city to repentance . . . while the reluctant prophet watched and pouted from a distance.

There has been a Christian presence in Iraq since the time of Jonah. The number is in decline today, down to about five hundred thousand believers, but nearly all of these Christians are of Assyrian descent. How about that! The great city Jonah bitterly led to repentance all those years ago still accounts for the presence of God's church in "Nineveh" today.

God built a little family home in the middle of what had once been the garden he provided for his creation. But that remnant of Nineveh is under fire today. Christians were once welcomed in Iraq; today they are seen as allies to the West and a threat to the religion of Islam. Over six hundred thousand Christians have fled to nearby Syria and Jordan. The remaining few need our prayers to sustain them as they continue to see their religious freedoms slipping away.

 Remember your brothers and sisters in Iraq in your prayers. Ask God for continued protection and for growth in the numbers of believers.

A Case of Mistaken Identity

Everyone who wants to live a godly life in Christ Jesus will suffer persecution. 2 TIMOTHY 3:12

It was a case of mistaken identity. My Bernese mountain dog did not bite the neighbor's cat. But the accusation felt terrible nonetheless. A sweet neighbor lady mistakenly believed we own two mastiffs and that one had put a four-hundred-dollar bite on her cat. There were several things wrong in this case:

1. We don't own mastiffs.
2. The neighbor said a "tall, handsome, well-dressed friend" of ours was walking our dogs when this happened. We don't have any handsome friends, and no one walks our beasts but us.
3. This petite older lady said she helped to corral the dog, holding the collar until the pup could be put back on his leash. No stranger touches Hero's head and lives to tell about it. Well, not really, but he doesn't like being touched around his face by people he doesn't know yet.

Our dog was innocent. The charges still felt terrible. Imagine Jesus on Good Friday. If the physical torture were not enough, he had been verbally mocked as well. The poignancy of a moment in the film *The Passion of the Christ* always strikes me: As Simon of Cyrene moves to pick up the cross, he, feeling persecuted, addresses the crowd saying something along the lines of, "I want it known that I am the innocent one here." Nothing could be further from the truth as Jesus is lifted up on the cross for our sins.

Persecution hurts, and it does require sacrifice. The World Evangelical Alliance estimates over two hundred million Christians are currently denied basic freedoms of faith in over sixty countries worldwide. These are people standing falsely accused, or perhaps accused of nothing other than the audacity to believe in the one true God. They are tortured, arrested, ostracized, mutilated, and often martyred for their beliefs. Paul says the godly will be persecuted. We must at some point realize our freedoms, though precious, endanger us. Very little is at stake in America, and believers risk little when there is little risk. But do you see the danger?

 Discuss with friends why we experience so *little* push back for our faith. Persecution is supposed to be part of the deal, right?

FEBRUARY 24
Free to Doubt

"What do you mean, 'If I can'?" Jesus asked. "Anything is possible if a person believes." The father instantly cried out, "I do believe, but help me overcome my unbelief!" MARK 9:23-24

I believe. I doubt. I believe. . . . I don't know! This seems to be the argument in the head of this desperate dad. He brought his son to Jesus' posse, having heard they were connected to a strong power. They had been performing miracles right and left. Hopefully they could do something for his boy. It was worth a shot. But the disciples failed (see Mark 9:17-18).

How embarrassing this must have been for the disciples! They were faced with not only failure, but failure in the presence of their enemies. Can't you just see the Pharisees snickering off to the side? Indeed, it seems when we read the account that Jesus rebuked his disciples—but he did not. His rebuke (see verse 19) was directed at the Pharisees who loved to see people fail, so that they might become more revered. The Pharisees believed they alone had it all figured out, but Jesus prefers those of us with enough understanding to know that is not true.

The father of this boy took a big risk in asking for deliverance. When he said, "I do believe," he was being honest. In spite of what he had just seen (failure) he was willing to risk failure a second time. Sometimes we have to obey first, and the belief will come along later. Giving Jesus the green light to heal his boy was a tremendous leap of faith, regardless of his obvious doubt.

There are traditions of faith in this world that leave no room for doubt. These are traditions built on the fear of alienating ourselves from God. Christianity is not fear based. Perfect love drives out fear . . . and perfect love does not fear doubt. Jesus tells his followers that this boy's demon could only be chased away by prayer and fasting (see verses 28-29). Why do we pray? Why do we fast? Because we have all the answers, we're all set, good to go, thank you very much? Or do we pray because we know our own failings yet have the guts to believe God loves us anyhow?

 Have you ever (or would you ever) be able to pray a prayer like this? "God, I have enough faith to believe you are God and nothing is impossible for you . . . but I have enough sense to look around right now and see it looks impossible." Has God ever met (or do you believe God would meet) you in impossible places?

It Is for Freedom

Christ has truly set us free. Now make sure that you stay free, and don't get tied up again in slavery to the law. GALATIANS 5:1

In the past I have looked at the NIV translation of our key verse: "It is for freedom that Christ has set us free," and have been confused. Isn't that a little like saying, "It is for ice skating I have taken you ice skating"? But I guess the point is this: what if I begged and begged to go skating, and when I finally got to the rink, I spent the entire time playing video games and eating corn dogs? I wouldn't be taking advantage of the gift.

We have not only been set free from the law of sin and death, but we have been given the opportunity to live in a country where (at least for now) anything is possible. We never have to sit back wide eyed, empty stomached, knowing we will never be able to achieve what the other guy has.

So why do we return to our old ways, our old habits . . . or vomit, as the Old Testament calls it (Proverbs 26:11)? Israel once had to make atonement for her sins annually. Most of the time the Israelites had to live under the weight of new sins piling up while they waited for the next Day of Atonement. The Pharisees used to call this their yoke, the hundreds of laws people had to obey in order to avoid guilt. But Jesus came along and said his yoke was light (see Matthew 11:30). Not too many laws, certainly not hundreds. *Love the Lord your God with all your heart, with all your soul, and with all your mind. And love your neighbor as yourself* (see Matthew 22:37-39).

Why aren't we telling people this? This is why we have freedom! Christ has already done all the work of saving. He has given us the work of telling and loving. I'm afraid sometimes the only work we engage in is chasing pleasure and sitting around. What are we doing? It is for freedom he has set us free. Get up off that couch, get out there, and live it!

 Limit your couch time. Freedom is out there, where the people are, so go tell others!
SW

FEBRUARY 26
Ah, Parents!

Grandchildren are the crowning glory of the aged; parents are the pride of their children. PROVERBS 17:6

Most teens not only love their parents, but they also desire a close relationship with them. About 80 percent of you say you even *like* your parents! Studies show teens having a significant bond with their parents experience greater success navigating the challenges of emerging adulthood than those who have less rapport with their parents.

At the same time, there is a generation gap at play, rapidly growing due to the Internet and cell phones. Almost 50 percent of teens say their parents are clueless as to what they do online.

Why does this cause a generation gap? The chief reason actually has nothing to do with technology. Every generation suffers a "gap" with the one that follows it. When you were a child, your parents were fully responsible for your well-being. The decisions they made were out of consideration for both your safety and their own values. You were at their mercy, and they were responsible before God for your formation. Eventually you developed a desire for independence, and in your quest for such, you met people and had experiences your parents could no longer "control." You made mistakes, and your parents felt powerless to protect you. It is a tough passage for teens and parents alike. The Internet and texting have simply upped the ante a bit—the process and the gap have been around for centuries.

A parent's life can end no more sweetly than to know you have chosen of your own free will and are fully sold out to a life of serving God. Likewise, what an honor for you to have parents who are loving you and guiding you toward adulthood, and who will continue to do so once you are "grown." Even as your parents move toward old age and its necessary discomforts, you can be there to encourage and bless them. It is your blessing today, and your own children will one day be your crown of glory!

Even if your bond with Mom and Dad is weak, find a way to bless them today. It can be as simple as doing something without being asked, writing a love letter to them, or even treating them to a meal or a night out on the town. If you do not live with your mom or dad, think of the adult who has helped you grow up. Bless him or her today.

Obey Is a Four-Letter Word

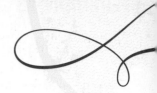

"Honor your father and mother." This is the first commandment with a promise: If you honor your father and mother, "things will go well for you, and you will have a long life on the earth." EPHESIANS 6:2-3

My father had a rule or two. And I'll be the first to admit that I didn't like some of those rules. I thought it was dumb we couldn't have food or drinks in his office. One day, I decided it was time to break down those walls of dumbness. And with a tall, cold glass of red Kool-Aid, I entered his office—and of course, the inevitable happened. I bumped my glass over and spilled my red drink onto the light gray carpet. Dad let me lie to him, though he knew full well I did it. I tortured myself with the weight of my secret, eventually collapsing into his forgiveness as I confessed and the burden came off my heart. Obedience is not always enjoyable, but disobedience has *nasty* consequences.

God's command is not to obey our parents when we think they are right or when it's convenient. The command is to obey because it is the right thing to do. The intent of the command is not to merely *do* what is right, but to do so gladly with love and affection in our hearts. It's not enough to walk the talk. We are called to delight in the opportunity to serve our parents this way.

Obedience is the first thing God required in the Garden. He created Adam and explained the tree situation. "You can eat from any tree in the garden, Adam . . . except this one" (see Genesis 2:15-17). Then he created Eve, gave the command to be fruitful, and repeated the tree rule. Before the first couple had managed to create even one little fruit, they stomped all over the tree rule.

Adam and Eve had been given eternal life. They were never going to get sick, never going to die. Disobedience changed everything. The first Adam blew the obedience gig, but the second Adam (Jesus) set it right again, and in the process he gave you and me another shot at it. There is a promise attached to the command to obey our parents, and that is so we might have long life filled with prosperity. Obey the ones who love us the most and get a life of blessing as a result? If they had the chance, Adam and Eve would tell us that that's a pretty sweet deal.

 **STEP** No grumbling today. *Yes, ma'am* and *yes, sir* only.
DG

Dropping Conditions

Now, most people would not be willing to die for an upright person, though someone might perhaps be willing to die for a person who is especially good. But God showed his great love for us by sending Christ to die for us while we were still sinners. ROMANS 5:7-8

Ashley was eleven when her dad left home. He had been unfaithful to Ashley's mom, and Ashley was angry. Though her dad sought a relationship with her for seven years, texting her each night to say he was thinking of her, Ashley had nothing to give in return. His texts went unanswered and his sin unforgiven. Then Ashley met Jesus and began to grow. She wanted her brothers to know this joy she had found, but a church-wide fast she participated in revealed something with great clarity: she couldn't lead her brothers to healing when something remained broken in her. She asked her dad for forgiveness, let him know she forgave him, and allowed God to begin healing everything conditional love had broken.

Relationships can't survive in conditional waters. Eventually, from your parents to your spouse to your girlfriends, people will disappoint you. The disappointment may come from a wound, a decision to move, or even from a loving confrontation. In other words, not every disappointment is borne of sin. Still, many are. And we are glad Jesus chose to love us without condition.

What nice, neat words are used in our Bible translations. We were "sinners." How about some synonyms? We were obnoxious, detestable, and vile. We possessed *nothing* we could use in payment for Jesus' goodness to us. He didn't say, "I'll rescue you once you prove you're worth it." He didn't ask us to clean up first or even make a partial payment in advance. He loved us, and he knew the impact his love would have. We would not remain what we had been, for love covers over a multitude of sins (see 1 Peter 4:8).

*Action* **STEP** Your family is likely far from perfect. Examine each of your family relationships carefully, and remove from each family member one expectation or condition you have imposed. Don't be surprised if you first notice a change in yourself!

MARCH 1

I Choose You

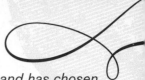

We know, dear brothers and sisters, that God loves you and has chosen you to be his own people. 1 THESSALONIANS 1:4

Rachel was raised in confusion. She was born to a black dad and a white mom but grew up with a white stepfather who loved to taunt her with racial slurs. Her anger led to fairly serious drug use by the time she was fifteen.

She met Josh during her junior year and was pregnant by her final month of high school. They married. She says marriage with Josh was "a couple of ill-mannered cats clawing at one another all the time." By the time Rachel was pregnant with child number two she found herself alone in a women's shelter wondering if anyone would ever love her.

Three days after her arrival at the shelter, Josh made an unbelievable choice. He chose Rachel, his children, and his marriage. The couple moved to Pennsylvania deeply in debt and without a clue of how to fix their brokenness. I was there the day Rachel gave her life to Jesus. I was in the delivery room on the day they welcomed their second child into this world. And recently I was filled with awe and wonder as I read this young couple's family Christmas letter—these "kids" had become a team I look up to! It all goes back to the night Josh chose Rachel, not understanding that Jesus had already chosen them both.

In our family we sign birthday cards "I *like* you!" My husband and I chose each other, promising we would remain together till death do us part. We chose to adopt our girls when they were teens. They chose to leave California and make a new home with us in Pennsylvania. We are stuck together now and figure we *have* to love each other . . . but we don't have to like each other. We want to know we would still choose each other today. We want to know, warts and all, we are chosen.

Relationships require unswerving choices, especially within families. There are moments when I do not *feel* like loving my family! There are times I don't want to forgive or to hang out. But my family needs to know after all is said and done . . . I still choose them. I desperately want them around. I like them.

Action **STEP** Write someone dear to you a little "love note" today . . . a family member if possible . . . but sign it "I like you!"

SW

Save Your Venom

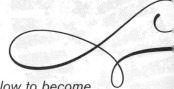

Everyone should be quick to listen, slow to speak and slow to become angry, because human anger does not produce the righteousness that God desires. JAMES 1:19-20, NIV

It was one of those dreaded long nights of driving. Our Secret Keeper Girl team was looking at a four-hour drive to our next hotel, and it was already eleven o'clock at night. We made one last pit stop before driving hours down barren New Mexico roadway.

Commotion at the front door of the gas station caught my attention. A huge tarantula was making its way across the parking lot, causing my tour mates to literally dance in combined fear and excitement. Screams filled the air as several of us came running with cameras.

From behind me a presence emerged. A woman wearing oversize basketball shorts and a football jersey, arms tattooed from the wrists up and head shaved except for the small ponytail banded high up on her skull, gently knelt beside the spider.

She began to talk softly, "Come on, little guy. Right in here." She cupped her hands. "I've got you." The spider jerked one massive hairy leg, an arachnid martial arts move, and went the other direction, into the outstretched hands of the woman's companion, a ponytailed, tattooed man. He continued to talk softly to the spider as he moved it toward safety.

"Don't they bite?" a grizzled trucker in our small crowd asked.

"Naw," the tough guy said. "They save their venom for their prey."

Unfortunately, too many of us do not behave like that tarantula. Oh, we experience threat, there is no doubt about that, but we do not always follow the clear instruction for defense in God's Word. We are to be slow to anger, slow to attack.

That karate move I saw the tarantula make? That was a readying-for-attack position. Tarantulas are famous for waiting, turning the other direction, and applying dry bites (no venom released). Only as a last resort will a tarantula release venom.

God asks us to consider the same defense if we wish to produce righteousness. Our duty is to listen and apply our hearts to what is being said—not to shoot the venom of our own opinion before we have a chance to consider whether we might be instructed by someone else's words.

 A soft answer turned away the wrath of this large spider. What might your listening ears and soft answers be able to accomplish today?

Friends and Family

Many will say they are loyal friends, but who can find one who is truly reliable? PROVERBS 20:6

Do you have one of those girlfriends who, the moment she begins dating someone new, completely ditches everyone else in her life? Wait for it. . . . Are you that girl?

The issue here is devotion. A garden left untended will never grow. Dinner isn't ready until someone cooks it. If you want to love your family more deeply and to maintain relationships with dear friends, you can't ditch them every time a new guy (or another interest) comes along. Devotion isn't a very popular commodity in today's economy. It's hard to find people who will stick with it (or you) for the long haul.

In this proverb, Solomon is just saying what we all know to be true. Most people will tell you they are good and loyal friends. Actions, however, speak louder than words. We chase what we are most fearful of losing. We neglect that which we are certain we possess. So we dedicate more time to guys out of fear. We neglect good friends and family due to comfort.

This is a time you are learning to live a little more independently of your parents. Not only have Dannah and I both been there as teens, but we have both raised teenage daughters. Though parents are far from perfect, no one desires success and blessing for you more unselfishly than the people who raised you. The flesh would have you pull away from your parents at this time, but we want to encourage you instead to step up your trust and dependence. It is still possible to trust and depend as you mature, and this is what we encourage you to seek. Parents aren't around forever. This is a key time to learn from them, to stave off any regrets of not enough time spent together, and oddly enough, to get some info on living as an adult.

 *Action* **STEP** Set up a couple of dates this week, one with your family and one with a bestie. Be sure to tend and water these relationships with great care!
SW

Loving the Fam

There was a crowd sitting around Jesus, and someone said, "Your mother and your brothers are outside asking for you." Jesus replied, "Who is my mother? Who are my brothers?" Then he looked at those around him and said, "Look, these are my mother and brothers. Anyone who does God's will is my brother and sister and mother." MARK 3:32-35

I remember the first fight my girls had. Having been adopted at fourteen, Autumn had been in the family less than a year. The two were immediate friends upon meeting in China, but back in the States reality set in. Lexi's sloppy. Autumn's a neat-freak. Lexi's germ-a-phobic. Autumn will eat anything. Lexi had friends. Autumn didn't yet. Finally, the ultimate girl move was made: the silent treatment.

A few months later the upstairs erupted. I looked at my husband and said, "Finally! This is good." From that day on, they were true sisters.

You have probably found you are "allowed" to say all manner of critical things about your family, but woe to the person who assumes it is okay to malign your family as well! Family is a place where we fight it out and live it out. But no matter what, we stay true.

Jesus threw a big paradigm shift into the concept of family. Jesus' family, even his mother Mary, must have thought he was a little deranged. Jesus was so far from the king they once thought he might be (one who would set up his Kingdom on earth and reign in power) that his family could not accept him for who he said he was. Several times they tried to derail his plans so they could bring the poor confused boy safely back home.

So Jesus pointed to those near him and around him. Imagine his hand circling around to include all who sat at his feet soaking in his teaching. . . . That circling hand included you and me. "You want to know what family is?" Jesus asked. "It's those who obey me. These are my mother, my father, and my siblings."

You have a family. "God places the lonely in families" (Psalm 68:6). If you are fortunate, you have two good families—the one you were born into and this family of God. The one you did not choose. The other you may hardly know, but there's plenty of time to remedy that. In fact, there is still an eternity.

 As you pray today, refer to other believers as brother and sister. It may feel old fashioned at first, but work on embracing the reality. These *are* the sibs!
DG

What God Hates

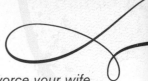

"I hate divorce!" says the LORD, the God of Israel. "To divorce your wife is to overwhelm her with cruelty," says the LORD of Heaven's Armies. "So guard your heart; do not be unfaithful to your wife." MALACHI 2:16

I love you. I love Todd. I hate divorce. Jenny repeatedly heard these three simple statements as she attempted to power walk her frustrations away. Her husband had been having an affair for two years. She had three young children at home. Did God even see her?

Jenny clearly saw two roads spread before her. The road to the left was "Divorce." It was loud, chaotic, and full of neon signs. It sang a song to Jenny, "Once a cheater, he's always a cheater." The landscape along this path was rough. Jenny saw gorges of financial difficulty, brokenness, and custody battles. The road was scarred with betrayal.

On the right was a road with a much different landscape, named "Forgiveness." It bore the earmarks of God's blessing: plush valleys of rejuvenation and family and lakes of life-giving reconciliation. Jenny's heart was scarred by betrayal and leaned naturally to the left. But two questions kept surfacing in her head. *If God hates something, why would I want to do it? How can I justify divorcing my husband to my children, especially when God hates it?*

The moment Jenny and Todd chose to take that road less traveled, they knew they were cleansed, free, and forgiven. Today they are fully restored and happily married, and they have *five* beautiful children. They have been invited to tell their story in church services; they have recorded a testimonial film and have had their story published in two books; and they have counseled many in similar circumstances, helping to rescue other marriages at a crossroads.

When one's relationship with God breaks down, every relationship suffers as a result. The seed of many broken marriages is not in the marriage itself, but in the vertical relationship between husband and God or wife and God. God warns us through Malachi to first guard our hearts . . . as our hearts go, we will go also. Anything entering the heart will find its way out through the mouth or actions. Thankfully, this is not only true of indiscretions we allow into our hearts, but also of things such as forgiveness and grace!

 *Action* **STEP** Take time to pray for the marriages around you today. Pray for your own parents—no matter what road they have chosen.

We're All a Little Broken

My people have done two evil things: They have abandoned me—the fountain of living water. And they have dug for themselves cracked cisterns that can hold no water at all! JEREMIAH 2:13

Eli was a powerful man. As the high priest of Israel, he was busy about the task of helping families and teaching truth. It seems he was a solid guy and would be a great dad, right? Wrong! Eli was a pretty awful dad. His sons were greedy and sinned sexually, and he let them get away with it. Why? Maybe he was too busy taking care of everyone else's kids. The Bible doesn't say. It only says he was a bad father and as a result there were terrible consequences. (Check out 1 Samuel 2:12-17, 22-25 to read some of the awful things those boys did.)

People who look like "great" dads or moms sometimes overlook their most important task—to raise great children. If Eli sounds like your dad—or your mom—you are not alone.

Eli was a cracked cistern. A cistern is like a well, but with a waterproof lining. When the Bible was written, cisterns provided water for cooking, drinking, bathing—they were a life source. The Israelites would line cisterns with lime plaster, creating a watertight seal, but sometimes these cisterns would crack and leak, causing all of the stored up water supply to drain.

Spiritually speaking, God is the only one who can provide us with a constant flow of fresh, eternal, life-giving water. His is not a limited source. It flows freely, and there is no danger of it drying up. If we choose to live by any source other than God, we have to take our sustenance from a cracked cistern, and this is where families meet their dried-up deathbed.

No matter how many times you refill a cracked cistern, it will again turn dry. You can't fix people. So what can you do? You can go to God's fountain of living water to be comforted, sustained, and made whole. You can know as much as you grieve for broken family members, God grieves even more. Is there hope? When people turn to God's fountain of living water, there sure is! We have seen it happen before. The cistern, however, is not yours to repair.

 One broken family member may kneel with you at the fountain while another refuses. But by all means, talk to someone about your family concerns. We were not created to walk alone!

A Recipe for Emotional Health

Brothers, if anyone is caught in any transgression, you who are spiritual should restore him in a spirit of gentleness. Keep watch on yourself, lest you too be tempted. GALATIANS 6:1-2, ESV

Our singer/songwriter friend Stephanie Smith grew up without her dad. She always wondered what he was like and if she looked like him; when she was fourteen she finally met him for the first time at a family funeral. Anticipation welled up inside as she saw him approach her mother. He touched her brother and spoke his name. Then, he came to Stephanie, shook her hand, and said, "You must be Priscilla!" He didn't know her name.

Years went by. Stephanie was in college and had run out of money. Her mom suggested she call her estranged dad. They met at a truck stop for lunch and traded numbers to stay in touch, but a few weeks later he wrote a letter saying it was better if she forgot him.

Some girls respond to a missing father by being boy crazy. Others respond by hating men. Stephanie didn't do either. Those choices would have made it hard to be in a healthy family in the future. The fact is, Stephanie is not only emotionally well, but she just married a great guy! The recipe for finding emotional health when you are from a broken family is simple, but not so simply followed. There's only one ingredient: forgiveness. Stephanie forgave her dad and even wrote a song about it. This freed her to love well.*

Stephanie did not *feel* like forgiving her dad. She *chose* it. It doesn't matter how you feel about your dad, mom, aunt, uncle, grandpa, grandma, brother, or sister. You can *choose* to forgive. And you must.

Galatians 6:1-2 says you must release anyone who has hurt you or you may find yourself guilty of sin as well. Stephanie released her father by writing a letter to her dad. A letter is a great way to say what you need to, only make sure everything is written in humility. We must forgive *gently*!

 Write a letter of forgiveness to a family member if needed. Rewrite until it is kind and gentle. Pray about whether you should give it to the person or if writing the letter was release enough.

---

*The name of the song is "First Words." You can get all the details of Stephanie's story in her book *Crossroads*.

Loved by Dad

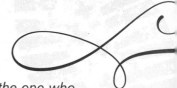

O Jacob, listen to the LORD who created you. O Israel, the one who formed you says, "Do not be afraid, for I have ransomed you. I have called you by name; you are mine." ISAIAH 43:1

My parents didn't grow up in perfect homes. Both lost their fathers when they were quite young. They grew up in the homes of single moms, and life was tough.

My mom's mom had to work multiple jobs to make ends meet. Her one pleasure was dating, and she did a lot of that in her time off. My mom became the housekeeper and cook by age twelve. In many ways, the relationship of mother and daughter was reversed and remained so through all of my grandmother's life.

My dad's dad died of alcohol poisoning. A family that goes through alcoholism may forget how to be intimate. Though my grandmother was an awesome citizen and did many good things for our county—including showing love for special-needs adults and adopting and fostering several children—I never heard her say, "I love you." She was loving but not expressive.

My parents didn't take their parenting cues from their own parents. They knew love mattered and saying it did too. I was told I was loved, was hugged, was photographed often, and was parented very well. At the stroke of midnight in the year 2000 my dad gathered all of us at his home. He'd written a "father's blessing" to speak over us. We listened intently, and then he asked us to sign the blessing to say we understood. It basically said, "You are mine" and "Everything I have is yours." That's what God says to us in Isaiah because he knows it is what every heart needs.

One thing is true for you as surely as it is true for everyone else: you need to hear you are loved. Hopefully you have parents able not only to show you love, but also able to verbalize it. If not, rest assured you *are* deeply loved and you are definitely in the position to break family chains, one day freely telling your children you love them.

 Imitate the great women in your church—ask them questions about their faith, study under them, and seek ways to spend time in their presence. It's imperative you know you are loved. And you are. DG

No More Abuse

This I declare about the LORD: He alone is my refuge, my place of safety; he is my God, and I trust him. For he will rescue you from every trap and protect you from deadly disease. He will cover you with his feathers. He will shelter you with his wings. His faithful promises are your armor and protection. PSALM 91:2-4

Gary (not his real name) lived with our family on and off throughout middle school. His younger sister had the courage to tell her teacher that Gary had been touching her inappropriately. Police showed up at the house, and in one night the entire family's life unraveled.

Gary's mom did a tragically difficult thing: she signed papers to have him taken from the home. That's when the church stepped in. Rather than the boy entering a foster home, he was able to stay with a few approved families. It took over a year of counseling and healing to obtain permission to return home, but we all rejoiced. Even his sister rejoiced, and she now felt safe. The painful process of protection almost killed the family, but in the end they were stronger for not hiding dysfunction under the rug.

One of your basic rights is to be safe. Your church family is commissioned to protect you and be your keeper. If you will choose to trust your true refuge and place of safety, *you* can possess the power in an abusive situation. You have the power to run to safety. You have the power to speak up and be rescued. You have an invitation to hide under the shelter of God's wings where no one can hurt you. From such a place, you are safe to refuse to return to an unsafe situation. There are plenty of adults who will help you if you speak up—there is *never* a need to remain in a place you feel unsafe or where you are likely to be hurt again. Never.

Maybe this doesn't seem to apply to you, but ask a friend if it applies to him or her. Sometimes our friends have secrets we just need to dig up so they can be free.

 Practice speaking up. You can choose the restaurant next time instead of saying, "I don't care," or you can tell the school bully to take a hike. The better you get at speaking up, the more likely you are to stay safe. DG

MARCH 10
Do It for Love

*I am boldly asking a favor of you. I could demand it in the name of
Christ because it is the right thing for you to do. But because of our love,
I prefer simply to ask you.*
PHILEMON 1:8-9

Onesimus had gotten himself into quite a fix (read the short book of Philemon).
A slave in the household of Philemon, he was treated as one of the family none-
theless. It was a *huge* betrayal, then, when Onesimus wronged his benefactor,
Philemon, and ran off. He had been entrusted with household affairs much as
a son would be, and most theologians believe his offense was running off with
Philemon's treasures.

Paul makes it clear in a short ditty of a letter that Onesimus has experienced a change. He once was "useless," referring in Roman culture more to a
person's moral fiber than their ability to perform work, but now Paul says he is
"useful." This is a character reference on Paul's part. Philemon had every right
to punish Onesimus severely. In fact, many Roman slaves were crucified for far
less than running away.

But Paul asks two incredible things of Philemon. First, he asks that
Philemon would receive Onesimus back into his household as his own brother.
No more master/slave, for how can anyone enslave his own brother? This
request effectively puts the practice of slavery to death in the Christian household. Remember, in Christ there is no slave or free. Paul asks that Philemon
forgive, and then astoundingly tells him that *he*, Paul, will pay back the dam-
ages Onesimus has caused.

Is this sounding familiar yet? Once a slave, now a member of the family?
Someone else offering to pay the penalty that rightfully belongs to us? Paul's
request is a mirror of the gospel! If we believe it, we must live it. If we have
benefited from this same kind of forgiveness, we must offer it to others. Paul's
second amazing request is this: *choose* to do this out of love. He could make
Philemon comply based on his authority over him, but love and forgiveness
must be choices, or what are they worth? God chose you and me while we
were still guilty. Choose love, and watch the bonds of slavery be shattered!

 **Action STEP** After reading Paul's letter to Philemon, help someone
you know choose love today. Maybe you need to receive
someone back to your heart. Remember that Jesus
paved the way for this kind of love.

Who Is Family?

Ruth replied, "Don't ask me to leave you and turn back. Wherever you go, I will go; wherever you live, I will live. Your people will be my people, and your God will be my God." RUTH 1:16

Ruth had a broken family. She had married a nice young man, and they were carving out a life for themselves when . . . he died (see Ruth 1:1-5). Ruth was left miles from home, with no family but her husband's mom. Ruth begged her mother-in-law, Naomi, to let her stick around, and it turns out, Naomi loved Ruth. She helped her find employment in the harvesting fields, and ultimately counseled her in regards to winning Boaz as a husband. When families are broken, God sees to it we are still rewarded with deep relationships. Psalm 68 even says he sets the lonely in families.

One group working for years to set kids in family relationships (when their own family can't swing it alone) is Big Brothers/Big Sisters. The concept of the program is simple. Kids who need an adult with time to give are paired with just that—a big brother or sister who hangs out with them once a week or so. The results of the program have been astounding. Kids who have someone with time to give are far less likely to miss school, smoke and drink, or even react to problems with violence.

The church can be its own sort of "big brothers/big sisters" operation. When I was in eleventh grade, my psychologist mom invited me to help her break a cardinal rule of counseling. She had a client a couple of years older than me who was one of seventeen children, a great Christian girl who was simply getting lost in the fray of a big old family too busy to say "I love you," and she wanted to know if I would approve of Jan coming to live with us. Did I want a big sister? Hello! I had wanted a big sister my whole life. So Jan became one of the family, going on vacations with us, spending holidays with us, and even going off to college with me as a freshman. She became my sister.

What Ruth and Naomi started isn't unusual. Family can be blood, but Jesus pointed out long ago that family is also the church. He "places the lonely in families" (Psalm 68:6). No one need be alone.

 **Action STEP** Read all about it. . . . Ruth is a short book. Who is your family?
SW

MARCH 12

A Personal Matter

We must all stand before Christ to be judged. We will each receive whatever we deserve for the good or evil we have done in this earthly body. 2 CORINTHIANS 5:10

What if prisoners could be exonerated by virtue of the fact their parents were neglectful? What if someone failing school could get a grade bump by explaining no one is ever home to help with homework? Or what if we could ride the coattails of someone else right through those pearly gates of heaven? Of course, you know it doesn't work that way—not heaven, not school, not even our prison system. One earmark of maturity is accepting that no one is responsible for your choices and your consequences except *you.*

Let's say you and your little sister are headed out for a walk. You have warned her that it is cold and have suggested she put on a coat. She insists she is fine and refuses to put one on. Soon she is whining and complaining about the cold. She says you never should have *made* her walk with you (it was her idea) and she'll never listen to you again. (Sound familiar?) You could give her your coat. You could call your mom and ask if she'll come pick the two of you up. Or you could make her walk home and freeze off her little hind end. Which choice would most likely help her to develop her character? (Hint: number three.)

Have *you* taken responsibility for your choices and even some of the circumstances you are facing these days? Maybe you are always late for school or the bus but blame it on your lil' sibs for hogging the bathroom. Maybe you are failing a class and blame it on the teacher. Maybe you feel lonely and blame the girls at school for being a clique.

We don't actually know anyone who *likes* to be wrong, but admitting your mistakes is a big step toward growth.

The heart that blames others for its bad choices has not humbled itself and has not grown up. Good thing we have time in our youth to learn . . . and to practice!

 **Action STEP** Practice admitting mistakes and taking responsibility. Try saying, "It was my fault." Attagirl!

Cooking Up a Storm

She is like a merchant's ship, bringing her food from afar. She gets up before dawn to prepare breakfast for her household and plan the day's work for her servant girls. PROVERBS 31:14-15

Story time! My boyfriend (now husband) Jonathan had come to visit my family, and I really wanted to impress him with a "home cooked" meal. Considering I had no kitchen skills, each course ended in a disaster. The times on the seasoning box were for bone-in chicken. I didn't know chicken tenders would cook more quickly, so they ended up dried out and crispy. Jonathan kindly informed me they were the tenderest chicken bones he had ever eaten. I never turned the heat on the green beans, so they were served ice cold, and my mom took the cake (literally) when she flipped my perfectly baked Bundt and it splintered into a thousand pieces. I was mortified.

Fast-forward a decade. Around the time my adopted teen girls came to live with us, I discovered the wonderful world of *recipes*. I began experimenting and discovered I could actually knock my family's socks off with my culinary skills. A couple of good cooking magazines, the Internet, and my growing family led me to discover a new hobby I'm surprisingly in love with: cooking!

This brings up a cultural judgment: we have not only become accustomed to fake or fast food, but we have forgotten *how* to cook.

Why does this matter? Let's look at two benefits derived from learning to cook. The first is that of blessing your family. No matter how professional, busy, or sports minded you may be, your family will still need to eat. Loving your family more than the couch is a beautiful thing. Ask any man. He may be liberated in his thinking, but the way to his heart is still the stomach! Second, the ability to provide a table for friends and family is priceless. It seems food and the soul are connected. Food gives us the chance to grow in both hospitality and in generosity, and it turns out dinner tables are a great setting in which to feed not only the stomach but the spirit.

You know, it's not that difficult. Just find a recipe and have at it. You might like it!

 Cook up something yummy and challenging tonight or tomorrow. Enjoy the work God has given your hands to do!
SW

Choosing Growth

When I was a child, I spoke and thought and reasoned as a child. But when I grew up, I put away childish things. 1 CORINTHIANS 13:11

There are some fun road signs out there to entertain travelers. Electronic signs can be hacked, allowing people to see messages like "Zombies Ahead" or "You'll never get to work on time!" Fun-loving township supervisors sometimes provide signs like "Beware of invisible cows" (Hawaii). But one of the best is rumored to exist in the Alaskan wilderness: "Choose your rut carefully. You will be in it for the next 200 miles."

Your next few years will require *you* to carefully choose ruts. *Now* is a great time to choose a "rut" of high involvement in church and the habit of a daily quiet time. You are already establishing a priorities list in your heart. You may not realize this is occurring, but—where your treasure is, there your heart will be also (see Matthew 6:21; Luke 12:34). Today, when you are still young and under someone else's roof, is the day to decide your church family and time alone with Jesus are priceless.

Today is a good day to choose health. Regular exercise and healthy eating choices are rut material; any notions of "I'll start tomorrow" are deflections. It takes about a month for a new behavior to become a habit. This means at least one month of regular exercise and a "no more eating after 9 p.m." mindset, or it won't stick.

Here's a great rut—spend at least thirty minutes a day reading. And when we say reading, we mean good material, not vampire fantasy. Pick up a memoir, some juicy history, a missionary biography, or a book on ballet or business or whatever happens to float your boat. Did you know watching most television shows actually puts part of the brain to sleep? To make matters worse, the frontal lobe (the part of the brain responsible for processing information critically) is the part taking a nap!

You are not too young to choose good ruts. It's time to think and reason like an adult and leave those childish ways behind! God *has* a purpose and a plan for your life, but your good ruts help him accomplish what he has in mind.

 **Action STEP** Make a daily to-do list. Be sure to include mental, physical, intellectual, and (most importantly) spiritual growth activities. Ready, set, grow!

To Grandmother's House We Go

Take care of any widow who has no one else to care for her. But if she has children or grandchildren, their first responsibility is to show godliness at home and repay their parents by taking care of them. This is something that pleases God. 1 TIMOTHY 5:3-4

My mom has always been there to teach me the ins and outs of life, but we lost my dad to cancer in August 2010. My life is flooded with memories of him—playing catch, skiing for countless hours, walking on the beach, laughing together. . . . I had a good dad. But as much as I'm flooded with memories, my mom has far more. She met him at fourteen; she tried to hit her neighbor with a pear and hit my dad instead. *Hello. I'll be your wife and the mother of your children for the next sixty years.*

Just twelve days after Dad died, Mom had to encounter her fifty-fifth wedding anniversary . . . alone. After that it was the first Thanksgiving and the first Christmas. By the second year, Mom says, everyone moves on with normal lives, but she hasn't fully moved on, and the phone calls to check in and see how she is doing have slowed way down.

God is specific in requiring care for widows. If you have a widowed grandparent, you are first in line as caregiver. Look at our verse today. You'll see it's not just children who are mentioned but grandchildren as well. It is not the church's job to care for those who have family. It is the family's job. Even now be sure you are fulfilling your duties to call your grandparents; check in on them and spend time with them. I learned some stunning things about my grandma just after she passed away. I had always seen her as the perfect Christian. I had no idea things in her past had wounded her or how much she had grown from big mistakes she made as a youth. I appreciate, even more now, her legacy as a Christ follower.

There are harsh words in store for those who forget lonely family members. They "have denied the true faith. Such people are worse than unbelievers" (1 Timothy 5:8). So many times God's Word reminds us if we want to wear this name tag of Christian, actions need to fall in line with the name!

 Set a date with Grandma or Grandpa. Let them know you will always be there for them.
SW

Don't Smoke, Don't Chew, Don't Go with Boys Who Do

I plead with you to give your bodies to God because of all he has done for you. . . . This is truly the way to worship him. ROMANS 12:1

Is it okay to light up? To drink?

Technically: There are laws dictating tobacco and alcohol usage. Unless you are eighteen, you cannot legally purchase tobacco. It is understood you should not use it either. Alcohol, of course, is illegal until you're twenty-one.

Socially: Smoking is not really socially acceptable. Drinking carries very little social disgrace, although alcoholism is not highly regarded. Funny, it doesn't seem you can get to the stigma of addiction without passing through a stage of participating in the really "cool" activity of getting blotto. There seems to be some hypocrisy here.

Religiously: Taken from the most black and white of stances, some would say a Christian cannot possibly smoke or drink. This is a risky judgment, for many who would seek Jesus may still be lighting up in the bars. Are seekers welcome in our churches?

Really: The Bible "allows" smoking and drinking as permissible behaviors. "'I have the right to do anything' . . . but not everything is beneficial," 1 Corinthians 6:12 (NIV) says. In God's system of free will, we have the "right" to do anything we choose. We are not to be micromanaged by our church, or by our Savior for that matter. But don't fail to look at this permission without looking deeply. Paul is using tongue-in-cheek sarcasm here. He points out that *everything* has a consequence.

Someone dies every eight seconds from tobacco use.* In one year, over ten thousand people died in car crashes caused by alcohol.** Very few of the drivers who caused those deaths realized they were drunk. Sure, you "can" smoke and drink if you choose it. There is no law against it (besides age limits and the command to not get drunk). But not all things are beneficial.

 *Action* **STEP**   Take a moment to make a prayerful decision about smoking and drinking when you are the legal age. Beneficial?

---

* http://smoking.ygoy.com/smoking-statistics-general-facts/
**http://sadd.org/stats.htm

Today Is the Day

[Jesus said,] "Come, follow me." The man agreed, but he said, "Lord, first let me return home and bury my father." But Jesus told him, "Let the spiritually dead bury their own dead! Your duty is to go and preach about the Kingdom of God." LUKE 9:59-60

You probably have a friend or two who do very little. After school, they spend endless hours on Facebook, wandering the mall, or zoning out in front of the television. They may report being bored on a regular basis. And this can become a problem. Psychologists have linked a new phenomenon to addictive and criminal behaviors—they've named it "Leisure Boredom." When people have too much free time on their hands and no plans for their free time, they will report feelings of boredom. Many will then seek to fill the mindless hours with smoking, partying, or even criminal behavior.

Surely there is something better to do with our downtime. Jesus said the harvest is plentiful but the workers are few (see Matthew 9:37; Luke 10:2). It's not like there aren't things to be done out there. So why are we still sitting, still bored, and still discontent? Are we procrastinating? Maybe we are failing to "put our hand to the plow" as today's verse challenges!

Though Jesus had twelve disciples, there were hundreds of people who had left jobs and homes and were following him as colaborers wherever he went. Several women with significant bank accounts helped to fund everything he did from their own pockets. This group was not bored. They were privy to life-changing miracles, part of a community making waves in the Judean countryside, and after Jesus rose again from the grave, they were primed and ready to be the first church the world had ever known. Occasionally, there were observers who approached Jesus expressing a desire to follow, but they weren't ready. One wanted to wait until his father passed away. *Then* he'd be free to follow. Another wanted to travel back home and have a little chat with friends and family, maybe get their opinions on Jesus. They *wanted* to follow. They just wanted to put it off for a little while.

Today is the day you have been given. What are you going to *do* about it?

 Try something new: ask the Lord how he wants you to use your "downtime" rather than watching TV or using Facebook as your default. Rest and leisure are important, but only in the right amounts.

MARCH 18

The Faith of Our Parents

The person who sins is the one who will die. The child will not be punished for the parent's sins, and the parent will not be punished for the child's sins. Righteous people will be rewarded for their own righteous behavior, and wicked people will be punished for their own wickedness. EZEKIEL 18:20

Being a drummer, I am amazed by the band Mutemath. After all, they are known for songs with some of the sickest time signatures possible. (For the nonmusical out there, that means their songs are hard to clap to.) The guys were raised in homes with a rule-based, legalistic faith, so it was a story from lead singer Paul Meany's teen years that most resonated with me.

Meany was on a street-witnessing mission in New Orleans. Rejected by person after person, he finally met someone who wanted to talk about Jesus. As he began to dispense his vast knowledge of the Christian faith, he realized he had no idea what he believed. Trying to repeat things he had been fed his entire life, he realized it made no sense to him. He had never developed a personal faith, and he came to the conclusion he was as lost as the man he was trying to convert. What's cool is that instead of blaming his parents for this, he took time to figure out what he believed.

The weight of *knowing* what we believe falls squarely on each of us as an individual. The merits of faith are nontransferable. I was raised in a half-Christian home. My dad was mute on the subject, but I had a mom who attended church and was completely intentional about her growth as a Christian. She told me more times than I can count, "Just because a person goes to church, it doesn't make them a Christian. I go to McDonald's every week; that doesn't make me a hamburger!" Mom made me define what it means to have a relationship with Jesus, and she challenged my views on a regular basis. I think I said so many foolish things that she had to help me set the record straight!

You're not going to be punished for your parents' errors. They aren't going to be hung for yours. On the flip side, their faith is their own, and . . . where does that leave you? This faith contract will be drawn up between you and God alone. Have you signed your name on the dotted line?

 Look in the mirror. Does the girl looking back at you own her faith?
SW

What Is Heaven Like?

I saw a new heaven and a new earth, for the old heaven and the old earth had disappeared. . . . I heard a loud shout from the throne, saying, "Look, God's home is now among his people! He will live with them, and they will be his people. God himself will be with them. He will wipe every tear from their eyes, and there will be no more death or sorrow or crying or pain. All these things are gone forever."
REVELATION 21:1-4

Many pet lovers often wonder if pets go to heaven. Before determining if Fido is going to get through the pearly gates, maybe we should first talk about the basics of heaven. Heaven is probably one of the most misunderstood places on earth. That's right—on earth. When you "go" to heaven, you won't be going anywhere. Heaven will be coming right here to you.

A few years back I was on a retreat with my church. The first night we talked about restoration. I was told to pick a plate from a pile of old, colorful dinner plates. They were cool, but they were old. Chipped. No one was going to be serving up meat loaf on them anytime soon. Next, I was given a hammer and was told to smash the plate into a bunch of pieces. Finally, I was given a frame in the shape of a cross and told to rearrange my plate into the frame. Now the shattered remains of that almost useless plate are framed by the cross. It hangs on my kitchen wall, and people tell me nearly every day how pretty it is.

Earth, as we know it now, is not our home, but that's only because the earth is under a curse, and it needs to be restored. It's barely useful to us, like those cracked plates. Our true home is the Kingdom of heaven. So are we going to be sucked off this planet just before it explodes into infinity? Or is the God who was existent even when there was no order or form, who spoke *this* world into existence, going to rebuild what is broken into something useful? Bible scholars favor theory B. The chaos of this broken world will be gathered up, framed by the Cross, and we will live in the glorious Kingdom provided by our God who makes all things new. The Bible is a nonstop depiction of a holy God who is *coming down* to be with his people. The Kingdom of heaven is the only one in which God comes down to where we are!

 See if you can make a piece of art out of something broken today. Let it serve as a reminder of what God plans to do with this earth.
SW

MARCH 20

Good-Bye, Sweet Tippy

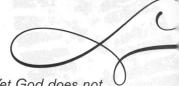

What is the price of five sparrows—two copper coins? Yet God does not forget a single one of them. LUKE 12:6

Tippy was the sweetest little copper-colored American cocker spaniel you ever would meet. I remember the first time I saw her at the county fair. She was in a little crate, and I don't think she'd been outside it once for the first six weeks of her life. She was terrified when we lifted her out and put her on the ground. No problem! Bob and I were happy to carry her as long as she wanted us to.

That dog lived with us and in our hearts for twelve years. She helped us welcome our babies, and she moved with us six times. It was heartbreaking when her body and mind became so weak it would have been inhumane to keep her with us. Bob did the brave thing and took her to the vet to help her go peacefully. Before he did, he drove through McDonald's and bought her an entire bag of hamburgers.

Is Tippy in heaven? I don't know.

Isaiah says the wolf will lie with the lamb, the goat will lie with the leopard (see Isaiah 11:6). As a horse lover and owner, I'm delighted that the book of Revelation talks about horses coming from heaven. Many scholars, including C. S. Lewis and Randy Alcorn, argue animals will be in heaven. And there's this from the book of Romans claiming that *all* of creation waits for God's next big move.

> The created world itself can hardly wait for what's coming next. Everything in creation is being more or less held back. God reins it in until both creation and all the creatures are ready and can be released at the same moment into the glorious times ahead. Meanwhile, the joyful anticipation deepens. (Romans 8:19-21, *The Message*)

Scripture seems to indicate all of God's creation will welcome him when he returns. What that looks like long term is a mystery to us. For now, I'm going to be a good steward of the animals he's entrusted to me, knowing he does not forget a single one of them. And he is wise enough to decide where they will be in the end.

 **STEP** Hug your favorite pet today. And thank God he doesn't forget our four-footed friends.
DG

Animal Servants

The LORD said to Elijah, "Go to the east and hide by Kerith Brook, near where it enters the Jordan River. Drink from the brook and eat what the ravens bring you, for I have commanded them to bring you food."
1 KINGS 17:2-4

Neither of us would ever want to be without pets. And there's a woman in Wisconsin who, we're pretty certain, would tell you she wouldn't even be alive if it weren't for her adopted cat. She and her son had just adopted the cat hours earlier when the woman fell into a diabetic seizure during her sleep. The cat pawed at her chest and nipped at her face to wake her, but she could not be roused. The cat then proceeded to do the same to the boy until he was awake and alert enough to call 911. Doctors say the woman would have died during the night if not for the persistence of her *very* new pet!

When God created Adam, the first observation he made was Adam should not be alone. "It is not good for the man to be alone," God said (Genesis 2:18). God knew his work was not done—Adam needed a helper and companion. God provided animals for Adam as companions. Adam even got to name them. And then, God created Adam's helper, Eve. When Eve was created, she was identified as the one who was "just right" for Adam (see Genesis 2:18). But from the start animals were included in the completion of our need for companionship.

Did you know most animals are happier when serving and in relationship with human beings? We don't know about the ravens that fed Elijah—there does seem to be something to the term "bird brain"—but there is ample proof domesticated animals derive joy from being a part of the "family" in every sense of the word. Cats will proudly display their hunting prowess to family members even if they have no intention of consuming their kill. Suzy's mom's cat, when taken from his native Indiana to live on a Florida beach, began catching geckos to present to the family. He may have been thanking the family for the warmer weather, but then again he may have been saying, "Thanks for letting me travel with you." We often pray when we leave for speaking tours for our dogs to be good companions to our husbands and to bless with joy all who walk through the door.

Action **STEP** Google "Pet Saves Owner's Life" and enjoy many good stories about pets saving their owners. If you have a pet, give it an extra treat today for good behavior.

Is Eating Meat Okay?

All the animals of the earth, all the birds of the sky, all the small animals that scurry along the ground, and all the fish in the sea . . . I have given them to you for food, just as I have given you grain and vegetables.
GENESIS 9:2-3

For what it is worth, vegetarianism was the rule of thumb before the fall of man. There is no evidence meat was ever consumed until after the Fall. Noah was the first human we see God granting permission to eat flesh, and this was not until after the Flood. Scientifically, the digestive tract of a human is better suited to vegetarianism than meat eating. It appears God's original and perfect plan for man was not carnivorous.

Noah was granted permission to eat only certain meats approved for the purpose of sacrifice. After Jesus' resurrection Peter was clearly given the green light for all meats. Why did God make a shift? There are probably a lot of reasons we could argue, but here is a big one: eating meat reminds us we are not in the Garden any longer. The wages of sin is death. For many of us animal lovers it is not uncommon to be sad yet grateful that something died to provide our sustenance.

There are limitations in man's freedom to eat all things. Humans can only digest small amounts of meat. Nutritionists say three ounces per day (no larger than the palm of one's hand) is more than enough. When we are with people who object to the consumption of meat for any reason, we should refrain, and without argument. (First Corinthians 8:13 actually spells that one out. Isn't it amazing how much God's Word has to say about meat?)

This is a lot to digest for animal lovers. Sin has really messed things up, not only for us as humans, but for animals as well. Look at Genesis 9 again. God says animals from this point on will look at humankind with fear and terror. They weren't afraid of humans before God allowed meat to be consumed! But God didn't cause this. We did. We believe the response belongs to us as well.

 *Action* **STEP** Pray about how you normally eat, and respond accordingly:

Red light = try a vegetarian diet for a short time
Yellow light = cut down on meats and increase veggies
Green light = remember to be thankful for meat and when you eat it, remember that we have fallen from the perfection of the Garden of Eden

MARCH 23
Cruelty

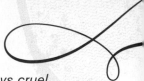

The godly care for their animals, but the wicked are always cruel.
PROVERBS 12:10

Care for animals has been modeled over and over by our loving God. Consider how the Sabbath was created not only for man, but also for working animals. When the land lay fallow for an entire year, farm animals were to be given free rein to eat from the fields. God told Israel to allow oxen to eat as they worked, and another proverb (27:23) says herds and flocks should be given close attention. God's eye is on the sparrow. A godly person (one who is like God) will imitate these careful behaviors.

Cruelty to animals is identified as wickedness in today's verse. Compared to humanity, animals are way down the curve in their abilities to reason, assert, or even protect themselves. Animals are at the mercy of humans, thus it would be a person of no mercy—no compassion—who would harm a defenseless creature. This may be why no crime other than child abuse raises so much ire among compassionate people. Who are we commanded to care for? Orphans and widows. The alien and stranger. Our flocks. A wicked person cares for no one but self, and this is why cruelty to animals is associated with wickedness.

Here's an area to consider if we want to live in the fullness of God's Word. What are we to think of the millions of animals who die excruciating deaths in traps each year for the fur trade? It's legal. It's big money. Is it cruel and there-fore wicked? How about the millions of animals suffering in laboratories with purposely inflicted cancers, abrasions, and mental illnesses . . . all in the name of research? Is there a difference between medical research and cosmetic research? These are all questions satisfied best by education on your part. Educate yourself. Avoid the temptation to offer strong emotional responses backed by zero information. Think carefully, prayerfully ask God, and then take a stand. You're called to care for the animals.

 Read up on animal industries such as ranching, fur trading, testing, circus involvement, big-game hunting, etc. What responsibility do you think we have to protect animals?

MARCH 24
Get In on the Rescue

*If you happen to find a bird's nest in a tree or on the ground, and there
are young ones or eggs in it with the mother sitting in the nest, do not
take the mother with the young. You may take the young, but let the
mother go, so that you may prosper and enjoy a long life.*
DEUTERONOMY 22:6-7

Some of my best memories are of animal rescue. My parents set an example
when I was young, rescuing a nest full of barn swallows. My dad had acciden-
tally killed the mother bird with our lawn mower. He and the rest of us spent
the next month diligently feeding those babies raw hamburger from the end of
a toothpick. By the time they could fly, we had a favorite party trick to show our
guests. Dad would go to the middle of the backyard and whistle. Then, young
birds would swoop through the air—from the north, west, east, and south—and
land on my dad! It was the coolest thing ever.

In my adult years we have been able to rescue baby ducks, more swallows,
a flying squirrel, and I'm still waiting for a fawn or a black bear cub! Friends in
Oklahoma raised an orphaned bobcat from a kitten. The day came when they
had to release the little guy back into the wild. It was tearful for the family, particularly due to the ease with which he dissolved into the night without looking
back. He was a wild animal. Given time he would have acted like one and hurt
someone, or another family pet. The family, however, has a memory book and
a slew of stories their domestic shorthair cat never would have given them.

Do we have a *responsibility* to rehabilitate injured animals and raise
orphaned ones? I believe we do. God sets a strong example of both taking
care of animals and using them to accomplish his purposes. God is an animal
lover. What he loves we are to love; when we rescue, we imitate his character.
Rescuing an animal in need may seem a small thing in comparison to rescuing people caught in human trafficking or women who are caught in an abusive relationship, but this little act of empathy and care is the very thing that
prepares our hearts for greater rescue. Remember, it is God who said those
who are faithful in small things will be entrusted with greater things! (See
Matthew 25:14-30.)

 How can you prepare your heart to be a rescuer one
day? Caring for a little animal may just do the trick. Be
on the lookout for your chance.
SW

Aslan and You

I began to weep bitterly because no one was found worthy to open the scroll and read it. But one of the twenty-four elders said to me, "Stop weeping! Look, the Lion of the tribe of Judah, the heir to David's throne, has won the victory. He is worthy to open the scroll and its seven seals."
REVELATION 5:4-5

The book of Revelation can be confusing. The Lamb who was slain becomes the Lion of the tribe of Judah. (See Revelation 5.) He alone is able to open the seventh scroll. Worthy is the Lamb that was slain! It is somewhat confusing that Jesus is at once both the Lamb *and* the Lion, but the use of the two animals is meant to be a clarification. Just as the Trinity is three persons, yet only one, the Lamb of God who takes away the sins of the world *is* the Lion of the tribe of Judah who was promised ages ago. All of heaven immediately begins to worship him as he opens the scroll, further placing Jesus (the Lion and the Lamb) and his Father at once on the throne as the God of heaven. (Does that make your head spin?)

C. S. Lewis helps us to see this duality of Jesus' character through his creation of Aslan the lion in The Chronicles of Narnia. Who hasn't read the books or watched the movies without wishing we could roll and tumble, run and chase, and generally have the time of our lives with a real live Aslan? Aslan, at once beautiful and fearsome, is the only character to appear in all seven of the Narnia books. Lewis had not intended to include this character, but he received a strong vision of Aslan in a dream. Lewis said Aslan was the lion and the lamb embodied in one character.

Think about it: a lion is seen as a symbol of strength and force. A warrior who can slay a lion (or a shepherd such as David, who could kill one with his bare hands) is a stud. But here's the thing about Jesus the Lion—he won his victory not through exerting brute strength or overthrowing a system, but by laying down his life as the spotless Lamb of God. His sacrifice was his victory.

 Offer up a time of prayer to Jesus, the spotless Lamb who took away your sins. Next, praise the Lion of the tribe of Judah who rose again to defeat death and the grave.

Hyperconnectivity

"Go out and stand before me on the mountain," the LORD told him. And as Elijah stood there, the LORD passed by, and a mighty windstorm hit the mountain. It was such a terrible blast that the rocks were torn loose, but the LORD was not in the wind. After the wind there was an earthquake, but the LORD was not in the earthquake. And after the earthquake there was a fire, but the LORD was not in the fire. And after the fire there was the sound of a gentle whisper. 1 KINGS 19:11-12

The first time I witnessed hyperconnectivity was after a quiet knock on my daughter's bedroom door. I knocked a little louder. Still no response. I opened the door to find Rachael on her bed with her laptop open to Hulu and Facebook open in another window, earbuds in both ears, and cell phone buzzing with text message after text message.

Granted, a lot of good information can come our way as a result of being connected to a larger world. The Internet connects me in real time to old friends, and I've become aware of so many social issues and ministry efforts (even continents away) I never would have known about otherwise. That's all good stuff.

However, the more time I spend online, plugged in and connecting, the less likely I am to hear the gentle knocks on my door. I check my phone every time it rings, no matter what I'm doing. How many people's phone calls do I really need to drop everything for? I check text messages every time they buzz in. Do I really need to stop writing this devotion only to find out a friend just saw the world's largest prairie dog in Kansas?

In the verses above, Elijah had just won a battle. It was 1 against 450. After this victory he took first place in a footrace with a horse-drawn chariot. Pretty amazing, right? But then *one* woman, Jezebel, said she would kill Elijah for what he had done to her 450 prophets, and Elijah became afraid . . . of one woman! Elijah needed to hear God knock on his door. He needed a word of encouragement. It was not in the wind, in the earthquake, or in the fire that Elijah found God's presence. It was through a gentle whisper that Elijah realized his God was with him and received a promise God would continue to walk with him. Do we need to be less connected to hear God's gentle whisper?

 **Action STEP** Arrange for a specific quiet time each day when you can be available (in real time and face-to-face) to God and to anyone else who may come knocking.
SW

MARCH 27
Worthy or Distracting?

Turn my eyes away from worthless things; preserve my life according to your word. PSALM 119:37, NIV

It's an amazing success story. Harvard sophomore Mark Zuckerberg begins messing around with social networking formats in the privacy of his dorm room with the help of a few friends. First the boys manage to get twenty-two thousand hits on their homemade site in only four hours, then the following semester they are launching Facebook, making Zuckerberg the youngest billionaire in the world. Now for The Question: Should we *use* Facebook?

In 1 Corinthians 10:23-33, Paul writes to the Corinthians who are a bit stressed out over meat sacrificed to idols. In his letter, Paul tells them that even though idols aren't real and nothing is inherently *good* or *evil* about sacrificial meat . . . the practice is still evil. Paul wants to be sure we don't do business *or* pleasure where evil is concerned!

Let us just say that we're on Facebook nearly every day. We use it to encourage friends, make new friends, share God's truth, and ask for prayer. Facebook in and of itself is amoral—it can be used for good or evil, like many things, and it doesn't care one whit which way you or I go. But there are a few modern-day dragons you and I could stand to slay: the need for approval, the tendency to waste time, and the failure to get in the Word of God each day. Facebook gives us opportunity for all of these. The key is filtering Facebook through Psalm 119:37. It's a question of doing the things of worth and avoiding the distractions.

Ask yourself, *Did what I posted or what I just read have worth*? An invitation to Bible study: worthy. A call out to a friend for prayer: worthy. Reading that a friend just ate Nutella: worthless, though fun. The bigger picture is this: while you were consumed with Facebook (and Nutella), were you distracted from being in the Word of God? Anything that pulls you away from God is, in fact . . . evil.

 Ask a trusted friend, mentor, or adult to keep an eye on your Facebook wall and photos. Give her permission to confront even the smallest breach of integrity she sees on your wall.

HARD-CORE ACTION STEP: Sit down with Mom and Dad and ask what boundaries *they* would like to see you put in place on your Facebook usage.

Mirror, Mirror on the Wall

Obviously, I'm not trying to win the approval of people, but of God. If pleasing people were my goal, I would not be Christ's servant.
GALATIANS 1:10

Marilyn Monroe was nearly thirty at the height of her sex-symbol status. Marketers used her image to sell makeup, clothing, and perfume. Women wanted to *be* like her. Today we have a multitude of sex symbols to pattern ourselves after.

This seems a little like worship. After all, didn't God say you and I were created in *his* image? Aren't we supposed to want to look like *him*?

The extreme celebrity culture we live in creates a strange sort of twist with technology like Facebook and Twitter at our fingertips. As we use technology to reflect our celebrity of choice, we can actually become one. And the person worshiping us? Ourselves! Don't think that sounds right?

- How often do you check your Facebook page?
- How often do you check Twitter?
- How often do you post a picture of *just you*? Same pose. Different place.

Each of these check-ins/posts can be an adrenaline drip as we seek to be watched, loved, and worshiped by others . . . and ourselves. It's not a lot different from the wicked queen in *Snow White* who checked in with the mirror every day, asking, "Mirror, mirror, on the wall, who's the fairest of them all?" She didn't like it when the mirror said Snow White. And sometimes we don't like it when a friend's posts get all the attention. (Have you ever posted something just to be competitive or passive aggressive with another girl?)

God's Word says we're not supposed to be seeking the approval of people, but of God. If we use our Facebook account to share what's up in our lives, connect to friends, encourage others, and even share Christ, it is a good use of technology. But when we cross the line into obsessively checking to see what people have written in response to our posts or continually posting pictures of ourselves, it's probably time to take a break.

 Get on your Facebook page right now and erase anything you've posted in the past week that might qualify as excessive, obsessive, or a search for approval. It will be a good exercise in moderating your future posts.

Some Things Just Shouldn't Be Said

Even fools are thought wise when they keep silent; with their mouths shut, they seem intelligent. PROVERBS 17:28

Oh snap, Solomon! Why don't you tell us what you really think? Maybe Solomon had just come from a viewing of *Bambi* and had heard Thumper's advice, "If you don't have anything nice to say, don't say anything at all." Of course not, but he was saying the same thing. Just because you have something to say doesn't mean it should be said.

Social media sites such as Facebook, Twitter, and YouTube have become the mecca of self-expression. In a sense they act as an instant press-release source for our lives. You can let the world know that you just ate the largest piece of apple pie ever sliced. You can post photos of your pets in hilarious poses or of the snack you're about to eat. This isn't really crucial news. And as we've said before, a little of this is okay, but not too much.

And far too many people cross a line into the inappropriate. There is the old argument that we don't have to look if we don't want to see it, but Facebook news feeds don't work that way. We *do* have to see drunken postings, passive aggressive (and foulmouthed) attacks, sexual poses that (one day) will be regretted when uncovered during a job interview process, temper tantrums, and pity parties. Perhaps the worst posts are those that name names and hurl personal information about others into the public forum. These things, too, show up on our news feeds. Sadly, the real news sites are full of tragic headlines like this one: "Iowa Teen Commits Suicide after Being Bullied on Facebook."

Solomon suggests we should keep more thoughts to ourselves. Does this mean we can't sometimes post a need for prayer? Or that we can't say we're hurting? Of course not, but let's slow down and think about it before we push that "post" button. Let's make sure it's something that should be said. And that it can be said without sinning. (In other words, it's not hurtful to someone else, not gossip, and not bullying.) And let's take time to be sure we aren't literally making fools of ourselves.

 Spend a week posting only once a day . . . make it count! Share news. Offer encouragement. Link to something important. No rambling!

MARCH 30
Make It Personal

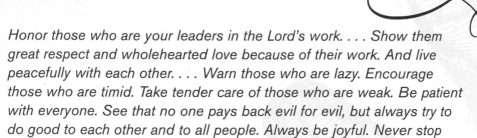

Honor those who are your leaders in the Lord's work. . . . Show them great respect and wholehearted love because of their work. And live peacefully with each other. . . . Warn those who are lazy. Encourage those who are timid. Take tender care of those who are weak. Be patient with everyone. See that no one pays back evil for evil, but always try to do good to each other and to all people. Always be joyful. Never stop praying. Be thankful in all circumstances. 1 THESSALONIANS 5:12-18

People receive on average 682 e-mails per week, but only one personal letter. Which is more likely to be valued? This is self-evident, right? It's so easy to jot a note online. A text is simpler yet. Neither can compare to the rarity and warmth of a personal note.

And texting or online messaging can't compete with time spent in person, right? I would never dream of checking in with best friends *only* online. When we say, "Let's get together," it communicates to the other person they are valued enough to warrant one of your most valuable resources: you.

We say this because we have been given the job of looking after one another! Today's passage from 1 Thessalonians is interesting because it delves into a few areas of caring for one another that may not come naturally to mind. Most could best be done in person or with a real live snail mail letter.

Let's look at a few: other than pastor appreciation month, when does it occur to us to write a note to our leaders letting them know how much we appreciate all they pour out for us? Have you ever challenged a close friend in an area of laziness or disobedience you've seen in his or her life? (That had better be done in person.) Paul tells us to stand behind those who are frightened or weak. (A little note telling them they have what it takes might be just what they need!)

Here's the thing: all of the things suggested above need the power of the personal behind them. While a typed note of encouragement on Facebook is not completely void of power, the thoughtfulness of a handwritten note is exponentially more effective. A quick text is sometimes timely, but there's nothing like meeting at Starbucks for a face-to-face chat about something deeper than the typical text message affords!

Action **STEP** Make it personal. This has to be an intentional goal these days or everything goes techno-shallow! (A new term. We coined it.) Make it a goal to encourage someone with one phone call or real letter per week.

Get Wisdom

The beginning of wisdom is this: Get wisdom. Though it cost all you have, get understanding. Cherish her, and she will exalt you; embrace her, and she will honor you. She will give you a garland to grace your head and present you with a glorious crown. PROVERBS 4:7-9, NIV

Not too many years ago my very adult uncle (that's a nice way of saying he is getting up there in years) admitted to me that he thinks church is kind of boring. "I've been going for so many years," he sighed. "I've heard it all. I've heard every sermon, every Bible verse. There's nothing new to it anymore."

He wasn't chasing wisdom. He was putting in his time at the religion factory, so to speak, punching in his time card every time he went to church. He chased his career. He chased accomplishments, entertainment, and happiness. But he wasn't chasing wisdom.

Wisdom is found in Jesus. It's not a by-product of going to church, growing up in a Christian home, listening to worship songs, or sitting through a bazillion sermons. The writer of Proverbs personifies wisdom as a girl and tells his son to chase after her! "Get her first," the wise man tells his son. "Chase her before you chase wealth. Consider her more important than your achievements. Don't bargain or haggle over her worth. Buy! Buy! Buy!" And it's a dizzying chase.

I've seen this chase at the dog park. My big Bernese mountain dog has a little collie girlfriend. He looks for her the moment his feet hit the ground at the park. The second they collide (that's how they greet each other), the chase is on. Around and around they go, my big guy in relentless pursuit though it seems he may never catch her, both of them completely spent and satisfied at the end of the race.

There is an old Latin saying: *Plurima ignoro, sed ignorantiam meam non ignoro,* which means "I am ignorant of many things, but not of my own ignorance." If only my uncle could have seen (maybe today he does—I should ask) that if he lives to be a million he will never cease to have new things to learn about his Savior! But the chase should leave him . . . and you . . . and me completely spent and satisfied.

 Chase after God hard today. Put in some extra time talking to him, writing to him, reading about him, meeting with him.

APRIL 1

The Twenty-Four-Hour Media Fast

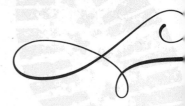

May the words of my mouth and the meditation of my heart be pleasing to you, O LORD, my rock and my redeemer. PSALM 19:14

I was sitting in the movie theater late last night. Ahead of me, a light was flickering with some regularity—not a big distraction, but enough to notice. Texting. The college student who had waited for hours to get a seat to this premiere couldn't pull herself away from her phone long enough to enjoy the movie. My daughter sat next to me, also texting occasionally. After she left early to feed my insatiably hungry new grandson, she and I began to text to relay how sorry we both were she had to leave early.

So . . . I can read the study by students from the University of Maryland saying an entire generation is incapable of living without their media outlets (smartphones, Facebook, Twitter) for even short amounts of time and go, "Tsk, tsk," but I have to face the fact that I am in the same boat.

The researchers asked two hundred students to give up all media sources for twenty-four hours and write a response about their experience. The students had plenty to say about their discomfort with a media-less existence. They reported mood swings, loneliness (though they were on a campus of thirty-seven thousand students), and a general feeling of being lost.

I recognize a significant value in the speed of connection we have with the world around us, so different from just a few years ago. Still, we are in danger of losing the ability to connect vertically, because a deepened relationship with God *is* necessarily practiced in quietness, solitude, and meditation. The psalmist in the verse above asks for only two things to please God. After all, everything that comes out of the first (the mouth) flows from the second (the heart). Our hearts need frequent opportunities to find stillness, a chance to dwell on all God has done and to be filled with gratitude as a result. Can we put down the media long enough to meet God in such a place?

 Try a twenty-four-hour media fast. Avoid it all—phone, texts, TV, movies, computer (yes, Facebook and the Internet!), magazines. Journal your experiences . . . after the twenty-four hours!
SW

Take a Personal Retreat

Jesus often withdrew to the wilderness for prayer. LUKE 5:16

Imagine spending three days with nothing in your possession but a sleeping bag, a Bible, a journal, and a pen. Oh, and a canteen. You are on the shore of Lake Superior, so far north in the Upper Peninsula of Michigan you are able to drink water directly from the lake without the need for any purification. The water is too cold to swim or bathe in, but the shore is washed considerably every day in sunlight. Large, flat rocks provide a warm bed; the jutted edges of some even provide comfortable "chairs" for meditation or journaling.

I'm really talking about an experience I had when I was eighteen and in the midst of a wilderness expedition. I had but one companion in those three days, a large bumblebee I named "Luci," short for Lucifer. This bee preyed on my fear of bees, my fear of being alone, and my fear of exposure. I had nowhere to hide but in the folds of my sleeping bag. I heard the bee first thing as I woke in the morning; it was the last sound I heard at night. Yet in the end I drew a surprising observation from our "relationship." *This* introvert doesn't like being completely alone. My real struggle was not with a bee, but with being forced to be alone.

The bottom line is that God requires a Sabbath, Jesus modeled retreat, and now psychologists everywhere are catching up on this thing God has already told us is good for our spiritual health.

But people who "get away" are doing just that—running from responsibilities and problems—right? The truth of a spiritual retreat is quite the opposite. Even Jesus—a man needed desperately by so many—took time to withdraw. What Jesus taught us by example is the need for a retreat. If you pour yourself out on a daily basis, how will you ever be refilled? Do your friends and family, your teachers and employers deserve the dregs of your cup—the coffee grounds on the bottom—or do they deserve the freshest and best you can give?

 1. Identify a time you can disappear for a few hours or even overnight . . . alone. 2. Choose a safe, quiet, unplugged, inspiring location. 3. Load up the journal and Bible. 4. Turn off your phone. Expect to meet God! SW

Why Do I Like Facebook So Much?

The LORD God said, "It is not good for the man to be alone. I will make a helper who is just right for him." GENESIS 2:18

Wait. That's a boy/girl verse up there. What does it have to do with Facebook? Genesis is, of course, the first chapter of God's love story with us. The Father, Son, and Holy Spirit (God, three in one) have been dwelling in community from the beginning of time. When God created man, he said, "Let *us* make human beings in our image, to be like *us*" (Genesis 1:26, emphasis added). And as he watched Adam strolling through the Paradise created for him, God decided Adam needed community too. He made Eve so Adam was not alone—so man could make a home on earth.

In his book *The Church of Facebook*, Jesse Rice notes that a few key elements of "home" are recognized through the Facebook experience and reinforce our connection to our home. "Home" is where we can keep the things most important to us. Just as the four walls of our bedrooms define us via our decor and personal items, Facebook allows us to store and display the things dearest to us. Go to our pages and you'll see our families, our pets, and our most recent adventures. Seriously! Go to our pages! Hold our feet to the fire. Do you see evidence that God is central in our lives? We're open to feedback on this one.

We feel safe at "home" because we have some control over the environment. Research has proven having choices in life is vital for healthy psychological development—a sense of powerlessness, on the other hand, is debilitating. Facebook gives us a place to be ourselves with no need for pretense. Do you feel safe enough to just be you? Ask a friend or mentor to check out your profile. How closely does it resemble the real you?

It's just like home. A place you can let your hair down and be known and loved just for being you. We don't display just anything on our home walls, and we don't let just anyone into our homes. Do you like Facebook for this reason, or for the world of pretense it allows you to build?

 Go to your Facebook wall and take inventory. What is most important to you as reflected on your page? Who are you inviting in? Who are you claiming to be? And while you're at it, message someone in your "community" and thank them for walking through life, your real life, with you.

Friends Aren't What They Used to Be

There are "friends" who destroy each other, but a real friend sticks closer than a brother. PROVERBS 18:24

Ever look at the picture of someone who commented on a photo you just posted and wonder, "Who in the world is *that*?" Facebook was initially a means for students to connect with friends, and friends of friends at neighboring universities. It has exploded, and we now often have no idea who some of our "friends" are.

Jay Baer created a company called Convince & Convert that helps large companies use social media sites like Twitter, Facebook, or Yelp for marketing and brand-name growth. In the course of studying the impact of these social networks, Baer made a poignant observation: today, we have both *more* friends . . . and *fewer* friends than ever before.

What Baer means is that social sites have given a new meaning to the word *friend*. How many Facebook "friends" do you have? How many of those do you know on a personal level—in other words, you know if they have siblings, and if they have a favorite song? On the other hand, how many have you met only once . . . or maybe not at all?

Baer says we actually have *fewer* friends than ever today. We meet online instead of at a coffee shop. Even when hanging out with friends, we are often not truly with them; we are texting several other people who are "hanging out" elsewhere. While we used to draw conclusions about a friend's character only after spending considerable time with him or her, we now win friends and exclude people based on the cleverness or offensiveness of status updates.

It's just not very . . . real. A true friend is willing to say hard things because she loves us. True friends are the ones who want to be with us in 3-D more than digitally. A true friend is the place to run in times of hardship. The more time we spend in cyber relationships, the less time we have to build what is true. The time comes for all of us when we need a true friend—it would be good to have a flesh and blood one nearby, wouldn't it?

Action **STEP**   Spend time today with a true friend, one who loves you enough to always be honest with you. Go get coffee or ice cream. Take a walk together. Play a game.

An Incubator for Drama

A gentle answer deflects anger, but harsh words make tempers flare. The tongue of the wise makes knowledge appealing, but the mouth of a fool belches out foolishness. PROVERBS 15:1-2

"You are so judgmental!"

"I hate hypocrites. And, _____, you know you are one."

"Was in a relationship. Now out of one. It's better this way."

"Maybe you should read your Bible once in a while."

Facebook can be covered with venom, judgment, and bitterness. If you want to start a fight, just post something airing your opinion on a controversial topic. At some point, social media users began to believe it is okay to make passive-aggressive comments online. They type what they would never utter out loud in the company of other people. Whether we say it or type it, we must believe a gentle answer will provide the off switch for a fight just begging to take place. The words we type on a Facebook wall have the power to build relationships or to tear them down. If we play the peacemaker, then the wisdom of our words not only calms the storm, but also makes the calm seem very appealing to those who are caught up in the fray. On the other hand, entering into the fray with a "belch of foolishness" can have disastrous consequences.

Conflict has always been handled best by gentle face-to-face conversation. Facebook will not change that fact. Actually, using Facebook, texting, and e-mailing are three of the *worst* possible ways to resolve conflict, for none of these methods allow you to read the nonverbal cues your "frenemy" is sending. There is no chance with the immediacy of the Internet to clarify what someone meant ("Was she joking or serious?") before shooting off a reply. Both wisdom and foolishness need clarification at times, and when a relationship is on the line, it's probably best not to leave clarification up to chance—maybe old-fashioned face-to-face communication is the best way to go!

 **Action STEP** Take someone you have had Facebook, texting, or e-mail conflict with out for a cup of coffee. Humble yourself and patch things up. And while you're at it, take a "no more arguing via my keyboard" vow!

APRIL 6

When Should I "Unfriend" on Facebook?

I meant that you are not to associate with anyone who claims to be a believer yet indulges in sexual sin, or is greedy, or worships idols, or is abusive, or is a drunkard, or cheats people. Don't even eat with such people. 1 CORINTHIANS 5:11

It's time for some very practical, no-nonsense advice. When it comes to your friends list on Facebook, who should be on there and who shouldn't?

The apostle Paul spends a moment in the verse above clearing up for the church a comment he had made to them at an earlier time. He had instructed them not to "associate" with people who are immoral. Time passed, and Paul was beginning to receive reports that the church was tolerant of *gross* immorality within its own ranks. Paul says his instructions were not to avoid *un*believers who were behaving in an ungodly manner—that would be like avoiding dogs who bark or cars with horns. His instructions were to cut off association with believers who . . . well, you can read the list above for yourself. It's pretty clear.

In terms of Facebook, there are two sets of people to look at on your friends list. The first would be acquaintances who are not believers in Jesus. They probably act and talk as they "should" given their current state of belief. The Bible says you once behaved like this, too, before you came into the light (see Ephesians 5:8). These people, as long as they are not posting obscene pictures or clogging your news feed with profanity, are okay to keep around. They *should* be before your eyes and on your heart so you can bring them before God in prayer.

The second set of people for you to consider are professing believers. Their use of Facebook should be held to a different standard. If your friends who claim to be Christians are using Facebook as a vehicle for engaging in sexual inappropriateness, idolizing the wicked adventures of certain celebs, or dishonoring God's holiness, you need to unfriend. This is not an invitation to chew them out online (see yesterday's devo) or to be snarky to them at school. It is a call to protect God's holy name. He is zealous for it, and it's time we get some backbone as well!

Clean up your friends list, but not until you have bathed this in prayer. Do you have the guts to stand with God for holiness in his church?

Check the Facts

Don't let anyone capture you with empty philosophies and high-sounding nonsense that come from human thinking and from the spiritual powers of this world, rather than from Christ. COLOSSIANS 2:8

Allow us to reveal the name of the most dangerous function in the Facebook universe—the "Share" button. Oh yes, with one little click of a button Facebook users are able to take extremely disputable "truths" from their news feeds and share them with every one of their friends. There may be a spell-checker on your computer, but no verification will be done on your behalf before you hit the Share button! Now you can propagate such infamous Facebook rumors as

Facebook is going to start charging!
Make-A-Wish will give seven cents to fight cancer every time you share this post!
JetBlue is offering two free tickets to Facebook users!

Here's a practical little secret: snopes.com. This little web gem has an extensive up-to-the-minute database on all Internet scams, hoaxes, and lies. If something sounds too weird to be true, check with Snopes. Use it before you hit Share!

What's the big deal? In the googol information age (we didn't misspell Google—the famed search engine is a play on the mathematical term for 1 with 100 zeros following) we have to be exceedingly careful to not surf around with a head full of mush. It's one thing if someone fools me into believing I could get a free iPad, but the stakes are going to go up dramatically as we near Jesus' return.

The Greek word *capture* in today's verse refers to illegal kidnapping. Pronounced, it sounds almost exactly like the word for synagogue; Paul was probably playing one of his word tricks here. He was telling us not to let people sneak their way into our minds with falsehood, particularly in matters pertaining to the gospel. We have been saved and set free, but the enemy would love nothing more than to enslave our minds again. I doubt your friends are out to trip you up, but don't assume they have done the fact checking for you. Trust, but verify. What you see on the Internet is shaky at best.

 Don't fall for just anything. Practice checking facts on the little things so one day it will be second nature to check the facts on the big things. Check out Snopes. It's so useful!

APRIL 8
Safety First

It is better to take refuge in the LORD than to trust in people. It is better to take refuge in the LORD than to trust in princes. PSALM 118:8-9

His name was Ryan, and he looked pretty normal. Not a hottie, but his wasn't a face only a mother could love. He was nineteen and appeared to be a great guy. Sadly, fourteen-year-old Megan (not her real name) decided to meet him. Ryan took advantage of her by having sex with her, though she was underage.

Megan's mom called the police. What they found wasn't pretty. Ryan had eleven different social media accounts through which he was targeting one thousand girls aged twelve to fifteen. Officials found he'd made face-to-face contact with eight of the girls. All eight had been sexually abused.

Facebook is as safe as you make it. It's not just the people you meet, but the information you offer to just about anyone. Did you know that every time you take a digital photo and post it, you're offering viewers information on where you are . . . or aren't? As I post vacation pics from Mexico, a criminal knows I'm away from home, when I began my vacation (because I checked in at the airport), and where my now unoccupied and unattended home is located (because I posted a GPS-enhanced photo of packing in progress).

In terms of sexual predators, the "good" news is they approach only 4 percent of teenagers online. They are typically up-front about what they want. They don't masquerade as another teenager; they approach lonely teens with promises of attention and affection.

The psalmist, musing over two thousand years ago about human integrity, knew this to be true: humans cannot be fully trusted. We would encourage you to think carefully and help your friends to think clearly when it comes to interacting online. You don't really know the people you are talking with—not truly. Take refuge in the Lord when you need affirmation, affection, and encouragement. Take refuge in real, godly friends. Running to the Internet when you feel lonely? You know that could end badly. Looking for romance or discussing inappropriate things online puts you in a very high risk category of being targeted by sexual predators.

 **Action STEP** If you don't know someone, is he or she a friend? Don't invest in mystery online connections. They are a red flag, not the pot at the end of the rainbow.

APRIL 9
A Built-In Prayer Team

[Jesus said,] "I also tell you this: If two of you agree here on earth concerning anything you ask, my Father in heaven will do it for you. For where two or three gather together as my followers, I am there among them." MATTHEW 18:19-20

When Bob and I were seeking to adopt Autumn (almost fourteen at the time), we ran into a huge obstacle. Autumn had to be removed from China before her fourteenth birthday or the Chinese government would close her case and we would never be able to have her.

It wasn't looking good.

A particular piece of paper from immigration services was going to take ten weeks to clear; we had only two until we would miss her birthday deadline.

Enter the beauty of social mediums. We asked dozens of friends to pray . . . who asked dozens of friends to pray . . . who asked dozens of friends to pray and call their government officials. A few days later when we called our congressman's office ourselves, his assistant asked, "Is this about that little teenager from China everyone is talking about?" She told me that they'd already been flooded with calls. Congressman John Peterson reclassified Autumn's adoption case into a humanitarian rescue, and we had our paperwork in a few days! That is a marriage of the power of prayer and the vast social network at our fingertips!

In Jesus' time two or three witnesses were required in order to bring judgment on the perpetrator of a crime. In today's Scripture we see Jesus turning things upside down, as he often did. He says to get two or three together and instead of casting stones . . . pray! This is an especially clear message occurring at the end of Jesus' instructions regarding how to resolve disputes.

If ever there was a breeding ground for disputes, it is Facebook. But let's not forget it is also a breeding ground (very fertile soil at that) for a prayer team.

The next time you have a prayer need, consider asking your Facebook friends to pray with you. Then, let the next post you make be about God's glorious answer to those prayers so you can not only rejoice together but testify in front of your unbelieving friends that prayer works!

 Put your next prayer request out to your Facebook prayer team, and let them go to work on it! Be sure to post again when God answers so they can join in your gratitude.
DG

A Rule for the Heart

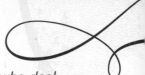

I will refuse to look at anything vile and vulgar. I hate all who deal crookedly; I will have nothing to do with them. PSALM 101:3

When I was in high school, a huge musical and social opportunity came to town. Van Halen was in concert . . . and all my friends were going. Van Halen was a great sing-along group, with lyrics like

> *Oh my my, I'm your ice cream man, stop me when I'm passin' by,*
> *See now all my flavors are guaranteed to satisfy.*

I didn't care about the concert. What I cared about was that *everyone* was going . . . and my mom said I couldn't!

The lyrics above are mild compared to today's standards. But there *are* other Van Halen lyrics I can't print. Mom was no pushover. Though I felt embarrassed by her decision then, today I have her to thank.

Psalm 101 is a ruler's psalm. (Go ahead and read the whole psalm.) These words would likely have been spoken as a king began his rule over a kingdom. Today it might be a household psalm—the promises made by Mom and Dad as they set up moral parameters for their home. Christian artist and author Rebecca St. James said her parents mounted this Bible verse beside the family television set. The TV couldn't be watched without the ever-present admonition to "refuse to look at anything vile." You know, Eve first *saw* the apple in the Garden of Eden and it looked good. Only after looking at its goodness did it gain admission into her hand and then her mouth.

My mom hated the darkness she saw in this group's lyrics and at their concerts. She hated it enough to be the ruler of our household and say no on my behalf. Eventually, I was able to say no for myself. There are a lot of concerts I don't go to today . . . even if everyone else is.

 What things are you watching or listening to right now that could be a doorway for sin into your heart? Do you have the courage to turn away from them? Place this verse above your TV and on your iPod for a week and see what this ruler's psalm does to protect your heart.
SW

APRIL 11

Everyone's a Preacher

If someone claims to be a prophet and does not acknowledge the truth about Jesus, that person is not from God. 1 JOHN 4:3

Everyone is preaching a gospel of some kind. If you listened to interviews with a few Hollywood directors, you might hear just how blatant their faith efforts are in the films they produce. Here's what one producer said:

> It's something in the human psyche, this desire for immortality. I think there are so many reasons that people are fascinated with this idea of eternal youth. That's every advertising image we see every day. Bella, for example, is obsessed. She wants to stay young, and be as young as Edward is. . . . It's crazy, but that is our culture.
> CATHERINE HARDWICKE, the director of the movie *Twilight*, in an interview with Salon.com

The end (immortality) justifies the means (forbidden fruit). This is not a Christian worldview Hardwicke is discussing, and it's exactly the kind of thing (worldview) we hope you'll begin to look for.

Movies express the worldview of a writer or production team, "worldview" being the individual's orientation to the world around him or her. When our worldviews are strong, we filter everything through that orientation. Exposing ourselves to conflicting views often muddles our worldview. For example, you can have a Christian worldview but believe sex outside of marriage is "not the worst sin in the world." Watching films such as *The Lucky One*, where an unmarried sexual relationship seems to set one woman's broken world back to order again, may not strike you as problematic. On the other hand, your Christian worldview may correctly alert you to the fact that *all* sin separates the one who sins from God. Then you would watch *The Lucky One* and say, "There was an untruth in that message."

Maybe we need to be reminded that the best way to enjoy our worldview and defend it is to keep a pure taste of it in our mouths. And looking at today's verse, we might care more deeply about *who* is preaching to us! God looks at worldview issues in one of two ways. Messages are from him . . . or the enemy. No in-between.

 *Action* **STEP** Test the words of modern-day "prophets" . . . film and music makers. See if they ring true. Know what you must do to accomplish this? You have to know the Bible and what it says! Learn God's Word.

APRIL 12

"$#!*!!#" Is Illegal Where We Come From

Obscene stories, foolish talk, and coarse jokes—these are not for you. Instead, let there be thankfulness to God. EPHESIANS 5:4

My son, Robby, was in first grade the first time he swore. The family was in his bedroom after school, getting the scoop on his first week of first grade. Robby picked up a toy, looked at his dad and asked, "What the *$#@ is this?"

Shocked, his father asked, "What did you say, young man?"

Robby again piped, "I *said*, 'What the *$#@ is this?'"

After we stopped giggling, we explained to our five-year-old that this was a bad word we didn't want him using. He told us that all the kids said it. Then, he told us a few other choice words he was learning. Sadly, my son later told us he struggled with profanity that whole year because he was always around it.

Two things turn my stomach most about R-rated films. One is sexual content. The other is foul language. There's a debate emerging in the church today about just how far we can go to meet the world where they are. To a degree, we're on board. But using foul language does not add up. God says six times in the New Testament not to let anything unholy come from our mouths. Let's just say he's vested in our abstention from gross talk.

Some of the things I think really cause God to grieve include the use of *OMG* all over Facebook. I think he's grieved when we watch a movie fueled by profanity for profanity's sake or for the sake of humor. And I'm positive he doesn't like it when we call our friends "B#$%*-es!" That offends him in the area of profanity *and* in our lack of kindness and respect.

Why do parents get upset about language in movies? It's imitative behavior. Though we need to be able to watch a film or TV show and engage our culture in conversation that leads toward redemption, a lot of people (not just teenagers) aren't mature enough to do so just yet. But all of us, even the littlest toddler, are ready to imitate what we see and hear. It's a tiny bit cute when a five-year-old does it. Not so much when it's you or me!

 Got a word or two you can trim out of your vocab beginning today?
DG

It Doesn't Affect Me

Your eye is a lamp that provides light for your body. When your eye is good, your whole body is filled with light. But when your eye is bad, your whole body is filled with darkness. And if the light you think you have is actually darkness, how deep that darkness is! MATTHEW 6:22-23

When Jonathan and I first moved to State College, we were definitely the new "kids" in school. We lived on a mountain about forty minutes from town. It really wasn't the ideal place for entertaining new friends. One night we asked another couple we didn't know very well to come up to the cabin for pizza and a movie—they had to bring both since neither business could be found anywhere near our little mountain nest. They showed up with three R-rated films.

Unknown to them, we maintain for the most part a non-R-rated-film existence. Since they were new friends, we found the least egregious of the three movies and settled in for what turned out to be a decent film. Afterward we talked about movies and TV, and our new friends struggled to understand why two mature, responsible, Christian adults felt it was in their best interest to avoid R ratings. Finally, the guy in the couple shrugged his shoulders. "They just don't impact me like that," he said.

A few days later we picked him up to play racquetball. After we arrived at the gym and stepped outside the car into the frigid air, it struck him: he had left his racquet at home. "Oh fuuuuuuuuuuuuudgggge!" he said (to quote *A Christmas Story*) . . . except of course he didn't say *fudge*. And yes . . . those movies, it turns out, did impact him after all.

In today's verse, Jesus says the light we allow into our eyes will affect the entire body. The first time he says *eye* (the good eye) he calls it *single*, healthy, and wholly devoted to God. The second reference to eye is the evil, or bad, eye. It signifies greed or stinginess, but is also wordplay for an eye that cannot see correctly. That is exactly what happens to our eyes, and our lives as a matter of fact, when we try to reconcile moral filth on one side of the body with a godly perspective on the other side. Is it possible to take in his light with one eye and the moral filth of the world through the other . . . and come out unaffected?

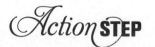 Pull the plug on R and TV-mature ratings for a while. How's it feel?

That Ain't Love!

There are three things that amaze me—no, four things that I don't understand: how an eagle glides through the sky, how a snake slithers on a rock, how a ship navigates the ocean, how a man loves a woman.
PROVERBS 30:18-19

A couple of weeks ago my daughter's friend posted a video of Adam Sandler's song "Grow Old with You" from the movie *The Wedding Singer*. She wrote above it, "This only exists in movies, right?" You know, even adults who should be able to tell the difference between movie love and realistic love sometimes get caught up in what is increasingly being referred to as "emotional pornography." It's not unusual for a girl to lose hope for love when she thinks she has to have a witty piano-playing songwriter fall for her.

Most of what you have seen on television and in the movies is not what your life is going to look like. When we are expecting one thing and then we receive something quite different, it's kind of like expecting milk in your cup and finding warm soda instead. If you've ever drunk something totally unexpected, you know it causes an involuntary gag reflex. You don't want to get three months into your marriage and have a gag reflex!

Real love is downright mundane at times. There are days when there is not a lot to talk about, when the only reason he's staring into your eyes is to help you find your dried up contact lens, and plenty of times you'll wonder why he can't complete a simple chore (translation—why he doesn't do things the way you would do things). But you have a chance at the *real* thing, which I can promise is *better* than any movie, unless maybe you're talking about a movie like *Fireproof*, where the husband is figuring out what it means to love his bride like Jesus loves the church and lay his life down for her. The kind of movie where the lead actor has his wife stand in as a body double for the actress playing his wife because he won't kiss anyone else. Now that is romantic (and that's what Kirk Cameron did in that movie).

Love in the movies is too much like the proverb in today's passage, verses about things untraceable and not understandable. The man and the woman stand up, brush themselves off, and move on to the next conquest. That ain't love, girls. That ain't love!

 **Action STEP** Take a break from romance movies. Study the real thing instead. Interview a few couples from your church who have been married for several years.
SW

APRIL 15

The Horror of Horror

Do not defile yourselves by turning to mediums or to those who consult the spirits of the dead. I am the LORD your God. LEVITICUS 19:31

One of my favorite plays is *The Crucible* by Arthur Miller. It relates the story of the Salem witch trials and is written with a decent measure of historical accuracy. A group of girls are caught frolicking nude in the woods. Though this would be an offense punishable by death (it was believed to be witchcraft induced), one girl sees an opportunity to punish the married man who rejected her sexual advances and creates a false spirit of possession. The ensuing hysteria brings the death of twenty innocent people, including the wife of the vengeful girl's obsession.

I was assistant director for the show in college, and I have a strong recollection of a horror story my director shared. He always began rehearsals with a read through followed by a day of entrenchment exercises—he wanted to be sure the actors were able to teach their muscles what it felt like to be persecuted, to be hunted, to be fearful. With *The Crucible*, he explained, he needed to be careful. These emotions must be explored without involving actors in the most dangerous element of the production—witchcraft. He didn't want a repeat of what happened to a colleague of his.

That director had to cancel his production of *The Crucible* before it ever left the ground. He led the girls playing witches in an actual séance. They created a potion and muttered curses . . . and went mad! Seriously—something came over them, and they were incapable of ever returning to the script.

Hollywood releases horror films at the rate of about one per month, a number that increases if you include supernatural thrillers. Entertainment? I don't know. Involvement with this stuff is listed as one of the one-way tickets to eternal separation from God in Galatians 5:19-21. In our key verse today, God says we are *defiled* by such a separation, as in made unclean in God's sight. Let's be repulsed by the things that repulse God. I hope knowing that such things are defiling makes you a little uneasy. And I hope God's caveat of "I am the LORD your God" convinces you that when it comes to the occult, he means business!

 *Action* **STEP**   Cross horror films off the list of favorite genres.

The Times They Are A-Changin'

Jesus turned to the crowd and said, "When you see clouds beginning to form in the west, you say, 'Here comes a shower.' And you are right. When the south wind blows, you say, 'Today will be a scorcher.' And it is. You fools! You know how to interpret the weather signs of the earth and sky, but you don't know how to interpret the present times."
LUKE 12:54-56

Have you seen *The Vow*? The movie tells a true story . . . but not entirely. (Spoiler alert!) In the movie (and in real life) a young married couple experiences tragedy when a car accident leaves her without any memory of him. (That's where the similarities end.) The movie couple fights for a while, but not too hard. Their marriage ends in divorce, and the promise of newly budding love rises only at the very end.

In real life, parents fueled by faith sat the couple down and say, "You made a vow before God and before us. We'll walk you through this." It was hard, and it hurt, and they cried. She got lost and couldn't remember where she lived, let alone the man she was married to. But after three years of never saying the D word, they renewed their vows at a wedding ceremony she *can* remember. The story is beautiful as it is. Isn't it even a lot more amazing than the movie?

Americans are gravitating toward the foulest of movies—vapid, gratuitous tales of unmitigated bad behavior. Adults are depicted as idiots or absent altogether. Love is relegated entirely to the emotions, which can be confusing for people who are expecting to be entertained and not necessarily molded.

Hollywood is not likely to change. But we can be smart and mature enough to read the signs of the times. We can submit ourselves to God's holiness to recognize good film (redemptive) versus bad (glorified immorality). (Incidentally, I still think *The Vow* is a really good film. It's just evidence that we live in times that don't honor goodness to the full extent.)

Jesus is exhorting the crowd to repentance in Luke 12. Get things right with God, and then walk in that right way. Movie ticket sales would suggest that we are buying into the notion that morality is not an issue with which to concern ourselves. But our holy God says morality is indeed to be our concern.

 Become familiar with one of the fairest, most balanced movie review sites we know of. Check out pluggedin.com. Use it to select your next movie.

Elevated

[John said,] "You yourselves know how plainly I told you, 'I am not the Messiah. I am only here to prepare the way for him.' It is the bridegroom who marries the bride, and the best man is simply glad to stand with him and hear his vows. Therefore, I am filled with joy at his success. He must become greater and greater, and I must become less and less."
JOHN 3:28-30

Signing autographs is truly one of the most bizarre things we have ever experienced. It's also one of the nicest feelings, realizing that people would like to meet us and talk with us. In a way, it is like meeting friends we didn't know we had but sure do love. But *never* do we feel like we deserve to sign an autograph.

Celebrities are people just like you and me. I know you have heard that a million times, but where would you assign the emphasis in that sentence? *Celebrities* are people just like you and me? Celebrities are *people* just like you and me? I want to suggest we look at it this way: celebrities *are* people just like you and me. In other words, if we take the celeb at her most basic composition, the essence of who she is, we find she is. She just is. Normal. Flawed. Scared. Needy. Plain.

Some famous people know this while others do not. The elevation of a celebrity is a dangerous business, both for the fan and the celebrity, and the stakes are even higher for a celebrity who happens to be a follower of Christ. The elevated stage or the big screen, the red carpet and bright lights, the autographs and the screaming fans. . . . We do realize, don't we, that these things stand in direct opposition to the humility commanded in Scripture?

The stage plays to an old human weakness too. Idolatry. Human beings have desired an object of worship from day one. The rock star with tragic good looks feels much more palatable than a God who asks us to take up our cross. Maybe we just want to *see* what we worship.

John the Baptist's followers were getting a bit uptight because once Jesus showed up, everyone was going to Jesus for baptism. John's star was fading fast, and with it the honor (for his followers) of being associated with him. John sets the record straight—something is way off kilter when the quotient looks like this:

created > creator

 **STEP** Set the record straight. Creator > All. Rid your life of anything that smacks of the opposite. You may want to talk through this with a mentor.

Dying to Be Famous

What do you benefit if you gain the whole world but lose your own soul? Is anything worth more than your soul? MATTHEW 16:26

> *"No matter how much fame you have, it's not something that belongs to you. If I'm famous, that doesn't belong to me—that belongs to you. If you can't remember who I am, I'm no longer famous."*
> MICHAEL J. FOX, as told to *Esquire Magazine*

If beauty is in the eye of the beholder, fame is even more so. Actor Michael J. Fox was a huge TV and movie star when we were growing up. You might remember him from a classic film called *Back to the Future*. But then Parkinson's disease knocked on his door. Thankfully, it didn't ruin Fox because he went on to be a spokesperson for the disease that he fights so valiantly. It is, perhaps, his perspective on fame that keeps him well.

Fame is addictive, but it's also destructive. There is a legend in music circles about a place called the crossroads. A famous 1930s blues guitarist met the devil at the crossroads; he allowed the devil to tune his guitar in exchange for easy money, fame, and access to beautiful women. All musicians know the legend, and many still refer to "selling your soul at the crossroads"— doing whatever it takes to become famous. The problem with fame is that it demands the soul. No one is wired to receive worship except for God. He is worthy and he is holy; there is no musician, actor, or athlete who can say the same.

Eventually the famous realize that no matter what they have been told, they are human through and through, and this becomes a very lonely place. We may tell celebrities all of the things we love about them, but they are acutely aware that we don't even know them. We are in love with an image . . . and they are aware of the sham.

I think celebs deserve compassion. They are not to be imitated, this is certain, but the reason goes deeper than irresponsible behavior. I think that behavior can be linked to the fact that deep down they know they are not living a dream, but a lie. And in all of our worship, we've made it a tough trap for them to escape.

 Pray for your favorite celebrities. Ask God to give them true friends, a foundation in him, and an escape from the snare of idolatry.

No Invitation to Fame

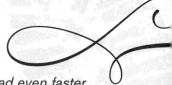

Despite Jesus' instructions, the report of his power spread even faster, and vast crowds came to hear him preach and to be healed of their diseases. LUKE 5:15

There are people in Hollywood famous for doing . . . nothing. A good number of people you might see on the pages of gossip rags have done nothing more than land a short stint on a reality show. Some have posed for ill-advised photos, have famous parents, or have managed to land a famous boyfriend or girlfriend. They can't act or sing, haven't produced a thing to benefit society; we often simply mistake notoriety for fame.

The astronauts of Apollo 13, a mission intended to be forgotten before it ever left the ground, earned fame long before a movie of the same title was released. America was in danger of being bored to tears by the space program at the time of Apollo 13's 1970 launch. The crew believed they were being broadcast on national television from outer space—in reality none of the three major networks had any intention of broadcasting the astronauts. America didn't tune in until the now infamous words you've perhaps heard came from the space commander: "Houston, we've had a problem." An onboard explosion endangered the mission and the lives of the astronauts. Those brave men never lost their cool, but commandeered the shuttle back to earth. They were instant heroes, though they'd never invited fame.

One group pursues intentional fame. The other has fame thrust upon them. The results are in, and studies show those who pursue their own fame register lower emotional stability than those who are pursuing things such as societal improvement or personal goals. *Please* tell me you are not surprised by this news!

Fame should never be invited. "The less good men say of themselves, the more will others say of them" (Matthew Henry). The Bible actually says, "Let someone else praise you, not your own mouth" (Proverbs 27:2). Only when humility is real will authentic honor follow as well. It's a foolproof plan God has set into place here! The proud will inevitably fall. Only the truly humble will be promoted.

Be slow to speak and slow to post online today. Before you say or write anything, be sure your motive is not to gain attention. Evaluate at the end of the day. How much did you have to edit?

APRIL 20
A Famous Story–
Identity

You Gentiles are no longer strangers and foreigners. You are citizens along with all of God's holy people. You are members of God's family. Together, we are his house, built on the foundation of the apostles and the prophets. And the cornerstone is Christ Jesus himself.
EPHESIANS 2:19-20

What would it be like to not be able to go *anywhere* without being stared at, whispered about, and criticized? Fame hit Daniel Radcliffe (Harry Potter) between the eyes like a speeding train at age eleven. He's handling it pretty well. He's decided not to drink. He wants to remain grounded. He has a girl-friend he wants to marry and proclaims himself a serial monogamist. Still, he is haunted by a spirit we first saw him battle as Harry Potter. Identity.

Radcliffe told *Parade* magazine that he doesn't believe there *is* a God. "I have a problem with religion or anything that says, 'We have all the answers,' because there's no such thing as 'the answers.'" Radcliffe adds, "Religion leaves no room for human complexity." If he's right, it's only because religion is something man has made. It is rigid and rule driven.

Radcliffe says he has learned to accept the fear celebrity creates, know-ing one day he will no longer be the biggest thing around. Instead, Radcliffe is looking now for a way to discover and fulfill his rich inner life. I have no idea what that means, but he says that "all that matters at the end of the day is that I'm happy with my life." I think he's looking for what the rest of us are looking for. We want to know who we are. We want to have purpose rising up out of the center of our being. We want the nagging empty feelings to go away.

Ephesians 2 is the perfect picture of both what Radcliffe is struggling with in the present and hoping to find in the future. Until we become part of God's family, there will always be a nagging sense of what Radcliffe calls "conning people" . . . and knowing we are not very good at it. We *should* feel awkward as we face the realities of this fallen world. It's not our home. We should feel at home as we face the realities of eternity. Once we were con artists, trying to convince everyone we had it all together. Now, our claims are true. That's way better than fame in my book.

 Take time to write down all the things you *are* according to God (you can start with today's verses). Would you trade all this for fame? For wealth? For anything?

Rejecting Fame for Notoriety

They brought the apostles before the high council, where the high priest confronted them. "Didn't we tell you never again to teach in this man's name?" he demanded. "Instead, you have filled all Jerusalem with your teaching about him, and you want to make us responsible for his death!" But Peter and the apostles replied, "We must obey God rather than any human authority." ACTS 5:27-29

As the words are coming together for this *One Year* devo that you can buy in public, read at Starbucks, and share at school, a man on the other side of the world sits in a prison. He did nothing more than declare that the people in his country have the same right you have to purchase, read, and share Christian literature. He defended their right to meet together as believers. For this, he has spent many years in jail.

His name is Gao Zhisheng. He is married to a woman he loves and has two beautiful children he has not seen in years. The family doesn't even know where he is imprisoned most days. A few years ago he surfaced briefly and spoke of the torture he endures.

Why would a man who has studied and practices law in China find himself in such a situation? He believes what Peter and the apostles taught: "We must obey God rather than any human authority." For this reason, Gao defends the right for Christians to meet together. He obediently risks the comfort of his own life to obey God rather than man.

Most believers across the world are persecuted. We live in Disney, comparatively! It is hard for us to understand that Christian leaders in other countries are not famous but are notorious in their culture. They are considered outcasts, and they are imprisoned and sometimes killed. But these Christians do not consider it too heavy a burden. They are obedient to God no matter what their government might threaten.

You may not be given accolades if you speak the truth of Jesus Christ in your public school. You may even find yourself an outcast for standing for purity and integrity in your *Christian* school. Compared to what some of your brothers and sisters in Christ are risking, it is not too much to give to Jesus. Don't be afraid of being notorious for your Savior.

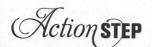 *Action* **STEP** Search online for "Gao Zhisheng" to get an update on his status. Pray for him and his family.

Being a Famous Christian

I planted the seed in your hearts, and Apollos watered it, but it was God who made it grow. It's not important who does the planting, or who does the watering. What's important is that God makes the seed grow.
1 CORINTHIANS 3:6-7

Katie Davis was only nineteen when she turned her back on our culture's celebrity-driven world. She left her cute clothes and her even cuter convertible, and a boyfriend she hoped she might marry one day. She left behind good-hair days and the gym she loved to frequent. She even left her parents—and her dream of attending college.

Why?

God called her to the red dirt of Uganda. Don't miss this: she was nineteen when she was called. Within just a few years, she became the adoptive mother of fourteen Ugandan girls. She left the "celebrity" of a good life in the United States for the grand promotion to do what God called her to do.

In a way, she is a celebrity. There's a *New York Times* bestselling book about her life. But not the kind that's self-made. She didn't invite fame. It came when she wasn't looking for it. It came while she was obediently living out 1 Corinthians 3:4-7.

Katie lives the truth that each of us should do the work God calls us to. No one person is more important than the other. One pastor preaches to a few thousand each week. Another, to a home church of fifteen. Both are important. One nineteen-year-old gets a record deal with a Christian label. Another goes to live on the red dirt of Uganda. Both are important. One teenage girl leads a Bible study club in her public school. Another prays for her. Both are important.

Fame tries to assign greater importance to one person than another. How do we fight that? It's true, some gifts are more *visible* than others, but we need to learn to regard gifts of service, prayer, and mercy as monumental forces in God's economy, because they are! Regard the people you are with at a concert as more vital than the artists on stage. Let's face it—you are not likely to get more than a passing smile from the artist, but you get to do life with your friends.

Check out Katie's story at www.amazima.org /katiesstory.html and learn about her exciting work in Uganda. Ask your youth leader to do a roundtable discussion of this topic at youth group soon.

APRIL 23
A Platform for Good

I, too, try to please everyone in everything I do. I don't just do what is best for me; I do what is best for others so that many may be saved. And you should imitate me, just as I imitate Christ. 1 CORINTHIANS 10:33–11:1

We're going to avoid names here, but consider this:

A female pop star OD's at thirty.

A reality TV star cites fame for his ability to attract beautiful women.

A sports icon tells media he didn't feel the rules should apply to him.

Now for some names. "I definitely think about a million people when I'm getting dressed in the morning. That's just part of my life now. It would be really easy to say, 'I'm twenty-one now. I do what I want. You raise your kids.' But it's not the truth of it. The truth of it is that every singer out there with songs on the radio is raising the next generation, so make your words count" (Taylor Swift, in an interview with *60 Minutes)*.

How about Dennis Quaid, who played the father of surfer Bethany Hamilton in *Soul Surfer*? Quaid took the role after nearly losing his twin toddlers from a medication error. Quaid said he knew people worldwide were praying for him and it renewed his faith, as did playing Hamilton. This famous man said the Hamilton family is an inspiration to him; he now embraces his role as one given a platform to inspire others.

We have a pastor friend in Nashville, Darren Tyler, who cofounded a company called Platform Artist Management for this very reason. Platform's web bio says, "We wanted to mentor [artists]. Our company is not based upon blindly doing whatever our artists want. Good management, we believe, is rooted in helping young men and women navigate a very difficult business, as well as helping to steer them in the right direction in balancing all aspects of their lives: spiritual, work, family, friends and rest."

The famous have a platform (wanted or not). It helps both the celebrity and the fan to understand how imitative behavior works: you and I are going to follow someone. We are going to embrace role models, whether they have asked to be one or not. Good marketers understand this. So did Paul. He tells us to imitate him because he is imitating Jesus. Actually, the only example worth following is one that is, itself, following Jesus.

 **Action STEP** Use Facebook, Twitter, or other social media today to thank a positive role model such as Tim Tebow.

Too Much Power

Jesus on his part did not entrust himself to them, because he knew all people. JOHN 2:24, ESV

We aren't without our fights. Suzy Weibel and Dannah Gresh have had a few. Well, actually not with each other. There was the friendship demanding so much of Suzy, she called Dannah for a midnight meeting at Denny's. There was the friendship unraveling so inexplicably, Dannah called Suzy for a trail ride to talk it out. It happens. It's the stuff girlhood is made of.

Why so complicated? Let's take one big important stab at it. We'd like to suggest that we give relationships too much power by having unrealistic and unnecessary expectations. Here are some expectations that we have seen break down friendships:

- Expecting a girlfriend to be exclusive with you
- Expecting a girlfriend to be available night and day
- Expecting a girlfriend to always agree with you
- Expecting her to say what you want to hear
- Expecting her to do what you want to do
- Expecting you will never hurt each other

We've had a few complicated friendships in our lives, and these have been some of the things we've seen end them. (We think this makes God very sad.) How can you avoid the same fate? Model your friendships after Christ's closest relationships.

In John 2:24 we see Jesus did not become overly dependent on people. He was free to be in relationships without constant favor or approval. Jesus knew people are sinful. They're capable of hurting each other, disagreeing and, well, making life complicated. We can make those complications easier to navigate by not expecting so much of girlfriends and by not insisting upon constant favor and approval from them.

The Bible also says that "a friend loves at *all* times" (Proverbs 17:17, NIV, emphasis added)—even when a friend hurts you, when she disagrees, when she doesn't say what you want her to say. You can build healthy expectations by committing to this: love your friend no matter what.

 Do you have any relationships where you expect too much? Which ones? How can you live in a place where you don't become overly dependent on a friend's favor?

Just Leave

Jumping up, they mobbed [Jesus] and forced him to the edge of the hill on which the town was built. They intended to push him over the cliff, but he passed right through the crowd and went on his way. LUKE 4:29-30

The Malaysian ant isn't the sharpest knife in the drawer! If it feels there is a threat to its colony, it'll blow itself up into a thousand pieces. Large glands filled with poison reside inside their bodies. By contracting their abs and releasing this glandular concoction, they spontaneously combust and spray poison all over the place. This kills not only their enemy, but also themselves and any little Malaysian ant friends who are nearby.

Unfortunately, I think that's often how we girls react when friendships begin to get complicated. We sense an attack of CAT-astrophic FIGHT proportions, and we let the poison of our hearts explode all over our frenemy, ourselves, and any nearby mutual friends. The aftermath is pretty ugly.

Jesus gave us a better example when people he could have easily expected to be friends made him feel attacked. In Luke 4, he had visited his hometown of Nazareth. He read a Scripture from the book of Isaiah in the synagogue. The passage prophesied of his arrival. After he read it, he said it had been fulfilled that day as they heard it (see verse 21). At first people marveled. But after a little while, when they had processed what he said, they couldn't believe it. "Who is this common man to say he is God's chosen Messiah?" Their peace turned to wrath, and they began to drive him out of town in violence.

Jesus—the omnipotent (all-powerful) God of the universe did something unexpected. In the shuffle of the crowd's fury, "he went on his way." Sometimes walking is the best course of action to take when people rise up against you. The Bible says we aren't supposed to confront a fool. Instead, we should simply stand firm in who we are and what we're called to be . . . and go on our way.

At the same time, remember Jesus still died for those people who drove him out. It's okay to walk away from a relationship and still hope, pray, and expect the Lord to one day restore it. But let's stop detonating ourselves, shall we?

Action **STEP** Have you been in any situations or friendships where it might have been beneficial to just walk away? Are you in any now? Prayerfully consider how you might "go on your way" when you need to.

The Depths of Depression

All praise to God, the Father of our Lord Jesus Christ. God is our merciful Father and the source of all comfort. He comforts us in all our troubles so that we can comfort others. 2 CORINTHIANS 1:3-4

Depression is nothing to sneeze at and nothing to ignore. If you suspect a friend is suffering from depression, make sure you talk with someone right away. Every living creature experiences ups and downs; some people are more susceptible to moping than others, and some have a greater tolerance for pain and hardship. How can you tell if your friend is legitimately depressed? Here are some signs to look for:

- Rather than basic sadness, she is expressing hopelessness.
- Normally calm and gentle, she is showing flashes of anger or hostility.
- She is crying more than usual.
- Lately she has not wanted to be with friends or her family.
- She shows less interest in fun activities or eating, more interest in sleeping.
- She has mentioned to you or someone else a desire to end her life.

These are common signs of depression. If even one of these is a newly observed behavior in your friend, sit down with an adult to discuss your observations. Only one out of every five teens struggling with depression receives help. Why so few? Depressed people don't typically seek help. If your friend is depressed, one of the first things to go would be her desire to address the problem!

Paul wrote more than two letters to the church at Corinth (though there are only two recorded in the Bible), and he likely visited them more than twice as well. At one point, Paul had to deal with some "pink elephants" in the church, and relations became strained. Unfinished business can complicate the best of friendships. But Paul reminded his friends of the benefits of comfort. If you have ever been comforted, he says, you can extend the experience of that comfort to someone else who needs it. Paul was ready to extend comfort even to those who in their pain had wounded him. If you are being wounded by the changes you see in a friend, turn to comfort rather than striking back in hurt.

Who would you go to if you needed to discuss a friend's concerning behavior? Establish a trusted, safe, godly counselor before the need even arises.

On Mediating for Others

Interfering in someone else's argument is as foolish as yanking a dog's ears. PROVERBS 26:17

Occasionally the Bible says something that just astounds me. It would seem to me a good thing to jump between two friends who have an argument and act as the voice of reason. Then again, those who do so often get bit!

Today's verse reminds me of the time I tried to help out our dog, Ruth. Somehow, Ruth had made her way into the 'hood. Ruth didn't like other dogs too well, a result of being nearly killed by a big dog when she was only four months old. I heard a commotion and ran to the street. Trying to grab Ruth by the collar, my hand was intercepted by the mouth of the beagle Ruth was "arguing with," and I suffered my first dog bite. This is a *painful* injury! I wince to this day every time I hear the words *dog bite*.

I think those dogs were just having a little argument. It was a spat. My dogs argue now and then. They weren't going to hurt each other, but I had to go and foolishly get in the way of their business. Mediating for friends can bring the same results if we aren't careful.

I'm not suggesting your friends need to fight to establish a pecking order. This kind of fighting is more likely sin and along the lines of James 4, which explains we fight because of evil desires warring within us we just can't lay down. What I am suggesting is the fights between your friends are better left to be solved by your friends so you don't get caught in the middle of something ungodly to begin with!

STEPS FOR *true* **MEDIATION**

1. Let each friend know you love her.
2. Tell them you will not be getting involved.
3. Suggest an objective mediator if appropriate.
4. Pray for them. If they can solve their issue and offer forgiveness, it's a win all around!

SW

Working the System

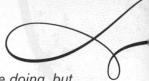

You may believe there's nothing wrong with what you are doing, but keep it between yourself and God. Blessed are those who don't feel guilty for doing something they have decided is right. ROMANS 14:22

I knew how to work the system when I was a teenager. By that, I'm talking about the network of homes that were my friends'. I knew where the best meals would be, where I could stay up all night, and where I could watch movies I wasn't allowed to see at home. I knew which parents would sit and talk with me like I was an adult, which ones would play sports with me, and which ones to avoid altogether. Of course, I only had to work the system because *my* mom was the one saying no to certain things.

"I'm not _____'s mom!" (Bet you've heard that one too.)

What my friends were allowed to do was of little consequence to my mom. She answered to God, and that's all that mattered to her. Sometimes it bugged me that her rules for me didn't apply to others. She would tell me she didn't think it was a good thing if they had no curfew, but she never told those kids to go home. She told *me* to come home plenty of times, and if I were even five minutes late I'd be grounded. But she was perfectly okay with the fact that other parents did it differently.

The issue at stake when Paul wrote the verse above was similar. One group of Christians was looking down on another for being less spiritual. It would be like me looking down on you for having cable TV because I've chosen not to have it. Paul cautions us in dealing with other Christians in three ways:

1. God has accepted other believers as his children, even though their ways may not be like yours. *You and your TV have God's acceptance.*
2. Even if they are wrong, God will help them to stand justified before him on the last day. *You and I are both justified by Christ, regardless of our viewing habits.*
3. Be sure of what you are doing. If any of us think we might be in the wrong, we may as well slink around like guilty puppies.

Action **STEP** Do you hold your parents' values? If not, can you respect them while living under their roof? Can you avoid playing the values of other families against your parents?
SW

New Kid in Town

You must not covet your neighbor's house. You must not covet your neighbor's wife, male or female servant, ox or donkey, or anything else that belongs to your neighbor. EXODUS 20:17

I can't let my dogs have chew treats at the same time. Within moments of receiving his prize, the Bernese mountain dog sneaks around the edge of a tree, hoping to catch a glimpse of what his nemesis has. In the meantime, the golden retriever has left his rawhide to creep on the Bernese's treat. The two will circle each other's position for a good half hour, constantly exchanging treats but never chewing, until the Bernese realizes that he outweighs the retriever by twenty-five pounds! The attack is never pretty.

Girlfriends can be the same. One of my best friends arrived at my school during sixth grade. She came from exotic California, introducing me to new fashion styles, new kicks, and parents who were a lot of fun to hang out with. She was cute and fun, and you'd better believe other friends noticed the amount of time I was spending with her . . . and *not* with them. Fights broke out, and though we never drew blood, there's no doubt covetousness was at the root of it all.

The word for *covet* in Exodus 20 means the desire to have something so badly that it takes the rightful place of God. God is our hope. And the Bible says that when we let go of hope, we cast off all restraint. In other words, if we want something badly enough to take our eyes off God, we will do whatever it takes to get that thing; the moral rules God once helped us to live by go out the window. I would have done anything to impress my new friend, including things I once deemed immoral or unkind. That was my fault, not hers. In the meantime, some of my oldest friends got lost in the shuffle.

We do this when the new kid arrives. We do this when the new crush arrives. Our old friends who have loved us through thick and thin, who have seen us at our worst and love us anyhow—they deserve better, don't you think?

 Take your oldest friend out for coffee, dinner, a movie. . . . Let her know how much you appreciate her and your history as friends.

APRIL 30
Secret Keepers

A gossip goes around telling secrets, but those who are trustworthy can keep a confidence. PROVERBS 11:13

Do you consider keeping secrets to be a virtue? The writers of Proverbs do. Here we have a disclaimer that gossips break up friendships, but people with integrity keep secrets. When we were in school, a lot of our friends were more adept at the gossip part than they were at the secret-keeping part.

We should not keep company with gossips. But what about the girlfriend able to take the most volatile secrets from your heart and hold them safely in her own? Do you have that friend? If not, where do you find her?

She is going to be a friend able to rejoice when things are going well for you. A girl who exhibits tinges of jealousy may be a friend, but she's not likely to be the secret keeper. The motives of a secret keeper must be free from jealousy.

She will not be a girl you have heard sharing stories about other girls. If a girl is gossiping about someone else, she will let your secret slip too. Just be aware as you watch your friends interact: they are telling you who they are. If we expect a gossip to keep our secrets simply because she is our friend, we are the foolish one every bit as much as she is the gabby one!

She must be wise. Wise and smart are two different things. Smart people may read a lot, know a bunch of trivia, and get good grades. Wise people make good decisions and have a good reputation as a result. It isn't easy to keep a secret. The Bible says a foolish person can't do it (see Proverbs 10:14).

We all need to have some secrets. They don't have to be dark—in fact, hopefully they aren't! But our dreams and certain opinions, our hopes, longings, fears, and even a mistake here and there need a safe place to rest. As long as you have one friend who fits the bill of "safe place," you can count yourself fortunate. Not every friend can be a secret keeper, and that's okay.

 Who is your confidant? Work to find her, because you need her! Ask God to bring her to your attention today. And make sure you're a good secret-keeping friend too.

To Date or Not to Date . . .

Our present troubles are small and won't last very long. Yet they produce for us a glory that vastly outweighs them and will last forever!
2 CORINTHIANS 4:17

When I cowrote *Lies Young Women Believe* with Nancy Leigh DeMoss, we asked girls what lies they might believe about guys. Number one answer: "I *need* a boyfriend."

It's actually a biblical paradigm under the law of sin and death. Way back in Eden, God said one of the consequences of sin would be that women would desire to control a husband. Some describe this desire as a "violent craving." (I write about it in *Get Lost: Your Guide to Finding True Love.*) Does the "need" to have a boyfriend feel like a "violent craving"? Then you are human. And female. But you are living under the paradigm of the law of sin and death.

When we go to God's Word for counsel, we find the answer in a paradigm shift. Stop looking at things in the here and now and start looking to eternal things! Obsessing on the perceived need to have someone to love us causes us to overlook the fact there is one who *has* loved us and made a way for us to be with him forever. It's the greatest romance ever! It's not about making things better or even bearable now; it's about being rescued from a horrible future (separated from God because of sin) and brought instead into a Kingdom fit for the bride of a King!

The question isn't, To date or not to date? The question is, What's your motivation? If the motivation comes from a violent craving, then take guys off the table until Christ is all you need. Spend some time building that eternal relationship, and you'll find he truly is all you need.

 How about a little fast from dating? Not because dating is evil or unbiblical. But because the only thing truly eternal is that relationship you have—or do not have—with Jesus. Choose your intensity:

Regular fast = No activities except with girlfriends or in groups for a month
Intense fast = The above plus no texting guys for that same month
Super fast = All of the above for more than one month
DG

Your Crowning Achievement

I love you, LORD; you are my strength. The LORD is my rock, my fortress, and my savior; my God is my rock, in whom I find protection. He is my shield, the power that saves me, and my place of safety. PSALM 18:1-2

Before writing these devotions, we asked some college girls who remain close to our hearts what truths they would have loved to understand before leaving high school. We're going to let you hear directly from Lydia's "pen":

Even though I actively pursued a strong and close relationship with God throughout high school, I could never quite mentally accept that I was adequate. Why? I did not have a boyfriend. It sounds silly (especially now that I am married), but I felt as though I didn't quite measure up. I wanted that special kind of attention, and I never really accepted the truth that God could fill that void. The funny thing is that I had countless reminders in my life that God was enough, that a girl absolutely DOES NOT need a boyfriend in order to feel fulfilled. I knew in my head that this was true, but I could not convince my heart.

It wasn't until the summer after my freshman year in college that I finally surrendered this insecurity to the Lord and felt completely at peace. Fortuitously, I met my future husband one week later. Amazingly, he had just been wrestling with God about the exact same issue! Apparently, God wanted both of us to find 100 percent assurance in him, before we were allowed to meet one another.

The crowning achievement of a Christian's life is to come to this realization: God's grace and his love for you truly are enough! Jesus alone. He is enough.

I don't know if you'll have the same experience Lydia did. I did. After years of chasing relationships throughout high school and college, I gave up. I chased God instead. While I chased after God instead of guys, I met my husband. I had already met the one who satisfies, and I was set for life by the time I met Jonathan. May you learn to breathe, "I love *you* Lord. *You* are my strength!"

 Take time today to read God's love letter to you in Psalm 18. Write one in return. He is enough. Each day. SW

MAY 3
Honorable Dating

If you keep yourself pure, you will be a special utensil for honorable use. Your life will be clean, and you will be ready for the Master to use you for every good work. 2 TIMOTHY 2:21

This weekend I am at the wedding of a girl from our youth group, but she's not just any girl. My husband is walking her down the aisle, because she grew up without a dad. This girl waded through a lot of heartbreak and loneliness to find Mr. Right; she's twenty-nine years old today, her wedding day. But she's walking down that aisle with her eyes fixed directly on a man who has honored her from day one.

What does it mean to honor someone in relationship? First, it would involve no "stringing along" from the get-go. Isn't it kinder to say, "I'm sorry, but I'm not interested," than to accept a prom date with a boy you know is looking for a girl-friend? Being kind is not the same thing as never hurting someone's feelings.

Second, it means observing boundaries. But we're not just talking sexual boundaries. Purity is a heart condition, not merely a sexual term. Practice observing all kinds of boundaries—curfews, speed limits, budgets, confidential conversations—anything that will help you get used to denying the almighty you, the unrealistic and insatiable need to get anything and everything you want! Relationships are about putting other people's needs ahead of your own.

Finally, it means being real. It's not difficult to be the eye candy hanging on a cute guy's arm—the right clothes and a little bit of makeup will transform anyone into Cinderella for a night. But we honor others, girlfriends and guys alike, when we agree to be real. One of the greatest compliments we can pay others is to admit that we like them—not in a romantic, gooey sense, but for who they are. Spending time with others because you legitimately like their sense of humor, playing board games together, or learning how they think is way better than using people to establish image. Choose the people you hang with for interpersonal reasons . . . including those you date!

 **Action STEP** Evaluate your relationships, girlfriends included. Are there any you are in simply to get a step up in the social realm? Gently and kindly walk away from those relationships—they do not prepare you for honorable service.

Serial Dating

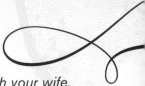

Drink water from your own well—share your love only with your wife.
PROVERBS 5:15

"Bet you can't eat just one!"

That was the taunting slogan Lay's potato chips used to sell their addictive snack foods back in the day. The marketers at Frito-Lay know human beings have never been fond of limits.

God told Adam and Eve that they could have the fruit of any tree in the Garden. There was only one tree forbidden to the couple, yet it was the tree from which they just had to eat. But you know, boundaries are healthy for us, no matter how little we like them.

Suppose we consider your life a delicious, delectable chocolate cake—cheesecake if you prefer. Every time you date someone, you offer a little piece of that cake to the guy you are entrusting with your heart. Maybe it's just a sliver of a piece, or a bit of the frosting gets swiped away for the tasting, but the cake is disheveled nonetheless. By the time I went to the altar, I am afraid I offered Jonathan something like leftovers of a child's first birthday cake . . . and I was a virgin on that day! Physically, that is. In the course of only two years I once "told" my diary I loved something like nine guys. *Loved*—I used the word *loved*. You can berate me for being shallow all you want; I will agree with you. But the average college girl is hooking up (and I mean sexually) with multiple guys during college, often times not even bothering with words like *love*.

Serial dating is bad news. Especially if sex is involved. It proves to your future husband you're perfectly okay with having sex with someone to whom you are not married. *Hello!*

Doesn't a future where your husband rejoices in you, the one and only wife of his youth, sound promising? Don't you want to be able to look him straight in the eyes and tell him he has always been the only one? It's not impossible. It's not even old fashioned. It's sane. And romantic. And beautiful.

 Ask a friend or mentor to talk with you about what you can do *now* to ensure your husband will truly be your one and only, even if he's your one and only from this day forward. Remember, God washes us as white as snow!
SW

Why Girls and Guys Can't Be Just Friends

Talk to younger men as you would to your own brothers . . . and treat younger women with all purity as you would your own sisters.
1 TIMOTHY 5:1-2

Can girls and guys be just friends?

A couple of young film artists named Jesse Budd and Patrick Romero decided to take the question to the streets on the campus of Utah State University. Perhaps in order to find only the best and the brightest, they chose the campus library as their interview field, asking every guy and girl who would tolerate their über-fuzzy microphone, "Do you think men and women can be just friends?" The results were flabbergasting. Every girl said yes. Every guy said no.

When the girls were pressed with the question, "Do you think your guy friends secretly like you?" most admitted they had sensed a tension something like attraction. The girls also admitted their guy friends would likely "hook up" with them if given a chance.

The guys who were interviewed seldom hesitated with their answers. All were quick to admit they would go after a relationship if they thought their female friend would allow it. In a clip of the film, one guy is being interviewed sitting next to his female "best friend." The filmmakers ask him point-blank, "Would you hook up with her if she let you?"

"Yes," he immediately says. "I mean, look at her." (She looks irritated.)

Look at what Paul tells Timothy, our teenage apostle, about the matter in the verses above. He tells Timothy to look at young girls as if they were sisters. One might argue Paul was giving Timothy instructions for ministry here—did he really need to be cautioned against seeing younger girls in the church as a possible fling? Yes. The warning was necessary.

Given the number of moral failures in the church today, the warning is still necessary. Paul understood men. Your dad probably understands men. Some of the older, wiser women in your life understand men. Hey, we're just the messengers. It's the guys who actually said they can't be friends with us. So, whoever he is, he cannot be just your friend. Be careful.

Find a (girl) friend or two to watch this YouTube video with: "Why Men and Women Can't Be Friends." Discuss the problem and ways you have been contributing to it. Agree to hold each other accountable.

Phone Tag

My dove is hiding behind the rocks, behind an outcrop on the cliff. Let me see your face; let me hear your voice. For your voice is pleasant, and your face is lovely. SONG OF SONGS 2:14

Much of the Bible is one big living metaphor—a picture of Jesus and his bride. This mushy love story, much like the one described in the Bible in Song of Songs, is one that gets to be lived out by you—pursued by your prince, wooed and swept into a lifelong covenant of marriage.

It is not only marriage being mirrored by Jesus and the church, but your engagement, too, and even the mad chase for your attention! As you read the book of Hosea (read it as a contemporary love story in Francine Rivers's book *Redeeming Love*), you have to shake your head in wonder. Hosea pursued Gomer though she was an unfaithful lover who prostituted herself to others. In all our unfaithfulness, Jesus pursues us just like that! All of Scripture is an endless pursuit. Translation: if you want the fullest of satisfaction in your own love story, you will let the guy pursue you.

The verdict is out as to whether guys like it when girls call them. Guys say they like it if they like the girl, but it's a pain when they don't. Thanks, guys. We couldn't have figured that out on our own. But it doesn't matter. A godly guy, which is the only kind you should be waiting for if you want the love story of a lifetime, is going to enjoy pursuing you. He needs to be the hunter.

This isn't a popular stance. Should you choose to adopt it, your friends may question your decision. One prominent politician said she does not allow her girls to call boys. In a nationwide poll, 70 percent of respondents said the politician was old fashioned and outdated in her attitudes. Maybe the new "normal" is for girls to pursue, but let's talk about normal. What grade would you give the new normal dating relationship these days? The new normal emotional state of your girlfriends who are boy crazy? The new normal is broken. It doesn't work. He who began a good work in you, every type of good work, is able to carry it to completion (see Philippians 1:6) . . . if only you will trust and obey by letting a guy pursue you!

Action **STEP** For one week (minimum) refuse to initiate contact with a guy. He calls first, texts first, makes the suggestions, the plans; he takes the first step.

How to Plow

Do not be unequally yoked with unbelievers. For what partnership has righteousness with lawlessness? Or what fellowship has light with darkness? What accord has Christ with [the devil]? Or what portion does a believer share with an unbeliever? 2 CORINTHIANS 6:14-15, ESV

Farmers train animals very carefully for the yoke. The yoke is the bar lying across the shoulders of two animals pulling a load together. To yoke (verb) means to put animals together to carry a load. Farmers don't yoke a baby to the plow, expecting the little one to carry a big load. And when he is older, they don't suddenly slap the yoke on his back. He has to try it on a few times to become acclimated. When finally hooked to the plow, he is not partnered with another animal his age, equally inexperienced. He's partnered with an experienced animal that gently pulls and pushes the newcomer, teaching him the ropes.

Paul teaches that we should not be "unequally yoked." It is easy to see how putting two different species in a yoke would be a disaster. An ox and a mule would not work—the mule would be dragged to his death by the stronger, more brutish ox! No, a "team" (verse 14, NLT) signifies two animals of the same kind. This definition of "unequally yoked" represents Paul's truest intent: don't even waste time dating boys of a different faith system.

But it's also easy to be unequally yoked by age and experience. When an older girl (say, a senior) dates a younger boy (say, a sophomore), she is bound to deal with a bit of immaturity. At fifteen/sixteen a boy is at the height of biological idiocy. He can't help it. (You were probably that way at about twelve!) There are parts of his brain not developed enough to draw logical conclusions about the consequences of his actions. When you ask a fifteen-year-old boy, "What were you thinking?" and he says, "Nothing," he may be telling the truth!

When a girl (say, a freshman) dates an older boy (say, a senior) she is not equally yoked either. He has experience and confidence far beyond hers and is ready for a type of independence she is not ready for. The result is likely to be serious bumps and bruises in ego and possibly purity. Is it a sin? No. Is it always a bad idea? No. But be careful. Take time to imagine you and that boy in a yoke. Who is stronger? More experienced? More confident? If the difference is too great, someone is going to get hurt, and the field you tread together will be a wreck!

*Action*STEP Look up pictures of oxen in a yoke. Can you see Paul's intent?

Love Isn't Jealous

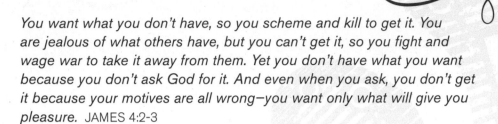

You want what you don't have, so you scheme and kill to get it. You are jealous of what others have, but you can't get it, so you fight and wage war to take it away from them. Yet you don't have what you want because you don't ask God for it. And even when you ask, you don't get it because your motives are all wrong—you want only what will give you pleasure. JAMES 4:2-3

Jealousy and love aren't going to fit together in the same shopping bag, so let's unpack and move on. If you are in a relationship with a guy and experiencing jealousy toward other girls (or he is experiencing jealousy toward other guys), what you have is not love. Love is not jealous. James gives us a peek at the things jealousy more closely resembles. So let's unpack that bag by testing your actions against a few definitive signs of jealousy.

Jealousy involves scheming. Scheming is an activity done under the table; it's never an honest activity. If you are scheming ways to get a guy to yourself, to make him disinterested in other girls, to get him to commit to you, to get him to notice you—you are inviting disaster.

Jealousy leads to murder. You don't have to scan newspapers too long to see this is a truth. In our home county right now there is a case on trial where a man tried to kill his ex-girlfriend's new beau. Of course in God's eyes he committed murder the moment his anger burned against the new guy. If you find yourself "hating" on girls who talk to your guy, that's not love. It is the seed of murder.

Jealousy is coveting what someone else has, which means we are not content with what God has given to us. It's ingratitude. It may not seem ingratitude is related to relationships, but remember in Romans 1 it was ingratitude that made God turn people over to their lustful passions. If you are not content with what you have, then it's not love. Real love breeds real contentment.

Brace yourself for this test: *Prayers of desperation reveal jealousy.* Do you spend all of your time praying he will talk to you more, notice you more, notice only you, kiss you, hold your hand?

Yep, it might be time to unpack that shopping bag, including the guy. While we don't say that lightly, we are eager for you to experience a jealous-free love when it is the right time. Sometimes you have to step away from a counterfeit to do so.

 *Action* **STEP** Love isn't jealous. (Found that in the "Love Chapter"!) Look at 1 Corinthians 13 and write down a few things love *is*.

MAY 9

Accessorizing Your Brain

If what I eat causes another believer to sin, I will never eat meat again as long as I live—for I don't want to cause another believer to stumble.
1 CORINTHIANS 8:13

I was swimsuit shopping with Lexi and Autumn. My girls are really tasteful fashionistas. I'm proud of what they wear, and I believe that God is too. But in the area of swimwear, they often tend to feel like the only ones not wearing bikinis. In fact, I was even once accused of being old fashioned because "back in the day," as Lexi phrased it, "no one wore swimsuits." I'm afraid that "back in the day," I was the only teen girl not wearing a bikini at the request of my parents.

Is it okay to wear a bikini? A study conducted at Princeton University revealed some very . . . well, revealing . . . information on wearing bikinis and other barely there fashion trends. Test subjects were placed in a brain scanner and shown photos of women clothed in bikinis and women dressed modestly. Even though some images were shown for as little as two-tenths of a second, the most memorable shots were of women in bikinis.

A startling discovery was when men viewed photos of women in bikinis, their median prefrontal cortex was deactivated. This meant the guys stopped thinking about the women as humans, but rather as commodities. The ability to consider the women's thoughts, feelings, or intentions was actually turned off in the men. Instead, their thoughts turned to how they might take action with the women. (And they weren't thinking about studying for history together.)

This wasn't the case when the guys looked at girls dressed modestly. When the girls were dressed modestly, the guys tended to have thoughts about the girls' abilities. As opposed to their bodies, the guys were thinking about the girls' brains!

The bottom line is that when you dress immodestly, you cause your brother to struggle with impure thoughts. The apostle Paul said he'd even stop eating something he liked a lot—meat—if it would help his fellow believers not struggle! Isn't it kind of a no-brainer? If wearing waterproof underwear in public makes it hard for your Christian brother to think straight, maybe you should stop.

 **Action STEP** Throw out your bikini today.
DG

Touching Too Much

Let your wife be a fountain of blessing for you. Rejoice in the wife of your youth. She is a loving deer, a graceful doe. Let her breasts satisfy you always. May you always be captivated by her love. PROVERBS 5:18-19

Can we *just* touch the forbidden fruit?

When I was writing *What Are You Waiting For?: The One Thing No One Ever Tells You about Sex*, I found out some people think that's just fine. One youth pastor said anything "above the belt" is okay. I can't agree. Let me tell you why. God created a sexual superglue inside you: oxytocin. It's a brain chemical that washes over you when you have sex with someone so you'll bond to them. Dr. Joe McIlhaney, founder of the Medical Institute for Sexual Health, says, "The desire to connect is not just an emotional feeling. Bonding is real and almost like the adhesive effect of glue—a powerful connection that cannot be undone without great emotional pain." God created you to have sex with just one person, and he designed oxytocin to protect that bond.

Oxytocin isn't created only during intercourse. A woman's body creates it during all meaningful skin-to-skin contact. Your guy holds your hand? Oxytocin! You enjoy a quick, innocent kiss? Oxytocin! He brushes your hair with his hand? Oxytocin! Each touch creates emotional glue.

When you've touched too much, you'll find it emotionally impossible to break up without deep depression. This is why "friends with benefits" is impossible. Unattached sex just can't happen. God created you to be glued to the people you have sex with!

A college-aged girl drove me to the airport after I spoke on sexual purity, tears streaming down her face. Her story was one of purity. In high school she had dated a guy for five years; he remained a friend though they'd gone different directions. But then, she dated another guy only a few months, and he touched her breasts. "Why can't I get over him?" That's what she wanted to know. Well, it's because God created her breasts to be a tender source of interaction, causing her body to produce a chemical that would bond her to one man. Proverbs 5:18-19 claims a man should be captivated by *one* woman. So, how many guys do you think God wants you to captivate with your body?

 Take some time to develop a short list of dating boundaries. Be specific in deciding how far you'll go. DG

Decide or Slide

Give honor to marriage, and remain faithful to one another in marriage. God will surely judge people who are immoral and those who commit adultery. HEBREWS 13:4

Is it okay to live with a guy? More and more, Christian girls are exiting high school and moving in with boyfriends. Even more common are overnight visits. It's more convenient to stay in a guy friend's apartment when you travel for the weekend, so you stay. Or, you want to go camping for the weekend, so you stay in the same tent.

Before we look at right or wrong, let's just consider the question: Does living together work? The research seems to indicate it leads only to frustration.

"I felt like I was on this multiyear, never-ending audition to be his wife," said one woman who had lived with her boyfriend. "We had all this furniture. We had our dogs and all the same friends. It just made it really, really difficult to break up." Yep. Why buy the cow when you can get the milk for free?

There's a name for the increase in divorce related to living together first. It's called the Cohabitation Effect. The fact is, a lot of your friends will decide to live together. If you love them, you'll try to convince them to hold out.

What does God say about it? He says the marriage bed should be held in special honor and those who approach that bed better be in it for life. He treasures marriage, and he wants you to treat it like the treasure it is. As much as you may want to believe the guy you are dating is going to be the one for life, if he likes it, he'd better put a ring on it.

Allow us to introduce the concept of sliding versus deciding. Many couples live together because "he doesn't have any place to live," or "she can't afford her rent." They "slide" into it, rather than having made a decision based on values. Sadly, it's easier to slide into living together than it is to slide out of it. As the young woman quoted above said, you have a dog and all the same friends . . . and, we might add, entwined hearts.

 Decide whether you will live with a guy or not. (PS Don't leave yourself open to sliding into it!)

Dear Abby

A time is coming when people will no longer listen to sound and wholesome teaching. They will follow their own desires and will look for teachers who will tell them whatever their itching ears want to hear. They will reject the truth and chase after myths. 2 TIMOTHY 4:3-4

When we want something, we accept any justification allowing us to continue with ill-conceived plans. Adam and Eve really wanted 100 percent access to the Garden. When the serpent told them God was afraid they would become just like him, they embraced what they were told. Down the hatch went the apple.

Enter the girl writing for advice from Dear Abby. Her boyfriend said he loves her and he wants to marry her, and while they are waiting they should go ahead and live together. As she writes, they have already moved into their new home, but he is no longer talking marriage. He explains he is happy with things the way they are; he's okay with having kids and starting a family. He just isn't interested in marriage anymore.

Should she stay with him, Dear Abby? Does he love her? Funny thing: when she writes to the advice columnist, she is writing to a *stranger!* Anyone can qualify as an adviser when we simply want our behavior to be justified.

Paul told Timothy a time would come when people would not listen to truth but only want to hear what supports decisions already made in their hearts. (See the verses above!) We have to assume since you are working your way through a devotional, you are willing to be instructed and molded by truth. We urge you, then, to seek mentors and friends who will speak *truth* to you about your relationships in the future.

It's always going to be a good idea to ask godly women both your age and older for their read on your guy. Listen when they say hard things or raise red flags. Listen when they insist upon godly decisions from you. How far is too far? Well, you've gone too far anytime you extend past the boundaries your godly friends help you identify as God's best. Put aside the itch to be justified! Hunger instead to hear the truth.

Action **STEP** Are you up for the truth? Put it to the test now if you are in a relationship, or make a covenant with God that a litmus test like this will be part of your decision making in the future.

MAY 13
Philematology Facts

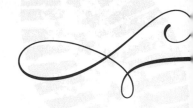

It's not good to eat too much honey. PROVERBS 25:27

Philematology is the scientific word for the study of kissing. No kidding. And here are some facts to consider the next time you pucker up.

- A kiss quickens your pulse up to one hundred beats a minute!
- A soft, little kiss will actually burn three calories!
- It is illegal for a husband and wife to kiss on Sundays in Connecticut.

Remember oxytocin? (See May 10.) Your body is created to respond to sexual stimuli. This response occurs in the autonomic nervous system, not by you thinking about things, but by you simply taking in an environment. The same system controls fear. When you got lost as a little girl out shopping with your mom and your pulse began to race because you couldn't see her anymore and you felt like you might sweat to death—that was the autonomic nervous system. The environment, not your mind, controls what happens in your body. This same system controls sexual response. Once it's activated, it's hard to shut down.

Now, consider a tasty kiss of the French variety. What happens? You just initiated the body's sexual response system into frenzied overdrive. There are very specific changes happening in your—and even more so in his—body. You're quickly approaching the point of no return.

Is kissing bad? The Bible says that all things are "'permissible'—but not everything is beneficial" (1 Corinthians 10:23, NIV). So yes. You have permission to kiss before you are married. The question is always going to be, Is it beneficial? A measure of gentle, loving kissing may be a good way to express affection and diffuse sexual tension in a pure relationship. (Like a gentle kiss on the cheek.) But be careful with that kiss. It's powerful!

The Bible speaks of having moderation in *all* that you partake of. This may be one area where it's extra wise to consider such counsel. "It's not good to eat too much honey!" (Or to have too much of a kiss.)

 *Action* **STEP** Take some time to write down what kind of kissing is okay and what kind of kissing is not, prior to being married. If you're in a dating relationship, communicate your boundary to your guy!

They Don't Call It "Oral Friendship"

Among you there must not be even a hint of sexual immorality, or of any kind of impurity, or of greed. EPHESIANS 5:3, NIV

Once when I was speaking at a Christian campus event at Penn State, a couple approached me. He was a football player—all but worshiped in a town where the blood runs Penn State blue. Proud as could be, he stood beside his girlfriend to tell me they were using his "celebrity" status to encourage purity on campus.

"Whenever we get the chance, we share *our* philosophy!" he said with pride.

Noticing a look of distinct shame on the girl's face, I felt the need to clarify. "What is *your* philosophy?" I asked.

"We just stick to oral sex," he said.

She burst into tears.

Roughly 50 percent of fifteen- to nineteen-year-olds have given oral sex a try, according to one study. I'm saddened by how common this has become and mortified that it could be passed over as if it's not sex. Oral sex exposes a woman to the same emotional connection and intimacy as vaginal intercourse, as well as the same sexually transmitted diseases. In recent years, HPV (the primary cause of cervical cancer) has also been linked to throat cancer because of the rise in oral sex.

And, last I checked, they don't call it *oral friendship*. It is sex.

God's Word says this: "Among you there must not be even a hint of sexual immorality, or of any kind of impurity, or of greed, because these are improper for God's holy people" (Ephesians 5:3, NIV). Looks to me like the virginity line is not our standard for purity. (I know a lot of virgins who are anything but pure. But, I know a lot of nonvirgins who are living beautiful lives of purity after learning from their mistakes.) We aren't supposed to be finding out just how close we can get to that virgin line without sinning. Instead, we are to be pursuing a life that is free from any "hint" of sexual sin. The question therefore is probably more reflective than practical, and should be directed to the Lord, not us: Lord Jesus, how have I *hinted* at sexual sin?

 What would you have said to that couple at Penn State? Write it down. You'll need it someday.
DG

Source: This devo is excerpted, in part, from *What Are You Waiting For?: The One Thing No One Ever Tells You about Sex.*

Playing with Fire

Kiss me and kiss me again, for your love is sweeter than wine.
SONG OF SONGS 1:2

Is it okay to just flirt? A quick definition of *flirt* is "to tease or toy with another; to make romantic attention without serious intention." You've probably seen the girl whose body language promises something she'll never actually give. How about the girl who sends a sext message, knowing it's not ever going to lead to anything? Maybe you've even been that girl.

Matthew 5:37 would be a good verse to check out. It reads, "Just say a simple, 'Yes, I will,' or 'No, I won't.' Anything beyond this is from the evil one." We should mean what we communicate, whether it's with our words or our body language. Anything less is evil.

So, does that mean you can't express your desire to a guy? Not at all. In Song of Solomon, the virgin maiden starts the song with an invitation for a kiss. Is this flirting? Nope! She means what she says. Their relationship has been going on for quite a while at this point. In fact, they're engaged. And she really wants him to kiss her! This isn't considered flirtatious at all because her romantic attention is fueled by intention! (It's also been fueled by his intention. She's not leading the way, but following him!)

I might have flirted a time or two with Bob Gresh during our dating years. (Does putting on red lipstick and kissing the window of his white sports car count as flirting?) In the context of a relationship where a guy is leading by asking you out and making his desires known to you, it's cruel not to throw the poor guy a bone now and then!

The point is this: leading a guy—*one* guy—on is going to be a really fun part of your courting and engagement experience. But if you're not in it for the long run, leave the body language and enthusiastic hugging to someone else.

 What's underneath that flirting? Could it be you're looking for value and affirmation from guys instead of looking for it in Christ? Take some time today to determine what's at the root of any flirting going on in your life.
DG

MAY 16
The Way Out

If you think you are standing strong, be careful not to fall. The temptations in your life are no different from what others experience. And God is faithful. He will not allow the temptation to be more than you can stand. When you are tempted, he will show you a way out so that you can endure. 1 CORINTHIANS 10:12-13

I recall a time as a high school girl, squinting my eyes in a dark room, seeking to make sense of the squiggly shapes on the porn channel. That room had a light switch and a door that was tightly closed. If only I'd made the choice to turn on the light, open the door, walk twenty feet to settle on the nice comfy couch and snuggle up to my mama. It would have been *Fox News* on the TV, but I would have survived that. Instead, I kept the door closed, electing to miss the opportunity to flee temptation.

Paul flat-out says there is no such thing as a temptation we can't withstand. You know what this means, right? We can't say, "The devil made me do it." We can't blame the strength of the temptation or the charm of the tempter, because God always provides a way out.

When temptation ends in sin, sin was never the first station the train could have stopped at. All along the way there are physical and spiritual "outs," with God as our biggest advocate on the sidelines saying, "Get out now! Right here! I've given you another option." I know you can hear him. I hear him every time.

When a younger Billy Graham would travel from city to city, he would ask hotels to remove the television set from his room. Did Graham think TV was evil? No. He simply knew he was most vulnerable when alone and away from his family. He knew the greatest danger to his integrity would be a false belief that he was beyond giving in to temptation. "The best way to avoid giving in to temptation is to flee from it the moment it appears," he said.

There is never, in any circumstance, a time when you can't turn on the light, open the door, and walk your way into a better situation. Listen to Paul one more time: "When you are tempted, [God] will show you a way out so that you can endure" (1 Corinthians 10:13).

 Write down your two or three greatest temptations. Next to each, write down the escape God has given you. You know what it is—you see it every time you travel that road!
SW

I'm Sorry

The kind of sorrow God wants us to experience leads us away from sin and results in salvation. There's no regret for that kind of sorrow. But worldly sorrow, which lacks repentance, results in spiritual death.
2 CORINTHIANS 7:10

One summer spent with a professional theater company out east rocked my life. I have told my husband about it. I have told my girls. I have never told Dannah. But now I am going to share the story with you.

I received some relationship wounds my sophomore year of college. You don't get details on the wounds, just on my response, which was to hurt the guy who had hurt me. How would I hurt him? By tossing out every boundary I had ever set up in my life! I was going to live wild all summer long and boy, would he be sorry! I hope you see the fallacy of my thinking. Who was I going to hurt but myself? He wasn't even around! But I set about it with a vengeance. To this day I realize only divine intervention prevented me from being a victim of date rape. Near the end of the summer I was tired of it all. I was embarrassed and wracked with shame.

Who should come along one night to share with our dormitory but a group of college kids on a missions trip! I grabbed the first few girls on that mission team that I could find, and I poured out a summer full of confessions. It was a long, ugly rant, congested so badly by snot and tears that I couldn't breathe any longer. It was the truest moment of brokenness in my life. The girls gathered around me, laid hands on me, and prayed God's redeeming love right back into every muscle of my body.

There is no sorrow like godly sorrow. When we are sorry from the depths of our souls, repentance occurs—the kind that makes us hungry for obedience. It's said that repentance is proven when we turn and walk in an entirely different direction. The rest of my life was fueled by better choices, defined by obedience to God. You can have a clean slate too. And it begins with godly sorrow.

 Ask God to make you a person of genuine sorrow. Will you allow him to break you when he needs to so you will choose forgiveness over spiritual death?
SW

Out from under the Rainbow

Once you were slaves of sin, but now you wholeheartedly obey this teaching we have given you. Now you are free from your slavery to sin, and you have become slaves to righteous living. ROMANS 6:17-18

Are people born gay?

Science would have us believe that this is so, and we are not going to argue with science. It is a fact that the brains of those with a genuine leaning toward same-sex attraction have a small differentiation from those who prefer heterosexuality. Does this mean the argument is said and done? That we can simply celebrate homosexuality?

Not really.

God defines marriage and sexual expression in the book of Genesis as that which should take place between male and female. There is no place in Scripture where he says that he loves those who struggle with same-sex attraction any less, but he encourages them to look back at his original intention for sexuality before they give free rein to their physical desires.

The fact is, almost every sin can be traced to a biological underpinning, and a person's brain will look very different when they are embracing or being tempted to embrace something other than God's best. (Ever get violent or verbally abusive during a really bad bout of PMS? Guaranteed, a brain scan would reveal a biological difference at that time of the month compared to the rest of the month.)

The bottom line is always that we have a choice to make—am I going to obey God or my body? The book of Romans says that we will become a slave to whatever we choose to obey.

When God calls a young man or woman to override a biological desire for same-sex attraction, he will also provide a way for him or her to do so. "If you love me, you will obey my commands," Jesus said (see John 14:15). If you want out—of homosexuality, of pornography, of self-mutilation, of self-righteousness—you have a way that has been made for you! The choice to obey is that which will set you free. Is this simple? No, so here's the first step in your new journey: tell someone.

 Tell someone today if you are struggling with same-sex attraction. Go to your parents, your pastor, or a close Christian friend who can help you walk well.

Kiss and Tell

Don't use foul or abusive language. Let everything you say be good and helpful, so that your words will be an encouragement to those who hear them. EPHESIANS 4:29

I was sitting in a counseling room when a pastor encouraged me to start using four-letter words. He said they were "just words" and I was repressing anger by not using them. He wouldn't let me leave the room until I called someone I was mad at a "bleep!"

Over the next few weeks I "wove a tapestry of obscenities that as far as we know is still hanging in space over Lake Michigan" (borrowed from *A Christmas Story*, of course). I knew I was owned by my sin when a moment of road rage had me shouting obscenities at someone I'd never even met. I asked the Lord for his opinion, and he directed me to the passage where Isaiah stands before God and cries out, "Woe unto me, for I am a man of unclean lips!" (See Isaiah 6:5.)

It's becoming popular to use profane or sexual language. The "cool" Christians do it. They are living in "freedom." But I wasn't really free. I was a slave to anger, fury, vulgarity, and impurity. Are you?

Our key verse reminds us to check the type of language we use. You may not use coarse language, but you know what we are talking about. You hear it—maybe so often you are unaware of how inappropriate it is! We encourage you to give great thought to your own language as well as what you willingly expose yourself to through friends, music, and television. It's not prudish. It's wise.

It is a rare occasion when sexual jests or coarse phrases can be spoken in a group of people and leave no one uncomfortable. This is one of the main reasons Paul cautions us against salty language. It ends up dividing rather than unifying. It invites judgment rather than encouragement. People don't need to lighten up. We say hooray for those who are offended by coarse talk! It's right along the lines of God's own heart to love what is pure and hate what is evil.

 **Action STEP** We are instructed to hate the things God hates (see Psalm 97:10). Yes, God is love, but wickedness is one thing you are encouraged to be allergic to. Walk away from the next foul words you hear. Seriously—leave the room.

The One and Only Boundary

A man leaves his father and mother and is joined to his wife, and the two are united into one. Now the man and his wife were both naked, but they felt no shame. GENESIS 2:24-25

According to the Myers Briggs personality test, there are sixteen dominant personality types, which we find to be eerily accurate. Just for fun right now, Google "Myers Briggs free test" and complete one of the free assessments. Warning: You may spend the next few days showing your friends this assessment and comparing results. This really is such a great exercise for understanding friends, family, and all relationships! (Both of us are ISTJs. Go figure.)

As you read your profile, you will see it is not only uncannily accurate, but that it gauges you on a number of things, one being flexibility. Our personality type of ISTJ tends to resist flexibility. We don't compromise much, due to a certainty that we are right. That doesn't sound good now that it's on paper, but we know it's true. We have to check ourselves all the time to be gentle. Compromise can be a good thing when one friend (Suzy) wants to eat at Bob Evans and another (Dannah) wants to eat at Cracker Barrel. It can be deadly, however, when it comes to the arena of romance and sexual behavior. If you have been willing to compromise or be flexible in these areas, you may have made statements such as

- I'm only going to try it this once.
- She did it, and it didn't seem to hurt her.
- At least he's not as bad as _____.

There are dire consequences attached to such compromise, like regret, family fractures, disease, a ruined reputation, embracing of lies, unplanned pregnancy, and so many more.

God's boundary for sex has always been marriage, not physical desire, not need, not engagement, not even "love." You either are married or you'e not. If you're married, have sex with your spouse. If you're not married, you're *compromising* if you have sex.

Make a list of things important to you when it comes to your future husband. Put a star next to "no exceptions" items and start living by them *now*. If you wouldn't marry him, don't flirt with compromise!

MAY 21

God's Plan A

You are the light of the world—like a city on a hilltop that cannot be hidden. No one lights a lamp and then puts it under a basket. Instead, a lamp is placed on a stand, where it gives light to everyone in the house. In the same way, let your good deeds shine out for all to see, so that everyone will praise your heavenly Father. MATTHEW 5:14-16

George Gipp played for legendary football coach Knute Rockne at Notre Dame. He still holds three unbeaten records today! But fame came in a tragic manner—two weeks after being named an all-American in 1920, he died of strep throat. Antibiotics were not yet available.

Legend says Rockne went to visit Gipp on his deathbed, where Gipp said, "I've got to go, Rock. It's all right. I'm not afraid. Some time, Rock, when the team is up against it, when things are wrong and the breaks are beating the boys, ask them to go in there with all they've got and win just one for the Gipper. I don't know where I'll be then, Rock. But I'll know about it, and I'll be happy." Rockne used this speech to rally his team to beat undefeated Army in 1928.

There are days when it may seem there are no great transcendent truths worth going to battle for. You get up in the morning and go to school where people have nothing more to discuss than the prom and who is going with whom. No wonder it all seems rather empty.

But what if you could believe God has a part for you to play in his redemption plan? What if you could become convinced there is a legacy waiting to be created by you and God, that the meaning of life exists somewhere outside yourself and you were meant to be a part of it? Because this is what God tells us in his Word. Here is our pastor's (Suzy's husband) "Big Gipper" speech: *You are God's plan A to reach a lost and dying world for Christ, and he doesn't have a plan B.*

Jesus said it this way: "You see that darkness out there? Your job is to shine and dispel it. You cannot help but shine if you have been with me, and the darkness cannot help but disperse when it comes in contact with light. Now get out there and win one!" (See Matthew 5:14-16.) We don't develop character and integrity and become a light unto ourselves. We do it to fulfill God's plan A.

 **Action STEP** Write out today's key verse and keep it on your mirror. Read it daily!

MAY 22

Get Busy

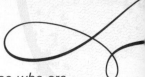

Be careful how you live. Don't live like fools, but like those who are wise. Make the most of every opportunity in these evil days. Don't act thoughtlessly, but understand what the Lord wants you to do.
EPHESIANS 5:15-17

For a number of years there was a prevalent philosophy in youth ministry: if we provide enough after-school activities for teenagers, we can keep them out of trouble, particularly away from alcohol, drugs, and sex. Boredom was seen as the enemy to purity.

Boredom, however, is not caused by too little to do. Boredom is caused by an inability to connect emotionally (passionately) with a specific activity, or by feeling "forced" to participate in unwanted activity. One psychologist recently wrote a fascinating treatise on the problem of boredom. He believes boredom is an offshoot of wrestling with the meaning of life, particularly when an individual comes face-to-face with the possibility of life being meaningless. He thinks you get bored because somewhere inside you have determined there is nothing out there defining who you are.

He may be on to something. Apart from Jesus, there is no purpose to existence. But in Christ, there is fulfillment. Paul tells us to be wise and to make the most of our chances, understanding what it is God wants us to do. God has provided for us a pair of tasks we are well suited for. He made us for this: to love him and to love one another. Here are some ways you can get busy on center stage and, yes, keep yourself pure as the white-hot spotlight follows your every move:

- Get a small group of friends together for ten minutes a day at school to pray for your friends, teachers, and one another.
- Volunteer your time with a charity you love.
- Go on a missions trip.
- Set a goal to meet one new person at your school each month. This means reaching out in ways that may stretch you.
- Get into a leadership position at school or youth group.

This stuff won't keep you pure in and of itself. But it might help restart your engine and remind you how very much purpose you have.

 **Action STEP** Get busy. Don't accept a life of boredom!

Welcome to Graceland

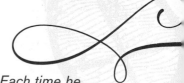

Three different times I begged the Lord to take it away. Each time he said, "My grace is all you need. My power works best in weakness." So now I am glad to boast about my weaknesses, so that the power of Christ can work through me. 2 CORINTHIANS 12:8-9

Apparently Paul had some kind of "thorn in the flesh"—we may more commonly translate this as "pain in the neck." No one knows for sure what the problem was. We only know he was completely vexed by this thorn, and he begged God three times to take it away.

So how would you like to receive God's answer? The verb Paul uses for "he said" is *legei*, a form of the verb *lego*, meaning to say or speak. But *legei* is typically reserved for the words of a ruler. God is speaking as king here . . . and he says *no*. Not only that, he speaks to Paul using perfect tense. This is what your parents do when they say, "And that's final!"

There are some hopeful elements in this passage. Isn't it good to know that when we are in need of God's grace, our struggle doesn't necessarily mean we lack faith? Don't get caught in the trap of saying, "I asked, nothing happened, and therefore God must not be real, or he must not care about me, or I must not be good enough." He is God. If we dictate his answers to our prayers, we're not really affirming his place as Lord of all.

God depicts our weaknesses as strengths. When we display a strength, it's easy to take credit, but what about when we succeed where all indicators say we should fail? Tim Tebow played his first real football game as starting quarterback for the Denver Broncos in 2011. Though Tebow is super easy to like, he doesn't play like an elite quarterback. He has a funny throwing motion. His arm isn't the strongest. No one expected him to have success. Yet in his first season, Tebow led the Denver Broncos into the play-offs. Tim Tebow will be the first to tell you that even on his worst days, God is racking up victories in his life.

It's okay if things are out of order in your life right now. You are a broken vessel. Let God do his thing, which is to glorify himself through you . . . in spite of your limitations. Let him be strong.

 Write your greatest weakness on a slip of paper and put it on your mirror. Every time you see it, ask God to glorify himself right there!

Big Forgiveness = Big Freedom

If the Son sets you free, you are truly free. JOHN 8:36

Could there be a forgiveness story as big as Corrie ten Boom's? Corrie was imprisoned in a Nazi concentration camp along with her sister Betsie, who died there. Five years after the end of the war, Corrie was speaking at a church in Germany. Imagine her horror at recognizing one of her camp's most vicious guards in the audience. The man explained he had become a Christian since the war. He knew God had forgiven him, but he needed to hear it from her. Corrie ten Boom determined she could at least extend her hand to the man, though she felt nothing even remotely like forgiveness in her heart:

> And so woodenly, mechanically, I thrust my hand into the one stretched out to me. And as I did, an incredible thing took place. The current started in my shoulder, raced down my arm, sprang into our joined hands. And then this healing warmth seemed to flood my whole being, bringing tears to my eyes. "I forgive you, brother!" I cried. "With all my heart!"

Our friend Andrea was called to the same place of forgiveness. She had never told anyone that as a girl she had been sexually abused by a friend's father. Andrea was also confronted with the presence of her abuser in a church when he sat directly in front of her during Communion. Andrea was tempted to walk away from the body and blood of Jesus before agreeing to share it with one who had hurt her.

"The pride that came from my pain had deceived me," she says. "I believed I was more deserving, more worthy to receive the body and blood of Christ than my abuser. Our sins—both mine and my abuser's—hung Jesus on the cross. My pride had to die, or the cross of Christ would be meaningless for me."

Big forgiveness is a miracle, and it's one the God of the universe invites us to participate in wholeheartedly. He promises he will bring healing—every time—to those who choose the high road.

Action **STEP** Do you need to be set free? Simply admitting your bondage to unforgiveness is the first step. Have an honest talk with God to get things rolling.

Who's the Fool?

You cry out, "Why doesn't the LORD accept my worship?" I'll tell you why!
Because the LORD witnessed the vows you and your wife made when you
were young. But you have been unfaithful to her, though she remained
your faithful partner, the wife of your marriage vows. MALACHI 2:14

My husband and I once took a sunset walk on the beach with my brother and his
now ex-wife. Somehow we stumbled upon a Coppertone photo shoot. There on
the soft expanses of sand were two amazing female physiques, tanned to perfection, in snow-white bikinis. My brother's eyes were glued to the scene, and his
wife was furious enough to give him a tongue-lashing.

"Jonathan," my brother said in exasperation to my hubby, "tell me you didn't
notice!" My husband said something I will never forget. "Oh, I noticed," he said.
"I'm just not stupid enough to keep looking."

Raise your hand if you think my husband is a hero! But let's be sure to
admit as women we need to make some brain adjustments too.

Maybe we need to *stop* reading so many romance novels? (Yes!) Perhaps we
should *stop* taking our cues on romance from movies or TV shows that encourage us to root for the extramarital affair? (Yes!) We could even *quit* reading
gossip rags that leave us panting for the next juicy story of yet another celebrity
relationship shot to pieces. (Please!) They may be there for our convenient voy-
eurism, but we'd better not stay focused on them. Someday the stakes will be
much higher. Someday you may have a marriage to protect.

Why do we need to stop doing these things? They are formative behaviors
standing in direct opposition to God's Word. We need to begin to understand
we are literally formed not only by things we participate in, but also by things
we choose to observe. What you practice as a manner of viewing and hearing
now will be what you live out in your marriage. Do you really think you'll stop
wanting to lust after the half-naked Abercrombie & Fitch model just because
there is a ring on your finger?

Want to protect your marriage *now*? Remain faithful to your husband, even
if you have not yet met him. Your relationship with him is a picture of Jesus'
relationship with the church, a holy picture for which God is quite jealous.

 Begin protecting your marriage bed *today*. Refuse to
look at things causing you to long for romance, root
for unfaithfulness, or celebrate broken ties!
SW

MAY 26

Are You Crazy?

The LORD hears his people when they call to him for help. He rescues them from all their troubles. The LORD is close to the brokenhearted; he rescues those whose spirits are crushed. PSALM 34:17-18

We wish there were another word for counseling. There are a lot of myths associated with counseling that keep people from reaching out to experience the fantastic growth it allows. Here are a few of the myths:

Myth #1: Only weak people talk to therapists. Then both of us are weak, because we have both sought counsel. The truth is, it takes a lot of chutzpah (that's guts or strength) to be honest about the things in your life. Psalm 34 is not only God's promise to be near when you are troubled but a general statement that you're going to be in trouble a time or two in your life. It *is* the human condition to know times of trouble, hurt, and brokenness.

Myth #2: Crazy people go to counselors. Most people with true mental illnesses are unable to admit or recognize a need for help. It's a sign of sanity to be able to affirm your need for help! Counseling is for people who feel stuck in a rut or who need a little nudge to get things moving in a better direction. It's a good sign to want to talk with someone.

Myth #3: Talking to my friends or my youth leaders is enough. Friends are great, as are youth leaders. But counselors have been professionally trained in listening and in utilizing techniques that can help you get to the root of your questions or issues. We have been in youth ministry many years and have loved the girls we work with, but we are not trained to help people unlock the mysteries of their minds. Double ditto goes for your friends!

Myth #4: Talking won't change anything. Ironically, the most harmful decision you can make when stuck is to keep your mouth shut. Talking things through allows the muddle to untangle; silence leaves you caught in a place where bad can grow to worse.

 Counseling may or may not be for you, but ask this question: *Lord, if I feel stuck, would you point me not only to your truth, but to a solid counselor who would help me unpack my thoughts?* Thank God today for his rescuing spirit!

Save It for the Stage

A person without self-control is like a city with broken-down walls.
PROVERBS 25:28

I graduated from high school with eleven plays under my belt. People wrote all over my yearbook that they expected to come see me on Broadway one day. I believed the hype, which is why I came crashing to the ground pretty hard when I failed to earn a spot in the school of theater my freshman year of college.

I went to the program director, curious as to why I had been cut for the first time in five years. He was able to tell me exactly why I ended in the cut pile—I had been acting. Say what? You don't *act* sad when you play a jilted girl, he explained. He went on to say that instead of acting sad, you recall a time when you *were* sad and you recall how that impacted your speech, your muscles, etc. If the actress is merely *acting* sad, well, the audience may end up snickering at her "pain" because it looks like an "act."

You may want to snicker at your school's resident drama queen as well—she "acts" like her problem is so big, like what just happened is the biggest thing in the world. But, the drama queen's behavior probably deserves empathy more than snickers. The drama queen is not one who behaves in a truthful manner. She seeks attention, so she will act out an exaggerated emotion to gain empathy. Why would I say she deserves your empathy? This behavior of hers is going to account for a lot of loneliness unless she can get it under control. Hopefully you can be her friend and gently help her see the truth.

This drama queen may be you. If such is the case, understand this: as long as lack of self-control and public pleas for attention are the choices you make, misery will be your company! There are a myriad of healthy ways to deal with your fears. Talk to a trusted adult. Take it to God in prayer. Confide in a friend over coffee. Take time to learn what God says about you in his Word. But do not fall for the lie that drama equals life. The drama is a fraud masquerading as the real thing. You deserve the real thing.

 Talk to someone about renouncing public displays of big emotion. Check yourself to see if you're the one who needs to give up the drama.
SW

You Can't Take It Back

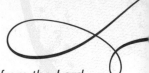

Once you were full of darkness, but now you have light from the Lord. So live as people of light! For this light within you produces only what is good and right and true. EPHESIANS 5:8-9

Every day eleven teens take their lives, making suicide the third leading cause of death among teenagers. As much as teen suicide is an absolute tragedy, we believe kids who take their own lives want their pain to stop more so than life itself. If people want to live, there exists a foundation for change and healing.

In the winter of 2012 a local college student committed suicide in his fraternity bedroom. His actions were premeditated only by a drinking binge and a fight with his best friend. His mother says alcohol had medicated his reasoning and "all that was left was thoughtless pain." Without alcohol, the young man's mother believes, he would still be alive today.

Pain blinds us to the realities of hope. Our enemy, the devil, would love nothing more when we are writhing in pain to deprive us of the life-giving presence of hope. There is an old maxim that man can live about forty days without food, three days without water, eight minutes without air, but only one second without hope. Think about the amazing things people have been able to survive when they keep hope afloat:

financial ruin
diseases
natural disasters
breakups

It isn't hardships in life that do people in. It's falling prey to the lie that there is no hope. Proverbs 13:12 says when hope is taken away our hearts grow sick. God is the giver of hope. Satan is a thief. God is the giver of dreams. Satan is the father of lies. God is our rescue, an ever-present help in time of need (see Psalm 46:1). Satan is a murderer. So what could the enemy do if he could get us to believe that even God is against us?

The world is in great darkness, but the Light has come into the world. John 1:10 says the world did not recognize the light, but as followers of Jesus we have recognized him, we identify with him, and we reflect him.

 If you cannot see hope in the light of Christ, let someone know immediately. If a friend talks of hopelessness, lead her right away to a counselor.

MAY 29

Masterpiece . . .
Part Deux

We are God's masterpiece. He has created us anew in Christ Jesus, so we can do the good things he planned for us long ago.
EPHESIANS 2:10

Imagine ordering an original work of art from a master painter and waiting breathlessly for your tour de force to arrive. You have spoken with your insurance agent and cleared a spot on the wall, and finally the big day comes. You sign for the package, tear open the box, and . . . the canvas is torn. Someone has smeared coffee grounds or ink across a portion of the work. It's clear this is ruined. Insurance will cover it, sure, but that won't get you a new painting.

Your phone rings. The artist has heard what has happened, and he encourages you to send the painting back to him. "Can you fix it?" you ask.

"No," he says. "This one has been ruined. But I can paint you a new one. It will be perfect this time, because I'll deliver it myself."

When God first made a blueprint of you, before the creation of the world, he knew his plan was a masterpiece. He was enthralled with your beauty and the wonder of you even before he knit you together in your mom's womb (see Psalm 139:13-14). Of course, by the time you arrived, sin already had a grip on the world, so you were born flawed from day one. (Says so in Psalm 51:5.)

God is in the process of making a new and improved you and me. One day we will be made complete like him. For now, everyone who has been redeemed by Jesus' blood is like painting number two being redone in the master artist's studio. And the Master is excited, because you are finally allowing him to prepare you for the things he created you to do all those years ago.

Pain from mistakes and bad decisions does go away with time and the magnificent stroke of the Master's brush. It fades as a matter of course for every human being, but it is snatched away and thrown immediately back up on the easel for redoing for everyone who surrenders the scratched, stained, brokenness of their lives to the Master. He is the only one able to make us anew!

 *Action* **STEP** Thank God for who he is making you, how he is making you anew, and all of the good he has prepared for you to do.

You Might Be Greedy If . . .

Give freely and become more wealthy; be stingy and lose everything. The generous will prosper; those who refresh others will themselves be refreshed. PROVERBS 11:24-25

You might be greedy if . . .

- you keep a wish list around at all times.
- you will do a job if money is involved, but not for free.
- you are always looking for get rich quick ideas.
- you play the lottery.
- you are hypercritical of people who have a lot (or little) money.
- you are jealous of others' new purchases.

God loves turning all conventional wisdom upside down on its head. The world says that if you give away too much money, you will become poor. God says just the opposite. If you give freely, you will simply obtain more wealth. He is the giver of all good things.

Greed is one of those things we have to check on now and then. It's kind of like dogs during tick season. It's only once a tick is feeding that it can be felt or seen; prior to feeding, it's only about the size of a pinhead! But once it latches on, it's a hassle to get rid of. That's what greed is like too. You don't feel its bite; you only notice it after it swells up a bit.

Here are a few ways to take a bite out of greediness if you find it's taken a bite out of you.

- We all struggle with greed, so just admit you are in the same boat as everyone else.
- God says to pray at all times (see Ephesians 6:18). Ask him to remove your greed.
- Say "thank you" more and complain less.

Greed will never truly go away. Not until we walk on the streets of gold. Until then it's a day-by-day investigation of the heart. We can't go a day without checking the dogs . . . can we go a day without letting God examine our hearts for greed?

Action **STEP** Take ten minutes to meditate on Psalm 139:23-24. Focus on the question of greed.

MAY 31

Where Did All My Money Go?

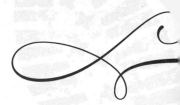

Don't begin until you count the cost. For who would begin construction of a building without first calculating the cost to see if there is enough money to finish it? Otherwise, you might complete only the foundation before running out of money, and then everyone would laugh at you. They would say, "There's the person who started that building and couldn't afford to finish it!" LUKE 14:28-30

Every two weeks a ritual takes place in the Weibel household. We drive two blocks to the neighborhood bank, put the ATM card in the little slot, and take out enough cash to buy groceries, feed the dogs, eat out, and have some fun. It's more cash than I have ever carried around in my life! But because of that cash and our written budget, I can tell you where *every* penny we have earned over the past two weeks is going to go. Some of it will pay for our house, our electric bills, gas for our cars or scooters (we rock the Vespas to the tune of seventy miles per gallon); some will go into savings, to the church, for home improvement . . . but the point is, I can tell you exactly where every penny goes.

I'll bet 60 percent of retired NBA players wish they could say the same, because that's how many have to file for bankruptcy within five years of retiring, according to the *New York Times*. That means *millions* of dollars have been squandered on lavish homes, cars, parties, jewelry, child support payments . . . all without a plan. Apparently it's worse in the NFL. Their players' bankruptcy rate, according to the *New York Times*, is 80 percent two years after retirement!

Perhaps we don't ever have enough because we have never stopped to ask the question, "Enough for what? What exactly is it that I want?" Do you want to buy a car while you are in high school? Do you want to wear designer jeans? Do you want to be able to give thirty dollars a month to a child in need? Do you want to go out for breakfast at midnight with your friends every Saturday? Whatever it is, it requires a plan.

You may only make a couple hundred dollars a month, but you can have the peace of knowing what you can or cannot do if you just build a plan. This peace will follow you when you get a job or go to college because you have learned the discipline of building a budget and of spending only what you have earned.

 Find a simple budget worksheet online and work through it. Better yet, sit down with an adult who has some budgeting experience and get serious!

JUNE 1
Learning to Say No

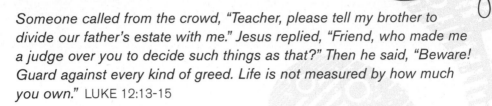

Someone called from the crowd, "Teacher, please tell my brother to divide our father's estate with me." Jesus replied, "Friend, who made me a judge over you to decide such things as that?" Then he said, "Beware! Guard against every kind of greed. Life is not measured by how much you own." LUKE 12:13-15

There is a guy named Dave (his blog title is just that: *guy named dave*) who is encouraging people to take "the 100 Thing Challenge." Sickened by rampant consumerism, Dave Bruno has spent the past few years paring down the possessions in his life to a mere one hundred items. The 100 Thing Challenge has a Facebook page you can check out.

Dave seems so normal. We like his honesty. Here he has started this movement and has written a book and has been featured in *Time* magazine . . . and yet he admits he doesn't know whether he can accomplish his own challenge. Is there any way you and I could live with only one hundred personal possessions? (Keep in mind each piece of clothing, or each pair of shoes, equals one possession.)

The 100 Thing Challenge is extreme, as it is meant to be. The most acute question it poses is whether our discontent with "stuff" we don't have actually arises from the fact we *have* too much stuff! How many times have you caught yourself saying you *need* this or you *need* that, when the word you were looking for was *want*?

There is such a disease as wanting more than God provides. It's called covetousness, or *pleonexia* in Greek. This is what Jesus is warning the man in today's passage against, and what Dave is fighting in his own life. The number of toys we possess in this world is no indicator of our happiness. One of the most important words we can learn to say to ourselves is *no*! Recognizing the difference between what we want and what we need is key, and many people find themselves in the position of being unable to do what they need (pay tuition bills and fill the gas tank) because they have not learned to say *no* to what they want.

 Practice paring down. Find at least two items you can throw or give away, or even sell. Start there. Put at least a twenty-four-hour hiatus on your next purchase (other than food). If this action step blesses you, do it again tomorrow! Remember, your life will never be measured by how much you own.

JUNE 2
Marketing 101

Beware of these teachers of religious law! For they like to parade around in flowing robes and love to receive respectful greetings as they walk in the marketplaces. And how they love the seats of honor in the synagogues and the head table at banquets. LUKE 20:46

As the heat of summer hits, you might be planning to earn a little spending cash. Maybe you'll babysit or don the lovely uniform of a fast-food joint. (We think a great place to get that first job is Chick-fil-A. They're closed on Sundays to observe the Sabbath—a great example for us all!) Whatever it is, be careful, or that money you make will get sucked right out of your hot little hands faster than you can say "sunscreen." Before you know it, the slowly increasing savings account for a new car can turn into . . . nothing significant.

Let's say a few years back your forward-thinking parents bought you the first version of the Kindle hot off the shelves. For a while it was the coolest thing you had ever seen. But then some friends started showing up at school with this new device from Apple. They didn't need a Wi-Fi signal to download books. Or music. Or movies. Or Angry Birds. Suddenly your old Kindle seemed pretty primitive. But, fortunately for you (or so you thought), a new shipment of iPads just came in at Best Buy! *Good-bye car fund!*

Why do we spend money we don't have on things we technically don't need? Someone has managed to get us to bite the apple of prestige, promising we'll be loved more or thought better of or envied if we manage to have the best. Marketers make us feel dissatisfied with what we have, and we're selling our futures to run after the next soon-to-be-outdated piece of technology.

At its root, this is the thinking of a Pharisee. The Pharisees loved to be thought of as important, so they wore ostentatious clothing and strutted about where they could be seen and admired. They, Jesus said, have received their reward in full (see Matthew 6:2). It's okay to think the iPad is cool. Save for it. Buy it only after you have tithed and taken care of your responsibilities. Enjoy it for its merits, rather than using it to garner esteem. And hold it loosely, so that it may *never* become your god.

 Take some time to decide what your summer earning will look like. Don't be haphazard about it. Plan. Determine how much you need, and what you need to do to earn the money.

Who Do You Love?

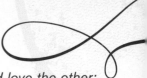

No one can serve two masters. For you will hate one and love the other; you will be devoted to one and despise the other. You cannot serve both God and money. MATTHEW 6:24

Imagine standing at the edge of a vast prairie. The night air is warm and breezy. You can see for miles and miles. As you breathe quietly, the night sky begins to emerge on the canvas of the heavens, right before your very eyes. Confronted by its enormity, you break. *How could I have ever been so self-centered? How could I have ever believed it was all about me?* This is exactly the setting in which recording artist Stephanie Smith found herself near the end of her years in college. Instead of singing and touring and signing those autographs, she was cured of their effects in a small African village.

The African family Stephanie was living with did not care much for her American success story. In fact, they found it humorous. *What do you mean you don't know how to kill a chicken? Don't you eat chicken?* Here was Stephanie, accustomed to shopping in air-conditioned superstores stocked with enough food to feed multiple African villages . . . and she was being mocked for not knowing how to prepare her own meal from field to table.

There is a big world out there consisting of billions of people. Some are "privileged," but millions are not. Millions earn only enough to get by from day to day, and millions more earn even less than that. Here's the riddle: the millions who have the toys, the machines, the ease, and the comforts of life are no happier than the millions who have little.

Money was one of Jesus' favorite topics. He never encouraged people to store up a pile of it, though. In today's verse he even warns that loving money could compete with worshiping him. In fact, we end up serving the god of money if we are not careful.

Stephanie learned to slay that giant in her life by living with people who had very little. What might you need to do in order to be sure you do not worship the god of money?

Begin to save for something that builds the Kingdom of God. Support a missionary. Contribute to a ministry. Serve victims of a natural disaster. A glass jar or a new savings account—either will do the trick!

JUNE 4
Who Is Better Off?

Don't love money; be satisfied with what you have. For God has said,
"I will never fail you. I will never abandon you." HEBREWS 13:5

Asha is a fifteen-year-old girl living in Swaziland, a small country on the continent of Africa. Her name means "life," and she knows she is lucky to have it. Asha, her two siblings, and three cousins live in a one-room sunbaked mud hut. Their parents have all fallen to AIDS. Only the oldest boy, a cousin, attends school. Asha works twelve hours a day as a maid for a European family to pay her cousin's school fees, including one fee for a seat in the front of the classroom and another for having homework checked. Hopefully Asha's cousin can one day earn enough to move the family out of the slums, but they will be content regardless. The family is alive and together—for now, it is enough.

Karina is also fifteen, living in Denver, Colorado, and has been a competitive skier from a young age. Her family has moved west to support her pursuit, which tends to be expensive. Karina leaves school early each day and heads an hour west to train. Though Karina is hoping to win a spot on the next Winter Olympics team, she worries about her parents. They are fighting a lot about money, and Karina's dad has just taken a higher-paying job on the East Coast, meaning he will be with the family only one weekend each month. The family stress is high, and the pressure to succeed intense.

Is Asha or Karina better off? That's what we call a rhetorical question. There's no true answer, but the question should cause us to think. Are you satisfied with what you have, or has the drive for "more" overtaken your family?

Philip Yancey once said that if you can buy a book and have the education to read it, you are among the world's most elite. You're sitting here with a book you own, reading it. Add it up. You not only have enough, but you are among the world's elite.

Rather than staying on the rat race to nowhere in an effort to have more, pause often today to focus on being satisfied.

 *Action* **STEP** Write a prayer or poem of contentment to God.

Burned

When the ground soaks up the falling rain and bears a good crop for the farmer, it has God's blessing. But if a field bears thorns and thistles, it is useless. The farmer will soon condemn that field and burn it.
HEBREWS 6:7-8

I live surrounded by fields. Soy. Wheat. Corn. That's what the Penn State agricultural department grows around me each summer. I've never seen the fields barren. Because the fields are tended, they are not overtaken by weeds, which makes for some wonderful trail riding with my horses, Trig and Truett.

Our verses today say that at some point all the water falling on a farmer's field *has* to cause the crop to come up or the field is useless. Worse yet, thorns and thistles could be the farmer's crop. That field is going to get burned.

We are a field, called to produce fruit.

Whether you believe the fruit we produce refers to the fruits of the Spirit listed in Galatians 5:22-23—"love, joy, peace, patience, kindness, goodness, faithfulness, gentleness, and self-control"—or to producing other disciples who produce fruit is a moot point. This is about the realization that we exist to produce. Something. Anything. Out of us should come something others can use.

Why do you think God has placed us in the midst of such wealth? Some believe life is short and to the victor go the spoils—she who dies with the most toys wins. This probably isn't a conscious thought in the minds of most people, so it's not meant to be a verdict of "evil" we are passing down. But many times we live as if we believe life is about accumulating stuff. God says the farmer burns the field yielding such selfish results.

Some would say we have been dropped in the midst of such wealth in order to serve, bless, heal, and proclaim freedom for those who are destitute, both physically and spiritually. Looking up and seeing the needs around us is the only way to recognize that we can be part of the solution. "When someone has been given much, much will be required in return" (Luke 12:48). Please don't wait until you are a millionaire to give. You'll never give then if you can't give now. You have something right now to give. What is it?

 Keep your head up for a day or two. What needs are you seeing that your particular riches can meet? Have the guts to do something about it.
DG

JUNE 6
The Problem with Greed

Not that I was ever in need, for I have learned how to be content with whatever I have. I know how to live on almost nothing or with everything. I have learned the secret of living in every situation, whether it is with a full stomach or empty, with plenty or little. For I can do everything through Christ, who gives me strength. PHILIPPIANS 4:11-13

The day after Thanksgiving has a name known to shoppers everywhere—Black Friday. Lately, the hour at which doors open to shoppers has stealthily crept backward into Thanksgiving Day. Some shoppers will stop at nothing to land the big deal. Recent altercations have included shoppers stepping over the body of a man who had had a heart attack at a West Virginia Target store and a woman in California who pepper sprayed a group of fellow shoppers reaching for video game deals.

What is going on?! Greed. Plain and simple. And lest we too quickly point a finger at Pepper Spray Woman, let's admit struggles with greed seem to be shared by all, the rich and the poor alike. Theologian Matthew Henry says, "The temptations of fullness and prosperity are not less than those of affliction and want." We shouldn't assume getting more of what we want or think we need could ever satisfy the feeling of wanting or needing more.

We know greed is bad, and we hate it when we feel it creeping in, but how do we make the desire for "more" go away? It seems we would have to become monks to avoid these things, because they are everywhere! Should we just give everything away as Jesus instructed the rich young ruler? (Read Luke 18:18-30.)

In today's passage, Paul talks about the secret of living with contentment, which in the Greek here means to be strong enough to accept one's lot, though it may be little. When we lack, we are not to look to others to meet our needs, but instead to God and say, "I can do this, with you." When we have plenty, we are not to look to "stuff" to feed the perpetuation of our happy outlook. Again we look to God and say, "How can I use this blessing in my life to serve someone else today?" Notice one other thing: Paul doesn't say he *knows* the secret. He says he *learned* it. This is one attitude that might just take us some time to acquire!

 **Action STEP** Practice saying no to yourself and yes to the needs of others. Just for fun, catch the "Stuff Mart Rap" with the VeggieTales' Madame Blueberry on YouTube.

Is "Rich" Bad?

True godliness with contentment is itself great wealth. After all, we brought nothing with us when we came into the world, and we can't take anything with us when we leave it. So if we have enough food and clothing, let us be content. But people who long to be rich fall into temptation and are trapped by many foolish and harmful desires that plunge them into ruin and destruction. For the love of money is the root of all kinds of evil. And some people, craving money, have wandered from the true faith and pierced themselves with many sorrows. 1 TIMOTHY 6:6-10

No one knew her name. She was a homeless Jewish woman wandering the streets of New York City. Some knew she'd survived a Holocaust camp in her younger days. Everyone knew she lived a life in the streets. What no one knew is that through the years she'd collected and saved about $300,000.

No one knows how she earned the money. She wasn't employed. It's believed she saved it penny by penny as people made donations to her in an effort to feed her and keep her warm with coats and blankets. Even those pennies were, it appears, more than she needed.

By legal will, she assigned her fortune upon her death to several charities and causes. One of those was Hebrew University, which she instructed to use her donation of $100,000 to fund scholarships for medical research. It's obvious she was an intelligent woman who wanted to do good in the world. And that she was content with very little.

Could you be content living without a home? Without your mom's famous breakfast rolls or your dad's fantastic steaks grilled to perfection? Would it be okay if you didn't have your own bedroom but had to share with a few sibs? How about if you had only one computer in the house? Goodness. We have a lot!

When Paul speaks of "contentment," his instruction is for us to live independent of *things*—neither our happiness nor our worth should come from possessions. Paul never condemns wealth. He simply says contentment and wealth are not related. If it is dangerous for the world to forget this, how much more dangerous is it for you and I as believers to fall for the lie?

We brought nothing with us when we came in to this world, and we can take nothing with us when we leave. One simple, anonymous Holocaust survivor lived that truth quite literally.

 *Action* **STEP** Pick one *simple* pleasure to enjoy today and forgo all others. Is your one thing enough?

JUNE 8

Who Is Rich?

Hasn't God chosen the poor in this world to be rich in faith? Aren't they the ones who will inherit the Kingdom he promised to those who love him? But you dishonor the poor! Isn't it the rich who oppress you and drag you into court? Aren't they the ones who slander Jesus Christ, whose noble name you bear? JAMES 2:5-7

I have a dear friend in Zambia, Africa. Her name is Brendah, and she is raising seven children. Three of these are her own. The others are the children of her brothers and sisters who died of AIDS. (Brendah's husband died from a "headache" long ago.) Brendah walks an hour each day to teach a class of one hundred kindergartners using only chalk and a blackboard. She walks another hour home. Her pay is less than you'd make working a few hours a week at a fast-food chain!

You would think she'd be worn out by the weekend and need rest, but Brendah is fueled by compassion and faith. On Saturdays she volunteers to teach orphaned children who cannot afford school fees. On Sundays she worships and serves the Lord.

When I visit her, she fills my arms with gifts. Brendah is truly very rich.

No one is awarded a kingdom, riches, or a name that is eternal except for God alone. Every all-American athlete, singer of a number one hit, and winner of an Academy Award will one day be relegated to a nearly unsolvable clue in a crossword puzzle. Google is the burial ground for the fame of most people—one day it will be the only place you can find their names.

Why do we give so much preferential treatment to the rich and famous? Why do people who make millions of dollars get the best seat in the house and served a free meal? Their renown is the antithesis of the Kingdom of God—your homeland! Why do we honor them and neglect the poor and lowly? It is the Brendahs of this world who deserve that position of honor.

Look around you. Do you see someone like Brendah? Is there a way you can honor that person? Perhaps the only honor needed is that of your friendship. But let's stop vying for the seat next to the popular girl and maybe start fighting our way to the one who has little but gives much.

 **STEP** Take the word *idol* out of your vocab. Put the energy you used to idolize certain people into worshiping God and loving your neighbor.
DG

Forgetting the Blesser

Those who are wise must finally die, just like the foolish and senseless, leaving all their wealth behind. The grave is their eternal home, where they will stay forever. They may name their estates after themselves, but their fame will not last. They will die, just like animals. PSALM 49:10-12

Hello! How's that for some happy verses? But as the playwrights say, *You Can't Take It with You*. It's okay to have some money. Saving is good. It's okay to have some things you enjoy, as long as you recognize the principles of the psalm above. Eventually we all die, and everything we accumulated on this earth will be utterly worthless, at least as far as we are concerned. This life isn't the game. It's just the warm-up. There is an eternity ahead of us, lived either with the giver of all good things or eternally separated from him. If he has given you good things during this short stint before eternity, if he has blessed the work of your hands, or even if it has been your "good fortune" to be born into wealth, do *not* forget the one from whom the blessings come! Here's what it might look like if you do:

Exhibit A: *Singer.* Has filed for bankruptcy twice, owes $50 million in credit card debt, and has liens against her estate for unpaid taxes. Solution: She is starring on a new reality TV show.

Exhibit B: *Artist.* After her partner died, it was discovered she had $24 million in debt due to unpaid taxes, an incomplete book deal (publishers don't like it when you don't write what they've paid you for), and home improvement costs. Solution: None.

Those are actual celebs. Not going too well, huh? All the worldly woman thinks of is her possessions here and now. She may have a fleeting thought now and then of God, but her here and now consumes her. The godly woman, on the other hand, learns to train her thoughts on God, with only fleeting thoughts of this world and all it has to offer. There is plenty of time for ridiculous riches on the other side! For now, the truly rich girl is the one whose thoughts are fixed on Jesus.

 Take a tour of your home. Write down every material blessing you would like to thank the Blesser for . . . and do it!

Good Lending

Once I was young, and now I am old. Yet I have never seen the godly abandoned or their children begging for bread. The godly always give generous loans to others, and their children are a blessing. PSALM 37:25-26

Two case studies:

The first is Suzy (yep, me) as a sophomore in college. I had four roomies, and we settled into a comfy routine in most areas of community living; I can remember only two areas of contention, both due to *my* unwillingness to be generous. The first was when Terri wanted to borrow my car. Our fights usually involved the gas tank. The second was when Cam wanted to borrow my sweaters. She took great care of them, but they always reappeared in my closet smelling like Cam's perfume.

Now let's consider Marie (that's my daughter). Remember, we adopted our girls, and Marie was thirteen when she came to live with us. She had grown up with very little, but during her years in foster care she had several "angels" with deep pockets. The girls had learned, like the apostle Paul, what it was like to be in need and what it was like to have plenty. Marie has never had problems lending things to other people, and most of the time, she's not even upset if it doesn't come back. "It's just stuff." I've heard her say it more than once.

There seems to be this reverse principle in God's Kingdom: when we have little, we do not hesitate to lend; but when we have plenty, our fists want to close. Those who have little are still somehow making it. They know they get by every day by the grace of God and the generosity of others, and it builds in their hearts a principle of freely giving. Those who have plenty are more likely to think they have done something that has resulted in their good fortune. "I did this. I worked hard for it!" we might say. This attitude will not result in getting a "shares with others" gold star!

God's mandate is that we live with the open palm. It has to be open for anything to go out, but it also has to be open for anything to come in, right? We lend freely, and he takes care of us . . . and the fam. That's the deal.

 **Action STEP** Ask a friend if you are generous. Discuss together how both of you could become known as generous and gracious girls.

Spiritual Foreclosure

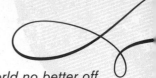

This . . . is a very serious problem. People leave this world no better off than when they came. All their hard work is for nothing—like working for the wind. Throughout their lives, they live under a cloud—frustrated, discouraged, and angry. ECCLESIASTES 5:16-17

Ever drive down a street and see that one house that just doesn't look like the others? Maybe the shutters are falling off and the lawn is overgrown with weeds. You may even see a piece of paper taped to a window or door. This house may be in foreclosure.

When you buy a home one day, you will likely sign a contract (mortgage) promising to repay what you have borrowed from a lender. If you fail to make payments according to the agreed-upon terms (a monthly amount and due date), the bank has the right to seize (foreclose) the home and sell it to satisfy the debt. If the bank's sale of the home does not cover the amount you borrowed, the bank can sue for the remaining amount owed! The reason foreclosures have become so common is because banks are in the habit of loaning people far more than their income and lifestyle can support.

Solomon alludes to this problem in Ecclesiastes. If we spend our time chasing only earthly things such as a nice home and the comforts of wealth, we leave no better than when we arrived. The lending habits of banks play on people's emotional attachments by offering them the chance to buy as much house as possible. The last time our family shopped for a home, the bank said they would give us $100,000 more than we applied for. This would have purchased a *significantly* nicer home! It also would have caused fights, worry, anxiety, and all kinds of other things that shouldn't be present in our home.

Be careful, well studied, and well advised as you seek to make purchases. This includes college costs and car expenses! It's possible to go for less and come out ahead. The banks tell home buyers, "Look at all you can have . . . if you'll just sign on this line." Greed says, "Yes! I have to have the best!" Wisdom says, "God's grace and this decent roof over my head, the affordable college degree, this old car that runs just fine . . . are enough."

 Next time you buy something, do not buy the most expensive option. Evaluate after two days. Was your decision good?

Wanting Too Little

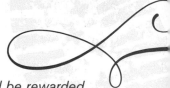

As for you, be strong and courageous, for your work will be rewarded.
2 CHRONICLES 15:7

It's so easy to want too much, but these days it has become just as easy to want *too little*. While the problem seems endemic with guys in your generation, girls are not altogether immune. In fact, we suspect the epidemic of college grads moving back in with mom and dad has as much to do with lack of vision as with a lack of jobs. The future is not something that will come riding in on a white horse and swoop you out of that basement bedroom.

God has a *calling* for your life. Does it take a bit of work to find it? You bet. And sometimes you'll journey many years before you find it, but each step of the way God is planting more of his purpose in your heart.

I was a yearbook editor at Cedarville University because it helped pay for my college tuition. It wasn't my life purpose, but it was a step in that direction. After college, my husband and I started helping local businesses with marketing. I wrote a lot of advertising copy and marketing plans. It wasn't my life purpose, but it was a step in that direction. I wasn't a published author until I was nearly thirty. Can you see how the jobs God gave me in advance prepared me for this career I love?

Nowhere will you find a Scripture encouraging Jesus' followers to be less than excellent or to desire less than excellence. When God's people honor him with their lives, personally and professionally, his response is to bless with excellence.

King Asa received the promise of our key verse in the beginning of his good reign. Asa insisted his people worship God alone—he even kicked his own grandmother off her throne as queen mother and destroyed her articles of worship to Baal when she refused to cooperate (see 2 Chronicles 15). Seek God and serve him, and the work of your hands will be blessed.

 Write your own obituary, just as an exercise. What do you want to fill in that dash between your birth and death? Do you have faith that if you relentlessly pursue God, he will bless the work of your hands? DG

How Much Debt Should I Have?

Just as the rich rule the poor, so the borrower is servant to the lender.
PROVERBS 22:7

Ask your grandparents if they remember getting their first credit card. They will, because they were the first generation to have them. Before that, people didn't buy something they didn't have cash in hand to purchase.

People have always borrowed and repaid money, even before the credit card. The practice of asking the borrower to pay back *more* than was borrowed (interest) is called usury and was actually made "illegal" by the Catholic church early in the first century. Today, there is no such thing as the borrowing of funds *without* usury attached. While the Bible doesn't come right out and call borrowing or lending money a *sin*, it does make clear the lack of wisdom and security found in the practice of debt. It simply is not God's best for us.

The Top Ten Reasons to Avoid Debt:

1. You surrender financial freedom until that debt is repaid.
2. It is immoral to leave a debt unpaid.
3. The ease of going into debt feeds greed.
4. Lenders have power. When leveraged against you, it doesn't feel good.
5. Lenders are not in business to help you; they are in business to make money. They make money when you cannot repay or by charging ungodly interest rates.
6. Debt makes financial growth impossible.
7. Today you make enough to pay on your loan . . . tomorrow you may be out of a job or injured.
8. The wealthiest people say the number one way to build wealth is to avoid debt.
9. The wealthiest people say it is good to give.
10. Romans 13:8 is an encouragement to owe nothing except a debt of love.

 Write out a commitment to yourself and to God to spend your life avoiding debt. It is just too uncertain, unlike a penny earned and saved!

JUNE 14

Credit Cards at Work

The person who strays from common sense will end up in the company of the dead. Those who love pleasure become poor; those who love wine and luxury will never be rich. PROVERBS 21:16-17

The moment your feet hit a college campus, you'll be invited to carry a credit card. Visa and MasterCard will be there giving away free pizzas and Frisbees . . . if you just sign up for a "free" credit card. Ninety-one percent of college students fall for it. Most will graduate owing over $4,000 on that "free" card.

People who carry a balance on their account are called "revolvers," and banks cannot make money without them. Interest is charged only on unpaid balances. Therefore, you can charge thousands of dollars at no cost as long as you pay the debt in full at the end of the month. This sounds like a great deal . . . until you remember the average person *cannot* pay the full bill. (How do you think all those smart college students ended up with over $4,000 still owed?)

Credit cards come with an annual percentage rate determined by risk—when you are a high-risk (inexperienced) borrower you are issued a high APR, sometimes as high as 29 percent! If you carry a balance of $8,000 on your credit card, you now owe that bank $2,320 in interest *plus* the $8,000. The bank has the right to change the interest rate anytime and for any reason. Your 29 percent APR could become 33 percent (now you owe $2,640 in interest). It is in the fine print of the contract. Of course you don't have to pay the full interest all at once. That would not work in the bank's favor. Instead, credit card companies allow users to make a *minimum* payment, about 2 percent of the total each month. Why? This keeps the user believing credit is "cheap" or "affordable" while keeping the balance nice and high so interest payments can grow.

God hates dishonest scales, and the scales of the credit banking industry are simply not honest. They are legal . . . but not honest. Loving fine things so much that we put ourselves at the mercy of lenders will eventually land us in the poorhouse. It's okay to have things, but not when the money isn't there.

 **Action STEP** Practice saying *no* to debt by tearing up or shredding credit card offers received in the mail. Remember this when you go to college.

JUNE 15
Saving for a Rainy Day

Ants—they aren't strong, but they store up food all summer.
PROVERBS 30:25

We didn't know too much about ants, so we decided to go on a fact-finding mission. Here's what we learned about the little wise creatures:

Ants can carry twenty times their own weight. (Maybe they are kind of strong!)
If they were human sized, they could run as fast as a racehorse.
Ants have two stomachs. One is for "personal use" and the other stores food to be shared with other ants. (How kind!)
The average life span of an ant is sixty days.

The work ethic of an ant is humbling. There doesn't seem to be any real fun built into their social system. It's all collecting food and moving from place to place and defending the colony. But there is a sort of wisdom possessed by ants. They know how to save for a rainy day.

Our human instinct is to consume all we have as soon as we have it. You probably make more money in the summer than you do during the school year. It'd be easy right now to feel rich, but that money has to last, right? We know something about this since we don't get regular paychecks for writing books. We have to plan the way that ants do.

Ants are identified as wise. Somehow they know the rains will come and the earth will grow cold and hard and food will be difficult to find. So they save. Jesus promises us in this life we will have trouble (John 16:33). It's not a matter of *if* you will need extra cash on hand to manage trouble; it's a matter of *when*. Things go wrong. Hard times hit everyone, and the wise person has some cash saved up for such a day. It's best to anticipate during good times and save the cash; it's neither wise nor fun to be caught unprepared. How sad to go into debt to take care of what a little bit of saving could have fixed from the get-go!

 **Action STEP** If you haven't already done so, open up a savings account. Put about 10 percent of the money you earn into the account, and don't touch it!

JUNE 16

The Twenty-Four-Hour Principle

Seek the Kingdom of God above all else, and live righteously, and he will give you everything you need. MATTHEW 6:33

It wasn't until my college years that I dared to beg my mom to buy me eighty-dollar boots (these would cost three figures today). Looking back on the situation, I can see she did one thing right and I did one thing wrong . . . or something like that.

I was head over heels in love with those boots, which was my big faux pas. I wore them for years, well past my wedding. I wore them after they no longer looked good. I guess you could say I got my money's worth (well, my mom's money's worth), but I think we need to be careful about emotional entanglements with *things*. It's a slippery slope.

What my mom did right was require me to wait a torturous twenty-four hours before purchasing the boots. She had never dropped this kind of money on shoes, and she kept trying to entice me to get the cheaper ones. It was the only time I held to my guns in eighteen years. I guess she knew I was sold when twenty-four hours later I asked if we could go get "my boots."

There are a couple of good principles to apply when you want to make a big purchase of any type. The hope in following these is that we could land in the middle ground Jesus directs us toward—do not value possessions so much that you *seek* them. The only thing we should seek is his Kingdom. At the same time, don't value things so much you worry about *not* having them. Find moderation in all things by taking these steps:

Seek counsel before you buy. Be sure someone responsible (not a friend with a bajillion in credit card debt) can tell you whether or not your purchase is wise.

Wait twenty-four hours. If you are still excited the next day and have cash for the item, then enjoy your purchase without remorse or worry.

Dannah has a name for regrettable purchases made hastily: post-purchase dissonance. It's that icky feeling you get after you've spent too much money on something you don't really want! Think about the last time you experienced post-purchase dissonance, and decide never to fall for it again.

SW

The Checkbook Says . . .

Don't store up treasures here on earth, where moths eat them and rust destroys them, and where thieves break in and steal. Store your treasures in heaven, where moths and rust cannot destroy, and thieves do not break in and steal. Wherever your treasure is, there the desires of your heart will also be. MATTHEW 6:19-21

You can't peek into everyone's checkbook (or online bank statements), but did you know if you run for office, your tax returns are public property? You can look up any incumbent or candidate's charitable giving records. Why? Because it says a lot about a person's heart.

When a person has very little charitable giving, it could mean that the person doesn't think it is his or her responsibility to give to charity. But the Bible says it is our responsibility to help others.

God's Word says we're supposed to be doing our own part to take care of widows and orphans (see James 1:27). (You might add single moms to that.) The Bible also talks about tithing—putting 10 percent of your money into God's hands to do what he wants with it—so yes, you should be giving to your church and other Christian charities.

Your checkbook will talk! Don't be afraid to take a good look at where you are sending your money. Yes, sending. Look at your checkbook if you keep one. Open your bank statements and actually study where you have used your debit card. If all the transactions are happening at Urban Outfitters and T.J. Maxx, you might consider what you're saying about yourself.

If you are still on a cash-only basis, put an envelope in your room and label it "Giving." Be sure you are putting a portion of all you make in that envelope . . . and then give it away! Only two things cause our checkbook to scream, "It's all about me!" One would be selfishness. The other would be lacking trust in God to take care of us. Neither are necessarily good reports!

Once you get the rush of how good it feels to help someone, you'll want to give more and more. Boy, will your checkbook have stuff to talk about then!

 Set up a giving system. Take measures to track your spending. What has your giving/spending said about you up till today? What do you want your giving and spending to say about you?

Five Words to Avoid

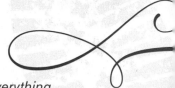

So you cannot become my disciple without giving up everything you own. LUKE 14:33

One of the most frequent reasons given for not tithing and not giving to outside ministries is budget problems: "I can't afford to give." Those are the five words we want to help you avoid, because, in most cases, they simply aren't true. What we are really saying with those words is either we have put ourselves in a bad spot with debt or we would have to make lifestyle changes we are not willing to make in order to add giving to our budget. But that's the thing about truly following God. Once he invites us to get in on his big adventures, he asks us to make life changes to do so.

The examples of this are as numerous as the people we know and love in the Bible. Abraham was asked to give his son as a sacrifice. Ruth had to leave her home and her people. The disciples dropped their fishing nets and walked away from everything they had ever known; by the time all was said and done, eleven of twelve had given their lives. There is no such thing as following God without making an adjustment in your life, and sometimes it's an adjustment that doesn't make much sense to you or others. There's a cost involved. Jesus isn't telling us in Luke 14 to literally sell everything we own. He's reminding us it's not ours to begin with.

The reason we can afford to give is *because* everything belongs to Jesus. We manage it well or we manage it poorly, as simple as that. The money we've been entrusted with is of varying amounts, but the principle remains the same—if we are managing whatever we have been given so poorly that we have none to give, even what we have will be taken from us. We can give. We may just need to make adjustments.

 What would you be willing to sell or give up so that you could be freed to give financially? How can you free more of your time to say yes to God's invitation?

JUNE 19
Sad or Inspiring?

Look, I am sending you out as sheep among wolves. So be as shrewd as snakes and harmless as doves. MATTHEW 10:16

David Klein invented Jelly Belly jelly beans a long time ago, originally offering only eight flavors. If you are familiar with the beans today, you know they are by far the best jelly bean on the market (in our opinion!), available in fifty flavors. Visit a store that sells them, and you'll see what I mean, but be warned—you'll have to break the piggy bank to afford these gourmet treats!

David Klein's story is a bit of a sad one. Jelly Belly was his *magnum opus*—his great life work. Four years into the life of the famous little beans, the factory could not make enough product to keep up with demand!

The sad part is that Klein was caught in what looks like a hostile takeover. He was led to believe he had no option but to sell his rights to his own company for $4.5 million. In the meantime, the candy company buying him out made $120 million off the company.

But the inspiring part of the story is in the character of David Klein. Though he failed to be as wise as a serpent, he remains as innocent as a dove. Person after person interviewed for a documentary about Jelly Belly claim their own business would not be what it is today if not for the kindness, generosity, and selflessness of Klein.

There are two legacies Klein could possess. He could be the brilliant, savvy business tycoon who not only came up with the concept for gourmet jelly beans but also took that company to billions in profits. He could be an elite, with a private jet and a name eponymous to the candy business. Or he could be a man who lived his life with radical generosity in mind, looking always for new ideas but only because he loved to see others succeed. I don't know Klein. Maybe the truth is somewhere in the middle. But I do know Jesus and his mandate for us in dealing with others. Never take advantage of someone you could lord it over. Do not provoke those who would love to harm you. Do good to all. Be fair. Bring life.

 **Action STEP** Watch a documentary about someone inspiring. How is/was integrity displayed in his or her life?

JUNE 20

Sweet Dreams

Study this Book of Instruction continually. Meditate on it day and night so you will be sure to obey everything written in it. Only then will you prosper and succeed in all you do. JOSHUA 1:8

When I started getting my family's finances under control, we didn't have much debt, but I was familiar with the dread often accompanying a stack of unpaid bills. I remember what it was to fear opening the mailbox. I am guessing you don't know these feelings just yet, so I rejoice at possibly having caught you in time!

Finances are not discussed in polite society. You don't go up to someone and ask if they have any debt or how big their car loan is any more than you ask someone how much they weigh. It's personal. For adults, it's often painful. I lead a finance class that breaks down some of those privacy walls and enables people to walk through the process of getting out of debt together. One woman in my class right now has almost a half million in unpaid bills. No wonder money woes are so private, painful, and able to rob us of any kind of peace.

When you decide to get serious about your finances, in a sense you have arrived at two roads diverging in the woods. God spoke directly to Joshua (facing a similar fork in the road) upon the death of Moses. Joshua was instructed to follow all of God's precepts, veering neither to the right nor the left. Do this, God promised, and you will have great success. But what does success mean? Was Joshua being promised great wealth? Will you be a millionaire if you follow all of God's precepts?

Becoming a millionaire is not the hardest thing ever. Biblical precepts plus certain behaviors give us good odds, but that isn't the point. The success God refers to in this case is his favor. What happens when we have the King's favor—the King who owns the cattle on a thousand hills, causes other kings and princes to bow in submission, and is tickled silly pink, madly in love with us? We sleep well. We have peace. He sees us, he knows our needs before we ever ask, and his precepts continue to teach us well.

 *Action* **STEP** Take a finance class with your parents. We highly recommend Dave Ramsey's Financial Peace University. We feel so strongly about this that the Christian school we helped found requires students to complete it before they graduate!
SW

You Are a Masterpiece

Look at the birds. They don't plant or harvest or store food in barns, for your heavenly Father feeds them. And aren't you far more valuable to him than they are? MATTHEW 6:26

I have an original painting in my house that has *no* idea how valuable it is. It began its life in 1980 hanging on the log walls of a little art gallery in Empire, Colorado. A few thousand dollars later it hung above a massive stone fireplace at my mom and dad's house in Fort Wayne, Indiana. Since I've inherited it, it has lived in Pennsylvania—in a log home, a Cape Cod, and now a really cool 1964 raised ranch. But like I said, it doesn't know anything about architecture, and it doesn't care where it hangs.

Its value has little to do with the painting itself. You see, my little painting is signed "Gregory Perillo, 1980." In 1981 the artist met President Reagan and his wife Nancy who took a liking to the artist and his work. One of his paintings, *The Cowboy and His Lady*, made it to the White House, and the rest is history. Everything signed "Perillo" shot up in value. His works hang in corporate offices and governors' mansions across America . . . and in my living room.

We are a lot like that painting. We have no idea just how valuable we are. We have these humble beginnings, formed from the rib of a man, but then a very powerful ruler proclaimed his interest in us. Our tremendous value has very little to do with us. We are valuable because of him, not because of anything we have to offer. If my painting's value was to be based solely on its own merits, there would be great debate as to its worth. I like it a lot. Others may not like it at all. But art collectors would quickly agree I have something of value on my hands.

You are so precious in God's sight—a masterpiece. God's delight is in you. You are his beloved. Your value is defined not by circumstances, but by virtue of the one who has made you. So here's the challenge: you are what God says you are. A masterpiece. Can you believe it?

What is the most valuable item in your house? Write out a prayer or letter to God thanking him for bestowing immeasurably more value on you. SW

JUNE 22

Heart Exam

The LORD doesn't see things the way you see them. People judge by outward appearance, but the LORD looks at the heart. 1 SAMUEL 16:7

Ever see a Jack Black comedy called *Shallow Hal*? Hal is chasing his vision of the perfect woman—she is thin and beautiful, has great legs, dances seductively. Problem is, none of these "perfect" women are interested in him. Then Hal meets a man who gives him the power to actually see as God sees—Hal can see the heart. He falls in love with a woman who is dangerously obese, but he can only see her for the beauty in her heart. The problem with this movie, as pointed out by many who have seen it, is that in order to understand Hal's shallowness, the movie itself had to go to the same superficial insistence that "beautiful" women sometimes have very ugly hearts while "ugly" women are often quite beautiful inside. The standard was still one of outward beauty . . . and thus the concept fell a bit flat.

The background of today's verse tells us that Samuel was sent by God to choose a king for Israel, and he was to make his choice from the sons of Jesse (see 1 Samuel 16). Initially, only the oldest son, Eliab, was presented to Samuel, who took one look at him and thought he was surely the one. Samuel seemed to have been hung up on looks, just like we can be at times. God took a pass on all seven of Jesse's oldest sons until only the teenage shepherd boy was left. Indeed, God looks at our hearts, not at our outward appearance.

It may always be this way with humanity; we look and see either beauty or unattractiveness. It may be that God does not necessarily find every one of us "beautiful" in our own way; he may be unconcerned altogether with physical appearances.

Our eyes are trained to respond to what is esteemed as beautiful. But God's eyes tell him what people really are. What do you want God and others to see when they look at you? Integrity, faithfulness, righteousness, gentleness, compassion, kindness, generosity. These are beautiful words, aren't they? It's time for a new picture to come in our heads when he tells us we are "beautiful."

 **Action STEP** Tell your three most beautiful friends how much you admire them today. Base your decision 100 percent on their hearts!

JUNE 23

When You Hate You

You made all the delicate, inner parts of my body and knit me together in my mother's womb. Thank you for making me so wonderfully complex! Your workmanship is marvelous—how well I know it. PSALM 139:13-14

"Well, I guess I'm ugly now since I got told that so many times today!!"

"It's been brought to my attention that I call myself ugly too much."

"So apparently I have a nice personality but I'm ugly? Nice, thanks."

"Confession #9: I'm so ugly."

Those are actual Facebook statuses. Wow, girls. We struggle with self-image, don't we? We wrestle with believing anyone could find us beautiful. The most common word spoken upon looking at our own image in a mirror? "Ugh."

This has got to stop. It's killing us. Here we are, created by the God of the universe with just a spoken word. Into each of us he built 206 bones, 106 of them in our hands and feet alone! With nothing more than a thought, our brains fire millions of synapses that tell our eyes to blink, our bodies to jump a hurdle, or our mouths to form and pop a bubble. The body is composed of over one hundred trillion cells, each performing several million functions each second of every day. No wonder we fall into bed exhausted each night!

God did this! And do you know what God said when he finished creating this masterpiece? He stepped back, and he said, "It. Is. Very. Good" (see Genesis 1:26-31). Everything else God created he pronounced, "It is good." He said that you and I are *very* good. And this is not just because we are useful to meet a purpose on this earth, like the ox and the horse. No, we are pronounced very good because we are the only things God has made in his likeness.

Ugly? Useless? Not in God's estimation. This world is full of counterfeits and false definitions; the chief among them would be the word *beautiful*, for God has already pronounced the awe-inspiring beauty of all he has created.

 **Action STEP** Put a dollar (or five) in a jar on your dresser every time you say "ugh" to the mirror or pronounce yourself "ugly." Give that jar to a charity or missions team when you don't need it anymore!

JUNE 24

Beauty Fast

[Joshua said,] "If you refuse to serve the LORD, then choose today whom you will serve. Would you prefer the gods your ancestors served beyond the Euphrates? Or will it be the gods of the Amorites in whose land you now live? But as for me and my family, we will serve the LORD." The people replied, "We would never abandon the LORD and serve other gods."
JOSHUA 24:15-16

If you're not afraid of some solid Facebook confrontation, read on. If you are feeling faint of heart today, you might want to stop. The endless photos you post of yourself are a *big* turnoff. We have videotaped proof of guys saying girls who post "come hither" photos are vain. Here are some examples of what turns the guys off.

"Nothing to do. Text me." (Sultry photo of you looking through your hair at your own phone camera. You do know what that says, right?) "Almost home." (Really? A picture of you driving that you took while you were driving?) "Ready for another long day at school." (Another photo of you looking into the mirror. Didn't we see that one a few days ago?)

Part of God's perfect and intentional design of *you* is that he created you to crave liberty—the freedom to choose what you will do and say and produce. Things forced upon us taste bitter, but what we choose for ourselves always tastes so sweet! He says that he created you and that you are good. Choose to believe and let that satisfy you!

The constant obsession with the mirror and camera is really an obsession with external beauty. Will you look less deeply into the mirror and more deeply into God's love letter to you?

The decision, as it was for Joshua and all of Israel, boils down to whom we choose to trust. Joshua offered Israel a choice: if you think another deity out there can meet your needs and protect you better than Yahweh, then by all means, have at it! Likewise, if we think those beauty magazines and fad diets and the Kardashian sisters have a better handle on beauty than the one who has created us . . . well, the choice is ours as to whom we will believe. Mirror or Bible? What will you look into?

 *Action* **STEP** Let's take a beauty fast. For one week, no looking in the mirror unless it is to get ready for the day. (No looking for looking's sake.) And no new photos on Facebook! God's love is unquenchable. For one week, we'll stop looking elsewhere!

JUNE 25
Classic Self-Mutilation

When I look at the night sky and see the work of your fingers—the moon and the stars you set in place—what are mere mortals that you should think about them, human beings that you should care for them? Yet you made them only a little lower than God and crowned them with glory and honor.
PSALM 8:3-5

There is the cutest little girl on YouTube, and I am going to send you to look at her now, but you have to promise to come right back. Go check out "Jessica's Daily Affirmation"!

Cute, right? Now, if Jessica (who was four in the video) did this same thing as a teenager, it would not go viral. For one thing, no one likes braggers, and the cuteness factor . . . let's just say we lose the cuteness factor as we get older. The thing is, I still wonder how *your* daily affirmation might sound:

I hate my hair . . .
I can't do anything . . .
Everyone else is better than me . . .
I don't have any friends . . .

Sound familiar? I hope not, but even if you don't struggle with having thoughts like these, I'll bet you know girls who do. I'll bet you know girls who verbalize these thoughts in public.

One luxury God does not give us is to define truth for ourselves. He gives the definitions, and if we are wise, we will live and move within his framework. Psalm 8 says he created you "only a little lower than *Elohim*" . . . only a little lower than the divine. At the same time, the psalm refers to you and me (in Hebrew) as *Enosh* . . . sinful and humble creatures.

There is a balance God demands we strike here. We must recognize we are sinful and wholly dependent upon God. Our hair is unruly, and we have zits. This is part of what it means to be human, and we don't have to rejoice in it. But God created us in his image. By this truth we must be humbled, and humility must not be mistaken for self-hatred! God is desperately in love with and pleased with what he has created in us. He craves fellowship with us, and he shares his eternal Kingdom with those who trust him. I don't know why . . . but we are marvelous beings!

 **STEP** Practice remaining silent when you feel like building yourself up. Practice remaining silent when you feel like tearing yourself down. Shhh!

The *Ins* and the *Uns*

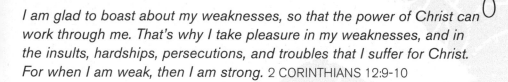

I am glad to boast about my weaknesses, so that the power of Christ can work through me. That's why I take pleasure in my weaknesses, and in the insults, hardships, persecutions, and troubles that I suffer for Christ. For when I am weak, then I am strong. 2 CORINTHIANS 12:9-10

Our friend came up with a pretty cool concept some years back. She couldn't help but notice that human beings struggle a great deal to have a sense of significance in their lives. You would think famous people or rich people might have a lesser chance of struggling with this, but no. It seems to be a human condition uncured by fame or wealth.

Our friend calls these our "*ins*" and our "*uns*." It sounds something like this:

I am insignificant.
I am unworthy.
I am unloved.

You get the idea? When there is an attack on our worth, the enemy loves to preface it with "*ins*" and "*uns*." And it's not very hard to get us to agree with such words whispered into our fearful little ears. I don't know if your "*ins*" and "*uns*" are real things—in other words, I don't know if your friends and family would agree. Sometimes we are the last ones to see ourselves correctly. In Paul's case, though we don't know what he suffered, we do know his sufferings were entirely real. He talks about having something sharp (*skolos*) in his flesh (*sarx*), and this could be anything from an actual physical ailment to having to deal with people who are regularly attacking his ministry and challenging his authority. No matter what caused Paul's pain, God met him with this one promise: "My grace is all you need."

Our weaknesses are perfect opportunities for God to show up in a big way. God chooses foolish things to shame the wise (see 1 Corinthians 1:27). Peter and John impressed people because they were "ordinary" and "unschooled" (Acts 4:13, NIV). If we were impressive in any way, why would people look to God? But when you, an average girl, allow God to power through the most basic version of you . . . heads are going to turn! Remember, there's nothing impressive about you until he shows up in your "*ins*" and "*uns*" to make you enough!

 *Action* **STEP**   Find a way to serve at the most basic level possible today. Do not worry about whether you are "good at it" or not—just make yourself available!

Time to Change

Now repent of your sins and turn to God, so that your sins may be wiped away. Then times of refreshment will come from the presence of the Lord, and he will again send you Jesus, your appointed Messiah. ACTS 3:19-20

Ever wonder why things don't get any better? I met a girl who broke my heart at one of our Pure Freedom events. The girls at school were ostracizing her. Classic mean girl stuff. They would invite her to sit with them, and as soon as she sat, they would stand up and leave. They would encourage her to make animal noises, laughing and clapping for her; only recently had she discovered they were mocking her. She had lost her best friend to that same gang—now she was alone.

The girls were not likely to change anytime soon. I told my new friend that she needed to fight bitterness. Don't fight them, I told her. That's the reaction they were looking for. And then I said one of the saddest things I've ever said in counsel. I told her as she asked God to send her a true friend, she may have to embrace books as her best friend for a time because these people were not friends.

Day after day those mean girls dished up the same punishments, and day after day my friend bit. Are you struggling to lose weight but slow to change your consumption habits? Are you short on funds but continuing to spend recklessly? Maybe you are in a relationship that produces hurt day after day, but the unknown is far more frightening than just putting up with it. One thing is for sure. If you keep doing whatever it is you are doing, you're going to keep getting what you are getting now.

Peter acknowledged the crowds were stuck in a place of sin. He went so far as to concede, "You've acted from a place of ignorance" (see Acts 3:17). But then Peter made them an offer they really should not have refused— about five thousand of them had already taken him up on it. *Repent.* Repent is a word meaning "turn around and go the other way." Peter is offering new choices. Look what he promises: "*Then* times of refreshment will come" (verse 20). Are you sick enough of the old yet?

Embrace change and set a new direction. What are three changes you could make to help you achieve a goal you've wanted to pursue but have felt stuck? SW

JUNE 28

Give Till It Hurts

There will always be poor people in the land. Therefore I command you to be openhanded toward your brothers and toward the poor and needy in your land. DEUTERONOMY 15:11, NIV

Did you know about sixty billionaires worldwide have signed a moral contract called the Giving Pledge? Each of these sixty mega-wealthy people have promised during their lifetime (or upon the hour of their death) they will give away 50 percent of their total wealth. You can read some of their fascinating letters at www.givingpledge.org.

We recommend you read the letter penned by Mr. Warren Buffett, who made his money by investing very, very well! When he dies, he will have given or designated 99 percent of his wealth for charitable contributions. This man has no moral obligation to give. He considers himself an agnostic. Yet his heart overflows with goodness to meet the needs of the poor.

You may not be a billionaire. But remember, if you had the money to buy this book and the education to read it, you are among the world's top 10 percent, and you have the same opportunity as Mr. Buffett to share the wealth.

Under the law of the Old Testament, God's people were required to tithe 10 percent of what they brought in to meet the needs of the poor. We no longer live under the law. There is not a legalistic standard for our giving. Instead, we are instructed to give sacrificially . . . or until it hurts. Acts 2:45 says the New Testament believers were so inspired they "sold their property and possessions and shared the money with those in need." That's what you and I are called to do. This requires us to be in constant communion with the God of the universe to know if we should buy that Starbucks or use the money to help sponsor a child in poverty.

When Mr. Buffett gives billions of dollars to charity, it doesn't impact his personal standard of living one bit. But he gives a shout-out in his Giving Pledge letter to average Janes like you and me . . . he understands when we give, whether it's time or money, we are sacrificing to do so. And this sacrificing pleases God. It's what he wants of you.

 Ask God how you can give till it hurts today. *Using your own money and your own time*, surprise someone with an act of generosity and kindness.

If They Ask, You Gotta Say Yes!

Give to anyone who asks; and when things are taken away from you, don't try to get them back. Do to others as you would like them to do to you.
LUKE 6:30-31

"Excuse me," the woman said sweetly, approaching me in the Walmart parking lot. "I don't want to be rude and certainly don't want to offend anyone, but I've come here to town for a doctor's appointment and now find myself without enough gas to get home." She went on to tell me that her husband was on disability due to a truck accident and seizures, and she wasn't able to work due to back pain.

I walked to the nearest gas station where the woman and her husband met me, and I put seven gallons of gas in the tank for them. They asked questions about my ministry and said when they need assistance they pray God will lead them to the right people. When they are able, they help others in need.

"You know that's a parking lot scam, right?" a friend asked me. I do know, and it is a good thing for you to know as well. We are called to be as wise as serpents. Apparently the scam of working large store parking lots for "gas money" accompanied by a convincing sob story is as old as the gas tank itself. Successful scammers can make hundreds of dollars in one day.

Was I scammed? I may have been, but according to God it's not my concern. I tried to be wise in the limits of my giving—I didn't just hand over cash. The couple was kind and polite, but only God knows if they were taking me for my money. If not, I was pleased to help a brother and sister. If it was a scam, I suppose it is between them and God, and boy, would I hate to be in their shoes when giving account for such deception and theft! But again, that's not my concern.

When Jesus went to the cross, he went for people who could never pay him back, for people who would never say thank you, and even for the ones who drove the nails into his hands. Self-sacrifice is an earmark of love. When asked to give, feel free to ask questions and use discernment, but give.

 Hopefully someone will soon ask you to give time, money, or a possession. Prayerfully and cheerfully respond with an open hand.

Hilarious Giving

Don't give reluctantly or in response to pressure. "For God loves a person who gives cheerfully." And God will generously provide all you need.
2 CORINTHIANS 9:7-8

How would you rate yourself as a giver? Take this quick "Giving Quiz" and see how you fare. Answer all questions on a scale of 1 = never, 2 = rarely, 3 = sometimes, 4 = usually, and 5 = always.

1. When an opportunity to give comes along, I always participate. _____
2. I feel a kind of pain or anxiety when I give things or money away. _____
3. I believe the main reason I have things is so I can share them. _____
4. I find it hard to spend money. _____
5. When I see people in need, I'm filled with a lot of emotion. _____
6. I worry when people borrow my things that they will ruin them. _____
7. I usually give more than the 10 percent tithe. _____
8. The thought of tithing scares me. What if I run out of money? _____
9. I like watching people receive things that I have given them. _____
10. I don't have much money—people who have a lot should give. _____

Add up your odd answers first. If your score is above fifteen, you have giving tendencies. If you scored above twenty, you likely have the spiritual gift of giving. Next add up your even answers. If you are above fifteen, you struggle with the idea of giving. It is difficult to give cheerfully from this place, so let's look at growth opportunities. The general rule of thumb is that weaknesses are not likely to ever become strengths. Still, we can grow and even become proficient in our weaknesses.

Paul's giving instructions are interesting: decide in advance what kind of giver you are going to be—decide so you can give cheerfully. Giving is supposed to be planned. A lot of people are scammed out of vast amounts of money because of emotional appeals. Like anything else financial, having a plan for your giving is the best way to manage it. The word *cheerful* in our passage today translates literally to "hilarious" . . . so laugh it up!

Decide how much you would like to give each week or each pay period. Transfer that amount of money into a cash envelope and carry it with you everywhere, planning to give it away, or send it directly to the charity or church of your choice.

What Will They Do with *My* Money?

Wisdom is even better when you have money. Both are a benefit as you go through life. Wisdom and money can get you almost anything, but only wisdom can save your life. ECCLESIASTES 7:11-12

After observing a need, my dad decided that he wanted to give a gift to our community. Our city had a pretty shabby Fourth of July fireworks celebration. It was one of those shows where a shell goes off to be followed by dead air to be followed by another lame shell to be followed by dead air. And on and on goes the torture! My dad thought he could choreograph the fireworks to music on the local radio station that he owned. The result was stunning. My dad and the engineers he worked with could time the explosion of a pyrotechnics shell to occur within one-tenth of a second of a musical note. The Great American Fourth of July Celebration was born, and it was all a gift to our community. Before we knew it, the whole world was using my dad's system and the *Wall Street Journal* was calling it "The Photoshop of the Pyrotechnics Industry." His system has shot off Super Bowls, Olympic celebrations, and New Year's parties across the globe ever since.

It took a lot of money to make it come to be. It was my dad's money that made it happen. But, after everyone saw how the whole world was watching and our local show had become the fourth largest in the world, people started to get greedy and to fight. A lot of unethical things happened. My dad had the wisdom to step out. He valued the wisdom of embracing integrity over protecting his money.

It's pretty much what today's verses say. If we can have both wisdom and money at our disposal, then things look pretty sweet. But Solomon, the writer of Ecclesiastes, knew this: money is iffy. Some of us have a lot of it, and some of us don't. Wisdom, on the other hand, is attainable by all of mankind, and she is a lifesaver!

Has a friend taken you for twenty dollars? Did someone forget to put their five dollars in the pot for pizza? Are you missing a skirt that you are sure your cousin has? Choose wisdom. Let go of the money!

 *Action* **STEP** Pray a prayer of release over anyone who has fought with you over money or disappointed you in how he or she has handled it. Let go. Hold on to wisdom.
DG

Taxes Are Due,
Love 'Em or Hate 'Em!

When you enter the land the LORD your God is giving you as a special possession and you have conquered it and settled there, put some of the first produce from each crop you harvest into a basket and bring it to the designated place of worship. DEUTERONOMY 26:1-2

Whether you have a job or not, you probably already know the date taxes are due in this country. Yep, we usually pay up on April 15. Here are some crazy facts about the anxiety surrounding the date taxes are due:

- The number of traffic accidents increases one week before April 15.
- An accountant will put in seventy-hour workweeks during tax season.
- About 15 percent of Americans think it's okay to cheat on taxes.

God calls us to be careful managers of the resources he provides. Maybe you have heard people chatting excitedly about the tax refund they are about to receive and big plans they have for all that "free money." But we want to let you know that we think tax refunds are actually poor fund management and a bad idea! The reason people get money returned is they are having too much withheld from each paycheck in the first place. In essence, what you have done is lent money to the government but charged no interest. If you put that money in your own bank or better yet in something called a mutual fund, you could be earning interest on it!

As to giving . . . America is one of the few remaining countries offering citizens a tax credit for charitable giving. To make this simple, if I earn one hundred dollars but have given away forty dollars, I only have to pay taxes on the sixty I didn't give away. You'll notice how this helps on taxes once you start filing more complex forms (not the normal teen-friendly 1040EZ). So giving to those in need is not only good management of money, but it also falls right in line with our character as followers of Jesus. We should seek to give as much as possible, and not just the leftovers. First fruits were the best, the ripest, and the most delectable part of the harvest. These were to be brought to the place of worship so God's people would learn to glorify God first and satisfy self later.

 Give before you buy this week. Until you have given your tithe or another charitable donation, sit on that Vera Bradley wallet of yours.

Best Things in Life

Give generously to the poor, not grudgingly, for the LORD your God will bless you in everything you do. DEUTERONOMY 15:10

If you're working a summer job right now, you might be getting minimum wage. This is the lowest amount that the government will allow anyone to be paid in the United States of America. It was established so that in our nation, unlike others, there cannot be "sweatshops" where people are not paid a fair wage.

Minimum wage is helpful and has put many people through high school and college with a little extra spending cash, but the minimum-wage job isn't of earth-shattering importance, and everyone knows it. Employers do not treat minimum-wage employees with the same respect a skilled employee would receive, and a worker earning hourly pay doesn't think much of taking a "sick day" to hit the beach. It's a mutual disrespect, if that's what you'd like to call it. I'm neither knocking minimum-wage jobs nor endorsing a disrespectful atti-tude. This is just how the economy of employment works.

On the other hand, there are jobs out there paying ridiculous amounts of money. The number one draft choice in the NFL each year receives something like $22 million for a four-year contract plus a $15 million signing bonus. How would you like to sign your name and make $15 million? Granted, these guys are worth a lot of money because they have worked ridiculously hard for years leading up to their NFL career. Success comes at a price sometimes. At the same time, if you're signing a $37 million package deal, doesn't money cease to be a motivator for you at some point?

Then there are people who do things simply because they love to create, they have a great idea, it's the right thing to do, God told them to do it, etc. This is the stuff the "best things in life" are made of. Money isn't the motivator when we go to serve those who are broken. The doctors who healed the des-titute in Haiti after the earthquake—they didn't do it for money. Mother Teresa, last we checked, didn't bring in seven figures as an income—but she did win a Nobel Peace Prize. No one paid Katie Davis exorbitant amounts of money to be a twenty-one-year-old mother of fourteen children in Uganda, but that is what she became—she is richer than you and I combined, I guarantee it. There is no greater gift than this, that a man would lay his life down for his friends. That's what Jesus says in John 15:13. Jesus gave freely. What could you give freely today?

 Find a YouTube video about Mother Teresa or Katie Davis to watch. Be inspired.

Look at Me!

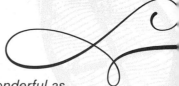

Oh, don't worry; we wouldn't dare say that we are as wonderful as these other men who tell you how important they are! But they are only comparing themselves with each other, using themselves as the standard of measurement. How ignorant! 2 CORINTHIANS 10:12

I couldn't believe I would say something that absolutely horrible! I truly didn't mean to, but I'd blurted out a backhanded complaint about my weight. "I love these jeans. They lie to everyone and take off two sizes!" Fact: I've gained a few pounds lately and don't feel great about it. Other fact: the friend I said that to has had a truly life-defining weight problem for most of her life. How obsessed with myself was I that I'd compare myself *to* myself without any sensitivity to who was nearby?

I'd just mastered the cruelty of the humble brag. The slang dictionary (urbandictionary.com) has coined the term. Humble brag is defined as "when you, usually consciously, try to get away with bragging about yourself by couching it in a phony show of humility." This might be your size two girlfriend posting a "complaint" on Facebook that she can only find jeans that look good on her for $110 at Express, or the new girl in school explaining you're so lucky to share a twelve-by-twelve-foot room with your sister because her house is so big she's not even sure which wing her sister's room is in!

Jesus dealt with similar attitudes of importance from the religious leaders of his day, as they loved to be admired. "Everything they do is for show," Jesus said. "On their arms they wear extra wide prayer boxes with Scripture verses inside, and they wear robes with extra long tassels" (Matthew 23:5).

Paul, unlike the Pharisees, refused to get into the comparison game. He had built a healthy church in the city of Corinth, but while he was gone, a new group of "apostles" rode into town and unleashed a barrage of "humble brag" that was starting to unravel things. The problem was these guys who had moved in on Paul's territory had nothing to back up their words. As you can see in today's verse, they compared themselves only to themselves, completely unaware of who might be around. Being obsessed with ourselves as our own standard of measurement is ignorant.

 *Action* **STEP**   Go through your last month of Facebook posts. Have you been falling into the *humble brag* trap? If so, make a mental note to learn compassion in how you communicate.
DG

Controlling Ourselves to Death

One Sabbath day as Jesus was teaching in a synagogue, he saw a woman who had been crippled by an evil spirit. She had been bent double for eighteen years and was unable to stand up straight. When Jesus saw her, he called her over and said, "Dear woman, you are healed of your sickness!" Then he touched her, and instantly she could stand straight. How she praised God! LUKE 13:10-13

A Girl Called Tim recounts the story of one woman's battle with a twenty-year eating disorder. It started when June, a tomboy whom her mom called Tim when she was good, was eleven and started to sprout breast buds. This was terrifying to her. She wanted to be good. So she did anything she could—even torturing her body—to avoid the oncoming curves of her body so she could be called Tim. Of course, she didn't know it was about controlling what her mother called her until she was in her thirties. She just thought she wanted to be skinny. Her story, like most battles with eating disorders, was about control.

How much control do you suppose a woman bent over from a spinal disorder for eighteen years tried to wield over those who saw her? Think she spent much time in front of a mirror making sure her hair looked just so? Her life was likely consumed with trying to find people merciful enough to feed her so she could live just one more day. But when Jesus met this woman, he immediately revealed her worth with two basic acts. He initiated a conversation (calling her "dear woman" no less), and he touched her.

The truly sad thing about eating disorders is how they are borne out of the lie that a human being has lost her worth. Perhaps a girl feels unattractive, unable to keep up with the world's high expectations for her, trashed by abuse of a sexual nature in her past . . . but Jesus knows the true worth of a human being. The only way to defeat the lies is by knowing the truth. Look at the truth Jesus spoke over this woman as he brought her healing, each truth crushing the lies the enemy had used to cripple her backbone to begin with.

Grab a little notebook and create a "Truth Journal." At the top of each page write a lie you are struggling to defeat. Below it write a Bible verse to smash that lie with God's truth!

The Neatnik and the Slob—Confessions of a Control Freak

Jesus said, "Come to me, all of you who are weary and carry heavy burdens, and I will give you rest." MATTHEW 11:28

Have you ever seen the television show *Hoarders*? Each episode features two families or individuals whose homes have become completely chaotic because they keep everything—like the tabs from their soda cans. I helped a woman struggling with hoarding clean her apartment once. We found her dentures under her sofa!

On the other side of the spectrum is the neat freak. I've seen children as young as three who couldn't stop lining up their shoes! Probably a sign of an obsessive-compulsive disorder (OCD). The neatnik feels she is out of control if things are not immaculate.

Hoarding and compulsive neatness are opposite spectrums, but they both stem from issues of control and anxiety. They are only considered disorders if they have impeded the individual's ability to function normally. And yet anxiety and control issues affect many of us.

Here's the thing: "Whoever fears God will avoid all extremes" (Ecclesiastes 7:18, NIV). In this case, that could mean avoiding extreme neatness and extreme messiness. But more than that, we should let God govern the circumstances of our lives. Jesus told his first followers to drop their nets and follow him . . . and they did! Is it possible God prefers to work through those who are willing to live lives a little "out of control"?

There is so little we *can* control, and there is *no* controlling what others say and do. We will always be impacted by the choices, good or bad, others make. We can't make people believe, behave, or change. Attempting to do so creates isolation rather than the community we were created to desire. The good news is Jesus invites us to be in partnership with him in this out-of-control roller-coaster ride called life. We can't pick and choose the turns and dips (or avoid them), but he promises he will bear most of the burden for us.

 Ask a counselor or mentor for tips on how to avoid behaviors that attempt to control others or your surroundings. Commit your findings to prayer.
DG

The Darker Side

The people who walk in darkness will see a great light. For those who live in a land of deep darkness, a light will shine. ISAIAH 9:2

Jillian Venters operates the Gothic Charm School. You got that right. We just used *gothic* and *charm school* in the same name. She says Goth is "a lifestyle. . . . For me it's about looking for beauty in dark and or frightening places." Goth Shane Jensen says Goths are frequently people who have been rejected by normal society long before actually adopting Gothic appearances. He says Goths tend to be free thinkers. "Goths check things out for themselves. They're very open minded and accepting of things/people that are different." Goth has proven to be one of the longest-thriving subcultures in American history.

As human beings one of our strongest desires is to belong to a community. Many who embrace the Gothic lifestyle say over time they have come to realize they will either never be embraced by the societal norm or are so offended by the aggression of the socially "powerful" they have chosen another, more somber way. Christian Goths affirm God has provided through Jesus an alternative to self-bondage, but Goths will only find this freedom after completely submitting to their Creator.

Where does this leave you and me? First of all, let's admit in the past the church has done an exceptionally poor job of welcoming people who look different than the norm. And while there's certainly a case to be made that Jesus is light and life and that the way we look should reflect him, there's no written rule that someone who likes to wear black is less spiritual than someone who wears button-down rainbow shirts. In fact, the only written rule is that we are called to love each other. No matter what we look like. Our key verse today promises that we can love someone right into the light.

*Action* **STEP**   Love on someone who is not "like" you today.

JULY 8
The Great Tattoo Debate

See, I have written your name on the palms of my hands. Always in my mind is a picture of Jerusalem's walls in ruins. ISAIAH 49:16

Many who oppose tattoos will point to the Old Testament law found in Leviticus 19:28 that says, "Do not cut your bodies for the dead, and do not mark your skin with tattoos. I am the LORD." The only problem with staking an argument on this verse is found in the verse preceding it. Verse 27 says, "Do not trim off the hair on your temples or trim your beards." Is it possible to lay down the law with one command while completely dismissing its neighboring command?

Part of the debate originates in the message differing generations assign to the practice of tattoo art. The Old Testament rules were given with the purpose of separating Israel from her pagan neighbors. Skin markings were made by early pagans to pacify angry gods. Our grandparents' generation acquired tattoos to send a message. The message may have been, "Stay away," "I'm tough," or "This is who I love," but there were not necessarily thoughts of superstition or paganism.

When it comes to tattoos, we simply want to leave you with a couple of practical thoughts. The first would be that of the fifth commandment—Mom and Dad's ruling on this must be, at least until adulthood and why not even after that, supreme. A tattoo is neither here nor there in terms of ultimate fulfillment, and if the motivation for getting one is simply, "No one has a right to tell me what I can or cannot do with my own body," . . . perhaps it is an act of rebellion after all.

And, though we may regard tattoos as *symbolic* of what is already inside us, we need to remember they are not the same thing as that which *is* inside us. The Holy Spirit dwells in *us*, not in images engraved upon our skin. God has our names not only preserved in the Lamb's Book of Life, but also engraved upon the palms of his hands. These are the only engravings truly eternal and significant!

 *Action* STEP Sit down with your parents and have a conversation about tattoos. What are their feelings on the subject? This time just listen and offer no opinion.

Talk about Extreme
Piercing . . .

What we suffer now is nothing compared to the glory he will reveal to us later. For all creation is waiting eagerly for that future day when God will reveal who his children really are. ROMANS 8:18-19

Why do people pierce the things they pierce? We have a few piercings between the two of us, but perforating your eyelid? Ouch!

The record for the most body piercings belongs to a woman living in Scotland. She has over nine thousand body piercings, over two hundred in her face alone. And there is one woman who has used piercings to redefine her face to be more catlike in shape. We have seen pictures and a video . . . she doesn't strongly resemble a human being any longer. Extreme piercing is truly mind boggling.

Some piercings are just a simple, fun way to dazzle up your ear. Or maybe your nose. (Did you know that the Bible records that Isaac gave Rebekah a nose ring as a sort of engagement gift? You can find that account in Genesis 24.) But be careful in your motivation for a piercing. There is a common thread of spiritualism in the practice. Some get piercings to ward off dark spirits. (The most-pierced woman offers tarot card readings.) A really important question to ask yourself before you pierce is this: "What's my motivation?"

If your motivation is pure—not rebellious and not fueled by spiritualism—and your parents approve, then it's probably okay to make an appointment to go under the gun. It's all about motivation.

Talk about ultimate extreme piercing! Jesus was pierced to cover our sins. His motivation was to rescue each one of us from the need to be superstitious and ward off darkness. He's already done that for you. All you have to do is embrace his piercing.

 If you have a goal to get pierced soon, write a few thoughts in your journal to analyze your motivation.

JULY 10

What Does It Mean to "Embrace Our Differences"?

Dear friends, let us continue to love one another, for love comes from God. Anyone who loves is a child of God and knows God. But anyone who does not love does not know God, for God is love. 1 JOHN 4:7-8

Her Facebook profile reads . . .

Religious Views: Love, love, love
Political Views: Besides being wildly Progressive . . . LOVE and PEACE!

Yet I cannot share most of her posts. Typically political in nature, most include profanities and slurs directed at politicians and ideologies she does not agree with. I simply do not understand such disconnect in regard to the word *love*. Does love apply only where agreement is present? I don't think this is biblical.

Dannah and I live near Amish country. The Amish do not drive often, so they hire "English" neighbors to take them on errands. I have no doubt the Amish think our ways are outlandish, materialistic, and prideful. I think the Amish ways are quaint, yes, but also a bit odd.

Yet as I recently watched a young Amish couple and their elderly neighbor interact with authentic camaraderie, I saw what I'm willing to bet God would like to see between Israel and Palestine, between the gay and straight student, between Republicans and Democrats. Do you have an opinion on any of the three conflicts above? Of course you do. Do you think your opinion is correct? Again, of course you do. Why bother to think at all if we do not believe we are forming solid conclusions? And the fact is, many times we are called to carefully and kindly defend something we believe to be true, especially if it is a black-and-white issue in God's Word. But we are never called to do it with profane, belittling, or hate-filled language.

As God's ambassadors we must be content to have the rock of his Word to stand on as a firm foundation. It is absolute truth. And today's passage says that anyone who does not love is not of God. Do your interactions with people who have different opinions than yours demonstrate that you are from God?

 **STEP** Spend time today with someone very different from yourself. Love him or her.
SW

JULY 11
Athlete's Advantage

Since we are surrounded by such a huge crowd of witnesses to the life of faith, let us strip off every weight that slows us down, especially the sin that so easily trips us up. And let us run with endurance the race God has set before us. HEBREWS 12:1

While we have no way of knowing whether Paul, a Roman citizen, ever attended the Olympic Games, all evidence points to the idea he would have *liked* to do so. He makes reference to athletic contests in Romans, Philippians, both letters to Timothy, and his first letter to the church at Corinth! Paul may have graduated a Pharisee, but it looks like he minored in sports information!

Athletes have a distinct advantage over other people when it comes to facing hurdles in life, both literally and figuratively. Even if you're not an athlete, we hope you'll get something out of this week's devotions. At any rate, here are four things we think we can learn from *elite* athletes:

- Elite athletes take responsibility for their own training. In the earliest Olympics, athletes signed a commitment to train for a minimum of ten months. If you're an athlete, you know this to be true. You have to consistently train or you will become out of shape.
- An effort of 100 percent is better than any other percentage—unless you want to talk about giving 110 percent. Athletes who train harder will typically get more playing time.
- Focus yields great results. It's okay to focus on just one thing and become great at it. This is why the author of Hebrews says to "throw off everything that hinders" us (Hebrews 12:1, NIV).
- Great athletes want the ball. Would you rather play for a big school and sit on the bench or a small school and play? An athlete wants to contribute.

In Matthew 9:37 Jesus says to his disciples, "The harvest is great, but the workers are few." Really? Are there so few of us who know Jesus we can't get the job done? The sad truth is more likely this—too many Christians are not in shape and give very little effort at "practice." Too many have lost focus, loving the world more than God's Kingdom. In too many cases . . . the Coach can't put us in the game.

Figure out where you are lacking in your spiritual training. Reading the Word? Serving? Learning? Make a plan so you can get in the game.

JULY 12
The Smell of the Lamp

She is energetic and strong, a hard worker. She makes sure her dealings are profitable; her lamp burns late into the night. PROVERBS 31:17-18

There was never a question for me as to how I should spend my time. Though my first word was *book*, I had an equal love for all things sports from the moment my chubby little legs hit the ground running. I am a tomboy with a competitive edge. My sports are basketball, golf, tennis . . . basically anything with a ball. While Dannah has been known to take up a tennis racket, her love of athletics takes her to less competitive options like horseback riding on her two beautiful geldings.

The stats are now in to support the advantages owned by girls who play sports. Girls who play sports earn better grades than girls who do not, are more likely to graduate high school and attend college, maintain better health throughout life, have lower rates of teen pregnancies, have lower levels of depression, and are more likely to earn higher levels of responsibility and pay in the workforce.

The description of the wife of noble character in Proverbs 31 is about a life focused on things profitable. This isn't just referring to finances, but the overall profitability from something she spends her time doing. If it doesn't earn this woman's family profit or honor, she doesn't mess with it. But if profit of any kind were to be had, that woman wouldn't hesitate to spend late hours by the lamp investing her time.

In the 1800s there was a saying that an excellent thing "smelled of the lamp," meaning someone obviously put a lot of overtime into creating it. Ah, sports . . . they smell of the lamp!

 **STEP** Make a list of your profitable/nonprofitable activities. Will you pray about dumping a few of the nonprofitable ones, making room for some exercise?
SW

Why It's Best to Be Yourself

Don't be concerned about the outward beauty of fancy hairstyles, expensive jewelry, or beautiful clothes. You should clothe yourselves instead with the beauty that comes from within, the unfading beauty of a gentle and quiet spirit, which is so precious to God. 1 PETER 3:3-4

Somehow I became convinced right around seventh grade that I had to become someone I was not, if ever I was to be esteemed beautiful. In my case the conflict wasn't about the details of a haircut or the makeup I wore or didn't wear—it was about sports. I grew up playing outside and loving all things athletic. Neighborhood friends were both male and female, but if they were going to play on my terms, we had to be active. By sixth grade this had all translated neatly to the playground. I wasn't into the "small group stand around and giggle" action. I wasn't one of those girls who said, "I'll play if you do" to my girlfriends. At heart I was the kind of girl who was happy to simply roll in the grass and get bloody shins.

It's hard to explain, then, why I suddenly decided at the end of my eighth-grade year to throw in the towel. No more sweat, no more blood. I decided boys didn't like girls who were jocks or who could throw a ball well. . . . And I was done. A twelve-year moratorium on all things athletic followed.

Turns out I was wrong. Guys like a girl who knows who she is. That gentle and quiet spirit Peter talks about isn't the same thing as milk-toast meekness. This is not necessarily a fashion commentary or a prohibition on shopping, either. Peter is literally speaking to the "fashion" in which a woman wins a man's heart. External adornment is like wrapping paper on a present—it gives no clue to what actually resides in the box. Our family used to wrap hot cross buns that were over a decade old, and an ancient ratty shower cap as yearly Christmas gag gifts. The wrapping never gave away what was actually inside.

Let's be wrapped up to reflect what we really are inside. When we nurture a quiet confidence in the person God created us to be—athlete or science buff—investing in things eternal rather than external and temporal, we are likely not only to draw the right persons to ourselves in all kinds of relationships, but also to draw people to Christ.

Answer two questions: What did God create me to love? Can I accept this, trust this, and fully glorify him through it?
SW

Once upon a Time . . .

Jesus began a tour of the nearby towns and villages, preaching and announcing the Good News about the Kingdom of God. He took his twelve disciples with him, along with some women who had been cured of evil spirits and diseases. Among them were Mary Magdalene, from whom he had cast out seven demons; Joanna, the wife of Chuza, Herod's business manager; Susanna; and many others who were contributing from their own resources to support Jesus and his disciples. LUKE 8:1-3

You know that "Truth Is" thing people do on Facebook? Well, truth is . . . once upon a time women didn't really enjoy the same privileges men did. Historical discrepancies in sports are particularly glaring. Women were excluded from the first Olympic Games in 776 BC. By 396 BC a woman had won the "gold medal" in chariot racing (precursor to today's female Indy drivers), but the law prevented her from collecting her prize in person. It wasn't until 1892 the *Journal of Physical Exercise* published an article encouraging regular exercise for women, challenging the long-held perception that women were too weak for physical exertion. Whew! We've come a long way, baby!

Here's a cool factoid about Jesus, though. He was working to establish respect for women in his society long before the rest of the world caught on. Remember, Scripture declares that in Jesus "there is neither Jew nor Greek, slave nor free, male nor female" (Galatians 3:28, NIV). In today's passage, Jesus is found in Luke chapter 8 hitting the road on a missions trip with his twelve disciples and a bevy of ladies along. As rabbis refused to teach women, let alone speak with them, Jesus' actions were quite radical. There were a variety of women who followed Jesus. One (Mary Magdalene) has a historical reputation (earned or not) of once being a loose woman. One (Joanna) was from the upper echelon of society. One thing all had in common—they knew Jesus accepted them as one of his own, and their response was to give in return.

Action **STEP**   Watch the movie *A League of Their Own* with some girlfriends. How can you work for justice as a grateful response to those, especially Jesus, who have paved the way for you? How can your freedom turn into support for the growth of God's Kingdom?

JULY 15
She Plays like a Man

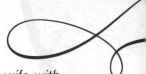

You husbands must give honor to your wives. Treat your wife with understanding as you live together. She may be weaker than you are, but she is your equal partner in God's gift of new life. Treat her as you should so your prayers will not be hindered. 1 PETER 3:7

A female tennis player at the French Open most likely pulled a big interview no-no when she claimed she lost her match because her opponent "played like a man." She probably doesn't play like a man. Even though yesterday's devo talked about the equal opportunities a woman can enjoy, we are different physically.

My husband is a beast of a tennis player. Though he has never played on a team, he was a college athlete. College athletes are the cream of the crop—put them in a new sport, and they will still outperform every other average Joe. Then there is the female college athlete. She, too, is the cream of the crop, and will outperform all of the average Joes out there, often beating the male weekend warrior. All things being equal, however, the elite female athlete is going to lose to the elite male athlete. I have to face the facts—I will likely never beat my husband in tennis. I can ace him now and then, hit winners he cannot return, and place a drop shot where he cannot reach it, but I will never (thank God) be the beast he is.

The International Olympic Committee (IOC) has been considering some controversial rulings lately, among them a required testosterone measurement for female athletes to see if they are enhancing their performance. The thing is, high testosterone levels are not enough to guarantee the win; focus and determination are huge factors in athletic competition. The field of women's athletics is actually dominated by women with normal testosterone levels, not by those with high levels. Girls, you've got game. Just as you are.

You will never, however, have game in quite the same manner as the guys do. Sure, there will always be guys you are able to outperform, but this is a reflection of skill. Peter's use of the word *weaker* in this verse is a *physical* reference. This is a somber reminder to men to treat you with special care and gentleness. Oh, we can go at one another on the playing fields, but the moment the game is over, this is the relationship God prefers.

 Praise God today for the strength and prowess he has given your brothers in Christ. It is truly for your mutual protection and edification!
SW

Princesses All

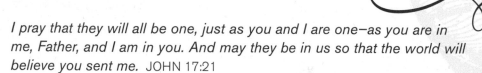

I pray that they will all be one, just as you and I are one—as you are in me, Father, and I am in you. And may they be in us so that the world will believe you sent me. JOHN 17:21

If I am more interested in sports than anything else, does this make me a feminist? How do I approach these nontraditional passions of mine? Am I less of a girl because I like to have a fantasy football team?

We can answer a lot of confusing, seemingly unrelated questions with one simple sentence: God is the King. Anyone who believes in him is called his child. What do you call the female child of a king? A princess. I'm not talking about a Disney princess—after all, a glittering dress and glass slippers do not a princess make. A princess is defined simply by the fact that she is the daughter of a king. And the King gets to call the shots. He's the authority in the Kingdom.

We know a princess who has won the Wade Trophy for basketball—that's the award for the best player in women's collegiate basketball. She's the head coach at Providence College, a Division 1 school in the Big East conference now. We know a princess who is a personal trainer—she will *hurt* you if you ask her to work on your core. These two athletes are princesses because their Father is a King, and they live lives in subjection to him. It's as simple as that.

Femininity is good. But being a princess has nothing to do with liking pink, shopping for shoes, playing with Barbie dolls, or learning to play by a set of cultural rules for "how girls act." Check out today's key verse. Are you and the Father one in the way that you conduct yourself?

Explain to someone today what it means to be a true princess.

Why We Need Girls

You have heard me teach things that have been confirmed by many reliable witnesses. Now teach these truths to other trustworthy people who will be able to pass them on to others. 2 TIMOTHY 2:2

It's funny that Dannah and I are best of friends. I am your quintessential athletic tomboy, and Dannah is the poster child for girly girls . . . unless she is mucking stalls in her barn. We are worlds apart in the way we dress and the condition of our cuticles. Nevertheless, we both love animals, books, ideas, and talking. Besides that, she has one of my favorite laughs on the planet. We need each other. I need her when I feel like maybe I'm not a great mom. She needs me when she's feeling nervous about a confrontation she needs to have with someone. We may not be card-carrying members of an official women's ministry, but we are in the ministry of making significant relationship deposits into each other.

Don't get stuck in a box and think your best friend has to be an athlete because you are . . . or an artist because you are. You may be surprised, but a much better connecting point will be your relationship with Christ and a grounding in his Word.

Even in his youth, Timothy was instructed to find people he could pour his life into. Do you have that kind of person in your life? Not every relationship is a good fit, and that's okay. Both a guy named Barnabas and Timothy had a chance to watch Paul at work. Timothy was the right match for Paul, Barnabas wasn't. God is good and blessed Barnabas's work elsewhere. Chances are, if you are in a good church, you can find a girl or two (and a grown woman or two) who tend to unpack things the way that you do. Just don't fail to recognize that these are relationships you need!

 Identify two girls/women who process things like you do. Invite each to spend a little time with you . . . drinking coffee, hiking, doing crafts . . . whatever. And when you are with people *unlike you*, keep those ears open all the same!
SW

How Guys Work:
An Instruction Manual

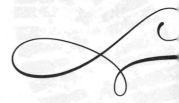

God created human beings in his own image. In the image of God he created them; male and female he created them. GENESIS 1:27

Lean in for a little secret about guys and sex: it's been said that sexually speaking, men are like microwaves. Women are like Crock-Pots. Yep. Guys cook a sexual idea up pretty fast. We tend to process one like a slow cooker. To understand this, let's look at their brains!

The brain is an unbelievably sophisticated machine with each of its portions responsible for different tasks. The deep limbic system processes emotions, the amygdala manages pain, the parietal region deals with spatial relationships; the female brain produces more of the hormone estrogen and the male brain produces more testosterone. . . . Getting the picture? God was intentional when he created two genders, and one of his greatest purposes for this disparity was *sex*. Immediately upon creating the man and the woman, God told them to be fruitful and multiply (see Genesis 1:28). Trust us, he's God, and he could have set this birthing program up any way he chose. He chose for men and women to be attracted to one another and to procreate through the covenant of marriage in a *very* pleasant manner.

When it comes to sex, men and women are worlds apart. Though the brain is the primary sexual organ for both genders, men are stimulated quickly and through the visual portion of their brains while women take much longer to arouse and do so via the deep limbic system, the seat of their emotions. It's been said that men have a sexual thought about every six seconds of the day, but there's no research basis for that statistic. The truth is, men seem to think about sex twice as often as women do. Why? A man is visually stimulated, so that billboard on the highway and that Super Bowl commercial get to him . . . while you could care less.

 Take a few girlfriends out for ice cream and discuss these questions: Have we ever purposefully chosen outfits hoping to get a sexual response? Why?

JULY 19

He Told You Who He Is

Pattern your lives after mine, and learn from those who follow our example. . . . There are many whose conduct shows they are really enemies of the cross of Christ. PHILIPPIANS 3:17-18

Ants are stinkers. Really. They contain at least ten different sacs of phero-mones, each with a unique scent, and each intended to communicate a differ-ent message. The strongest scent the ant possesses is that of death, and it is only released as the ant is dying or when severely threatened.

The other day I was waiting for my Bible study partners to arrive, and my waiting spot was overrun by zealous ants. Every now and then I would take off a flip-flop and smash an ant that was getting too close. Soon I began to notice strange behavior. As a new ant would approach, it would stop in its tracks about two feet away from the killing fields. It would lower its antennae to the ground, move them back and forth a few times, and then it would launch into hyper-speed mode, running in frantic circles with no purpose in mind, a terror-ized race to nowhere. Ants can smell death, and it causes them to lose their minds with fear.

My mom let me have fairly free rein with the guys I chose to crush on, but there was one particular saying she came back to over and over again whenever I chose poorly, which was unfortunately more often the rule than the exception. Here's what Mom would say: "He told you who he is!" Mom was basically saying, "Suzy, he emitted that death pheromone the first day you met him. He let you know what you were dealing with. Why did you expect different?"

Why don't we know to run away like the ant? And why do we get upset when we offer pheromones of another kind only to find them working their magic upon the intended target? If we wore bikinis only to stave off heat, our argument—our pretense of being offended when we get the attention—might carry weight. Truth says we wear a bikini in order to put off our "I'm so sexy" smell so all the right ants can find us. We dance the way we do to let loose that "pay attention to me" perfume. When these "smells" achieve the effect they were intended for, whose "fault" is it? Paul says we make it pretty plain what we are after. We are known by our fruits, our behavior.

What does the conduct of the guys around you say? How about your con-duct? You can trust your nose.

 **Action STEP**
What do you say by the way you dress? The way you interact with guys?
SW

Boys Will Be Boys

Do not let any part of your body become an instrument of evil to serve sin. Instead, give yourselves completely to God, for you were dead, but now you have new life. So use your whole body as an instrument to do what is right for the glory of God. ROMANS 6:13

All that locker-room talk is bound to happen, magazines are going to be looked at, and a guy just can't resist the invitation to "take a peek" on the Internet. Untrue. All of it. Still, the statistics on this matter are discouraging. About 70 percent of American men confess to using porn, which of course does not account for those unwilling to confess. What is really upsetting is that about 60 percent of men who attend church will confess to monthly pornography peeks.

In case you're not clear yet on this issue . . . pornography is highly destructive to the health of relationships. It is one of those behaviors the Bible talks about that people "do in secret" (Ephesians 5:12). The majority of men (and women) who "use" pornography are not trumpeting their activities on their Facebook wall. Rarely does a man say to his wife or girlfriend, "Hey, honey, guess what I just watched?"

It is destructive because pornography creates an increased dependency on its users, escalating the need for greater and greater stimulation. It is not unusual for a casual viewer of pornography to find himself a user of prostitution years down the road (and then he wonders how he got there). The incline is gradual, and the cost to personal relationships is devastating.

Pornography is destructive because it leaves no nonvictims. Those participating in the industry have often been trafficked (as close to slavery as it gets today). Those viewing it are being trained to objectify other people. Some call pornography a training manual for abusers. And those whose spouses are addicted find themselves caught in webs of lies, deceit, and empty promises, such as "I'll quit tomorrow."

With our bodies we can praise and serve our Savior, or with them we can satisfy the desires of the flesh. One leads to life and the other to destruction, and there is no happy middle ground. Paul says we have new life—this means a new set of rules, of standards, and even companions.

 Is it possible to find a guy who will keep his way pure? Confess both your desire for this and any skepticism you may have to a trusted mentor.

No Means No:
Beware of Scoffers

People will love only themselves and their money. They will be boastful and proud, scoffing at God, disobedient to their parents, and ungrateful. They will consider nothing sacred. They will be unloving and unforgiving; they will slander others and have no self-control. They will be cruel and hate what is good. They will betray their friends, be reckless, be puffed up with pride, and love pleasure rather than God. They will act religious, but they will reject the power that could make them godly. Stay away from people like that! 2 TIMOTHY 3:1-5

She knew her parents' rules like the back of her hand. She was not to be in a car alone with a guy. The rule made no sense to her. For the most part she embraced her parents' value system. She was going to go to the altar a virgin. So when he asked for a ride home, she figured what her parents didn't know wouldn't hurt them. Their rules were silly. What she didn't count on was that when she said *no . . .* he wasn't going to listen.

Rape and sexual abuse are never the victim's fault, though the first question to enter a victim's mind is often, *What did I do to invite that?* The girl above chose weeks later to go to the park with one of the "sketchiest" guys she knew just to prove she could be alone with a guy and nothing would happen. She had to prove to herself that she had not caused or invited the assault.

If you know someone who has been the victim of sexual assault, *you cannot remind her enough that she is not at fault.* There is wisdom you can lean on as a young woman, however, and that is to recognize the world in which you live. Your values help you make wise decisions, but they will do little to protect you once you are out of the public eye. You have probably been given a number of rules having very little to do with what your parents think of your own integrity. Consider the wisdom of your elders. They are sharp enough to know that you will meet people like those described in 2 Timothy.

Be patient. Follow the rules. Wait for a guy who is chasing God so hard it takes him a while to notice you. Be assured of who you are and who God is so you are not an easy target for snakes. Know that you are forgiven and loved by God, and remember that there is always a way out, because *no* will never mean *no* to a scoffer.

 Respectfully ask your parents *why* they have the rules for you that they do.

JULY 22

Erotica . . . More Than Fifty Shades Off

Take no part in the worthless deeds of evil and darkness; instead, expose them. EPHESIANS 5:11

While we were working on this book, another book hit America and became a fast bestseller. I wrote a simple blog post at purefreedom.org entitled "Why I'm Not Reading *Fifty Shades of Grey.*" And I could not believe how many Christian women and teens were infuriated at my choice. Over one thousand comments later, the conversation is still fueled with both applause and disapproval. Let me explain.

Erotica is a type of fiction expressly designed for the purpose of arousing sexual desire in the reader. God meant for one person and one person only to arouse sexual desire in you: your (future) husband. Jesus says when we look lustfully at someone we are not married to, we have committed adultery in our hearts (see Matthew 5:28). Can we commit adultery with a fictional character? All I can say is I was amazed how many girls were fantasizing about a steamy relationship with a beautiful, brooding vampire.

Defenders of erotica say things like "It's just a love story!" or "Isn't this okay if I'm married and it makes me desire my husband?" They might also say, "It's just fiction." Is it?

While I was doing a radio interview on this topic, a listener called in to tearfully share how she believed that erotica was just fiction and so she enjoyed it early in her teen years, thinking how fun it would be to live it out someday with her husband. When she got married, the sex wasn't as exciting as the stories she read. Several years down the road she'd lost her husband, her children, and her job because of her addiction to fantasy. Fiction had destroyed her reality. Lust is the destructive vice that God turns people over to when they refuse to acknowledge him or to be filled with gratitude. "God abandoned them to do whatever shameful things their hearts desired. As a result, they did vile and degrading things with each other's bodies" (Romans 1:24). The problem with turning to something like erotica for sexual fulfillment is that it makes *real* relationships almost impossible.

Action **STEP** Clean the bookshelf and magazine rack. Be sure anything that can't be a read-aloud with Mom and Jesus gets the boot!
DG

Guys Need a Few Good Elephant Dads

Fathers, do not provoke your children to anger by the way you treat them. Rather, bring them up with the discipline and instruction that comes from the Lord. EPHESIANS 6:4

My dad was a member of a fraternity. He was a Sigma Alpha Epsilon. I know this because burned into my sensory perception as a child was fear of the SAE paddle that hung on our kitchen wall. The board of discipline. My brothers knew the paddle well—I met it only once.

It was a hot Midwest summer day. I was outside sweating, and I realized I needed water pronto. I went to the front door. Locked. I pounded. My dad came to the door and told me to go around back. I argued a bit, but he shut the door on me, telling me his word was final. So I did what any nine-year-old would do . . . I kicked in that glass door, shattering it into a million little pieces. Suzy, meet SAE.

Dads are of huge importance in a kid's life. Let's look at animals. All kinds of research has been done on animals typically raised by two parents. What happens when the father is removed? Degu pups, which are kind of like guinea pigs, have certain nerve cells that fail to grow normally in the brain when they don't have a father present. The pups display more aggressive behavior than pups raised by two parents. On an African elephant reserve where the bull elephants were removed, the juvenile males went on a rampage that tore up the park and left several smaller female elephants trampled to death.

Dads have been charged from the beginning of time with instilling moral values in their kids. Kids don't exist for parents. Parents exist for kids. It is a dad's job to instill discipline into his children. Remember that the next time your dad steps in to do his job. And, if a guy you know is running amok with his words and behavior, consider grace in your attitude. Perhaps he grew up without a bull elephant in his life.

 If your dad's around, do something special for him today.
SW

JULY 24

Where Are the Real Men?

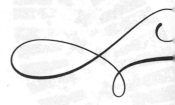

[King David said to his son, Solomon,] "I am going where everyone on earth must someday go. Take courage and be a man. Observe the requirements of the LORD your God, and follow all his ways. Keep the decrees, commands, regulations, and laws written in the Law of Moses so that you will be successful in all you do and wherever you go."
1 KINGS 2:1-3

Guys are experiencing somewhat of an identity crisis right now. The average age of marriage for a guy has risen to twenty-nine. A lot of grown guys are spending years living with Mom and Dad and staring at a TV screen an average of six hours a day. It's no wonder then that 17 percent of your fishing pond are weighing in with technical "obesity" and less than 59 percent are sticking around to be a father after getting a girlfriend pregnant.

This is not to villainize guys. It's just that they don't have many good role models these days. It looks like a lot of guys are going to the Hollywood School of Manhood. This means they are taking classes such as Sexual Conquests 101, Preventing Intimacy, Money and Power, Being Put in Your Place by Dominant Women, and 101 Guns You'll Never Even Be Allowed to Own. What about instruction in justice, loving what is good, serving rather than taking, and speaking tenderly to his wife and children?

Today's verse recorded King David's parting words to his son, Solomon. He told his son to "take courage and be a man." His wisdom called his son to step up and lead. And Solomon did. He wasn't perfect, but he did demonstrate goodness.

Be sure you wait for a guy who has had the advantage of Solomon . . . a wise and life-tested mentor against whom he has been able to measure, test, and develop his own manhood. It's funny how we expect guys who have never had manhood modeled for them to be the perfect picture of chivalry. And why do we go for the bad boy who seems to be more exciting? Choosing your guy for life is the single most important decision you are going to make other than following Jesus as your Savior. The real men are out there. And most of the time, they have a real man teaching them.

 Have your dad or an adult guy you respect help you make up a list of "manly" traits that you should look for in a guy.

What If I Don't Have Any Gifts?

God has given each of you a gift from his great variety of spiritual gifts. Use them well to serve one another. . . . Then everything you do will bring glory to God through Jesus Christ. All glory and power to him forever and ever! Amen. 1 PETER 4:10-11

Not everyone is gifted. The *technical* term "gifted" refers to people who consistently and naturally perform within the top 10 percent of one or more domains, whether these are academics, performance, or sports oriented. Granted, it's not easy to measure how a person performs in the top 10 percent as say, a dancer, but experts would likely argue it is not difficult to identify true giftedness.

Everyone does, however, have gifts. My daughters did not have a chance to develop many gifts in their early years. By the time we adopted them, they had been in four different foster homes as well as having experienced years of migrant living with their birth family. But both took to sports immediately and both lamented the fact they had not been a part of our family from birth. Imagine what Rachael's booming leg could have produced if she had been able to play soccer from age three, or how Marie might have excelled in ball handling if she had played basketball from the time she could toddle!

Instead, we had to fight through a couple of years of "I don't have *any* gifts." No one questions whether the guy winning all the photography awards or the girl who always gets the lead in the school play has a gift. But what if you're just really good with kids? What if you like to read and can put away a classic novel each week? What if you have no idea what you like to do or what you're good at? Do you have any gifts?

One thing God has bestowed on *each* of us is spiritual and practical gifts. Some spiritual gifts, by the way, are even quite practical. Take *hospitality* for instance. The ability to make people feel welcome in your home or in a new setting is a *gift*, even though you may not end up celebrated in the Clubs section of your yearbook. True, some gifts are "ordinary." But ordinary is important. Extraordinary is *never* accomplished without ordinary. What's more, God has told us he prefers the ordinary. We are treasures in jars of clay, true? (See 2 Corinthians 4:7.) Trust you have a gift . . . and he will extraordinarily use it!

 Use a search engine to find and complete a spiritual gifts test online.

Do You Really Want to Be Prom Queen?

When you are invited, take the lowest place, so that when your host comes, he will say to you, "Friend, move up to a better place." Then you will be honored in the presence of all the other guests. For all those who exalt themselves will be humbled, and those who humble themselves will be exalted. LUKE 14:10-11, NIV

"Whom the gods wish to destroy they first call promising."
CYRIL CONNOLLY

Forgive us for citing such an obscure quote by an obscure man in the annals of literary criticism. Cyril Connolly apparently became a literary critic because (1) he was very good at it, and (2) he was never disciplined or humble enough to complete the classic novel he had always dreamed of writing.

Connolly seemed to believe the "gods" had given him a *great* talent, a desire to perform that *great* talent, a lot of kudos when he was young about how *great* he would one day become . . . all so they could crush his spirit by taking the dream of writing fiction away from him. But Connolly was right. One of the surest ways to crush a "talent" is for the talent to begin believing he or she is indeed something quite special.

As humans we want to be noticed, be honored, be revered, and be admired. The desire seems almost insatiable at times. One of the most difficult things you and I may ever have to quietly endure is watching someone who has the same skill set as we have receive the accolades.

You want to rise high? The place to begin is with humility. The one who wants to tell the world how gifted she is will place herself where she thinks she may be noticed. And noticed she will be! Not only whatever measure of gifts and talents she may have, but also her flaws, her warts, and her pretense. This is a sure recipe for disaster. On the other hand, the one who is content to take the seat of lowest honor will also be noticed. It's hard to miss someone who has integrity, who quietly soars above the rest in quality. The Lord and those around her will pluck her from obscurity—after all, a light shines brightest in the darkest of corners, not in the brightness of a self-prescribed spotlight!

 Humble yourself today and tell another girl who sings, who dances, who cheers, who runs, who acts (you get the picture) that she is truly gifted and that you are pulling for her . . . and hey . . . be sure you mean it!

Confidently Humble

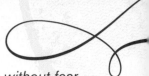

She is clothed with strength and dignity, and she laughs without fear of the future. When she speaks, her words are wise, and she gives instructions with kindness. PROVERBS 31:25-26

Don't you just love a good oxymoron? That would be two words appearing to be opposites, yet when paired with each other they represent a completely separate and recognizable concept. Here are some examples:

Act naturally
Alone together
Pretty ugly
Diet ice cream

Leadership experts have begun to define the best leaders as those who are both humble and confident. Humbly confident—they seem like two completely different concepts, but even in the wife of Proverbs 31 fame we can see that these two words working together actually pack a knockout punch.

Humility alone is not enough to make you a Proverbs 31 woman. Without knowledge of your unique gifts, you may end up with what many call a doormat mentality. Confidence is an emission from the engine of skill. Find what you are good at, even if it is one thing, and let your skill breed a confidence in you that God is using you and will use you to bless your family and others around you.

If instead you struggle with humility, understand this: you cannot grow without humility. You cannot grow in relationships, you cannot grow professionally, and you cannot grow as a person. Humility allows room for growth.

The truest proof of humble confidence is it makes everyone around you look good. "Her husband can trust her, and she will greatly enrich his life" (Proverbs 31:11), and "her children stand and bless her" (verse 28). God has great things in store for you, but his design is not likely one of ridiculous wealth or paralyzing fame. It's more likely this—that you would be clothed with both strength and dignity, and (as a result) you would face the future without even a hint of fear.

How can you improve in the area of your two greatest strengths? Find out by asking your mentors/coaches/teachers. Humble yourself enough to begin such growth. Your family will rise up one day and bless you for it!

JULY 28

The Strengths of
an Introvert

Make it your ambition to lead a quiet life: You should mind your own business and work with your hands, just as we told you, so that your daily life may win the respect of outsiders and so that you will not be dependent on anybody. 1 THESSALONIANS 4:11-12, NIV

There are two types of people in this world. Okay, that is what is called a sweeping generalization, but one basic way to divide people into two groups would be to use the principles of introversion and extroversion. Introverts are charged by time alone but drained by too much stimulation. Extroverts are charged by stimulation and drained by too much time alone.

Our society is skewed (biased) toward extroverts, but perhaps that is fair as they outnumber introverts two to one. There is a misconception, however, that extroverts make better leaders and have more confidence than introverts. Employers uneducated in the matter may tell you they would rather hire an extrovert for production purposes, but introverts are, generally speaking, more creative than extroverts. Group work can be painful for introverts. Every time the introvert takes a stance in opposition to a group, something similar to pain registers in his or her brain's amygdala; working alone frees the introvert from having to shield himself or herself from the pain of expressing independent thought.

Introverts also make great leaders, credited to the fact that introverts are great big-picture thinkers. While an extrovert may love micromanaging all aspects of a project, the introvert is more comfortable allowing people to run with their own ideas. Introverts are good, therefore, at fostering creativity in others.

Introverts in the animal kingdom—yes, there are introverted and extroverted animals—will often quietly observe from the sidelines when predators are present. The result? Introverts have a greater survival rate in crises!

Greek culture rewarded those who made public shows of generosity or wealth. Paul turns this attitude on its head when he says God honors the one who has a quiet and unassuming manner. This is about as close as the Bible is going to come to telling us to mind our own business—one-third of you may now breathe a sigh of relief, as this is much easier for the introvert than the extrovert!

 Introverts, know this: it is okay and even good that you need downtime! Extroverts, cheerfully give your introverted friends the space they need.

The Strengths of an Extrovert

There are "friends" who destroy each other, but a real friend sticks closer than a brother. PROVERBS 18:24

Extroverts crave new things; the monotony of a routine may absolutely drive them to the point of insanity. Thus the extrovert is a great starter.

The animal kingdom has both introverts and extroverts. An extroverted animal is highly involved in the pursuit of food. While this may put him in great danger if a predator is nearby, the extroverted animal rarely goes hungry. Human extroverts are so prolific in social networking that they have less trouble finding or creating work while unemployed. Extroverts are perceived to be friendlier. When it comes to inviting people to "come and see" Jesus, the extrovert is unmatched.

Extroverts need to be cautious, however, that friendships do not run shallow. Listening may prove difficult for some extroverts; let's face it, sitting down over a cup of coffee to listen to a friend's woes doesn't exactly provide high stimulation. The conversation in the booth halfway across the room may even prove more interesting to an extrovert than the one right in front of his or her face.

God's Kingdom does require authenticity, and it would be unfair to my extroverted friends to suggest they are not authentic or even transparent. They often are. But the extrovert needs to be careful not to spread herself too thin. Another version of our key verse says, "A man of too many friends comes to ruin" (NASB). Impulses can get extroverts into hot water, particularly if they are listening to too many counselors!

 Extroverts, slow down enough each day to engage one-on-one with Jesus and at least one good friend! Practice listening. Introverts, be sure you are occasionally the instigator of time spent with your extrovert friend. It will help her to know you value her friendship.

JULY 30
Relating Is a Gift

"To what can I compare the people of this generation?" Jesus asked. "How can I describe them? They are like children playing a game in the public square. They complain to their friends, 'We played wedding songs, and you didn't dance, so we played funeral songs, and you didn't weep.' For John the Baptist didn't spend his time eating bread or drinking wine, and you say, 'He's possessed by a demon.' The Son of Man, on the other hand, feasts and drinks, and you say, 'He's a glutton and a drunkard, and a friend of tax collectors and other sinners!'" LUKE 7:31-34

We have a friend who tours with us to teach at our Pure Freedom live events for teens and their moms. Her name is Erin Davis, and if she doesn't make you laugh within five minutes of meeting her, you have no sense of humor. She lights up the stage with laughter from the audience. But at times when she's prayed with us backstage, she feels that her gifts are lesser because she's the "funny girl." That's tragic! Are you a funny girl? Lean in for some courage.

The ability to make other people laugh isn't listed on most spiritual gift inventories, but boy, does it play a key role in winning people to Jesus. There's no denying Jesus had a way about him that was deeply welcoming. And in Luke 7 he is using humor when he points out the accusations against him. "You're like a bunch of kids holding a pouting festival," he tells the Pharisees, who are upset that the crowds see the value in the repentance message of John the Baptist, whom they have imprisoned. "No one will play the game the way you want to so you're going to cry and moan about it. Really? Who can win with you guys? John won't dance so you say he's demon possessed; I dance and you say I'm a sinner!" One of the Pharisees, Simon, must have been disarmed by Jesus' humor, because Jesus was invited to have dinner at Simon's house that same night.

We believe Jesus was funny. After all, he was fully human, and people can be just flat-out funny. More than that, we believe Jesus was *purposefully* funny. God is full of surprises and Jesus also happens to be fully God. Jesus knew bringing the surprising truth of God to life with humor helps people be more receptive. And we believe he wants you to know that relating easily to others . . . is a gift.

 The musical *Godspell* is a great example of the gospel presented as relationally and humanly as Jesus likely lived it. Check out a scene on YouTube!

Learning to Live Bored

Make it your goal to live a quiet life, minding your own business and working with your hands, just as we instructed you before. Then people who are not Christians will respect the way you live, and you will not need to depend on others. 1 THESSALONIANS 4:11-12

Apparently teenagers who get bored are 50 percent more likely to get into drugs, violence, and a world of trouble. We don't condone that kind of behavior, but we're going to suggest that being bored is good. And you should learn to live with it. (I, Dannah, even prayed you might be a little bit bored on the day that you read this so the message will sink in.)

It's not that there are no adventures to be had. We get to travel all over the world every year teaching at our Pure Freedom and Secret Keeper Girl live events, but the average day finds us in sweats for most of the day, walking aging doggies through the woods, wondering what to cook for dinner. Most of life is not lived in the fast lane.

Paul was the master of word choice—the more I learn about him, the more I admire what a clever writer he was. Our translation simply says, "Make it your goal . . ." to live a simple life. But Paul used a word typically found in connection with wealthy people doing good things to enhance their reputation. Maybe we could compare the concept with the People's Choice Award. "You know what trophy you should go for?" Paul is asking. "You should go for the one that says, 'She may not have seemed like all that from the outside, but we never had to lift a finger to help her and look at everything she accomplished!'"

I, Suzy, played my drums in a basement cubicle for a lot of years before I ever got to play in an arena. I ran sound for Dannah long before she put a microphone in front of my mouth. God's plan for our lives, at least for today, is local and simple. Where are you right now? You are where God has planted you, at least for this season of your life. Your school, your friends, your family, your job—that's your mission field. It may be "boring," but it's 100 percent real life. Get used to it, because in my experience, it stays pretty real.

 Take a quiet, thankful walk through your mission field today.

AUGUST 1
Dropping Your Nets

One day as Jesus was walking along the shore of the Sea of Galilee, he saw two brothers—Simon, also called Peter, and Andrew—throwing a net into the water, for they fished for a living. Jesus called out to them, "Come, follow me, and I will show you how to fish for people!" And they left their nets at once and followed him. MATTHEW 4:18-20

Some time ago my mom decided to cover up the camera on her laptop. She has heard too many stories about people spying on others. Unlike Mom, I'm not slapping any tape on my camera, so all you cyber-geniuses can consider this an invitation to get your spy on. But, at the same time, this gets me thinking. If I'm just sitting in front of my computer, you could conclude I am not *doing* much about the things I complain about. You'd be right. I don't like poverty, gossip, waste, ignorance, illiteracy, or injustice. But you have the right to ask me, "What are you *doing* about it?" That's the deal with change. We have to *be* the change. We can't insist other people do it, we can't complain rich people aren't funding it, and it isn't wise to keep saying, "I'll start tomorrow."

Jesus' choice of disciples was odd. He went to one of the most remote portions of Israel and chose guys who did not have honored professions. The speech patterns in Galilee were so unrefined that today Peter and Andrew might be called "hicks" or "rednecks." Their response to Jesus' calling was equally astonishing. He made an invitation, and *they immediately dropped their nets and followed him*! This kind of spontaneity today would be considered crazy, but there is no doubt God had prepared Peter and Andrew through a life of hard work for what he was calling them to. He sought after and found hard-working men who were willing to live without many comforts; they were intelligent yet not already exposed to a bunch of garbage printed in books. Brilliant!

God is preparing you right now to *be the change*. When he calls, you will be fully equipped to drop whatever you are doing and follow. Just remember—once your eyes are opened to a need, a problem, an injustice, a dark reality . . . you are part of the solution. But the needs are huge, you say! Yes. Yet your matchless God has prepared you and is calling you to join him.

 What would you be unwilling to leave in order to follow Jesus? Now is a good time to find and address such a roadblock.
SW

Dealing with Tough Teachers

You who are slaves must accept the authority of your masters with all respect. Do what they tell you—not only if they are kind and reasonable, but even if they are cruel. 1 PETER 2:18

Robby had one bad grade in high school. One. And he didn't deserve it. As his mom, I wanted so badly to go to this teacher and explain to her why her grading system was not fair. And I could have. She worked for me. My husband and I started the Christian school that my kids have all attended. This was no small thing. It would be the one grade that would keep him from having a 4.0 for his full four years of high school. After a lot of prayer, we decided to let the grade stand even though we believed it was not fair.

Why?

Because the lesson Robby learned in submitting to his authority is more important than protecting a perfect 4.0.

Why submit to authority even if we are wronged? Because we are free! In the realm of God's Kingdom, there is no slave or free man. All have been set free from the law of sin and death; therefore there is no need to respond with anything other than the same grace and patience Jesus showed as he paid for sins that he had not committed. "He is your example," Peter says, "and you must follow in his steps" (1 Peter 2:21). God's Kingdom is a kingdom, not a democracy. There is a hierarchy of authority that goes along with every kingdom, but the irony of this Kingdom is that we get to choose to submit.

And God remembers your willingness and rewards it. You may remember how Joseph submitted again and again to ruthless leaders when he was in slavery. Because he submitted, he was continually promoted. What might God do for you if you choose to submit rather than strike out in anger?

 Read the rest of 1 Peter 2. Identify your toughest (most unfair) teacher and make a list of ways you can respond to him or her with grace. Be sure your list includes only doable ideas! See if a couple of friends will join you in your quest to respond with humility—even if you are truly wronged.
DG

But They Are the Authorities, Right?

Dear friends, do not believe everyone who claims to speak by the Spirit. You must test them to see if the spirit they have comes from God. For there are many false prophets in the world. 1 JOHN 4:1

Early in my career, I taught in the public schools in Tulsa, Oklahoma. Typically for me it's "the older the better," but my one year of teaching fifth graders before moving up to middle school showed me that the trust and reverence they displayed for me as a teacher was precious . . . and not long for this world.

Several parents came in (amused, thankfully) and told me they had debated an issue with their fifth grader at home in which their child had refused to believe the parent . . . unless Mrs. Weibel corroborated the parent's point of view. Apparently I knew everything. Wow. But this is a child reasoning like a child. We know we have to grow up and reason like an adult. Does your favorite teacher know everything? No. Is your least favorite teacher a blooming idiot? No. But your teachers don't always know God's truth, so where does this leave you as a student who sits under the authority of teachers but who wants to be a follower of wise counsel?

First, remember that "our struggle is not against flesh and blood" (Ephesians 6:12, NIV). People do offer poor counsel, but it is most likely offered from a place of care. The problem is not with the person per se, but in the fact that the person (often an authority) may be embracing philosophies or tenets that God's Word has identified as false. Test what your teachers say by holding their counsel up to the light of God's Word.

Second, the best defense you have against swallowing the bad advice pill is to first know what God's Word actually says and then to determine whether *you* believe the Bible truly is the standard against which you should weigh all teachings. This is a faith you have to own—by very definition of the word, you cannot use someone else's faith. There's an old saying: If you stand for nothing, you will fall for anything. First establish a baseline for truth. Then hold all other teachings up to its measures. Many of us do not know God's Word. Teachers included. Politicians included. Musicians included. Athletes included. Get my drift?

 **Action STEP** What are you doing about *knowing* God's Word?
SW

AUGUST 4
Do Not Judge

You may think you can condemn such people, but you are just as bad, and you have no excuse! When you say they are wicked and should be punished, you are condemning yourself, for you who judge others do these very same things. And we know that God, in his justice, will punish anyone who does such things. Since you judge others for doing these things, why do you think you can avoid God's judgment when you do the same things? ROMANS 2:1-3

Statistics say your basic personality will not change much over the course of your lifetime, but such a statement fails to take Jesus into consideration! Take, for example, Saul of Tarsus who was rejoicing that Christians were being killed and helping to plot their deaths! (See Acts 9.) He met Jesus on the road to Damascus and was so changed that he was now known as Paul and went about recruiting believers. Had you asked him before that encounter on the road if he'd ever be a Christian, he'd have told you, "No!" Jesus makes all the difference.

Even though your personality may not experience the dramatic change Saul's did, you *are* likely to change jobs and even careers more than a few times in your adult years. No matter how many times you have watched your teachers in action and said, "I will *never* be a teacher. . . ." you may decide someday to teach.

I don't know where *your* teachers are today in terms of their dreams, gifts, encouragement received from home, disappointments, fears of failure . . . but you don't either. It is so easy to jump to conclusions about "bad" teachers, who could be failing to realize their life circumstances are bleeding out into their jobs. I know that I've had very, very bad days in ministry where I wish I could take back something I said or did. Do your circumstances ever bleed out? Teachers cry, feel frightened, and suffer anxiety like everyone else, right? How about giving them a break today and praying, if they need it, that they might meet Jesus on the road to someplace so they'll be changed too?

 *Action* **STEP**
Pray earnestly for each teacher you'll have this school year.
SW

AUGUST 5
First Impression

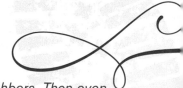

Be careful to live properly among your unbelieving neighbors. Then even if they accuse you of doing wrong, they will see your honorable behavior, and they will give honor to God when he judges the world. 1 PETER 2:12

We hear a lot of freethinking mosaics (that's your generation's nickname) declaring they don't care what anyone thinks about them, but we think that's kind of a self-lie. We all care what people think. In fact, we take great pains to paint a picture for others detailing precisely how we wish to be viewed.

You'll soon be making first impressions on some of your teachers. One of Dannah's earliest college speech teachers pegged her as a poor public speaker. She was either dead wrong or she was a great teacher, because I (Suzy) believe Dannah puts together a great speech today! One of my high school teachers assumed I would give him the same troubles my older brother had given him and treated me unfairly for a couple of weeks as a result. Bad first impressions, right?

There are a couple of ways to secure a good first impression. The first is to be committed to listening. Whispering and goofing off during instruction is not just a high school phenomenon. It has reached almost epidemic proportions across all age groups in our culture, and it never fails to communicate one very clear message—*I don't care at all about what you are saying.*

Take time to remember and use names. Names are important to every-one's identity, including your teachers. Dannah (pronounced Dannah) is called Dana more often than not. It rubs a little, because she is not Dana. Sometimes people take the liberty of shortening my name to "Sue" as soon as they meet me. But that is not who I am. Remembering, using, and correctly spelling a teacher's name is an indicator of respect . . . ahem, which they deserve.

Finally, don't talk too much in general! Talking shows off how much we know, which to our embarrassment often turns out to be very little. Listening proves we are willing to become wise.

In today's verse, Peter is exhorting a church often accused of disloyalty to the Roman government that they should be making every effort to prove God's goodness through their behavior. Our good reputation, in other words, belongs also to God if we claim to belong to him. The classroom is a great place to start practicing a life that draws others to the person of Jesus.

 *Action* **STEP**   Ask a friend to be brutally honest with you about your reputation with adults.

AUGUST 6

Surefire Ways to Lead Even a Teacher

Obey your leaders and submit to them, for they are keeping watch over your souls, as those who will have to give an account. Let them do this with joy and not with groaning, for that would be of no advantage to you. Pray for us, for we are sure that we have a clear conscience, desiring to act honorably in all things. HEBREWS 13:17-18, ESV

I am a huge fan of Christian schools. As a lifelong Christian school student, however, I did not have the burden of living out a life of integrity before unbelieving teachers, which would have been a good challenge to my character.

If you have teachers and friends who do not know Jesus, you have the opportunity each day to take Jesus to school with you. What's the best way to do this? Wear Christian T-shirts? Correct everyone's language before it gets even more out of control? Hand out tracts? No, no, and no. There are some practical ways in which you can lead even those hired to lead you:

Be real. All people have broken parts, including you. The good news is you know the one who has come to repair all of the brokenness. Be honest about your struggles.

Do the little things well. Little things both show and earn respect. Do your work on time, show up on time, don't cheat, don't rat people out, don't participate in gossip, keep your mouth clean—you'll stick out from the crowd like nobody's business!

Learn to pray all day long. When we pray the way Jesus taught us to pray, no one but God and us even knows it's going on. Keep a running talk with God going in your head all day long. It's hard to feel cheated, bitter, hopeless, anxious, etc., while attached to the vine (see John 15:1-8).

You be you. Let God be God. Find out how God created you to serve him best and become great at that. But don't steal God's job. His job is to convict of sin and to cause things to grow. Let him do all the judge and jury work.

Know why you believe what you believe. Make Bible study part of your daily work. You'll get run over without this one in place!

 **STEP** Which of the five things above are you strongest in? Weakest? Ask a good, honest friend to confirm your answers.
SW

AUGUST 7

Today Is the Day

The Kingdom of Heaven will be like ten bridesmaids who took their lamps and went to meet the bridegroom. Five of them were foolish, and five were wise. The five who were foolish didn't take enough olive oil for their lamps, but the other five were wise enough to take along extra oil. When the bridegroom was delayed, they all became drowsy and fell asleep. MATTHEW 25:1-5

"Never put off till tomorrow what you can do today."
THOMAS JEFFERSON

Jesus teaches in Matthew 25 the wise are ready when they are supposed to be ready. This parable hearkens back to a time when the bridal party had to be ready at a moment's notice for a wedding to break out. After the bridegroom had secured permission from his beloved's father to take a girl as his bride, he immediately began building a home for her. All of the couple's friends and family were put on notice . . . this wedding could start at any time. The second the bridegroom had put the last nail in the roof, he was coming for his woman! And the rejoicing would begin.

Only in this parable, the story doesn't end quite like it should. Ten bridesmaids had gone out to meet the groom and his buddies. Five had taken extra oil, but five had been a little lazy. Sure enough the groom was a little late in arriving, and five of the girls hadn't prepared. They ended up missing out.

Procrastination is a dangerous game. In high school, procrastination on one little assignment or at your McJob may not seem like a big deal, but keep in mind how the game works. "If you are faithful in little things, you will be faithful in large ones. But if you are dishonest in little things, you won't be honest with greater responsibilities" (Luke 16:10).

Can you imagine telling your best friend you weren't fitted for your bridesmaid dress in time to have it for the wedding? Or missing her bridal shower because you were late to catch your flight? This is the degree of insult that procrastination may communicate not only to friends, but also to bosses.

There are a lot of ways to beat procrastination. Set deadlines. Reward yourself every time you get a job done. Tell someone to hold you accountable. Consider it a challenge. But beat it you must. You don't want to miss the wedding!

 *Action* **STEP** Write and follow a to-do list for a week. How does this help?
SW

Let Me off the Merry-Go-Round!

Those who are wise will shine as bright as the sky, and those who lead many to righteousness will shine like the stars forever. But you, Daniel, keep this prophecy a secret; seal up the book until the time of the end, when many will rush here and there, and knowledge will increase.
DANIEL 12:3-4

What is up with graduation ceremonies featuring three valedictorians, all with a 4.6 GPA? Is that even possible? Aren't we just inflating the grades? (Sorry if we're stepping on your 4.3 toes.) It's a sign of our times, as if knowledge has become a commodity with no end, and we can barely keep up.

The book of Daniel prophesied it would look like this in the final days. The Hebrew words for "rush here and there" were travel terms, implying a lashing at the ocean with oars. The promise that knowledge will increase speaks not of slow growth, but *exponential* growth. Modern knowledge doubles every two years, it is said. The father of one of my former students is working closely with the Pentagon on supersonic travel. He says it won't be long before businessmen will fly from New York City to Japan . . . for lunch.

In such a volatile world, how can you possibly prepare for your future? First, study the Bible. Regardless of where and if you go to school or what you choose as a major, the promises of blessing from knowing and following God's Word are incomparable. Many Bible scholars believe this verse in Daniel actually refers to Bible study: the eyes of scholars will move furtively over the text of God's Word, and our understanding of its precepts will increase like crazy as the time of Jesus' return nears.

Second, pray about taking a chill pill when it comes to overloading on the academics. Maybe you believe that if you don't get into the perfect high school, take every AP class offered, and spend every waking moment working, no decent college will want you. There is such a thing as spinning your wheels, working for accolades that fade as fast as spring flowers, and finding yourself bitter about the rat race. God is good, and life is good. Be sure you have enough time to say so with conviction!

 Reset your weekly Sabbath if you've happened to let it slip.

The World of Bullying

Wash yourselves and be clean! Get your sins out of my sight. Give up your evil ways. Learn to do good. Seek justice. Help the oppressed. Defend the cause of orphans. Fight for the rights of widows.
ISAIAH 1:16-17

There are three positions we can take when it comes to the world of bullying, but only three . . . and each of us necessarily has something to *do* as a result.

You may be the bullied, and nothing feels lonelier than being singled out. Maybe it is clear you won't defend yourself, or maybe there is something unique about you that cruel hearts somehow get away with labeling "weird." Your job: refuse to walk alone. Tell an adult you are being singled out. Then be patient. Do not try to force friendships with mean girls or pawns of popularity. The Bible calls this "casting your pearls before swine" (see Matthew 7:6).

You could be a bully. You are a bully if you use your "power" to isolate other girls. You are a bully if you say words with the intention of causing pain, or if you work an entire group against a single girl who is weaker. You are a bully if you hide behind the anonymity of Facebook to deliver a message or a threat you would never have the guts to deliver face-to-face. Your job: you need to repent. Get on your knees and confess to God your participation in this cycle of meanness. As today's passage says, do not only stop doing what is evil, but also learn to do what is good. You need to begin to stand *with* the very girls you have tormented.

Finally, you may be a bystander. You are not bullied nor do you bully, but you certainly see it going on all around you. You feel compassion for the girls who are wounded. You feel impatience or even disgust for the girls who bully. But . . . you do nothing. Your job: like the bully, you need to learn to do what is right! It is not enough to merely disapprove when you see another girl being bullied. I am guessing that you don't want to be the "goat" Jesus speaks of (see Matthew 25:31-46) when he says, "I tell you the truth, when you refused to help the least of these my brothers and sisters, you were refusing to help me" (verse 45).

 **Action STEP** Identify your place above, and do your job!

AUGUST 10
Me? Gifted?

[God] has given each one of us a special gift through the generosity of Christ. EPHESIANS 4:7

According to Barna Research Online, over 20 percent of people in the church don't believe they have a spiritual gift. That's pretty sad, because God says he gives one to each believer. Including you. A spiritual gift is a supernatural ability given and empowered by the Holy Spirit. It's not a talent, but something you could not possibly do without the Spirit of God inside you.

I knew one of my daughter Lexi's gifts when she was very young. She kept having experiences where she knew something she shouldn't know. One time, Lexi came home from school with an interesting report. She said when she got to school, she was burdened to pray for her friend Piakene, who hadn't arrived at school yet. Her friend was only a few moments late, but Lexi felt it was urgent to pray for her. So she did. She even asked her teacher to pray during homeroom activities time. Later in the morning, Piakene came to school with a report that she'd been in a car accident. That's a spiritual gift of prophecy (sensing God talking to you about circumstances and his Word) operating in Lexi's life.

Some people get a little out of control with gifts like that one, so seek the fruits of the Spirit—"love, joy, peace, patience, kindness, goodness, faithfulness, gentleness, and self-control" (Galatians 5:22-23)—before you set out on a journey to be a powerful prophet or healer! On the flip side, don't think for a second the Spirit's gifts aren't alive and well and able to manifest in your heart and life. Gifts include administration (managing), exhortation (encouraging), giving (time and money), evangelism, healing, serving, mercy, wisdom, prophecy, knowledge, teaching, shepherding, and faith.

My top gifts are teaching, prophecy, and faith. I operate in them as much as I can because I serve God more effectively than when I try to do things on my own strength. That's the point—if you just try to serve God without knowing what your spiritual gifts are, you'll find yourself feeling like a rat on a spinning wheel . . . getting nowhere, when he has big places for you to go and big things for you to do!

 If you want to read about the gifts to see if you can recognize one in your life, check out these passages where several are mentioned: Romans 12; 1 Corinthians 12; Ephesians 4.
DG

Prophecy Is without Honor in Our Country

"In the last days," God says, "I will pour out my Spirit upon all people. Your sons and daughters will prophesy. Your young men will see visions, and your old men will dream dreams." ACTS 2:17

Years ago a boy was born to a young couple in South Korea. They named him Samuel Kang, prophesying over their young son that he would choose to follow Christ and become a great pastor in a time when alien Shinto beliefs were the norm in their nation.

Meanwhile, another gift of prophecy came to South Korea through a man named Billy Graham. In 1973, he didn't just share the gospel of Christ, but he predicted Korea would become a base for preaching the gospel throughout Asia. At the time, South Korea allowed little foreign travel. The nation was just beginning to let God in. How would they ever get the Word out with restrictions like that?

Years went by. In 1988, the South Korean government was forced to open the doors for their people to travel freely if the country was to have the chance to host the Olympics in Seoul. One of the pastors eagerly waiting and praying for a chance to be a missionary was a man named Samuel Kang. Today South Korea sends more missionaries worldwide than any country with the exception of the United States.

The gift of prophecy is often abused, and therefore disrespected and disregarded in our culture. But many still understand how the gift is meant to operate. While some say there will be a season of prophecy ceasing, it is hard to argue with Acts 2:17, which declares in the last days we *will* prophesy!

Prophecy is *forth-telling* the will of God. It is the knowing of something you can't see in the physical realm. God's Word says we can't mess around with it. We can't randomly say, "God told me _____" unless we are positive we have heard something from God. The Bible encourages us to "test" prophecy. In other words, if someone runs around prophesying events and they don't come true, that person is not gifted with prophecy.

Pastor Billy Graham and the parents of Pastor Kang were able to hear God's gentle nudge. It is quite possible you are able to as well.

 *Action* **STEP** Start a conversation about prophecy in your circle of friends. Being curious and learning from the Word is a good start to opening yourself up to spiritual gifts.

Two Ways to Be a Healer

By his wounds you are healed. 1 PETER 2:24

Summer camp is always awesome. Who can debate that? But this was a summer camp offered by a denomination that just doesn't talk about the more radical gifts God promises . . . things like prophecies, miracles of healing, or even general Pentecostal moments in time. Yet it was happening. To me. Around me.

The night had started like any other. About four hundred kids had gathered for evening worship under the humid canopy of an August night. About halfway through the set, prayer broke out, but not a usual type of prayer. This was a little more animated than usual, and even a little rowdy. One week later the news arrived. A seventeen-year-old boy with a ventricular septal defect had been present that night . . . and had been healed. The doctors confirmed there was no longer any evidence of a hole in the boy's heart.

It's not an everyday occurrence, though that is not the only healing I've encountered. A girl in our church was healed of cancer after a church-wide fast not long ago. And a complete stranger told me she had attended our church only once, but during worship she heard and felt a pop in her deaf ear, and she can now hear again. God heals. I know this.

Healing is a spiritual gift according to 1 Corinthians 12:9. Keep in mind, it is God who does the healing 100 percent of the time, and I believe he sometimes answers prayers with a "no" or a "wait." Why? I don't know—his ways are not our ways. Still, you might have this gift if you have a deep stirring to see sick people made well or if you are overwhelmed by confidence that God can heal at any time he chooses.

There's another way to join God in healing. Feeding the hungry, providing clothing for the poor, loving our enemies, remaining sexually pure, standing for justice, and believing God for miracles . . . all of these provide healing in a society rushing headlong down a river of destruction. Jesus is not merely an example to us; he personally bore the penalty for our sin so we can live for what is right. When we do, brokenness is mended.

 Do you need to ask God to increase your faith for healing? Read 1 Corinthians 12 and ask God for wisdom in understanding your gift.
SW

AUGUST 13
Got Faith?

Faith is the confidence that what we hope for will actually happen; it gives us assurance about things we cannot see. Through their faith, the people in days of old earned a good reputation. HEBREWS 11:1-2

The people written about in Hebrews 11 are crazy (take a few moments to read the whole chapter). You have to know that you know that you know God is good if you're going to

- build a huge ark in a country that has never seen a drop of rain.
- pick up and move your entire family across a desert after God says, "I want you to go, but I'm not going to tell you where. . . ."
- strap your son to an altar and raise the knife to take his life.

I've had to employ my gift of faith at times, sure, but it's been little stuff compared to Hebrews 11. Still, I have to wonder if God is preparing me now for something bigger down the road. The person who has faith is the one who will do the unthinkable when called upon to do so, not because she believes in herself, but because she knows God is true. Even when she cannot comprehend a good result, she says, "God, I know you love me and are walking with me, so I'm going to do what is right and wise and keep praising you. . . ."

In other religions, prayer represents what a human being asks a god to do for her. She hopes and prays that she is heard and that she finds favor. Christianity is the only expression of faith in which followers can ask God for help when we don't know how to pray—God actually steps in and says, "Since I know what you need, allow me to do this for you." So he prays on our behalf and then . . . he *listens* to himself. The reason we don't get to experience this more often is because we treat God like he is a vending machine that either says yes or no to our requests, as if there were nothing in between. As if God is only in the business of dispensing easy answers. The best question to ask may not be, "God, will you do this?" but "I know you'll do what is best, God; how can I be involved?"

 In the middle of the impossible, do you know that *God can*? Practice prayers that begin by asking God *how* he's going to do it.

How Should I Read the Bible?

I pray that your love will overflow more and more, and that you will keep on growing in knowledge and understanding. For I want you to understand what really matters, so that you may live pure and blameless lives until the day of Christ's return. PHILIPPIANS 1:9-10

In college I frequently encountered this one guy that just *had* to be a Christian. He was so full of joy. So I asked him, and he was shocked by my assumption. "I'm an atheist," he told me. A couple of days later he said, "Here's one of the reasons I don't believe. There's this story where Jesus tells a guy to be his follower, and the guy says, 'I have to go bury my dad,' and Jesus basically chews him out. What kind of God won't let someone bury his dad?" (See Matthew 8:21-22; Luke 9:59-60.) I was stumped. I was a youth pastor's wife, a small-group leader, a reader of the Bible . . . and I didn't know. That was when I realized I have to do more than just read my Bible. I have to *understand* what it says. I bought a big old concordance and a Hebrew/Greek dictionary and was off to the races at twenty-five.

You, my friend, should start now! The Internet provides every Bible commentary known to man at no cost. These are observations made by Bible scholars about everything from word origins and verb tenses to the cultural significance of God's words. It was from a commentary I learned the young man whom Jesus had invited to follow him had not yet lost his father. His father was likely old or ill, but it was customary to say, "I will do it after I have buried my father"; it may have been years before this guy would have freed himself up to follow Jesus.

In today's passage, Paul wants to be sure our relationship with Jesus is rooted in understanding. Only when we read the Bible for understanding do we really figure out what is important. Jesus demonstrated this when he released a woman caught in adultery (see John 8). The teachers of the law wanted Jesus to condemn the woman, but he began to draw in the dirt. Though we don't know what he wrote, Jeremiah 17:13 (NIV) says, "Those who turn away from you will be written in the dust because they have forsaken the LORD, the spring of living water." Is it possible he wrote that verse in the dust? The Pharisees knew the Word . . . but they were hard of understanding.

 **STEP** Ask around for the best online study tools and begin to *really* read your Bible!
SW

A Guy Who Was Basically Crafty

Look, I have specifically chosen Bezalel. . . . I have filled him with the Spirit of God, giving him great wisdom, ability, and expertise in all kinds of crafts. EXODUS 31:2-3

In the New Testament, the inspired writers mention about twenty-three specific spiritual gifts appointed by God's Holy Spirit. Most of the time, people have gifts from this list. But God can supernaturally gift *anything!*

In the Old Testament, when God was ordering his people to build the Tabernacle, he came down and offered a special spiritual gift to a guy named Bezalel. After all, God needed someone to carve the Ark of the Covenant, mold the lampstand, and set the stones. God's Spirit came into Bezalel and made him an expert in all kinds of crafts!

I used to think the artifacts and items in the Tabernacle must have been rather crude looking. I mean, what kind of tools would they have had to craft them? When I read Exodus 31:2-3, I realized God's Spirit was empowering Bezalel to make them. What amazing works of art they must have been! They'd have put any art museum treasures to shame.

Maybe you have a special passion or gifting. Working with animals, writing, singing, or swimming might be your cup of tea. God can supernaturally gift those areas if he sees a way you can glorify him. I believe he did just that with an Olympic runner named Eric Liddell who competed in 1924. Liddell had a special gift when it came to running. He was favored to win, but when Olympic officials scheduled his race on Sunday, he refused to compete. He was a firm observer of the Sabbath who believed, as I do, that God commands us to rest. Wanting to prove God could honor his gift, he pulled out of the Sunday competition—his best event—and planned to run in the 400-meter race, in which he had previously performed only modestly well. On the day of the race, he carried the words of 1 Samuel 2:30 with him: "Those who honor me I will honor" (NIV). That day Eric Liddell broke both Olympic and world records!

If we honor God in the things we love, he will honor us. If we invite him to lead us in every decision, he gifts us supernaturally with his power.

 Ask God to give you a heart like Eric Liddell, who spent the rest of his life serving God as a missionary in China.
DG

Rats on Spinning Wheels

They are like trees planted along the riverbank, bearing fruit each season. Their leaves never wither, and they prosper in all they do. PSALM 1:3

God intends for you and me to bear fruit when we are busy serving him. But too often today, I see fruitless Christians exhausting themselves because they aren't doing what *God* designed them to do, but what *people* ask them to do. They remind me of rats on spinning wheels. They are filled with dead works.

How can you know if you are caught up in a dead work? Here's a little test to help you know. Think about an area where you are serving God right now, then answer yes or no to each of these questions.

_____ Have you undertaken this work because of obligations to someone rather than an exploding desire ignited by God? (See Acts 13:2; 1 Corinthians 12:11; Galatians 1:12.)

_____ Do you find yourself unhappy and resentful when you do this work rather than filled with happiness and joy? (See Ecclesiastes 5:19; Hebrews 12:2; 13:17.)

_____ Do you find there's no long-term and significant fruit yielded from this work? (See Psalm 1:3; Matthew 3:10; John 6:27; 1 Corinthians 3:12-13.)

_____ Do you find yourself drained and emptied by this work rather than filled up and with time to rest between or after it? (See Genesis 2:2; Exodus 23:12; Deuteronomy 5:14; Romans 8:6.)

_____ Are you doing it to please man rather than to please God? (See Colossians 3:23.)

If you answered yes to most or all of the above, you're probably being distracted from being used by God in the way *he* intended. It's likely you're caught up in doing what *people* are asking of you. It might be time to make some changes.

 Pray about what changes you need to make, and then be brave enough to share this test with anyone you need to so you can get courage to make the changes.

---

*This test was previously printed in Dannah Gresh, *Five Little Questions That Reveal the Life God Designed for You* (Nashville: Thomas Nelson, 2007), 148.

Passion . . .
Out of Control!

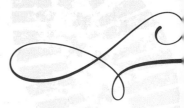

Don't be too good or too wise! Why destroy yourself? On the other hand, don't be too wicked either. Don't be a fool! Why die before your time? Pay attention to these instructions, for anyone who fears God will avoid both extremes. ECCLESIASTES 7:16-18

My husband met a college student with facial contusions while playing racquetball the other night. Though he didn't know the guy, Jonathan asked in his normal friendly manner, "What happened to your face?" (He once asked our fourteen-year-old daughter the same question about a prominent pimple on her chin. Ouch!) The student proudly explained he had gotten a DUI while riding his bicycle. His indiscretion had cost him his driver's license for ninety days, thousands of dollars in fines, and his name in the newspaper. He thought it was about the coolest thing that had ever happened to him.

Isn't it funny how people can seem proud of their indiscretions? Today's passage from Ecclesiastes contains a warning not to be too wicked. Ironically, it also addresses excess of passion in the other direction too. You shouldn't be an ultra "holy" child (think self-righteous) *nor* a wild child.

Solomon's first warning is to not become overly wise. Do not determine for both yourself and everyone around you that you are the judge and jury for all things right and wrong. Take note, those who consider themselves better than others are the ones who are warned they will destroy themselves! Let those in authority correct what is wrong. Find a place in the middle where you can simply win people to the truth through friendship and influence.

What a great verse for encouraging the middle ground (we used this verse in the July 6 devotion too . . . such a good reminder!). It isn't wise to pursue either extreme in your Christian walk. Steady as she goes. The wisdom God promises to give generously to all who ask (see James 1:5) is the same wisdom that will cause you to be a stable and sound, yet passionate, disciple.

 Ask someone who knows you well and will tell the truth, "Am I ever judgmental?" "Do you think of me as too wild?" Then be quiet and listen!
SW

What's in a Name?

The gatekeeper opens the gate for him, and the sheep recognize his voice and come to him. He calls his own sheep by name and leads them out.
JOHN 10:3

People are becoming more creative with name choices these days. Our friend Chizzy (pronounced "Cheezy" as a nickname for her Nigerian name Chizarouke) taught in an inner-city school where creative names were epidemic, so she fit right in. Chizzy talks of two unique names in particular: Abcde (pronounced "Absidee") and Female (with three syllables and the accent on the second syllable).

Names are important. They are inextricably connected to who we are. A good name, the Bible says, is worth more than gold and silver (see Proverbs 22:1, NIV). We get all shivery every time we read God's proclamation in Isaiah 48:9, "For my own sake and for the honor of my name, I will hold back my anger and not wipe you out." God regards his own name with great zealousness.

The image Jesus paints in John 10 is clear. He knows our name not only collectively (as in *my children*) but also on an individual basis. He is our Shepherd. (We recommend you pick up a great little book called, *A Shepherd Looks at Psalm 23* by W. Phillip Keller.) One thing we have learned about shepherds is that they work together to experience community and lighten the workload. They did this in Jesus' day too. Shepherds would often allow the sheep to have "sleepovers" where all would be kept in one community pen. One gatekeeper would be assigned to watch for predators and thieves. The shepherd comes for his sheep through the gate, of course, and the gatekeeper knows who is a shepherd and who isn't. The gate flies open, and the shepherd calls out his sheep. He may use a whistle, a song, a noise he has created on his own, or simply the names of his sheep. The miracle as one watches a true shepherd is that though these animals are dumb, they only come running out if it's their own shepherd calling. They know their shepherd's voice.

Your name may be boring, embarrassing, unique, or plain, but the point is that Jesus knows it. Do you know his voice as that of your shepherd? Are you wearing *his* name well?

Have some fun exploring the meanings of names, yours and your friends', taking time to thank Jesus that your name is known!

God . . . Selfish?

I will rescue you for my sake—yes, for my own sake! I will not let my reputation be tarnished, and I will not share my glory with idols!
ISAIAH 48:11

We have a friend who leads a small discipleship group of teenage girls. Her group is a hodgepodge of age, race, and spiritual backgrounds. Though many days she sticks to benign topics for the sake of her spiritual rookies, she decided to tackle an age-old discipleship question one day. "Whether you like it or not, whether you want it or not, you have a spiritual relationship with God," she told the girls. "So," she continued, "what is your spiritual temperature right now?" Here are some of the responses she got:

"I just really love God."
"I don't care."
"Honestly? I've never thought about it."
"I think God is kind of selfish. . . ."

Hold the phone! Selfish? Selfish technically means "caring only for one's self." Seeing as God loves the world so much he gave his only Son as a sacrifice (see John 3:16), he is generous in love (see James 1:5), and doesn't withhold good gifts from his children (see Matthew 7:11), we can certainly choose a better word to define God's character.

And yet, if you look at our key verse above, it might appear that God is selfish. He's certainly motivated by desire. Look at it this way. Do you have a best friend? Do you spend time with her purely out of duty? Is it because she demands your time? No! You do it because you like it. The verse above is telling us that God's motivated in the same way. He likes being with you!

Here in Isaiah, as God is about to lead Israel out of her captivity to Babylon, he makes one other thing perfectly clear—he gives good things because he is good. He protects us and gives us good things because we bear his name . . . and his name is Holy. "I cannot let you call yourself by my name," he says, "and yet live like I don't exist." Our God is serious about his name. If we are going to share that name, it looks like he still gets top billing.

Action STEP Find a way to put God first in everything today. How can you give him top billing?

AUGUST 20

The Greatest Love Story Ever

May you have the power to understand . . . how wide, how long, how high, and how deep his love is. May you experience the love of Christ, though it is too great to understand fully. EPHESIANS 3:18-19

My husband and I have a love story with a quirky beginning to say the least. Jonathan was the administrative assistant at the church I attended. He decided to ask me out via a nursery duty reminder. A couple of weeks went by and he hadn't heard from me, so when we bumped into each other on the street, he asked me about it.

I told him I never signed up for nursery duty. He argued, insisting he had seen the sheet with his own eyes. "If you knew me, you'd know the last thing I would ever sign up for is nursery!" I insisted. At that moment his big round eyes revealed how little we truly knew each other.

"What's your last name?" he gasped. He had sent the card to a married woman he thought to be me.

You are already in the middle of the greatest love story ever. Theologian Søren Kierkegaard wrote a parable of God's love for humanity called "The King and the Humble Maiden." Kierkegaard was concerned with free will. God loves us for certain, but will we love him in return? It's important to God that we choose him, just as it was important to Jonathan to know I returned his affection.

In Kierkegaard's parable, a king is deeply in love with a humble maiden girl. If he simply commands her to be his wife, he will never know if she really loves him or if she is simply afraid of his power. And if he impresses her with the fullness of his royalty, he will always wonder if she merely loved his wealth. He decides to surrender his royal status to be a pauper himself so both will experience the fullest of all loves—one chosen by both parties.

God loved you first. He comes to you as the King of kings and extends his offer: that you would accept his love, evidenced by his death on the cross. You will offer him a home in your heart. And you will love him only, forsaking all others. It's the perfect love story, and it's yours in the making. I pray as Paul did that you will have the power to understand it!

 *Action* **STEP** Write down your love story: how you first met the King. SW

AUGUST 21

Can We Have a Christmas and Easter Love?

I am convinced that nothing can ever separate us from God's love. Neither death nor life, neither angels nor demons, neither our fears for today nor our worries about tomorrow—not even the powers of hell can separate us from God's love. No power in the sky above or in the earth below—indeed, nothing in all creation will ever be able to separate us from the love of God that is revealed in Christ Jesus our Lord.
ROMANS 8:38-39

I'm not sure, but it may be that Katy Perry and Russell Brand's marriage didn't make it simply because they didn't have time for each other. Documented in Perry's 2012 tour movie, you see the singer desperately trying to see Russell as much as she can during a yearlong concert tour. But it doesn't happen much. And the marriage didn't make it. It happens a lot to those Hollywood types, and I feel sorry for them. It's hard to maintain a relationship long distance.

Sometimes we try to have a love relationship like that with God. We make time for him twice a year. Easter and Christmas. Those are the two Sundays the majority of Americans will choose to pay God the tribute of a home visit. But it's not really about church attendance or observing Lent or going to a midnight service on Christmas Eve. The question is whether or not I am going to reciprocate the relationship he wants to have with me. He wants to be, in the best possible way, all up in my business. He wants my heart—to own it. He wants to be the first and last thought of my day, my baseline for health, and my one and only first love. This isn't going to fly if I want to be with him only two times a year.

I am thrilled some people make it to church a couple of times a year. I want them to taste and see the Lord is good (see Psalm 34:8). I want them to feel welcomed and leave knowing beyond the shadow of a doubt they are loved. But these are visitors. These are houseguests, and God wants to *occupy* us. Church services are important, but the issue truly isn't whether we attend or not. Attendance measures, like a thermometer, what is already cooking in the heart.

 On a scale of one to ten, where is your passion for Jesus? He's checking in with a ten for you.
DG

Don't Skimp on the Good Stuff

Don't be misled, my dear brothers and sisters. Whatever is good and perfect comes down to us from God our Father, who created all the lights in the heavens. He never changes or casts a shifting shadow.
JAMES 1:16-17

I wonder what you would do if suddenly a very wealthy benefactor showed up and offered you unlimited riches. Would you even be able to take the offer? You may feel pretty strongly that your answer is "Yes!" but a couple of years ago Marie taught us a lesson to the contrary.

It was Halloween night, and rather than go out with friends, Marie decided it was time to be the big kid and stay home to hand out candy. That night it was just Marie, two big dogs, and a ridiculously large bowl of Pixy Stix and assorted Hershey's chocolates. It was a feast of sugar any trick-or-treater would have drooled over. That's why Marie was left so incredulous by what happened.

With just a half hour of official trick-or-treat time remaining, Marie had seen only three visitors come to the door. When two boys she estimated to be around eleven years old came by, Marie employed drastic giving measures. "Take as much as you want," she told the boys. "Take the whole thing if you want. I don't think anyone else is coming tonight."

The boys' eyes got very big, their mouths dropped to the sidewalk in surprise, and they jumped up and down a few times, saying "Jackpot!" Then they approached the bowl, combed meticulously through its contents, and each selected three Pixy Stix. That's it. Three Pixy Stix. Marie said she spent the next hour alternately laughing out loud and shaking her head in amazement.

God has offered *everything* to us. The whole bowl of candy, so to speak. Take it! This is God's will for you, that you would lack nothing, but have everything, according to his glorious riches in Jesus. As you comb through that bowl of good things today, be mindful of what you will take. Others will not lack if you take too much. He won't run out, and you won't look greedy. There is no need to walk away from the throne of God's grace empty handed!

 Make a list of everything you would like to receive from God. Keep it limited to things achievable, measurable, and biblical. Examples might be joy, a giving spirit, a new friend, health, or discipline.

Serving in the Absence of Safety

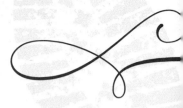

Don't be surprised at the fiery trials you are going through, as if something strange were happening to you. Instead, be very glad—for these trials make you partners with Christ in his suffering, so that you will have the wonderful joy of seeing his glory when it is revealed to all the world. 1 PETER 4:12-13

Moms are never going to cease to be moms. I recently returned from a trip to a third-world country. My mom worried the entire time I was there. Upon returning to the States, my flight was delayed, and I was alone in the New Jersey airport at one o'clock in the morning. She worried for my safety. She wanted a text the moment I was safely in my North Carolina hotel room . . . *with the door bolted*!

I don't begrudge Mom this. Our imaginations are always worse than reality. When she travels, I want texts too. But God never promised or called us to safety. This may be a hard pill for your own mom to swallow, so be patient as she mulls over your upcoming trip through the rain forests of South America!

Martyrdom is increasing worldwide. The greatest deception, however, is the belief we are safe at home. Far more people are involved in accidents only miles from home than while traveling. Most missionary travel occurs without incident, but in 2005 while training for dance ministry in South Africa, student Eddie Rector was murdered in an armed robbery. The philosopher in each of us kicks in here wondering why God would not protect a young man doing the Lord's work. Should parents oppose trips to dangerous countries? Should we seek to minister in the face of travel advisories?

Yet why should we expect to share Jesus' glory if we are not also subject to sharing his suffering? Peter goes even further than that in today's verses and says if we are blessed enough to share in suffering, we should be happy. I'm not going to pray to be persecuted or endangered anytime soon, and neither should you. But let's not be put off should we see it in our lives, particularly if we are seeking to live for Jesus. Common sense says don't walk into a clearly displayed trap. But wisdom calls us to something a little bit crazy. Are you willing to go where Jesus calls, even if safety isn't necessarily guaranteed?

 Find a few martyr stories with your search engine. Pray for the persecuted, but also that you would not refuse such a calling should it come.
SW

What to Do with Radicals

[Jesus] told [his disciples] to take nothing for their journey except a walking stick—no food, no traveler's bag, no money. He allowed them to wear sandals but not to take a change of clothes. MARK 6:8-9

Francis Chan is a pastor who has done some rather radical things. Several years ago, he and his family sold their house and moved into a smaller one so that they could have more money to give away. Then, he felt like God was calling him to leave his megachurch to start a ministry to the poorest of poor. His wife suggested they sell their home altogether so they'd be free to go wherever God wanted them to go. No strings attached. Even his fourteen-year-old daughter was on board with the radical idea.

Something in us longs to go crazy like this. I want to try the one-year "buy nothing challenge" where you go an entire year without purchasing anything other than food, books, and small gifts for others. I want to put an entire family suffering in poverty through college so that they might have a chance. You ever want to do crazy things like that? I hope so. We need more radical doers.

What Jesus sent his disciples out to do may seem extreme, but he set an example still being followed today. There is a yearly missions trip called the World Race where teams of twentysomethings sell just about everything they own, shove their few remaining belongings into a backpack, and hit eleven countries in eleven months. It's radical and intense and probably just what a lot of us need! It is guaranteed to be a trip that will wreck your life . . . in every good way possible.

God wants to ruin your life. If it were up to us, we would seek comfort and security. We would bury our heads in the sand, refusing to confront anything smacking of suffering or difficulty. That attitude has to die, or nothing radical will ever be born, which is likely why Jesus sent his disciples on such a mission. They were ecstatic when they returned. People had repented of sin, the sick were healed, the dead were raised, and these twelve men knew they could never again embrace the ordinary. God had ruined that. When we embrace radical assignments, we often see radical results! Do you have a taste for the radical?

 **Action STEP** What is the most radical way you are serving God now? Ask friends to help you think of ways to up the ante.

Are Emotions Even Okay?

We do not have a high priest who is unable to empathize with our weaknesses. HEBREWS 4:15, NIV

I marvel that God made it so that women who live together get their periods at the same time. What was he thinking? At our house, it can get crazy. Autumn does the silent treatment. Lexi gets short tempered. And I can't even talk lest I say something mean. It was at just such a time that Autumn stomped out to school for the day, slamming the door never having said good-bye. She was sulking. So, I did what any calm, cool, and in-control mother would do. I ran after her in a ball of fury and hollered, "You don't get to do that!" Autumn looked up, bewildered, and asked, "What?" "You don't get to not say good-bye!" I screamed, sounding like a demoniac. Later that night we were able to laugh that both of us had emotions that were not under control.

Most of our emotions and memory are seated in a part of our brains called the amygdala. This is connected directly to two other parts of the brain, one being the vision center. When we see certain things connected with past experiences, old emotions quickly flood our senses. This means many of our emotional responses are tied to memories. Let's say you are alone with a friend as she suffers a seizure and you have to stabilize her and find help. The next time you are alone together, your frontoparietal region may be on overload, leaving you in a hazy state of impending fear.

God gave us these emotional memories for a reason. A two-year-old cannot explain the workings of the heat elements on the stove that burned her, but she will display caution when she is near a stove in the future. Caution can be good. And who knows, maybe our bodies are remembering that our periods take a lot of energy out of us and by slowing us down, our emotions let us cope physically!

Here's what matters. Emotions themselves are not bad. Even Jesus experienced emotions like I have had. Well, he never ran after his daughter in a fit of rage, but he did know what it was like to feel the emotion that led me to that fit. And yet he didn't sin. He chose not to act on his emotions. (Wish I had done that!) Emotions are useful. Acting out on them can be sinful if we're not careful!

 *Action* **STEP** Record each major emotion you encounter today.
DG

Anxiety

Don't worry about anything; instead, pray about everything. Tell God what you need, and thank him for all he has done. Then you will experience God's peace, which exceeds anything we can understand. His peace will guard your hearts and minds as you live in Christ Jesus. PHILIPPIANS 4:6-7

Anxiety is a paralyzing emotion believed to be experienced by about forty million Americans, and women are twice as likely to suffer from an anxiety disorder than men are! That is not a Happy-I'm-A-Girl statistic! What in the world has us so worked up, ladies?

Part of the problem is that many who suffer anxiety don't even know what it is. They are like my friend Lori's four-year-old daughter. For years the family has been perplexed by Ella's clumsiness. But Ella has never complained or asked to see a doctor even though—unknown to all of them—she could not see well out of her left eye. Now, if you or I wake up tomorrow and cannot see out of our left eye, we are going to make some noise! I am going to cancel my entire day's schedule and get to the doctor. Right? But limited vision has been Ella's measure of normalcy from the start. She doesn't know any different.

How would a girl who has suffered from anxiety since birth (yes, babies can be anxious) know she feels differently from other people? Anxiety is easily misdiagnosed. It masquerades as racing heartbeats, frequent headaches, loss of sleep, fear of what others think of us, or just an unidentifiable feeling of dread. To be honest, anxiety is one of the most "normal" emotions a human being can encounter.

Will a Christian experience anxiety? This is a highly probable *yes*, but Paul gives us an answer to the racing heart, the fear, and the feelings of dread. "Pray about everything." You see, our all-powerful, generous-in-love God isn't far from each one of us. Our response to trials and fears ends up being a measure of our belief, or our trust, in God's ability and willingness to do for us exactly what he promised. Entertaining anxiety leads to sin in no time because it distracts us from trusting and being obedient to God.

 Memorize Isaiah 26:3 to battle anxiety: "You will keep in perfect peace all who trust in you, all whose thoughts are fixed on you!" Use it in prayer.

Anger

"Don't sin by letting anger control you." Don't let the sun go down while you are still angry, for anger gives a foothold to the devil.
EPHESIANS 4:26-27

Ever been so angry you have thrown something across the room? There's nothing like a little temper tantrum to relieve the pressure. Yep, it's all good; that is, until something breaks!

Counselors say anger is a "secondary" emotion, always masking a primary response. We feel threatened—anger. We have been wounded—anger. Someone embarrasses us—anger. The primary emotions would be fear, hurt, or embarrassment, masked by a reaction—anger.

Anger is never really what is "wrong" in a given situation; it is the light indicating something has gone wrong. The most productive thing to do when you are angry is indeed count to ten, using that ten-second breach to ask the question, "What is upsetting me right now? What just happened?" Chances are the answer will have something to do with being hurt, being frustrated, or feeling insecure.

The reassuring news is that God does not proclaim anger to necessarily be a bad thing. He says we should not be quick to get angry (see James 1:19), and he says he is slow to his own anger (see Exodus 34:6). The main instruction is that anger must be settled quickly—same-day maintenance. When addressed quickly, anger is pretty easy to settle. The longer anger roosts, the harder it is to dismiss. Anger burns in the hearts of all people now and then. It's only a foolish person who allows it to take root where it can blossom and grow.

 The next time you feel anger creeping in, try these things:

Write down on a note card or in a journal the answer to these questions: What am I really upset about? What just happened to make me feel this way?
Take the offense or hurt to God in prayer. Ask if any part of the problem belongs to you. Allow God (and friends and family) to comfort your hurt.
Offer peace to the one who has hurt or offended you . . . even if it's not deserved!

Chronic Sadness—
The Eeyore Complex

For everything there is a season, a time for every activity under heaven. . . .
A time to cry and a time to laugh. A time to grieve and a time to dance.
ECCLESIASTES 3:1, 4

Eeyore. He's like Debbie Downer from *Saturday Night Live* but without any of the hilarity. Winnie the Pooh's eternally negative equine buddy drags himself across the screen, colored an appropriate shade of gray, making everyone around him feel awful. "Why should Tigger think of me?" he moans. "Nobody else does." And off he goes, leaving poor Piglet, Pooh, and Rabbit feeling like the three worst friends in the world.

Chances are, you know an Eeyore. She is convinced things will never go her way, God can't see her, everyone else gets all the breaks, no one loves her. She may (are you sitting down?) be you. That's right, you may have just looked yourself right in the mirror of Pooh and seen one sad floppy-eared Eeyore looking right back at you.

There is a time to cry. Sadness is not an unhealthy emotion by any means. Jesus was sad when he looked at the people of Israel, because they were harassed and helpless. He was sad when his friend Lazarus died. He was sad in the garden of Gethsemane as he wrestled with his impending death. Sadness is a part of the human experience. Negativity or chronic sadness? Not so much.

To the Eeyores: know God sees you. Ecclesiastes 3 is not written to say there are times we choose to be sad and times we choose to be happy. It was merely written to say these things are common to *every* human life. The fact you don't get to control the circumstances or timing of this should be very freeing . . . you would not manage it well. God, however, is causing all of it to work together for good.

To Eeyore's friends: Eeyore has one thing right. This world is not our home. Be careful not to become so blinded by comfort and your enjoyments that you fail to see people who are legitimately hurting. Joy is around the corner, but hurting friends may need you to walk beside them until then. Some of your friends know a real and deep sadness. It simply calls for you to be Jesus with skin on.

 *Action* **STEP** Are you in a time of weeping or dancing right now? Ask God how you can embrace this place and time he has set specifically for you.

Doubting Thomas or Doubting (Fill-in-Your-Name)?

If any of you lacks wisdom, you should ask God, who gives generously to all without finding fault, and it will be given to you. But when you ask, you must believe and not doubt, because the one who doubts is like a wave of the sea, blown and tossed by the wind. JAMES 1:5-6, NIV

Can we doubt and still be saved? Most of our forefathers doubted at one time or another. Moses doubted God could use him to deliver Israel, for he was "slow of speech" (Exodus 4:10, NIV). Abraham doubted God could use him to establish a nation, for he was old *and* married to a barren woman. Even John the Baptist, as he sat in prison during Jesus' early ministry, wondered if he was wasting away in prison for nothing. "Are you *really* who you say you are?" he sent his disciples to inquire of Jesus (see Matthew 11:3).

It seems when considering all of the doubt suffered by the heroes of our faith, doubt must, at least in the long run, be an okay thing. But there is this one sticking point found in James. Though we are encouraged to ask for wisdom, we are also told not to doubt God will give us what we need.

It's confusing. Moses and Abraham doubted, but still made it into the Hebrews 11 Faith Hall of Fame. Zechariah was struck dumb when he didn't believe his wife Elizabeth would conceive a child in her old age. Which is it? Are we allowed to question or aren't we?

But look at God in the face of our doubt. He does not become belligerent. Where he could chastise, instead he comforts. Moses is given Aaron for a mouthpiece and probably the sweetest piece of "technology" ever—a staff that turns into a snake, parts oceans, and causes water to come out of rocks. Abraham, though he laughed, is given a covenant relationship with God.

The key is where we go with our doubt. John the Baptist did *one* key thing in setting him apart from many doubters. He did not go to friends, ask for a sign, or read the most recent Christian bestselling book. He went straight to the source. He asked Jesus, "Are you the one who is to come, or should we expect someone else?" (Matthew 11:3, NIV). When we start with stubborn certainty, it often leads to doubt. Starting with doubt and going straight to the source allows us to be led to certainty.

 **Action STEP** Give it a try! Stop. Voice your doubt. Listen. Be assured. Permission granted!

Hatred . . . er, Extreme Dislike!

Never pay back evil with more evil. Do things in such a way that everyone can see you are honorable. Do all that you can to live in peace with everyone. ROMANS 12:17-18

The Great Plague killed approximately 100 million people. It's easy for us now to understand what happened. Rats were infected, and they would be bitten by fleas, which then bit people, passing the fast-killing disease on. Terrified, people didn't know what to do. With no understanding of the evil, they responded in extremely strange ways. For example, they would carry around roses thinking that cleaner air would save them. It was also thought if infected people could cough up the disease, they'd be saved, so they were spoon-fed ashes. From these responses we got the children's song, "Ring around the rosie, pocket full of posies. Ashes! Ashes! We all fall down."

When we don't understand evil, we respond in ignorance. There are people we don't like. Sometimes it is because they are, in fact, rather evil. Mean girls. In our ignorance, when we don't like someone, we assign ourselves a place of power over her. We do unusual things. Giving her the silent treatment. Gossiping about her. Dressing up when we might run into her so we look better. Stealing her boyfriend (or attempting to). None of these things help! It is like putting roses around a person with the Great Plague.

Paul helps us in today's verse by speaking directly to the difficult situations. Someone has done you evil, he begins. Never respond with a reciprocated evil. Instead be the one who, when the story is retold, will be regarded as honorable. It may be possible to restore peace with an enemy.

And it may not. Some people are so bitter they will never allow peace to be drawn. The point is not that you actually create a good relationship, but that you do everything possible to try!

 Identify one shaky relationship in which you have been acting like a child. Choose today to become a woman in regard to how you treat that other person.

Shame

The LORD is still there in the city, and he does no wrong. Day by day he hands down justice, and he does not fail. But the wicked know no shame. ZEPHANIAH 3:5

I hereby own the following moments:

- Walking into a men's bathroom . . . in use!
- Performing a one-hour play in eight minutes flat . . . "some" dialogue got skipped.
- The old "bra comes unhooked" situation . . . while on the pitcher's mound. With an incredibly cute ump behind the plate. Try explaining that one!

Ah yes, the good old embarrassing moment. Everybody has at least one. But note that while embarrassment and shame are both regarded as negative and may seem interchangeable, they are not the same thing. Embarrassment is a perceived loss of dignity we experience when we have said or done something against a societal norm. Many people feel as if they are holding on to "normalcy" by a thread to begin with, so any behavior noticed by an outsider is mortifyingly embarrassing. Is this wrong? Not necessarily, though it can be a sign of immaturity. One sign of growing up is the ability to laugh at oneself.

Shame, on the other hand, is also a loss of dignity or honor, but not "perceived." It should be real. Shame is a good indicator for us not only that we have done something wrong, but also that we live in a society that will correct us if necessary.

Before Adam and Eve were banished from the Garden, sin had not yet entered the world. Genesis 2:25 says Adam and Eve were both running around the Garden in their birthday suits . . . and "they felt no shame." What was the first thing they did when they encountered God after their sin? They hid, telling him they were ashamed because of their nakedness.

The fact that people are not shamed by sin today is problematic. But it is no surprise to God. He has already told us this is how it will be in the last days (see 2 Timothy 3:1-5). In an ironic twist, shame turns out to be a positive emotion after all! Think about it—if the *wicked* know *no* shame, what does that say about the girl who *is* able, when necessary, to experience it?

 **Action STEP** Take time to thank God right now for the emotion of shame. Here's hoping you never have to feel it, but praise God that you can! It's a good sign.

Sneetches Are Sneetches

How can you claim to have faith in our glorious Lord Jesus Christ if you favor some people over others? JAMES 2:1

Dr. Seuss was an absolute genius with an eye for both pictures and stories to entertain the youngest of children, while simultaneously teaching those of us who are more mature a deep truth. Take the Sneetches for example.

The Sneetches live on beaches. Some have stars on their bellies and some do not. Those who have stars look down upon those who do not and exclude them from everything. Suddenly, along comes a man who (for a fee) is able to put stars on the bellies of the non-starred Sneetches. Soon, all of the Sneetches have stars.

That same enterprising man then convinces the original star-bellied Sneetches that stars are so yesterday, and he is able (for a fee) to remove their stars so they can once again establish themselves as the best Sneetches on the beaches. Throughout an entire day, every Sneetch on the beach runs through an endless process of having stars put on and then removed until they can no longer tell who is an original star-bellied Sneetch and who is an original naked-bellied Sneetch. By then it is too late—the man with the marvelous star machine is driving off with all of their money, laughing and proclaiming, "You just can't teach a Sneetch."

Oh yes, girls, we are Sneetches. Our stars are many different things, but somehow we have become convinced others can in fact be less than we are based on completely shallow criteria. Not only are people profiting off of our ignorance (for a fee they will make you believe you look like all the other Sneetches), but we are falling for the lie that those who don't look like us or who can't afford the same things are somehow less than we are.

How then do we justify regarding others as greater or lesser? Do you see the problem? It's not that differences between us do not exist. Some *are* better athletes than others. Some *can* sing, and others cannot. Some *have* the ability to study astrophysics, and others (like me) would never have that ability. Yet none of our abilities or attributes makes us greater or lesser in the Kingdom . . . it's time to kiss the Queen Bee mentality good-bye!

 Reach out to someone whom you have previously regarded as lesser (or better) than you.
SW

SEPTEMBER 2

Gossip

A troublemaker plants seeds of strife; gossip separates the best of friends. PROVERBS 16:28

Quick quiz . . . don't even think twice about your answer. Is gossip good or bad? Did you say "bad"? Sure you did. Then would you be surprised to find there are actually *defenders* of gossip out there?

> "But if you had to find a positive side to negative gossip, it can really bond people together."—A student at the University of South Florida

> "First, it's a really useful source of information, and secondly, it's the way we form and maintain alliances."—Andrew O'Keeffe, principal of Hardwired Humans

Admittedly, there is a lot of sociological truth to the statements above. When we share a salacious negative story about a common enemy, we do feel like we have made a connection. I don't like Person A. You don't like Person A. Excellent! My dislike is therefore validated! Not only that, but the more dirt we know, the more popular we are likely to become.

Does it work this way in the real world? You know, it may. But it also works this way: a gossip separates friendships. Gossip is a sin of fear at its root. People are at their most vulnerable when fearing they are alone. "Please tell me I am not alone. Please tell me I am not at the bottom of the social food chain!" These are the cries of the gossip's fearful heart, and she knows instinctively she can gain community simply by getting someone else to agree with her.

Jesus gives us new ways to overcome fears and gain community. The best way to win friends and influence people, according to God's Word? Encouragement. Keep meeting together. Encourage one another. Bear one another's burdens. The result is actually the same result gossip brings—community, but with honor and dignity rather than fracture and dissension. It is not likely a friendship will end due to over-encouragement.

 *Action* **STEP** Write a note of encouragement to someone who is often the subject of gossip. Keep it simple, honest, and real. Don't make promises, just be encouraging.

SEPTEMBER 3
Revenge

Never take revenge. Leave that to the righteous anger of God.
ROMANS 12:19

A few years ago, I hired a guy to completely reproduce my live event for tween moms and daughters. It was more money than I'd ever spent in my ministry. We set an exciting date for a debut in Nashville, and I couldn't wait to see my new event in lights. But as the day drew near, the man never seemed to gain momentum in preparation for the day. With only days until the event to which we'd already sold tickets, we had no show.

I worked with this man through the night to write a script, design multimedia graphics, pick out music, and more. The things I'd paid him thousands and thousands of dollars to do, I was doing myself. On the day of the event, he pulled some things out of an old trailer and put them on my stage in a last-ditch attempt to earn his money, but they weren't things I could use long term. We pulled the event off, but I was completely embarrassed by what had happened. I'd been robbed. In all integrity, he owed me nearly $20,000. But he was not going to pay. In fact, he was saying I'd ruined his life and reputation by not using "his show." (Translation: the old, used-up parts he'd pulled from storage and the script and graphics I had created myself.)

I felt God tell me to just walk away. No demands. No lawsuits. No unkind words. So I just let him go, trusting God would make him a man of greater integrity. Here are some things to consider when you get crossed, whether it is someone stealing clothes from you or stealing a friend from you!

Avoidance isn't always a bad thing. Jesus was confronted by a hurtful crowd, and he chose to simply walk away (see Luke 4:29-30).

It's okay to receive the hurt and acknowledge it with a friend who also loves the person who has hurt you or, at least, will not speak badly of him or her.

Speaking up for yourself is not the same as revenge. Sometimes it's enough to remind someone calmly what they are doing is wrong or unfair.

The most radical response of all might be to do something good in return for the harm done to you. Send a letter of encouragement to or buy a cup of coffee for the one who has wounded you.

 Tell that dorsal striatum of yours you are claiming your real reward—try one of the above responses to conflict today!
DG

The Art of Listening

I tell you this, you must give an account on judgment day for every idle word you speak. The words you say will either acquit you or condemn you. MATTHEW 12:36-37

What are some of your pet peeves when talking with others? Do any of these ring a bell?

- people who talk with their mouths full
- people who interrupt
- people who never laugh at your jokes
- people whose eyes dart all over the room as you are speaking

Ding ding! We've just hit mine right there. I remember trying to have a conversation one time with a friend who had just put a fake pile of vomit on the floor of a cafeteria. We hadn't seen each other for a couple of years, but he was fully focused on his puke pile instead of on our conversation! His eyes and ears were everywhere except the words I was sharing. I have since forgiven my little ADD friend.

Writer Doug Larson said wisdom is the reward you get for a lifetime of listening when you'd have preferred to talk. Maybe friendship is the reward you get for listening when you really don't feel like it, when you've heard your friend's complaints a hundred times or when no one else will. Want to play a quick game of "Truth Is"? The truth is, most people would really prefer to have their own needs stated before they prefer to listen to someone else's. And the truth is, friendships can only grow when both people are willing to do some sacrificial listening.

Jesus is speaking here of "idle" behavior—words we may not even remember speaking. Times we turned a deaf ear but thought nothing of it. Even in the moments we pay no attention, Jesus is present. We are not saved by works (see Ephesians 2:9), but that is not the heart of Jesus' message. It's not that listeners go to heaven and ignorers do not. Jesus' point here is that our words (and in turn our silences), even the idle ones, reveal the condition of our hearts. It's impossible to have a heart ready to be a friend if we have lips unwilling to silence themselves long enough to hear someone else out.

 Practice listening today. Share your opinion only when asked. Ask others a lot of questions, then shut your mouth and listen!
SW

SEPTEMBER 5

Lying

Now is the time to get rid of anger, rage, malicious behavior, slander, and dirty language. Don't lie to each other, for you have stripped off your old sinful nature and all its wicked deeds. Put on your new nature, and be renewed as you learn to know your Creator and become like him.
COLOSSIANS 3:8-10

One of my closest friends, Donna, worked with me on a big project that required both of us to put up a lot of money and time and heart. In the end, we weren't as successful as we'd hoped to be. It was hard on our friendship, but I really wanted it to be okay. So, I kept acting like our life (mine and Bob's) was fine. One night, Donna got tired of hearing that. Her life wasn't fine. She was hurt by what had happened and still felt the impact of it. It was the end of our friendship.

Until. . . .

I told her I wasn't fine. Then, I shared with her how hard it still was for us, and it was a lifeline to our relationship.

Lying within friendships often occurs as a result of one person's attempt to protect the relationship. The twisted logic goes like this: if I tell her the truth about what was said or what I did, it may hurt her feelings. If I hurt her feelings, I compromise our future friendship. It's best to protect both her feelings and our future, so I will hide the truth. We end up forgetting that lies protect *nothing*.

God identifies exclusively with truth. In him there is no darkness at all. Titus 1:2 flat out states that God *does not lie*! On the other hand, lying is exclusively associated with Satan in the Bible. Lying is his native tongue, and he is the father of all lies (see John 8:44). It would seem there is a clear line drawn in the sand between truth and the lying tongue, with not much room left for middle dwellers.

 Before you answer questions or tell stories today, run them through this litmus test: Is what I am about to say 100 percent *true*?
DG

SEPTEMBER 6
Negativity Part I

Now, dear brothers and sisters, one final thing. Fix your thoughts on what is true, and honorable, and right, and pure, and lovely, and admirable. Think about things that are excellent and worthy of praise. PHILIPPIANS 4:8

On a recent missions trip, Gina (not her real name) was the resident drama queen. She complained when her team didn't have time for a sit-down meal in the airport. Then, she verbalized her stress again and again about how nervous she was about missing the flight. When the team decided to shop for a while, she told everyone they had to go to the gate. On and on and on the negativity went, and the teens hadn't even left the United States yet. She drained the life right out of the team, and no one wanted to spend time with her.

There is so much to be positive about, though if we spend too much time focusing on the drama of our circumstances, we might miss this fact. Paul's words are refreshingly positive. As long as something, anything—whatever floats our boat—passes the litmus test of being excellent and worthy of praise when held up to the light of God's truth, Paul exhorts us to think on these things. Not focus on what could go wrong or what is wrong with something, anything.

The only time a negative comment is needed is when what you are saying passes Paul's test. And here's the test:

- Is what you are saying true?
- Is it honorable?
- Is what you are saying right?
- Are your motives pure?
- Are you acting in a lovely manner?
- Is this criticism admirable?

By asking yourself if what you're saying passes this test, you'll be more positive. For example, there's no need to complain about missing a flight until you are less than fifteen minutes away from departure and nowhere near the gate. Until then, what you are saying isn't true!

 **STEP** Which of the above questions do you need to work on the most? Spend a day thinking about all six, and select one to work on over the next week.

SEPTEMBER 7
Negativity Part II

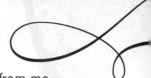

Keep putting into practice all you learned and received from me—everything you heard from me and saw me doing. Then the God of peace will be with you. PHILIPPIANS 4:9

A pastor in Kansas City, Missouri, realized he could not ask his people to imitate him without initiating a lot of negative talk. And so he set a goal for himself. He was going to go twenty-one days without saying anything negative. To track his goal, he placed a bracelet on one wrist. Any time he caught himself saying something negative, he would take the bracelet off, place it on the other wrist, and begin his count again. It proved to be a simple system . . . but not easy. He finally did make it to twenty-one days, but not before breaking three bracelets and watching nearly three months of his life pass by! Three months to reach twenty-one days of pure positivity.

Today's devotion is sort of one big Action Step. Paul concludes his lesson on thought life and unity with an exhortation to imitate him. How great would it be to have the kind of countenance and reputation where we could say to other people, "Do what I do," and not have to worry one bit about the results of that?

If you choose to take this challenge, there are a couple of things to consider. What you are undertaking is a promise to speak blessings rather than curses. Speaking a blessing over a situation is not the same thing as condoning it. To speak a blessing is to find the good (whatever is true, lovely, right, etc.) and give voice to it. You do not need to change your stance on a friend's unholy relationship, in other words, in order to stop bathing everyone around you with your negative views on it.

Speaking truth is not the same thing as speaking negatively. Again, let's look at the friend who is in an unholy relationship. To tell her privately her decisions are not right in God's eyes is not the same thing at all as speaking negativity. Your convictions can be spoken with complete grace and truth without an ounce of negativity present.

We hope you make your goal in twenty-one days flat! Even more, we hope you learn the riches of a life spent as a blessing and the joy of having the favor of all who know you!

SEPTEMBER 8

Passing the Blame

The man said, "The woman you put here with me—she gave me some fruit from the tree, and I ate it." Then the LORD God said to the woman, "What is this you have done?" The woman said, "The serpent deceived me, and I ate." GENESIS 3:12-13, NIV

I have no idea why I did this, but when I was a teenager I basically stole from my cousin. He was younger, and he'd spent days collecting empty soda cans so he could cash them in at a campground where we were staying. One night, I took those cans, cashed them in, and spent the money.

And then, I acted as if it were someone else's fault! The saddest part is that I sort of believed it. It was easier for me to believe that the friend who had been with me had talked me into it and that I had no control. I was not protecting my relationship with my cousin when I could not confess my sin.

Adam and Eve did the same thing when they found themselves in trouble. Adam blamed Eve for his disobedience, and Eve said it was the serpent's fault. No one wanted to own up, which is complete silliness since God knows each person's heart inside and out. There is something glorious about the humility of a person who does not hide behind others but will accept full responsibility for what he or she has done.

When I finally confessed to what I'd done, I was relieved. My relationship with my cousin was restored. Until then, I was absolutely miserable!

 *Action* **STEP** Next time you are in such a position, *own up to your responsibility.* Grit your teeth and refuse to pass the buck.
DG

How Do I Achieve Excellence?

They were completely amazed and said again and again, "Everything [Jesus] does is wonderful. He even makes the deaf to hear and gives speech to those who cannot speak." MARK 7:37

Imagine this: you are at a training session at your job that could potentially result in a promotion, and the boss stands before you holding six Ping-Pong balls. He explains that as he tosses the Ping-Pong balls in your direction, you are to catch them. He tosses the first, and you snag it from the air. Before you can blink, he makes the next toss . . . all five remaining balls have been gently lofted in the air at once. Panicked, you immediately try to gather all five, and in the process you drop the one you have already caught. Afterward, you meet the newly promoted assistant manager, who had also attended the training session. Wondering how she won the job so quickly, you ask her about it. "I was the only one who reached out for just one ball when all five were tossed," she says.

I hope you want to be regarded as living with excellence in this world where most people settle for average. The key to excellence is to identify your two Ping-Pong balls, so to speak. That's all you can catch. The areas in which you can excel are endless. You may be a gifted evangelist. Perhaps you have a gift for math or you would like to write. You may love cars, hair design, or dog training. Any of the above can be done to the glory of God's Kingdom. Any can be done with utmost excellence—that is, if you're willing to let the other balls drop.

It is possible to live a life of excellence, and today we want to key in on one element of such a life: simplicity. You cannot be good at everything, but everything you do can be done well. The main thing keeping us from being good at everything we do is that we don't know how to say no!

 Trim that schedule of yours! School and _____ = excellence. Keep a hobby or two, but identify the *one* area to chase and produce excellence in your life.

Benefits of a Team

All the believers devoted themselves to the apostles' teaching, and to fellowship, and to sharing in meals (including the Lord's Supper), and to prayer. A deep sense of awe came over them all, and the apostles performed many miraculous signs and wonders. And all the believers met together in one place and shared everything they had. They sold their property and possessions and shared the money with those in need. They worshiped together at the Temple each day, met in homes for the Lord's Supper, and shared their meals with great joy and generosity. ACTS 2:42-46

Did you know that when a band or army marches over a suspension bridge, they stop marching? They can walk normally over that bridge and it'll hold them just fine, but if they march in cadence pounding their feet onto the surface of the bridge at the same time, they would weaken the structure.

Together humans can do amazing feats. Miracles.

Jesus' little band of believers, if you think about it, did amazing things like this. They banded close together. They prepared and shared meals with one another and witnessed miracles like seeing dead people walk again. People sold their possessions voluntarily and put the money in a pool from which anyone who had need could draw. Every day they gained new brothers and sisters in Christ.

Being part of a team, part of something larger than you could ever accomplish on your own, is an amazing experience. You may or may not be an athlete, but there are other kinds of teams as well. The debate team or mock-trial team is a great place to hone skills in argumentation and order. A dance or cheer team could provide key female relationships and a sense of oneness. Sports provide the opportunity to plan, practice, and execute skills that require perfect timing and synchronicity.

Then there are all of the physical and psychological benefits of teams. Teamwork teaches us new skills and lets us employ them under a bit of healthy competition. Being a teammate teaches us humility—there's always someone better than us, and there's always someone not quite as accomplished. Oh, and the refs and judges—they teach us to handle persecution or unfair judgments with grace, don't they?

 **Action STEP** Are you on a team? Maybe you are on too many teams? (Remember yesterday's devo!) Get the balance right . . . and enjoy!

Self-Taught

The words of the wise are like cattle prods—painful but helpful. Their collected sayings are like a nail-studded stick with which a shepherd drives the sheep. But, my child, let me give you some further advice: Be careful, for writing books is endless, and much study wears you out. ECCLESIASTES 12:11-12

Ken Jennings is regarded as one of the greatest "trivial" minds in the world. It took six months to kick him off the quiz show *Jeopardy!* By the time he finally lost, he had earned a spot in the *Guinness World Records* for earning a record fortune on quiz shows—$2.52 million. Jennings didn't learn all of his information in school. He learned by exercising curiosity every day of his life. Jennings says those who have a thirst for knowledge live far more interesting lives. We have to agree.

Solomon mentions the pain of being goaded by wisdom. It's like exercising for the first time when you are terribly out of shape. It hurts! Exercising breaks down muscles, wounding them, so they can heal themselves and come back stronger than before. Solomon says the acquisition of wisdom is like a nail-studded board poking you in the hiney—that'll get you up and moving!

Let's see if we can get you up and moving . . . from the couch, from your bed (in the morning), or wherever you tend to go for vegetation! Try something new this week to "take your mind to the gym." Here are some of our favorites:

- Do a crossword puzzle.
- Try sudoku.
- Read a "self-help" book (nonfiction).
- Watch a TED Talk.

 Set aside a portion of each day to "take your mind to the gym." Not just for today or a week . . . as a lifelong habit.

What's Your Guilty Pleasure?

Well then, should we conclude that we Jews are better than others? No, not at all, for we have already shown that all people, whether Jews or Gentiles, are under the power of sin. As the Scriptures say, "No one is righteous—not even one." ROMANS 3:9-10

Nerd Alert! A few years back I began to notice I had a morning routine that had gotten me into a rut. I would pour myself coffee, grab the paper, and do the crossword puzzle. Why am I calling these harmless things a "bad" morning routine? It ate up most of every morning—I was finding time to meet with Jesus perhaps only one day a week. For that reason, my fun neutral activity had become a bad habit.

What do you stumble to first thing in the morning? Facebook? Your cell phone and text messages? Your three-mile run or diet supplements? Anything you reach for before or in place of your time with God is going to be a stumbling block for spiritual growth. The writer of Proverbs 25 said, "It's not good to eat too much honey" (verse 27)—it tastes good as the first few tablespoons go down, but eventually the body says, "No more!" in a very unpleasant way. So who provides the moderation for your habits? No one can do it but you, so here are some practical suggestions:

- Use your "guilty pleasures" as a reward for completing other tasks.
- Commit your habits and hobbies to God in prayer.
- Make time in God's Word your first priority.
- Ask, "Is this bringing me closer or taking me further away from God?"

Large or small, anything we regularly turn to for a pleasure rush masks our need for the sustenance that can be found in Christ alone.

 Subject your number one guilty pleasure to the four suggestions above for a day.

BONUS ACTION STEP: "Friend" me (Suzy) on Facebook today. It's my birthday!
SW

School Pride: Good;
Self-Pride: Bad

If you think you are too important to help someone, you are only fooling yourself. You are not that important. Pay careful attention to your own work, for then you will get the satisfaction of a job well done, and you won't need to compare yourself to anyone else. GALATIANS 6:3-4

The first day runner Ryan Brown appeared on the front page of the local paper was because he was favored to win a couple of races at district. The next day, there was Ryan again. This time he scored the front page because not only had he won at district but he had won both races. The 3,200 is his best event, but he also won the 1,600. Ryan was planning on running both races at state, but only the top two qualifiers are taken in each event. His teammate finished third in the 3,200 so *of course* Ryan chose to give up his best race so both he and his teammate could run in the state meet.

Of course? No, not "of course." Your school, Hollywood, the music industry, professional sports, my church . . . we can all be so full of pride that it isn't funny, so Paul steps in and gives a grave warning. You are not and I am not all we think we are! We are supposed to learn to look at ourselves with "sober judgment" (Romans 12:3, NIV). If at any time we compare ourselves to others, we can't have good judgment. Each person, God says, will be judged as an individual, not on any kind of a scale.

Ryan is better at both of those races than any of his teammates, but he's not godlike—and he knows it. But there is a kind of pride Ryan has, allowing him to shine like a superstar. He wants to see another guy get the goods, and not just himself. He chose love over glory. (School pride, not self-pride.) The Bible actually gives us permission to boast over this kind of victory—look what the cross of Christ has done in my life! But we don't think Ryan will boast. He'll probably just keep cheering on his buddies.

 *Action* **STEP** Where has pride seeped into your life? See if you can find a way to step aside or down this week so someone else can "run."

Busybody
or Busy Body?

Some of you are living idle lives, refusing to work and meddling in other people's business. We command such people and urge them in the name of the Lord Jesus Christ to settle down and work to earn their own living. 2 THESSALONIANS 3:11-12

Lexi, my daughter, couldn't seem to get a job the summer before she left for college. She wanted so badly to work at Rita's (for the free Italian ice treats). But they didn't want her. She tried a few other places, too, but no one wanted to train a girl who was leaving in just a few months. As a last-ditch effort, she went to the local convenience store and got the job no one else wanted. Ever. The 5 a.m. coffee-girl shift! Each morning she woke up before the crack of dawn to go warm up everyone's caffeine. There were days when she was discouraged with the pay. (It was low.) And then her hours were cut back. (Her pay was even lower.) One morning she whimpered, "I'm getting out of bed in the dark to make twenty-four dollars today."

But, at the end of that summer, she had the most amazing sense of accomplishment. (And enough money to go buy an Italian ice at Rita's!)

Working is one way we bring honor to the Lord. Work does not have to be defined in traditional terms such as wake up, drive to a place of employment, and receive a paycheck at the end of the week. If you are blessed enough to know you have a future in athletics or the arts, your work may be to practice, practice, practice. There is great value in volunteering and short-term missions. The average household takes more time to run and manage than your parents, your grandparents, or that sweet older neighbor lady likely have available. Helping them is employment, whether it's compensated or not.

Maybe your parents are ready to let you take on the commitment of a summer job, or even part-time work during the school year. Good for them, and good for you! And I'm sure you know what the opposite of employment looks like. It's the butt on the couch, the brain dead from too much TV or Facebook; it's that feeling of boredom and ingratitude. It's the constant whine of, "I don't have a life. . . ." And it's completely within your reach to make that malady go away!

 **STEP** If you were to allow yourself only one hour of TV or Internet usage per night, how would you use the rest of your time? Write out your list of options. DG

SEPTEMBER 15

Balancing the Secular and the Divine

When I am with those who are weak, I share their weakness, for I want to bring the weak to Christ. Yes, I try to find common ground with everyone, doing everything I can to save some. 1 CORINTHIANS 9:22

I had a plane actually reroute midflight on the way to Grand Rapids, Michigan. Stuck in Indianapolis, Indiana, at one o'clock in the morning was not where I wanted to be. There were plenty of other customers who wanted to get to our final destination, so two college-aged girls and I decided to go together to rent a car. I took the wheel, and the girl talk began. It included not too little profanity, and I even got to listen in as the two girls shared alcoholic drink recipes. One of them shared how she'd found her live-in boyfriend with a girl in bed, so she bleached the carpet in his apartment and slashed his tires.

Then they asked why I was going to Grand Rapids. I said it as tenderly as I could: "I'm going to record a television interview on a book that I wrote." They prodded until they understood that it was a Christian book on sexual purity, and then their faces turned white. One of them apologized. I told her there was no need. They could just be themselves.

And they were. It ended up that one of them spent the night in my hotel because she wasn't old enough to rent a room herself. When I drove her to her final destination the next day, she said she'd never been near a Christian who accepted her as she was. She said she might rethink faith.

Paul was sent as an apostle to the Gentiles. As such, he was rubbing shoulders constantly with nations steeped in sinful traditions. One of the key things to see in Paul's life is that while he was adept in appealing to popular culture, he never confused the issue of rights. His own rights he would lay down. He did this rather than judge so that his kindness might lead people to repentance. Conversation will always trump condemnation. He would do life, like they did life, and he would honor God.

 **Action STEP** Think about conversations you've had with nonbelievers. Do you think you acted like Paul? Why or why not? Be sure that those who do not know Jesus would feel comfortable being with you . . . then you might get the opportunity to introduce them to Christ!
DG

SEPTEMBER 16
Teen 'Rents

[Jesus said,] "Let the children come to me. Don't stop them! For the Kingdom of God belongs to those who are like these children. I tell you the truth, anyone who doesn't receive the Kingdom of God like a child will never enter it." Then he took the children in his arms and placed his hands on their heads and blessed them. MARK 10:14-16

Cassie didn't plan to get pregnant, but she did. And when she did, she chose the right thing: to give life to her precious Chad. She was only eighteen. Sadly, she did not get loved on for this good choice at one place that she should have: her church. Her mom, a long-standing member of the congregation, was told it might be better if she left. You can imagine that Cassie didn't feel very safe at church.

We just want to say that there are a lot of worse things than getting pregnant. Getting cancer from sexual activity is worse (and common since HPV causes cervical cancer). Having an abortion is worse (and easier in some ways since no one really sees it).

Having a baby is actually courageous. And when we met Cassie backstage at one of our teen Pure Freedom events, we told her so. Our arms welcomed her back into fellowship with the church. But our arms only go so far. Yours could do well to welcome a teen mom into the church or back in if she has felt shunned.

Jesus loves children. Or as Colton Burpo, whose story is found in *Heaven Is for Real* and *Heaven Is for Real for Kids*, said after his experience in heaven during a brief physical death on earth, "Jesus really, really loves children." When a little one comes to God, he or she comes as one who is a blank slate. The Artist is free to draw on the child's heart whatever he wishes. There is not already the graffiti of a million regrets and opinions written there. Teen pregnancy isn't the most ideal way to become a parent, but it is a brave choice. But let that child come into the world, into family, and unto Jesus.

 *Action* **STEP** Do something to help a teen mom today. It's a lonely place to be.

Leadership 101

All glory to God, who is able, through his mighty power at work within us, to accomplish infinitely more than we might ask or think. EPHESIANS 3:20

One high school in New York City has taken the call to leadership completely to heart, naming the school Leadership and Public Service High School. Each student is paired with a Syracuse University graduate living and working in the area, and together the pair navigate high school curriculum, college selection, community involvement, and what it means to forge relationships. In other words, each student is given a role model and the chance to be trained in leadership in a real-world setting.

There is a lot of well-deserved hype out there for student-based leadership. The idea of youth leading the way is nothing new. Most people who count themselves as disciples of Jesus make a decision to follow him before the age of thirty. Most historically significant revivals have begun among people in their twenties and younger.

But what happens when you are told that you are expected to be a leader . . . and it feels too soon? We see this happen every year to girls at our Christian high school. These girls ooze confidence. They are wide eyed, full of life, and easily approachable. They are go-getters and good salespeople. As the saying goes, they could probably sell ice to an Eskimo! Yet when challenged by the mantle of leadership, it becomes clear they are burdened by the weight of it all.

Are you a leader? To some degree as a follower of Jesus the answer must be *yes.* At the very least you are called to live a godly life inspiring others to praise God (see 1 Peter 2:12). Have you been equipped to be a leader? The answer to that is also *yes*—God is the well from which you and I draw our strength and abilities; yet all of the saints working around the clock together could never cause God's well to run dry. He can do even more than you imagine. Test his power—the same power raised Jesus from the dead, and his gifts are *always* accompanied by power!

 Pray about one area at school where you can pursue stepping up in leadership. But don't stop there. Sign up. Step up. Seek out a mentor.

Sugar and Spice

Since God chose you to be the holy people he loves, you must clothe yourselves with tenderhearted mercy, kindness, humility, gentleness, and patience. Make allowance for each other's faults, and forgive anyone who offends you. Remember, the Lord forgave you, so you must forgive others. COLOSSIANS 3:12-13

My daughter and I were watching an episode of *Celebrity Apprentice,* and it didn't take long for me to figure one thing out—I would *not* want to be on the girls' team. Here I am comfortably into my adult years, and I'm thinking I would still rather hang out with the guys! What's up with that? In this case the answer was simple. The girls were mean.

The problem we run into is this mean-spirited thing sells when it comes to television and movies. Writers have even become famous for nothing more than posting snarky blogs about trouble-filled celebrity lives. Maybe this is why meanness garners popularity for high school girls. It leaves a girl like you and me wondering if we are somehow missing the boat by choosing to walk on God's side. Thank God it's still fair to say nice girls finish first. Women in positions of real influence in our society rarely display consistent tendencies of snide or ill-willed behavior.

Morality is not defined so much by what we do as it is by who we are becoming. The apostle Paul focuses on our transition out of darkness (who we used to be before Christ) and into light. If you are a follower of Jesus, you must begin to look like him. The invisible wrestling match for power in the halls of your high school is one you are called to forgo. If being mean and wielding power earns popularity, then kiss that social status good-bye. Your call is to be full of compassion and tenderness toward others, particularly toward those who cannot stand up for themselves.

 **Action STEP** Run your words and attitudes toward others through a filter today. Before speaking, ask this question: Will this tear someone down? If so, zip it!
SW

SEPTEMBER 19

Cheating

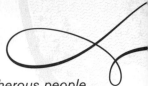

Honesty guides good people; dishonesty destroys treacherous people.
PROVERBS 11:3

It seems we have a crisis of ethics here in America. ABC's *Primetime* ran a story on cheating in schools. Turns out three out of every four high school students (75 percent) reported cheating at least once per year in 2002. By 2012 the numbers had risen to 85 percent. If those numbers aren't chilling enough, these statements by students should put the icing on the cake:

> "The real world is terrible. People will take other people's materials and pass it on as theirs. I'm numb to it already. I'll cheat to get by." —Joe, student at a top college in the Northeast

> "Everything is about the grade that you got in the class. Nobody looks at how you got it."—Business student subsequently hired by a top US investment firm

Now for the partially good news: we who know God are far less likely to jump on the cheating bandwagon. Sure, it may earn us better grades. But the fear of a good and holy God allows us to hear just enough of the warning siren to stop us in our tracks sometimes, which is a good thing.

Why is it only "partially good news"? According to a study done by a research group at the University of Oregon, belief in God is not what stops us from cheating. What keeps us from cheating, the study found, is our *perception* of God. If we view God as a fierce punisher of wrong deeds, the likelihood of cheating is drastically reduced. However, if we view God as a loving and forgiving God . . . we are more likely to cheat.

Hmmm. We believe God is *indeed* loving and compassionate, forgiving to a thousand generations, yet we also believe cheating is outright rebellion. Girls, we need a paradigm shift in our thinking! It comes down to *who* we are. Notice the proverb says we are guided by honesty itself, a trait of God's we have taken on as our own. What if *who I am becoming* could actually be greater than the desire to sin?

 **Action STEP** What would be enough to keep *you* from cheating? Include some friends in this discussion.

SEPTEMBER 20

Epidemic

"Physical training is good, but training for godliness is much better, promising benefits in this life and in the life to come." This is a trustworthy saying, and everyone should accept it. 1 TIMOTHY 4:8-9

Weight a minute. First Lady Michelle Obama developed an initiative to use government programs to curb obesity. Fifty-seven percent of Americans supported her idea. The group most likely to reject her plan? Evangelical Christians. Meanwhile, Northwestern University School of Medicine released a study showing those who frequent "religious activities" are 50 percent more likely to be obese by middle age. Guess we need to take a look at our hearts and our waistlines.

Not long ago I spent some time with German students in Berlin. When I asked them their perception of Americans, they had two words for me: rich and fat. Though their answer could hardly be called scientific, I can see how they arrived at their conclusion. Germans walk or bike whenever possible, and I was hard pressed to find Germans I would call obese. Americans are weightier, which brings a slew of health problems to the forefront. Heart disease, diabetes, and even certain types of cancer are weight related. If the church is at risk due to our weight, perhaps we should sit up (or at least do a sit-up) and take notice.

Several years ago the Southern Baptist Convention responded to a study from Purdue University, showing results similar to the Northwestern study. Both groups had found the SBC at the axis of evangelical obesity. The convention chose to come clean. We need to change, they wrote in a 2007 report, acknowledging that attacking other sins while ignoring their own gluttony is shortsighted and dishonest.

I love to work out and play sports. Athletic prowess or pride in our beautiful physiques, however, would fall under the category of pride if these were our motives for being "in shape," and pride is a sin. It's clear our bodies need to be sharp for one superior motive alone—when we are at our physical best, we have the strength to train for godliness, a condition of utmost worth and one that instead of pointing people to beautiful physiques, points them to the beauty of our Savior and King.

 *Action* **STEP** Do you have elements of both physical and spiritual training in your daily routine? Adjust your schedule to be certain you can fit both in.
SW

College Degree or High School Diploma?

Intelligent people are always ready to learn. Their ears are open for knowledge. PROVERBS 18:15

I had a Korean daughter for a while. I first met Christy when she was a sophomore and in my English class. She had no accent, so it took me a while to figure out that she was not an American. Before long, however, I came to realize her lack of accent was due to a good ear. On paper I often caught her employing hilarious misuses of American colloquialisms. I can't repeat some of her honest mistakes in polite company; you'll just have to trust me.

Midway through Christy's junior year, her parents returned to Korea, bravely trusting me and my family with their girl! For a year and a half I watched an amazing dance play out before my eyes. Tradition is extremely important to Korean families. Christy was expected to attend a celebrated university, preferably an Ivy League one. I am a night owl, but when I would go to bed at two o'clock in the morning *and* stumble back through the hallway at seven o'clock in the morning, Christy's light would be burning bright with SAT preparations.

Christy likes school, but what she loves is music and fashion. She is an accomplished pianist and violinist. She created a fashion show for her senior project reminiscent of *Project Runway*. Thus the dance: Christy wanted to go to college, but to study in her passions. Her parents loved her and wanted her to be happy, but tradition and expectations were breathing down their necks. Christy said that if she didn't study something "respectable," go to a time-honored school, and marry a Korean boy, her grandfather would disown her.

The key is for Christy to remain a lifelong learner. If she is a fashion designer one day, I hope she is well read. If she writes music, I hope she is a reader. If she is a foreign diplomat, I hope her nose is often found in a book. Leaders are readers. Do I think everyone is meant to go to college? No, though I think it's a good place to be! What is of greatest value needs no degree. Read. Crack the books. We're talking the building of brain cells here!

 **STEP** Commit to reading a half hour or more every day. Make it a life habit!
SW

SEPTEMBER 22

Calling 911 for Our Nation's Schools

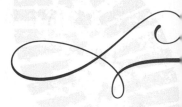

The fear of the LORD is the beginning of knowledge; fools despise wisdom and instruction. PROVERBS 1:5-7, ESV

We have a problem to discuss. Our nation's schools are in absolute crisis. Every president in the past one hundred years has promised to make education a priority. As proficiency scores for students continue to hang in the balance, the promises that are made seem more frantic and fantastical as the years go by. Nothing proposed has worked as of yet.

Ironically, laws once put in place to make our education system better or more efficient are now the very roadblocks to success. One New York superintendent secretly videotaped teachers in his failing district and found a percentage of *them* to be failing. He fired the poor performers only to find he had to rehire them with back pay due to something called tenure, which is awarded to teachers after a certain amount of service in the classroom and guarantees employment for life (barring illegal activity). Tenure was designed to protect teachers from willy-nilly firings; it's unlikely anyone ever imagined it would protect a teacher who basically refuses to work.

A great teacher who is changing lives right and left, working twice as hard as her peers, doing what she was born to do . . . will make the same salary as the tenured teacher reading a *People* magazine while her students are practicing their Facebook stalking techniques. Students pay the price. In California, though the top one-third of high school students earn college placement, 50 percent of these freshmen take remedial classes before they are ready to do college work.

No matter what level of education your school provides for you, here is the true crux of being mad-intelligent: to fear the Lord. God allows all people to grow in knowledge. Only those who love his precepts are privileged with wisdom. People in low-income areas would do anything to get their children into exclusive, high-performing schools. Here we have God promising a full scholarship in wisdom . . . ours for the taking. The wise will run to it. The fool will despise it. Which are we?

 *Action* **STEP** No more complaints about school! What a gift it is to grow wise! Eat up every bit of knowledge you can get at school, and wisdom from God's Word, too.

The Many Faces of Poverty

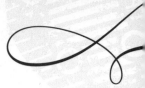

Share your food with the hungry, and give shelter to the homeless. Give clothes to those who need them, and do not hide from relatives who need your help. ISAIAH 58:7

I distinctly remember a horrifying experience from years ago. Hanging out in a Chuck E. Cheese's kind of place, I was watching little children play. As I reached over to hand tokens to children that I knew, a tiny little dirt-crusted fist reached out and touched mine. I'm sad to say that I withdrew. The smell. The sight. It was all so shockingly out of place in this rich kids' playland. I'd been to poor neighborhoods to minister to kids and expected to see them there, but this was so out of place. And it revealed my heart. It was ugly.

It may be accurate to say one of the main arenas in which our attitude in the church has grown away from God's own heart is poverty. God's heart is for the poor. Our hearts, if we are honest, are for comfort, safety, and assurance.

God's heart is for the downtrodden. He has revealed over and over again in Scripture his plan to rise up in their defense, a defense much needed by people hammered by unfortunate circumstances, disability woes, or prior bad planning. The need for assistance knows no gender, no race, nor a level of education. The one thing honest recipients of public aid have in common is the desire to be understood, and they want just enough help to get back in the game.

"I was hungry and you gave me something to eat" (Matthew 25:35, NIV). This mandate was originally given to the church to be certain no human being would suffer. Isaiah's command was for Israel to give food out of their cooking kettles, rather than the scraps from their plates. The instruction to give lodging was to take the outcast into one's own home, not to provide a tent on the back of one's property. When the church will not or cannot provide, the government is left to take up the job. Perhaps if we could stave off our fear of the poor, the church could take back the job rightfully hers to do.

 **STEP** Confess before God any prejudices you have regarding poverty.

DG

SEPTEMBER 24

You've Gotta See This

Taste and see that the LORD is good. Oh, the joys of those who take refuge in him! Fear the LORD, you his godly people, for those who fear him will have all they need. Even strong young lions sometimes go hungry, but those who trust in the LORD will lack no good thing.
PSALM 34:8-10

On a recent trip to Haiti I saw people who were hungry . . . yet who also trust in Jesus. So what's the deal with this verse?

It's interesting to note David didn't write this psalm from the marbled halls of his palace. He was in exile, wanted by madman King Saul. He had been captured by the Philistines and was playing the part of a mentally ill man in order to escape imprisonment. Isn't it impressive when a man or woman in dire straits praises God for his lavish provision? It's as though the person in distress is able to see with his or her heart what we aren't able to see with our eyes.

Visiting a family in Haiti, we noticed a quote painted beautifully across the top of the typical village home—two rooms, outdoor kitchen and outhouse, no electricity, two to three people per bed, very sparse belongings. The quote stated surely Jesus could see this family, cares for them, and soon their day would come. As Golette, who lives there, spoke about the phrase, her eyes danced. She has no doubt her God can see her and that he loves her deeply.

But her family hadn't eaten for three days. How is it possible they will "lack no good thing" if they aren't even eating? Her girls will never know what it is to go "back to school" shopping or to be asked where they would like to eat on their birthday. They will never have reason to complain, "Mom! Tell Rose Carmel to get out of my room!" How do they lack no good thing? Is it possible we have a messed-up view of what a "good thing" looks like? Or . . . what if *we* have been given so *many* good things that we might supply good things to the poor out of our abundance?

These questions about our priorities and responsibilities to the poor cannot properly be answered from the comfort of our 2,500-square-foot homes. The only way we will get a proper view of our wealth and the impoverishment of so many . . . is if we go get a look at things for ourselves.

 *Action* **STEP**   Begin praying for an opportunity to see the third world with your own eyes.
SW

Gendercide

There is no longer Jew or Gentile, slave or free, male and female. For you are all one in Christ Jesus. GALATIANS 3:28

"You've come a long way, baby." That's an old marketing campaign for Virginia Slims cigarettes, created specifically to target young professional women. We have come a long way . . . if you are talking about American women. Women in other countries, particularly in the East, are still not so fortunate. In fact, many countries are flat out committing gendercide—the systematic elimination of the members of one sex. Over fifty thousand little girls are aborted in India *every month*. And we are not talking about sophisticated drug-induced abortions such as are common in the United States. In India, newborn baby girls are often thrown into rivers or left to die in garbage dumps.

Why single out the girls? Girls hit the family in the pocketbook. When a girl is married in India, her parents pay a dowry to the young man's family for the wedding. Giving birth to a boy, on the other hand, means the family will gain wealth. Many people in India encourage pregnant family members to abort for purposes of population control. While India is less than half the size of the United States in square mileage, its population is three times that of the United States. India is one of the poorest nations on earth, faced with over-population, illiteracy, vast unemployment, virtually no natural resources, and a clean-water crisis.

This is not government-forced birth control as it is in China. This is a desperate people, often with low levels of education and even less hope, trying to right something much bigger than themselves that has gone terribly wrong. Until all of India ceases to think of women as a burden, it is unlikely this can be successfully done.

The light of Christ must be brought to places like India hand in hand with the knowledge that God has removed every barrier for those who seek him. There is one God. One Savior. One Kingdom. Praise be to God, Jesus made a way for all mankind to approach him from an equal vantage point and to enjoy him, as one, forever.

 **STEP** | Pray for the women of India. Pray for an end to gendercide. Pray for the nation's leadership. Pray Indian women would come to know their value.

We Are the Same

Jew and Gentile are the same in this respect. They have the same Lord, who gives generously to all who call on him. For "Everyone who calls on the name of the LORD will be saved." ROMANS 10:12-13

Be honest: Have you ever said something negative about someone's race? Perhaps you were mad at someone's behavior and they just happened to be of a different race than you. Or have you been around friends telling seemingly harmless jokes about a racial group? It might seem harmless, but stereotypes about race can lead us to think one group is less than another—just because of the color of skin!

We pray, "Your Kingdom come, your will be done, on earth as it is in heaven" (Matthew 6:10, NIV), but race on earth is *not* as it is in heaven. The Bible doesn't address a situation between races as we know them today, but it does talk of Jews and Gentiles. Take black and white race relations in America at its most volatile period and there you have the Jews and Gentiles of Jesus' time. What a radical teaching Paul introduces: they—Jews and Gentiles, black people and white people and people of any other race—are the same! God loves them with an equal dispensation of grace. This is the Kingdom of God. How in the world do we ever get earth to see race through heaven's eyes? It doesn't do any good to deny reality—the race issue remains broken in this fallen world. But it's been said the world changes one person at a time.

Action STEP Ask God's forgiveness for any prejudice you have harbored in your heart. Can you love people on earth as they are loved in heaven?

Number One Killer

Are any of you sick? You should call for the elders of the church to come and pray over you, anointing you with oil in the name of the Lord. Such a prayer offered in faith will heal the sick, and the Lord will make you well. And if you have committed any sins, you will be forgiven. JAMES 5:14-15

Odds say your life has been impacted by what is now the number one killer in the world. It used to be heart disease, but cancer has waged a valiant war for first place, and all signs point to a photo finish if the race were to end today. I lost my dad to cancer not long ago. My grandma died of the same cancer four months before him. How is it possible statistics are now saying four out of every ten persons will be diagnosed with cancer in their lifetime?

And what about prayer? Is James saying faith and prayer will yield a 100 percent rate of cure? To suggest so would be an insult to friends of mine who just lost a wife, a mom, and a sister. I was part of those fervent prayers going up on behalf of my dad and my grandma. God said no. Two years ago, our church prayed and fasted for a girl with cancer. God said yes. In our humanity we naturally look for a formula—the right combination of words to bring before God in prayer so he'll say yes. The problem is that this leaves the responsibility in our hands, rather than recalling that he is God in heaven. His ways are not our ways. Why bother praying then? One big reason is because prayer reminds us that God is in control . . . and that can bring peace.

We may not always know God's reasons for certain things, but we do know of his love for us. Life lost in this world is not equivalent to being unloved. When we are right with God, neither death nor life is a threat.

 **Action STEP** Find out if the elders in your church have a ministry of praying for the sick. Do you have prayer concerns to submit on behalf of yourself, a friend, or a neighbor? SW

Why Johnny Can't Read

"But a beautiful cedar palace does not make a great king! Your father, Josiah, also had plenty to eat and drink. But he was just and right in all his dealings. That is why God blessed him. He gave justice and help to the poor and needy, and everything went well for him. Isn't that what it means to know me?" says the LORD. JEREMIAH 22:15-16

When bestselling author Rudolf Flesch (*The Art of Plain Talk*) offered to give a friend's twelve-year-old son some "remedial reading," Flesch discovered that the boy was not slow or maladjusted; he had merely been "exposed to an ordinary American school." Author Flesch decided to investigate how reading is taught in the United States. . . . He published his findings in a 222-page book, *Why Johnny Can't Read—and What You Can Do About It . . .*, that will shock many a US parent.

The above quote is from a 1955 book review. It's a book title still well known today, possibly because illiteracy remains a massive problem. Only 15 percent of Americans are considered fully literate, operating at the level of someone with a college degree. The majority of Americans operate at an eighth grade literacy capacity, and just over 20 percent remain fully illiterate. About 40 percent of illiterate Americans live in poverty.

The problems associated with literacy are many, affecting not only the illiterate, but the entire population. Somewhere around 70 percent of the people imprisoned in the United States are functionally illiterate. The inability to read means an inability to find and maintain a job. Many turn to crime in order to meet needs. Think of all the things we have to read to survive for a day—it's not just books people have lost. They can't read street signs, labels on food, menus, warning labels, ballots, welfare forms, or job applications. The inability to read is crippling.

Is it possible this could be an area where God would call us, like Josiah, to deliver justice to the poor and needy? The true king is not the one who has the biggest cedar palace. True kingship is not about conquering and building wealth—it is about setting captives free, proclaiming the day of justice, and delivering the oppressed (see Luke 4:18-19). This is what it means, after all, to know the Lord.

 *Action* **STEP** Comb through your home library and deliver your books to an organization that will get them into eager hands.

SEPTEMBER 29

When Children Are Prey

[Jesus said,] "But if you cause one of these little ones who trusts in me to fall into sin, it would be better for you to be thrown into the sea with a large millstone hung around your neck." MARK 9:42

One of the happiest endings to an American tragedy was the rescue of Elizabeth Smart. She was taken from her home when she was only fourteen years old and forced to live eighteen miles away from her home with a married husband and wife. Happily, she was one of the blessed ones who was rescued and returned home, but it was a few years later. Much had been lost.

Most abuse today is from people known to the victims. Imagine knowing that something is wrong, that it felt wrong, and that the only way to make it stop might be telling another adult . . . but feeling a strange loyalty to the one who hurt you.

Another aspect of this epidemic of child sexual abuse is that victims are typically not singular, and there is often at least one outside adult who knows or is suspicious of the abuse. Abusers in recent years have received a protection program we have failed to offer the victims. It's the mask—our family, our school, our church must appear to be perfect at all costs. Woe to those who agree to wear such a mask, for the cost will not only be to that little child, but also to their own soul.

ACTION STEP A: If you have been the victim of childhood sexual abuse and have still not told anyone, find a safe adult to confide in. The repercussions of remaining silent are too great. Have you noticed you avoid touch, eye contact, or deeper relationships? Maybe you have turned your fears and negative feelings inward and no longer like the person you see in the mirror. That girl in the mirror is precious. She deserves to be believed and loved. Let someone begin walking you through that process.

ACTION STEP B: One day you may become privy to or suspicious of child sexual abuse. Remember that silence is not an option, and there is no reputation so precious that it deserves to be protected over the well-being of a child.

Wars and Rumors of Wars

[Jesus said,] "Don't let anyone mislead you, for many will come in my name, claiming, 'I am the Messiah,' and saying, 'The time has come!' But don't believe them. And when you hear of wars and insurrections, don't panic. Yes, these things must take place first, but the end won't follow immediately." LUKE 21:8-9

I remember exactly where I was when I heard the United States had declared war for the first time in my lifetime. Never before had I been faced with the possibility of friends and family being called to the front in a war zone. I was driving up "the hill" in Lawrenceburg, Indiana. I pulled my car off to the side of the road and cried.

Is war okay? It depends what the word *okay* means. Is it good? No. Is it necessary? Sometimes. Have there been unjust wars? Entirely. Wars have been happening since humankind got booted from the Garden. War brings bloodshed, and innocent people lose their lives. The problem is, we often don't know the whole truth about why wars have been declared. In a sense, simply having "the vote" does not give citizens any real power. I have not been consulted once in my lifetime regarding wars that have impacted my family, the economy, and my kids' futures.

What I do know is that wars are bound to come and we cannot stop them. The only true remedy for unrest was provided by Jesus on the cross, and that's the other thing I know—sometimes shed blood paves the way for God and for good. The United States became free from tyranny only by the shedding of blood. Slavery was ended only by the shedding of blood. The genocide of Jews in Europe was put to an end only after blood was shed. And back to the cross . . . without the shedding of blood there is no forgiveness of sins.

 Surrender your fear to God. He's got the whole world, wars and all, in his hands.
SW

OCTOBER 1
Abortion's National Toll

Children are a gift from the LORD; they are a reward from him.
PSALM 127:3

Kim couldn't believe she was pregnant. She was only seventeen, and she had her whole life ahead of her. There was no way she could tell her parents. So she made an appointment at an abortion clinic and had the baby killed.

No one told her that her baby wasn't the only one who'd be hurt. For years Kim struggled with depression and emotional grief, never realizing it had anything to do with what happened in that abortion clinic. Then, one day she confessed the abortion to the Lord. What grief came out of her then, but it was also the turning point. She began a series of counseling and prayer therapies, and today she is one of the happiest and funniest women you'd ever meet . . . and she has two beautiful daughters.

What if one of every five babies conceived was aborted? Actually, that's not a hypothetical question. In 2005, one of every five pregnancies in America ended with abortion. A current study from New York says 41 percent of New York City pregnancies are ending with abortion. Though no chapter and verse are dedicated specifically to the practice of abortion in God's Word, it is helpful to be able to answer the two most common pro-choice arguments biblically.

Argument #1: It is a woman's body, and therefore it is a woman's choice. Read 1 Corinthians 6:19-20 and write the main idea here:

Jesus paid the price, the Bible says, one time and for everyone. Though many do not recognize this truth, we belong to God. We are his, and he made us.

Argument #2: It's better for the child to never be born than to be unwanted. Read Jeremiah 29:10-14 and write the main idea here:

Israel was in exile when God spoke these words to her—homeless, enslaved, and utterly destitute! Was she better off dead? God said he still had plans for her; plans to prosper her and to bless her.

 Buy a plastic baby bottle and take some time over the next few months to fill it with quarters, dimes, and nickels. Once it's full, take the bottle to your local crisis pregnancy center as a donation.

Happy Twelfth Birthday

[Jesus said,] "I tell you, her sins—and they are many—have been forgiven, so she has shown me much love. But a person who is forgiven little shows only little love." LUKE 7:47

Somewhere in India a little girl is turning twelve. She has been raised in a village where her twelfth birthday is special. It is the day she gets to choose if she will follow after the footsteps of her ancestors to be an "entertainer." The girls who've gone before her return from the big city where they are "entertaining" and have cell phones and designer clothes and expensive hairstyles. Who wouldn't want that?

But it is an evil too great to understand.

You see, this village is the tribe once brought before kings in India to jest, dance, and play. But when the palaces and kingdoms slowly disappeared, these people felt they only had one form of "entertainment" to offer. Now they breed daughters to sell as prostitutes.

I know this because my daughter Lexi raised funds and wrote a character-building curriculum in an effort to stop the travesty as a part of her high school senior project. I can picture the faces of the girls Lexi and I prayed for whose twelfth birthdays arrive this year.

It's so easy to view those in prostitution as sinful people. The Pharisee in Luke 7 did. When a sinful woman came into the room where Jesus was dining and washed his feet with her tears, the prideful Pharisee was shocked! He could not understand why Jesus would let this woman touch him.

Jesus knew who she was. And perhaps Jesus also knew that so often what leads a woman to the vile act of selling herself is a journey making her more of a victim than an all-out sinner. He was quick to tell the Pharisee that this was a woman who had a great capacity to love. He also said the Pharisee's own capacity to love was very small.

We cannot endorse, empower, or use the services of the sex and porn industries. But we can be in contact with the victims of them through prayer-filled, authority-driven ministries existing to reach out and collect their tears.

 *Action* **STEP** The next time you drive by an adult bookstore, take a moment to pray for the women who are involved in inappropriate activities in there. Ask God for a heart to see what may have brought them to this place. DG

Human Trafficking in Your Backyard

[Jesus said,] "If you cause one of these little ones who trusts in me to fall into sin, it would be better for you to have a large millstone tied around your neck and be drowned in the depths of the sea." MATTHEW 18:6

There was a recent bust just forty miles from my home; a teen girl was being forced into the sex trade. In York, Pennsylvania—a little farther—a nail salon was busted for bringing Vietnamese women from their homeland and forcing them to work for free in the salon. We tend to think of human trafficking as something happening only in Third World nations. It's not. This year about one hundred thousand to three hundred thousand people in the United States will be sold into slavery or the sex trade. Most of them will be under the age of fourteen.

Jesus said it would be better for someone to have a large rock tied around his or her neck and dropped into a deep lake than to be one who would cause a child to sin. He hates human trafficking! We can't be passive about it.

What can *you* do about it? Here are some creative ideas.

1. Use Facebook and Twitter to raise awareness.
2. Find out what groups in your church or community are on the front lines of the battle, and find out how you can help.
3. Host a *Slumdog Millionaire* viewing party. (Get your parents' permission first. It can be graphic, but it's very educational.) Seeing what trafficking looks like can change your heart.
4. Buy fair trade—those companies guaranteeing no human slavery was used in the labor or production of their products.
5. Buy products from ministries producing goods to help trafficking victims start over.
6. Ask your youth pastor to preach about it.
7. Write a paper on it for school.
8. Invite your friends to donate to a cause instead of buying gifts for you.
9. Ask God how you can be involved in a big way in the future.
10. Pray.

Google "Human trafficking in (name of your state)." You'll find news stories about real crimes in your own backyard. Pray for the areas you read about. DG

It's as Simple as Soap

Teach those who are rich in this world not to be proud and not to trust in their money, which is so unreliable. Their trust should be in God, who richly gives us all we need for our enjoyment. Tell them to use their money to do good. They should be rich in good works and generous to those in need, always being ready to share with others. 1 TIMOTHY 6:17-18

We have just found the simplest way possible for you and your family to make a difference out of your riches. You are not rich? Well, according to the Global Rich List, an online tool computing income rankings worldwide, if your family brings home the median US income (about $50,000), then you are in the top 99 percent of money earners worldwide. Your family has cars and televisions, there is food in your refrigerator, and you know what the inside of a hotel room looks like. Stop! That hotel visit is the opportunity we have found for you.

Clean the World (CTW) is a nonprofit organization with a super-soapy simple plan. We both travel a lot, so we know for a fact hotels provide more soap than even the dirtiest traveler could use. We always leave a couple of barely used bars on the bathroom counter. The cofounder of CTW, Shawn Seipler, travels a lot, too, but he actually asked the right question: What happens to all of those lightly used bars of soap when I check out of the hotel? As suspected, he found the soap is tossed out once opened. So he asked another key question: Is there any way to recycle soap? Yep.

Seipler and his organization are now creating four hundred thousand bars of recycled soap per day and distributing them in Third World communities where basic sanitation prevents disease. Having access to something as basic as bar soap can reduce mortality rates by as much as 60 percent.

We think people like to do good things and serve others, especially when given clear and easy directions about how they can help. Many people are willing to be rich in good deeds. Here's Paul's take on the haves and the have-nots: all you have has come from the generosity of God's hand. You are to be a distributor, out of your own riches, to those who have not received the same comforts.

Organize a community soap drive. This is a great entry-level service project: it will be easy to recruit friends to serve with you, and it's nonthreatening for your school, so you can probably receive support there as well. All you need to succeed can be found at cleantheworld.org.

Spending to Save

If someone has enough money to live well and sees a brother or sister in need but shows no compassion—how can God's love be in that person? Dear children, let's not merely say that we love each other; let us show the truth by our actions. 1 JOHN 3:17-18

Buy some water . . . feed the hungry. Buy some mints . . . house the homeless. Buy some gum . . . save the earth. It's that simple, and it is being made possible by a company named Project 7. Founder Tyler Merrick began working with his father in the family business and was doing quite nicely for himself. He had a beautiful home, great job security, a membership at the country club, and the comfort of attending the church he had grown up in. But something was unsettling. Though Merrick is a staunch supporter of capitalism, he was also deeply concerned about oppressed people.

Welcome to the Project 7 brainstorm—why not produce items meant for consumption, but allocate 50 percent of the profits to one of seven areas: *Heal the Sick*, *Save the Earth*, *House the Homeless*, *Feed the Hungry*, *Help Those in Need*, *Build the Future*, and *Hope for Peace*. Any Project 7 product you purchase will have one of these seven catchphrases on the packaging. All Project 7 items are made in America and are high quality.

Let's encourage our local stores to carry Project 7 products. When companies like this make it simple to make a difference, it is love in action. But, you ask, shouldn't we just give money to nonprofit organizations so they can keep 100 percent of our gift rather than receive only 50 percent of what we spent on gum? Project 7 allows us to use our resources to bless nonprofits on an ongoing basis. The personal onetime gifts are just as important and should not be discarded.

Merrick is a businessman. He knows how to make money—that's a skill. What skills could you hone and then one day point in the direction of loving the oppressed? Never forget God's heart is for the poor. How can we say we know God if we don't have a heart for the poor and oppressed as well? In today's passage, John makes it clear we cannot. If we have no concern for those who are hungry, thirsty, homeless, unjustly persecuted . . . we cannot call ourselves "followers" of God. Makes it easy to spot a fraud, doesn't it?

 Go purchase a Project 7 product today. Research the company, and begin to dream about your future call to love those in need with your actions.

Make It Easy to Give

Keep on asking, and you will receive what you ask for. Keep on seeking, and you will find. Keep on knocking, and the door will be opened to you. For everyone who asks, receives. Everyone who seeks, finds. And to everyone who knocks, the door will be opened. MATTHEW 7:7-8

It's not unusual at all for kids to raise big funds for causes they believe in. Every year at Penn State the college students have a forty-eight-hour dance marathon to raise money for kids with cancer. THON itself is not an easy feat. Organizers work year round, as do dance teams and sorority and fraternity kids, to make this monster of an event take place. This year THON raised over $11 million!

Alex's Lemonade Stand started when Alex Scott, a cancer patient and only four years old, announced she wanted to start a lemonade stand and give the money to "her doctors" to help other kids who had cancer. Her first stand raised $2,000, and by the time she died at age eight, she had raised over $1 million for cancer research. The foundation has now raised over $50 million. Not bad for a four-year-old with a tender heart.

At the age of nine, Austin Gutwein became aware of kids in Africa who were losing parents to AIDS at the rate of 2,057 per day. He felt that the only difference between these kids and him was that they were suffering while he was in comfort. His plan was simple in the beginning. He'd ask people to pledge what would be the equivalent of one dollar per basketball free throw, hoping to earn $2,057 for orphaned kids in Zambia, Africa. The first year he raised almost $3,000 by shooting 2,057 free throws. His organization, Hoops of Hope, grew from there; $35,000 was raised the next year. Then $85,000; $211,000; $400,000 . . . and Hoops of Hope has turned into the largest free throw marathon.

How are these kids pulling this off? They were prompted by a passion to begin with. They are making an impact because their hearts were broken first. Beyond that, there is a simple answer. These kids are making it easy for you and me to give. They ask, and we have an opportunity to see to it that they receive. If you are feeling an urge to do something, do it! But keep it simple. Show people your passion and your brokenness. Tell them why you care and why they should care.

 *Action* **STEP** What are you passionate about? Chase down information to feed that passion. Don't know? Turn off the TV and find out. Nothing will bless you like making a difference in this world.

The Beanstalk Principle

Do not despise these small beginnings, for the LORD rejoices to see the work begin, to see the plumb line in Zerubbabel's hand. ZECHARIAH 4:10

You are familiar with the story of "Jack and the Beanstalk," right? Jack goes off to sell the family cow so he and his mom can eat, and a mysterious old man suckers him into trading Old Bessie for some "magic" beans. Of course Mom is furious with Jack, and in a fit of fury, she tosses the beans out the window. Up grows the beanstalk, and Jack repeatedly climbs up the stalk to the home of a rich ogre and robs him blind.

Perhaps it's not the most honorable example of wealth building, but here's the thing: Jack was faced with a lot of limitations in the beginning of this fairy tale. He and Mom were starving, and the cow had quit producing milk. From the pictures we've seen in fairy-tale books, the cow had limited prospects as a beef cow too. Jack is young and without any marketable skills. He comes home with nothing but a handful of small seeds—about what you'd expect when you send a kid out to save the family.

Small things, however, can set huge things in motion. Zechariah reminds us never to dismiss the small things or to judge what God is up to by our meager, human standards. You see, this is part of the same passage where God warns Israel, "It is not by force nor by strength, but by my Spirit" that he will deliver her (4:6). Zechariah prophesied about two olive trees on either side of God's dwelling place. One was Joshua—a less than imposing military figure. The other was the high priest Zerubbabel, who built a less than imposing Temple. Yet God said these two were mirroring his own story about his plan for humanity's salvation, accomplished as we know now by the humble servant King and High Priest Jesus, rather than the impressive military conqueror so many were expecting. God does not always use a massive show of power. In fact, he's saving that for the end of the book.

It started with a bean. God has graciously provided the stalk.

Action **STEP** Your gift is not too small. Find one small good deed you are passionate about and can do on a continuing basis. See if a big old stalk takes root!

Never Say Never

Moses pleaded with the LORD, "O Lord, I'm not very good with words. I never have been, and I'm not now, even though you have spoken to me. I get tongue-tied, and my words get tangled." Then the LORD asked Moses, "Who makes a person's mouth? Who decides whether people speak or do not speak, hear or do not hear, see or do not see? Is it not I, the LORD? Now go! I will be with you as you speak, and I will instruct you in what to say." EXODUS 4:10-12

We are about to share the most dangerous word in the English language. Grab a pen and take notes, because this one is a doozy. The word is . . . *never*. Suzy's husband said he would *never* marry an actress. They met while she was in a graduate acting program. Dannah said she would *never* speak in front of a live audience. She's got thousands of live audiences under her belt probably to the tune of millions of listeners. You don't say *never* and get away with it. *Ever*.

Moses told God he could never use him. He couldn't speak well. Some experts think Moses may have had a speech impediment. Others point out that God had already promised Moses success by the time this excuse came out. Moses wasn't lacking oration skills; he was lacking faith in God.

You may have plans for your future, and then again you may be in a time of floundering. Either way, know that God loves you and his intentions are to invite you to work with him to further his Kingdom. Most of the time the invitation is not a big surprise—he gifts us in advance for works he plans down the road. If you are a gifted athlete, dancer, or artist, this is likely where God will use you. But all roads have twists and turns. Suzy's friend Allison worked with Campus Crusade (Cru) after graduating from Purdue University. Allison had been a Division I water polo player, but she took a mighty and athletic jump over a wave and broke her neck, leaving her nearly quadriplegic. Ali has a platform now that she never anticipated. People are quicker to listen to her because she has a terrible story to tell; she'd say it's worth it, because she has an unbelievably perfect Redeemer to point the way to.

We don't know what you think you're cut out for or what you think you could *never* do . . . but don't count anything out. Could you be a missionary in a Muslim country? Does God have a difficult testimony waiting around the corner for you? Will he show himself sovereign in your weaknesses? Could be. Just don't stand in his way!

Action **STEP** There may be a world stage in your future. Relinquish your *nevers* today.

The Smallest Measure

Keep on loving each other as brothers and sisters. Don't forget to show hospitality to strangers, for some who have done this have entertained angels without realizing it! Remember those in prison, as if you were there yourself. Remember also those being mistreated, as if you felt their pain in your own bodies. HEBREWS 13:1-3

Have you ever heard of a TV show called *Amazing Adventures of a Nobody*? It's a reality show featuring a Brit named Leon Logothetis traveling across the UK on only five pounds per day. That is a little less than eight US dollars. He is not allowed to ask for or receive money, but he is allowed to work in exchange for food and lodging and to receive gifts. He must rely on the kindness of strangers.

Logothetis's film crew legitimizes him. If I'm managing a hotel, a guy asks for a free room, and there are two professional cameras in my face, I'm going to know this guy is legit. It's good publicity for my hotel, so I'm going to say yes. (Though it's surprising how many people look right into the camera's eye and literally say, "No way!") But what about when no one is around? What about the woman who is sitting by herself in the corner of the airport and crying? What happens when I see two older boys bullying a younger one?

Life is made up of little opportunities to care, and the Bible says we are not to despise small things. Hebrews 13 lays out a list of small ways we can care and thereby make a difference in the world. Little things feel good when you receive them as blessings, and to bless others is even better than to receive, so make it a priority to seize these opportunities:

- Love your brothers and sisters, showing particular grace and friendship to fellow believers.
- Show hospitality to people who are far from home. Find the exchange student and talk with her. See to it that she has the same comforts here she is missing from home.
- Remember in your own liberty those who have none. Remember them in prayer. Work on your own time to raise awareness. Do what you can in word, deed, and prayer to free them.

Find one way to reach out in a small way to the big world beyond, and act on it. This world is way too important to God for us to be consumed only with our own lives.

Am I a Hypocrite?

What sorrow awaits you teachers of religious law and you Pharisees. Hypocrites! For you are like whitewashed tombs—beautiful on the outside but filled on the inside with dead people's bones and all sorts of impurity. Outwardly you look like righteous people, but inwardly your hearts are filled with hypocrisy and lawlessness. MATTHEW 23:27-28

Eighty-five percent of young adults who have ever rubbed shoulders with the modern church say it is hypocritical. The number drops to 47 percent when the young adults are actually active within the church, but that's still half! What's going on?

For one thing, we are doing a terrible job convincing the world we give a rip about people who are hurting, and no matter how we try to spin things in our favor, we are going to have a tough time convincing people. We just can't boast about "fifty kids' salvation at our jungle-themed vacation Bible school" if we aren't helping some of the kids at Bible school whose single moms can barely make ends meet to feed them. Our efforts can tend to be about boasting of our great works rather than helping in small, practical ways.

The number of people in the world who can't afford food, live on dirt floors, and lack funds to buy simple preventative medicines is over a billion. The disparity between "us" and "them" defies decency. Author Tom Davis steps in and lays down the hammer, kind of like Jesus did. In a beliefnet.com article, he says, "When Christians care about their political views, what sexual preference someone has, or their bank account more than they care about the millions of people who die in the world because they don't have five dollars to buy the medicine that would cure them, something has gone drastically wrong."

Both the world and the church are full of hypocrisy. The Pharisees were greatly concerned with keeping the law, but they completely missed God's purpose of love. I know some in the world who claim no religion other than "love" but don't understand the love of helping people to abide by moral standards that keep them safe. Both are hypocritical. God is looking for a heart that looks like his own. His heart is not for us to grow rich. His heart is for the poor.

 *Action* **STEP** How does your pocketbook prove you share God's heart for the poor?

OCTOBER 11

What Makes Heaven Weep?

Suppose you see a brother or sister who has no food or clothing, and you say, "Good-bye and have a good day; stay warm and eat well"—but then you don't give that person any food or clothing. What good does that do? JAMES 2:15-16

What might an observant teacher conclude about a student who looks exhausted, wears rumpled clothing or the same outfit several days in a row, and often keeps late hours at school hanging out in such places as a locker room or student lounge? That's easy, right? There are thought to be about 1.5 million homeless teens and kids in the United States, but as you can imagine, counting people who have no permanent address is not quite an exact science! In 2005, the city of Minneapolis, Minnesota, alone estimated there were 5,500 homeless students enrolled in public schools!

Keith Green, an early pioneer of Christian rock, wrote these words in a song called "Asleep in the Light":

> *'Cause he brings people to your door*
> *And you turn them away*
> *As you smile and say*
> *"God bless you, be at peace"*
> *And all heaven just weeps*
> *'Cause Jesus came to your door*
> *You've left him out on the streets*

It sure does seem something is required of us, doesn't it? While it may not seem like a lot can be done—you are in school, you don't have much expendable income, and your parents may be wary of a radical response on your part to the homeless—the mandate is pretty clear nonetheless. We are supposed to take action on behalf of our brothers and sisters who have needs.

 *Action* **STEP**

1. Read Matthew 25:31-46. Where do you see yourself in this parable? Are you a sheep or a goat?
2. Check out www.clotheyourneighborasyourself.com. Is it true that obedience is not defined by what we don't do, but by what we do for the world that God so loves?
3. What is one simple thing you *could* do to help?

Blue Gold

The earth mourns and dries up, and the crops waste away and wither. Even the greatest people on earth waste away. The earth suffers for the sins of its people, for they have twisted God's instructions, violated his laws, and broken his everlasting covenant. ISAIAH 24:4-5

For a long time I failed to even try to understand my connection to the environment. I believed all "green" efforts to be driven by tree huggers (a real and somewhat disturbing phenomenon). Not wanting to be caught up in the hugging, I turned a blind eye, but I can't do that any longer. The earth is God's, and he's put us in charge of taking care of it . . . and we're not doing very well. Apparently one of the greatest areas of concern is with disposal of plastic water and soda bottles, which I have been guilty of in the past.

Bottled water sells to the tune of $100 billion per year worldwide. That's a great deal for bottlers, but not so much for consumers. The average bottled water sells at about five cents per ounce of water. At three dollars per gallon, even gas only averages out to two cents per ounce. Bottled water is a big-time business, and when profit margins are that high, it's hard to get manufacturers to pay attention to the environment.

Water has been dubbed "blue gold" in the twenty-first century due to the fact that clean water is becoming a rare commodity. This is bad news for underdeveloped nations, as deep pockets rush in to buy "gold" wherever it has been discovered. As corporations buy up sources of clean water, it will be more difficult for the poor to obtain what really should be a basic human right.

Finally, water bottles have created a massive garbage problem in the United States, accounting for over 1.5 million tons of waste per year. Water bottles are recyclable and made of a good quality plastic. The problem lies in the 80 percent of bottles that are not recycled but merely tossed. They won't decay . . . which means they won't go away.

How does this impact us? Nothing happens overnight—I'm not an alarmist— but given enough time our own public water sources will be threatened. We know the end of the book—God is preparing a new heaven and a new earth. For now, we are called to act with compassion and wisdom toward God's creation.

 **Action STEP** Purchase a stainless steel water bottle . . . if you don't already own one. Fill and refill it instead of using several plastic bottles of water each day.
SW

OCTOBER 13
Free Music

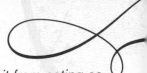

The Scripture says, "You must not muzzle an ox to keep it from eating as it treads out the grain." And in another place, "Those who work deserve their pay!" 1 TIMOTHY 5:18

Dannah and I have come to know a lot of people in Nashville and have some good friends in the music industry. And the industry, girls, is hurting. The artists in the music industry used to become overnight sensations because someone would buy an entire album of their music, then spend the night learning their lyrics and become die-hard fans. Today, you can download one song at the click of a mouse, and you might pick and choose who you listen to, not really getting to know anyone as personally as people once did. This makes it hard to make a living singing songs, especially in the Christian music industry.

There's something else that is making it even harder. When we illegally download or burn CDs loaned by friends, we are stealing from these artists, and the artists are not the only ones with families needing to be fed. In order for a song to be made available to you, all of the following require a paycheck: sound engineers, studio musicians, songwriters, producers, booking agents, managers, and the list goes on. The overhead costs for a musician are huge!

If the joy you feel when listening to your favorite bands or artists blesses you, consider it joy to contribute to their welfare! It's Dannah's and my privilege to travel a lot as we speak about the books we have written. We love meeting you, praying with you, hearing your stories. We also derive great joy knowing our efforts are helping to support our families and securing a future for those we love. It's a wonderful privilege to have not just a j-o-b but a calling from God, and one that pays the bills at that. My guess is, your favorite artist feels the same way!

The Bible verse above says a worker deserves his or her wages. It is refer-ring to paying leaders of the church. It's not about rock stars or construc-tion guys or people who work for Chick-fil-A . . . and yet it is. Paul's point to Timothy is "We pay all other workers, even the oxen for goodness' sake; why wouldn't we pay our church leaders?" Maybe we should also pay those who have been ministering to us through song.

 Make a covenant to pay for your music (and movies and books) from here on out. Consider it a joy to pay people for a job well done. (And if you have any stolen music, get rid of it today!)

When Will It Be Your Turn?

Everything that has happened to me here has helped to spread the Good News. For everyone here, including the whole palace guard, knows that I am in chains because of Christ. And because of my imprisonment, most of the believers here have gained confidence and boldly speak God's message without fear. PHILIPPIANS 1:12-14

We never thought we'd see it in America, but an Arizona man has been convicted for running a home Bible study. He began a sixty-day jail sentence and was fined $12,000 while we were writing these devos. The city of Phoenix and Pastor Michael Salman have vastly differing views of the situation. The Salmans had about fifteen people gathering weekly in their living room when the city let them know they were violating a code—their home was zoned as residential, not as a religious gathering place. An attorney helped the family determine they would not need to follow code for commercial buildings since they hosted friends and family and not the public at large. They were raided regardless of their attempts to comply, and a picnic with twenty guests was ordered to immediately break up.

Apparently it's okay to have large groups gather at your home if it is for the type of activity normally found on residential property. Hit rewind here. I've been to about a bazillion home Bible studies. I have also been to graduation parties, housewarmings, baby showers . . . all with well over twenty people present. The Salmans posted photos of their street during parties thrown by neighbors. Time after time these photos show cars double-parked and a street nearly impassable. Salman is the only one who has been cited for code violations. The city insists the fuss is over zoning alone—Salman says it sure feels a lot like religious persecution.

It would be easy to shrug this off and say, "It would be simpler to meet in a church building." And it would. But it's unlikely Phoenix will be the last city to produce this story. There will come a day when your religious liberties will be challenged. The enemy would love for us to go about with our lives never awakened to the impending culture shift, forgetting each of our few days on earth is a gift, lulled into a stupor. Be wise instead, and know that a change is blowing in the wind. It's all good. Jesus wins! But stay alert.

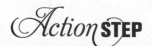 *Action* **STEP** Organize some friends to pray together for persecuted Christians.

You Have a Job to Do

*God said, "Look! I have given you every seed-bearing plant throughout
the earth and all the fruit trees for your food. And I have given every
green plant as food for all the wild animals, the birds in the sky, and the
small animals that scurry along the ground—everything that has life."*
GENESIS 1:29-30

The Bible says the earth is ill, groaning in her labor pains as she waits for her
own new birth in creation (see Romans 8:20-22). I think we can see that well
enough as we witness wildfires, tornadoes, floods, and droughts. But how do
you feel about it? Do you have compassion, or do you shrug your shoulders
and think, *Oh well!*

Romans 8 says the earth was forced into this condition against its will. *Our
sins against God's call to care for creation have, in part, brought this about.*
I read a story recently about a California family who produces only one liter of
trash per year! Compare that to the average family's 1,000 pounds of trash
each year. I don't want my life, or the dregs of it, to add to landfills. I don't want
to create waste and endanger soil or water supplies. But so much of my life
has been thoughtless in this regard. If I make a change, it will have to be a
big one.

God created an earth dependent upon our care, as we are dependent upon
the things the earth creates. This is called interdependency. Americans used
to understand this at a much more basic level before industry and technology
came calling.

We know how the book ends. All of this present earth will be consumed
by fire, and Jesus will present to us the inheritance of a new heaven and a
new earth. But still, nowhere in Scripture do we find license to disregard this
present earth. Instead, we find commands to care for it. We find a mandate to
work the soil and produce things both good for us and healthy for the soil, the
waters, and the creatures living in water and on land. This is the work he has
passed on for us to do. If a report card were to be issued on how well we care
for the earth, what might our grade be? What if we had been hired to do this
job of caring for the earth . . . would a firing be in order?

 *Action* **STEP** Look up *agrarianism.*
SW

No Exceptions to the Rule

Unjustly condemned, he was led away. No one cared that he died without descendants, that his life was cut short in midstream. But he was struck down for the rebellion of my people. ISAIAH 53:8

I don't know about your family, but mine has gone through some messy stuff. One brother went through a divorce only to lose his second wife to cancer. Another brother's best friend asked him to conceal a murder weapon; my brother turned him in. The young man was killed in prison. My uncle ran a red light and died. A cousin lost her fiancé in a motorcycle crash. Adultery. Rehab. Police records. Abortion. My little family has seen it all, and I'm guessing yours might have seen a little bit of mess too.

What Jesus did on the cross was a universal compensation for every one of us. There is literally not one human being ever to have walked on this earth who does not need the payment Jesus made on the cross handed over on his or her behalf. That's a crazy thought looking at the pastor in the pulpit or the worship leader on a Sunday morning. Or even Dannah and I, commissioned to write books, right? We are commissioned because we're beyond most of the drama and have things together . . . not! It's not unusual for confessions of "let me tell you how I blew it today" to fly back and forth between our texts. (Of course, Dannah loves to butt text me, but those messages—pbbesvhigthy—don't count.)

The reason we need to care about brokenness in the world around us is because it is our story. We may not be in need of clean water, but we need to know there is a way out of our misery. We may not be in need of medical supplies or disease prevention, but we need to forgive and be forgiven. Brokenness is not a regional problem. It is universal. It's easier to see it at some times more than others, but to be honest, when our brokenness cannot be seen, we are at a disadvantage. When we're broken and bleeding on the side of the road, others at least know to come to our rescue or to keep us company as we bleed. When we point to where it hurts, others can step up and say, "I had that happen too." It's when we wear the mask of "I'm fine" that we slip into a lonely place.

 **Action STEP** Tell someone today where you are hurting. Let that person be with you.
SW

The Corner Where You Are

From one man [God] created all the nations throughout the whole earth. He decided beforehand when they should rise and fall, and he determined their boundaries. His purpose was for the nations to seek after God and perhaps feel their way toward him and find him—though he is not far from any one of us. ACTS 17:26-27

When my mom was little, she would sing "*Right* in the corner where you are" to the song "*Brighten* the corner where you are." I guess she thought it was a song about being put in time-out. Still, Mom's lyrics are biblical. I know where God wants you to serve . . . right in your little corner of the world and with whatever resources he has given you. The problem is sometimes we let our dreams for big things get in the way.

When Phil Vischer first released VeggieTales, it barely made a splash. Then the right demographic got hold of it. The first rabid fans were college-aged coeds, and their hype skyrocketed the Veggies to overnight fame. Vischer began to think maybe he could be the next Walt Disney, setting his sights for theme parks and Hollywood; so he and his board of directors began to plan (and spend) based on money they *projected* rather than money they actually *possessed.*

Now Vischer has a radical take on following God. He tells *World* magazine that we are off track if we think we're called to be a people of vision. If we think *we* have the plan and the track for our lives . . . it's all about us. The reality is that God moves and then he invites us to join him. Vischer's new company is called Jellyfish Labs, because a jellyfish can't determine its own course. It has to trust that flow will take it where it needs to be. (I'm in Vischer's "fish boat" on this ideology!)

This world and its order are not an accident. This is a planned world, and one in which God still calls the shots. Your life of serving God begins where you are—influenced indeed by economics, race, education, and personal gifts—because this is how God created you and where he has placed you! Chase God with the means and the gifts he has given you, determine to work hard and learn, and seek wise counsel. He'll take you good places.

 *Action* **STEP** Can you sincerely thank God for the "corner" where you are today?
SW

OCTOBER 18

Live with an Economy of "Enough"

"No one is good—except God alone. You know the commandments: 'You shall not murder, you shall not commit adultery, you shall not steal, you shall not give false testimony, you shall not defraud, honor your father and mother.'" "Teacher," he declared, "all these I have kept since I was a boy." Jesus looked at him and loved him. "One thing you lack," he said. "Go, sell everything you have and give to the poor, and you will have treasure in heaven. Then come, follow me." At this the man's face fell. He went away sad, because he had great wealth. MARK 10:18-22, NIV

Here is something you might find . . . amusing? Many nonprofit organizations spend more money marketing their products than they are able to actually send for relief efforts. (RED), marketed by Gap, has provided about $20 million to fight poverty and disease in developing nations, and that is good work. But it has cost them hundreds of millions to do so. (RED) spokesman Bono from U2 explains how this disparity happens: "Some people won't put on marching boots, so we've got to get to people where they are at . . . in the shopping malls."

In other words, we can't get Americans to give money directly to relief organizations. We can't get Americans to *go* to Haiti, Africa, or India to see firsthand how others are living in abject poverty compared to our gross over-consumption . . . so we are going to appeal to that same consumerism and make people feel good about the money they spend on themselves. That's not really ha-ha funny, but odd, right?

I'm not knocking (RED), or TOMS (same type of philosophy). They are *doing* something, and we who do so *little* should perhaps lay off the criticism. The question raised is, Why do they have to do things the way they do? I believe the problem is partly in the heart, but also partly in our pocketbooks, meaning we love our comfort. We don't manage our money well. Jesus met with a rich young man who loved both God's Law and others well. He had kept all of the commandments, and Jesus loved him. But the man loved one other thing well. . . . He loved his wealth and comfort more than he loved his God. He left sad because he couldn't lay down his "too much." When we agree that God is enough, we are able to use all that he has given us, including our money, to do great things for his Kingdom, without needing the T-shirt or shoes!

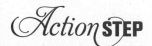 **STEP** Sell something this week, and give the money to a favorite charity or ministry.

Paying It Forward

Don't forget to do good and to share with those in need. These are the sacrifices that please God. HEBREWS 13:16

If the whole of the world were measured by "haves" and "have-nots" . . . you and I would be among the "haves." Scripture talks a lot about money, and God says there will always be both wealthy and poor people. But he says it's hard to be wealthy because we forget our need for him in times of plenty. It's hard to be poor, too; what if the only way to feed your family was to steal? Chances are your access to money is the result of a good work ethic on your part and the fortune of being born into your circumstances. The financial lack of the truly poor is often a result of circumstance alone. Some cultures make no exception for those who are willing to work—oppression is the standard.

What if you pulled a Mother Teresa, sold everything you possessed, and went to live among the poor in . . . (name your country)? A girl named Katie Davis did just that. At nineteen years old she decided she could not return to her life of comfort in Nashville, so she founded a ministry that allowed her to adopt eight Ugandan children and send hundreds of others to school. A mother of eight at nineteen, and a family that has since grown . . . Katie is one of our heroes (see April 22 and July 3 for more on her).

There's a simpler way to get into this habit of giving that may be more palatable to your parents until you are free to make such radical life decisions. What if you contributed a portion of each purchase to a person in need or an organization you can trust? For instance, after buying a $40 pair of jeans, your next expense is $20 toward a friend's missions trip. You buy a $200 iTouch . . . your next expense is a $100 grocery card for a single mom. The percentage you give is up to you. You may want to match 100 percent! Maybe 10 percent is a good place to start. This is, God says, a holy and pleasing act of worship.

 Will you set aside a percentage of your next planned expenditure to give to those in need? Make plans to do so now. Prepare the envelope, the jar, whatever!

Learning the Difference

I want you to know, dear brothers and sisters, what God in his kindness has done through the churches in Macedonia. They are being tested by many troubles, and they are very poor. But they are also filled with abundant joy, which has overflowed in rich generosity. For I can testify that they gave not only what they could afford, but far more. And they did it of their own free will. 2 CORINTHIANS 8:1-3

Poor and destitute are not the same thing. Most young couples are *poor* on the day they start their marriage. Jonathan's and my first home had mice and moles; it was across from a whiskey-bottling plant, and one night a drunk neighbor wandered in and demanded Jonathan preach to him. We were happy, though. And we were "upwardly mobile," meaning we had an education and lived in a society that allowed us chances for growth.

There are people out there who are *destitute*. The definition of this word would suggest these people own no home, have little if any education, and are subject to a society that does not allow their situation to change. This might include girls in India who are scheduled for the sex trade by age twelve or kids orphaned by AIDS in parts of Africa.

One key thing you can do is carefully study the difference between people who are poor and those who are subject to destitution. As "rescuers" we sometimes go to people who have a shot at upward mobility—the chance to gain a measure of education or find employment—and rob them of that bless-ing. Some people only need a hand *up*, a simple promise of stability while they fight to get their legs beneath them. This is far different than a hand*out*. It's important not to touch a developing butterfly as it emerges from its chrysalis. Likewise, assuming people are unable to do for themselves can be a crippling gesture of kindness.

In 2 Corinthians, Paul accepts money from a poor church. Consider this—the church at Corinth was not only fighting financial woes, but they were being persecuted for their faith. We might call their position "rock bottom" today. Still, they found ways to abound in both joy and giving. People who are in adverse circumstances are still blessed like you and I when they are able to give. The poor need only a hand *up*. The destitute are another story.

 **Action STEP**

Define what poor looks like in your neck of the woods. What about destitute?
SW

OCTOBER 21
Getting Weird

You are not like that, for you are a chosen people. You are royal priests, a holy nation, God's very own possession. As a result, you can show others the goodness of God, for he called you out of the darkness into his wonderful light. 1 PETER 2:9

Dannah and I live in a bit of a Christian bubble. That is, the majority of our time happens to be spent with Christians either discipling or being discipled. But we both know God has called us to burst the bubble at every opportunity. God called us to be in the *world*, not in a bubble. Even when Jesus prayed for us in the garden just before his crucifixion, he was not asking that we be removed in any way from the world, but that we would be protected as we go (see John 17).

But we have to know what we believe when we're out there, or we will risk being unprotected from false religion. Eighty percent of North American people *say* they believe in God, most referring to the God of the Bible. Here are other things they believe in and live by:

   *Forty percent of American Christians do not believe Satan exists.
   *Only 50 percent believe the Bible is accurate.
   *Sixty-five percent do not attend a worship service of any kind.
   *Seventy percent do not read the Bible.

The Christian bubble is a dangerous place to stay if it leads us to believe the rest of the world is operating just like us. One pastor in India prepares his workers by requiring they read the Bible an hour and a half each day. He explains his country is immersed in other gods, so it's important to teach them to immerse instead in the thoughts of the one true God. Then, he sends them out to be *in* the world! Guess what? This pastor's church is at twenty thousand people and growing. His leaders have faith to pray for healing. He has over five hundred home churches in operation.

Would that kind of radical commitment work here? What if we did something really weird and committed actual *chunks* of our day to knowing God in his Word? What do you think might happen?

 Make a dramatic increase in your personal quiet time for a week.

OCTOBER 22
Got Your Passport?

Don't take any money in your money belts—no gold, silver, or even copper coins. Don't carry a traveler's bag with a change of clothes and sandals or even a walking stick. Don't hesitate to accept hospitality, because those who work deserve to be fed. MATTHEW 10:9-10

I somehow managed to get into a "selective" college although I was not a National Honor Society member and I would be embarrassed to tell you my SAT scores. I remember asking my adviser shortly into my freshman year how I had been accepted despite my grades and test scores. She said I had written a good essay and interviewed well, they liked my involvement level in high school, and . . . I won bonus points for having traveled overseas! Lo and behold—college admissions offices like that.

Today Dannah's daughter Lexi posted pictures on Facebook of children from the Embera tribe in Panama, where she was visiting. The children are wearing colorful loincloths and no shirts. The tribe lives in thatched huts in the middle of the rain forest. Lexi and her friends took canoes to reach them. They were warmly welcomed and fed fish and fried bananas. Lexi and her friends received tattoos with berry ink. It's a life-changing summer experience. And I want you to know that kind of change.

The fact is, we live in a sort of Disney world. Our American lives are so plastic and perfect compared to the rest of the world. To really appreciate what God has given to us and to be responsible for what others in the world need, we have to get out and see it. We're boxed in by our lack of real (not Facebook) exposure to the world around us. Jesus sent the disciples out to share the gospel, but I think he also wanted them to know that the world his father created was not limited to the fifty square miles they had roamed with him. He urged them to stay in people's homes and to accept a bed and a meal. It prepared them to be the early church, and it will prepare you to be the church even today.

Action STEP Got your passport yet? Apply even if you don't know yet how or where it will first take you. A passport is a little pricey, so you might want to put it on your list for Christmas.
SW

Want to Do It? Learn How!

You have been taught the holy Scriptures from childhood, and they have given you the wisdom to receive the salvation that comes by trusting in Christ Jesus. 2 TIMOTHY 3:15

I have heard that it takes ten thousand hours for people to reach the top echelon of whatever they are practicing. That being said, if you want to do something, begin to learn it now. I am a drummer. The first time I sat behind a drum set was just before my thirty-second birthday. I can remember asking my husband after I had mastered my first exhilarating groove, "Will you buy me a drum set?" And do you know, my awesome man did just that? I don't know how many hours I've logged behind a kit, but it has been a lot. I'm mostly self-taught, and there were several years during which Jonathan referred to himself as a "drum widower"—that's how little he saw me. Just a few minutes ago I was watching a little six-year-old dude jam to Foo Fighters. He was *good!* The info under the video said he was self-taught, and that's what got me thinking.

He's not going to have any troubles reaching his ten thousand hours. He has found something at six that he loves, and he's going for it! What do you love, and what are you waiting for? A lot of things are out there with Internet instruction waiting for you to invest your first ten thousand hours. Making jewelry. Playing guitar. Gardening. Training dogs. Cooking. Horse farming (that's how Dannah learned). Learning a new language. You may choose something simply because it interests you, or you may see it as a head start for the change you want to make in the world.

Timothy had a head start in his knowledge of Scripture. His mother and grandmother laid the groundwork to prepare him for the colossal ministry God had in mind for him all along. Hebrew tradition was to start children on this path of learning the Scriptures at age five. Timothy certainly was not self-taught in the beginning, but look at the benefits of his course of study—he received the wisdom that led him to salvation in Christ Jesus.

 **STEP** If you are behind in your knowledge of Scripture, build that first. Next, turn off that silly TV and log on. What are you going to learn to do this year?
SW

On Breeding Spotted Mice

Work willingly at whatever you do, as though you were working for the Lord rather than for people. COLOSSIANS 3:23

In the early 1900s, a British lord died at the age of eighty-eight. Being a man of means, he had no reason to work, so for seventy years he did whatever he pleased with his time and money. He chose to breed spotted mice, consumed by wanting to engineer the perfect pet. He was widely criticized upon death for living a purposeless life.

A. W. Tozer, a contemporary of the man, wrote, "Not being a mouse lover (nor a mouse hater for that matter; I am just neutral about mice), I do not know but that a spotted mouse might be more useful . . . than a common colored mouse. But still I am troubled. . . . Made in the image of God, equipped with awesome powers of mind and soul, called to dream immortal dreams and to think the long thoughts of eternity, he chooses the breeding of a spotted mouse as his reason for existing."*

Here's the thing. Could he have bred spotted mice *for the glory of God*? Surely he could have sold them to raise money for missions. Surely these were conversation pieces proving the versatility of God's creation. Aren't we all called to contribute to the Kingdom whatever passion and skill we are given? Yes! Aren't we called to care for animals and to be good stewards of them in the book of Genesis? Yes! The key is that we do it *as if we are working for the Lord*.

The challenge as you decide what you will do with your life is not *what* you do, so much as *how* you do it. Ecclesiastes was written to make us wise to how useless and vain our lives can be if we are not careful; the writer calls us to do whatever we do "*with all [our] might*" (9:10, NIV, emphasis added). And I would add, with a focus on how it honors the Lord.

This important part of your future starts now. I see a lot of very talented teens consumed with their sport, the arts, their grades, or their pets. They're a lot like that crazy rich guy. They've forgotten it is all for the Lord and should glorify him. Don't be one of them.

 Think about your three favorite pastimes. Ask God to give you specific ideas about how you can participate in these activities in a way to bring him honor and glory.

---

*Source: A. W. Tozer, *Man: The Dwelling Place of God*, page 58.

Surrender

You can make many plans, but the LORD's purpose will prevail.
PROVERBS 19:21

Got plans for your life? I had it all figured out . . . many times. I began thinking I would study journalism. I had been the editor of my high school newspaper and had won some journalistic awards. One gut-wrenching semester of micro-economics convinced me otherwise.

I had no Plan B, but over the course of my freshman year one began to emerge. I had tried out for the theater program but hadn't made it. I thought I'd be a shoo-in having acted in eleven plays during high school. Turns out I had been doing just that—acting, ironically a bad word in serious theater circles! By my sophomore year I had worked my way into the group. I later auditioned for graduate programs and won a full ride.

Before classes began I had a bike accident and was trying to stop the bleeding as my doorbell rang. There I found a handsome young musician (my husband). He wasn't my husband yet—we were meeting for the first time—but he would become my husband. We married less than a year later, and I never finished that MFA degree.

Time for Plan C . . . but there was no Plan C. Jonathan and I moved to Indiana and took the reins as full-time youth pastors at a little church with five kids in the youth group. By the time we left four years later, I knew what Plan D was. I had gone back to school, earned an education degree, and was prepared to live out the rest of my years teaching. In case you were wondering, I'm on Plan G right now. Things change.

There are two ways to approach Proverbs 19:21. You could feel controlled. After all, he sees the road of your life in places hidden from you. Resistance is futile, as the evil Borg say in *Star Trek*. Or . . . you can believe God's plans are perfect and pleasing, thus seeing the verse as a comfort. The future you can-not see is wrapped in his blessing; why fight against his very best for you?

Confess to God that his ways are perfect and your own plans may well be *flawed*. Speak with a trusted mentor if you are struggling to accept this.

Wanted: Hedgehogs

Look straight ahead, and fix your eyes on what lies before you. Mark out a straight path for your feet; stay on the safe path. PROVERBS 4:25-26

Ever heard of Aesop's fables? Here is his fable "The Fox and the Cat":

A Fox was boasting to a Cat of its clever devices for escaping its enemies. "I have a whole bag of tricks," he said, "which contains a hundred ways of escaping my enemies."

"I have only one," said the Cat. "But I can generally manage with that."

Just at that moment they heard the cry of a pack of hounds coming towards them, and the Cat immediately scampered up a tree and hid herself in the boughs. "This is my plan," said the Cat. "What are you going to do?"

The Fox thought first of one way, then of another, and while he was debating, the hounds came nearer and nearer, and at last the fox in his confusion was caught up by the hounds and soon killed by the huntsmen.

Miss Puss, who had been looking on, said, "Better one safe way than a hundred on which you cannot reckon."

In the 1950s British philosopher Isaiah Berlin wrote a modern fable called *The Hedgehog and the Fox*, which asserts that hedgehogs are singularly focused people known for looking at the complex world and finding ways to simplify it. Foxes have many ideas, but the inability to settle on one often runs them into the ground.

When it comes to God's will for your life, the hedgehog approach is the one to take. Some people get distracted by everything the wandering eye can see. Fix your eyes on *one* thing—the author and perfecter of your faith (see Hebrews 12:2), the one who does not change like shifting shadows. Set one goal, and even though you may be presented with hundreds of opportunities (like a fox), be sure to weigh each against that one goal. If it does not fit the goal, even though it may appear to be harmless, toss it out!

 Be known for one thing. Write a life mission statement expressing the one thing you would like to be remembered for. For example, "She never met anyone without asking if she could help in some way."

What? Me, Worry?

Give all your worries and cares to God, for he cares about you. 1 PETER 5:7

For a period of several years I would wake up in the middle of the night filled with a faceless dread. I would ask myself, *What am I upset about?* The nights I could point to an actual cause of anxiety were rare. I finally found a portion of Scripture that helped me defeat it.

"Once I was young, and now I am old. Yet I have never seen the godly abandoned or their children begging for bread. The godly always give generous loans to others, and their children are a blessing" (Psalm 37:25-26).

Turns out my unidentified anxieties were about money and God's provision. Are those worries gone? No. But God has given me a way to dwell once again in his peace.

I believe worry (and anxiety) is the most common human struggle. I feel confident in saying I have a grip on worry in my life. This means only that I know how to fight it; it has not quit knocking on my door. Here are a few methods to consider:

Use Scripture. Nothing will strike a deathblow to the attacks of the enemy like the sword of God's Word! Internet search engines are the easiest route when searching for Bible verses by theme. Try it right now. Go to your favorite search engine and type "verses on anxiety." Write down your favorite, and put it by your bed.

Listen to reason. My daughter Marie and I both love quotes, maybe because they are the best of our thoughts and our reason as human beings. Consider these. Corrie ten Boom said, "Worry does not empty tomorrow of its sorrow. It empties today of its strength." Mark Twain said, "I am an old man and have known a great many troubles, but most of them never happened."

Allow other older, wiser people to speak to your worries. One time I was nearly paralyzed with anxiety over words I had spoken to a guy I liked. My mom looked at me and said, "Are you seriously so self-absorbed to think he's at home thinking about what you said?" Ouch! But she was right. I felt at peace almost immediately.

 Take your biggest anxiety to task using one of the three ideas above.
SW

When College Destroys Your Life

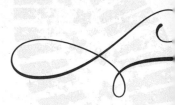

The LORD will send rain at the proper time from his rich treasury in the heavens and will bless all the work you do. You will lend to many nations, but you will never need to borrow from them. If you listen to these commands of the LORD your God that I am giving you today, and if you carefully obey them, the LORD will make you the head and not the tail, and you will always be on top and never at the bottom.
DEUTERONOMY 28:12-13

Ryan took two semesters longer to graduate from college than he had planned, but there's a good reason for it. He started his college career with a noble goal: to graduate debt free. To do so, he worked two jobs during the school year and two each summer. Twice he had to stop his education to work full-time. But he did graduate debt free, got a great job, and is having the time of his life now!

Student debt is a serious matter (and the time to think about it is *before* you are in college). Unlike credit card or car debt, student loans in default can be taken (garnished) right out of your paycheck. On the average, college graduates carry $25,000 in debt, the highest level of student debt in history. Let's put that into perspective. The average post-collegiate salary is about $45,000, so more than half of your annual salary would go toward debt (if you want to keep it from growing by paying it off aggressively). It's a mess. States are cutting funding to schools while the schools are raising tuition. The lowest income students get most heavily recruited by for-profit schools; and while the Pell Grant may cover part of tuition, students are responsible to take out loans to cover the difference. One girl graduated with $100,000 of loan debt from an expensive private school when she could have attended another university at no cost. Not everyone has the chance to attend school fully paid, but we do have options of where we attend school and how much debt we incur.

It is not accurate to say, "If I don't go to this particular college, I won't be able to make anything of my life!" This is simply not true. In fact, God will accomplish his purposes in many who follow him yet have *no* college education. The two ingredients in his purposes are obedience and a good work ethic. It's an if/then proposition—if we listen and obey, then he cannot help but send the rain that blesses the work of our hands.

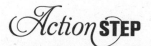 Have a serious talk with your parents about what you would need to do to get through school debt free.

What God Cares About

Whenever someone turns to the Lord, the veil is taken away. For the Lord is the Spirit, and wherever the Spirit of the Lord is, there is freedom. So all of us who have had that veil removed can see and reflect the glory of the Lord. And the Lord—who is the Spirit—makes us more and more like him as we are changed into his glorious image. 2 CORINTHIANS 3:16-18

Mirrors today require little other than a Windex wipe once a week, and even then it's only to remove the random toothpaste splash. In Paul's day, mirrors were much cruder. The more polished the metal of a mirror, the clearer the reflection. God's will for our lives is that we would submit ourselves to a continual regimen of being "polished." Why? So we can see him, not ourselves, and that remains true when we think of what we choose to do with our lives.

Does God even care what we do with our lives? To a degree, yes. The Bible speaks of good works he has "prepared in advance for us to do" (Ephesians 2:10, NIV). Many people report experiencing a "calling" from God. It happened to David, to Jonah, and to Paul . . . why not you and me? So have you ever wondered why God *hasn't* revealed more specifics for you? Is it too much to ask that he would tell us what career we will end up in one day or who we are going to marry or which college we should go to? Beyond some simple parameters, God cares far more about who we are than what we do. To be more specific, he cares a great deal about who we are becoming, because as long as we are sucking in air and letting it go again, we are basically construction zones.

As humans we are fixated on the "whats." What is your job? What are you studying? God is interested in the "whose." Who am I in Christ? Whose is he making me? We hope against hope that answering the "whats" will fill a desperate need for purpose in our lives. They won't—only in becoming more like Jesus, the "whose," will we stop striving and agree that he is enough.

There is a veil covering the eyes of every unbeliever. The veil is not removed when she figures out what she wants to do with her life, but when she turns to the Lord to figure out whose she is. As we seek God's will for our lives, we find his response to be this: he simply makes us more and more and more into the image of himself.

Action **STEP** Take out a journal and write a page defining "who" you are in Christ. Include an account of the last good "polishing" you allowed.

OCTOBER 30

Fighting with God

"Your name will no longer be Jacob," the man told him. *"From now on you will be called Israel, because you have fought with God and with men and have won."* GENESIS 32:28

The story of Jacob wrestling with God has to be one of the weirdest stories in all of Scripture (see Genesis 32:22-32). How is it that Jacob could be winning, and is God really so unfair that when he starts losing the match, he puts out his opponent's hip? We have to look into this one further, or we'll never be willing to wrestle with God!

Though Jacob was the second born, he came out holding the heel of his twin brother as if to say, "No way you're going out first, you dork!" Still unhappy with being number two, he was willing to lie and steal the birthright from his brother. This lie has something to do with that wrestling match. God could take out entire kingdoms with one word. But here's Jacob wrestling (the Bible says with God) for an entire night, and it *looked* like Jacob was winning. God wanted it that way. In the end, all it took to put Jacob out of commission was one touch from a finger. Poke! Your hip is out of joint. It wasn't much of a fight to begin with.

Next God asks Jacob, "What is your name?" Seriously? God doesn't know Jacob's name? Of course he does! But the last time his *earthly* father asked his name, he lied. "I am Esau," he told his blind father (see Genesis 27:18-19). Now Jacob's heavenly Father is asking his name, and surrendered, Jacob speaks the truth. "My name is Jacob," he says (see Genesis 32:27). Now that he has spoken the truth, God can use him. Now that he has stopped pretending and posing and demanding to receive things that do not rightly belong to him, God can make him a great nation.

What have you demanded from God? What have you schemed and wheedled and lied about so that it will come to pass? Go to battle with him. Wrestle until you know that you know you are not smart enough, experienced enough, strong enough, or even lucky enough to do this thing called life without him. Your surrender will be the sweetest thing that has ever happened to you!

 **Action STEP**   Ask God to show you any way in which you have been trying to manipulate circumstances while he may want you to simply wait . . . and trust.

OCTOBER 31
Go Ahead! Fail!

Don't wait in ambush at the home of the godly, and don't raid the house where the godly live. The godly may trip seven times, but they will get up again. But one disaster is enough to overthrow the wicked.
PROVERBS 24:15-16

There's room for many little failures on the way to big success. I read something brilliant about Wilbur and Orville Wright. Every time the brothers took their prototype airplane out to fly, they carried along a slew of spare parts. They knew two things. One day their plane would fly. And until that first successful flight occurred, they would need to endure countless crashes and make endless repairs. In other words, they would fail. A lot.

It's okay to fail. This is not permission to stop doing homework, do less than your best, or to stop studying for exams. But it's okay to take a risk, try something new, and fall on your face. Every success is built on a process just like that.

My husband and I are wired differently, yet both of us are willing to risk and fail. My husband is more likely to take calculated risks. If something is difficult and takes too much time, he scraps it. I am wired to not let a challenge get the better of me. I'll run late for appointments if I have to solve a problem. Failure is harder for me, because I'm wired with more of the "failure is not an option" mind-set.

It's not that you *might* have some failures on your way to success . . . your glory road will be *paved* with your failures. And really, if God is for us, what do we have to fear? Romans 8:31 says if God is for us, no one can stand against us. Proverbs 24 encourages us to realize that all people fail. We make mistakes financially, we show bad judgment, we place ourselves in the way of harm, we flat out sin . . . but there is always a hand up and restoration for the one who fears God. The righteous get to stand on the top of a shining mound of redeemed failures, while the wicked will only find themselves buried beneath it all.

 What was your latest failure or misstep? Write it down and stand on it; pray as you stand on it that God will use that failure to produce fruit in your life.
SW

Do You Love Him?

[Jesus said,] "Why do you keep calling me 'Lord, Lord!' when you don't do what I say? I will show you what it's like when someone comes to me, listens to my teaching, and then follows it." LUKE 6:46-47

Agnes Gonxha Bojaxhiu was born in Albania to a wealthy family devoted to the political life. But she would grow up to turn her back on her fortune as she answered the call of Jesus Christ to become a Catholic nun who took a vow of poverty. She lived in poverty and served those in poverty. You might know her as Mother Teresa.

If you know her story, you cannot deny that Mother Teresa chose to call Jesus Lord at any cost. For example, she went into the ministry when she was eighteen, and after that she never saw her beloved mother and sister again. When she won the coveted Nobel Peace Prize, she refused the $192,000 ceremonial banquet given to laureates, stating that the money should be given to the poor in India. She was obedient to the point of self-denial. She was not lord of her own life.

Take a moment to read Luke 6:48-49, Jesus' picture of what a life of obeying him looks like . . . and what refusal to obey looks like. Both are promises. This is what to expect. Why in the world would we receive both of these pictures—both of these promises—and still shake an angry fist at God when they come to fruition?

Following Jesus is not a free-for-all. Though he has given you a wonderful gift of free will, his precepts are not up for discussion. There's not your will and then his will, as if the two were equal. The truth is, if you follow him and obey, you will have a firm foundation. Furthermore, the Scriptures teach that our obedience really is the evidence of our love. John 14:15 (NIV) says, "If you love me, you will obey what I command." Do you love him?

 How are you doing in the area of "doing what Jesus says to do"? What can you do to align yourself to Jesus' will?

Living Lonely

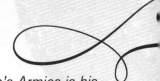

Your Creator will be your husband; the LORD of Heaven's Armies is his name! He is your Redeemer, the Holy One of Israel, the God of all the earth. ISAIAH 54:5

Corrie ten Boom, Holocaust survivor and author of *The Hiding Place*, never married. She loved and lost, but then she surrendered that pain and her life to God's plan. She once told a bitter, unmarried missionary, "Those called by God to live single lives are always happy in that state. This happiness, this contentment, is the evidence of God's plan." Contentment, however, should never be mistaken for ease. Single is hard. Married is hard too.

The single life should be one of service. One guy who had no plans to marry pointed out that the single person should expect to have *less* free time on her hands than the one who marries (see 1 Corinthians 7:32-35). That's certainly not what it would seem. It might make more sense to think that someone who is married and has children would be busiest. But God is more demanding than a spouse. The vision given to many who choose not to marry is the ability to live like the disciples—owning no home and having no family, they are free to drop everything and go the moment they are asked, no need to check with a spouse or put a home on the market. They can spend themselves for God.

The verse above declares that God is your husband. Today. In the future. Married or unmarried. Be careful to make him your ultimate priority. If God were to reveal plans for a future marriage to you today, don't lose focus. And don't be always on the lookout for Mr. Right. Still, don't be relieved for him to say, "You'll never marry." Instead, just let him lead you one day at a time and focus on your relationship with him. If that is your focus, you will be content like Corrie ten Boom.

 *Action* **STEP** Rate your life happiness quotient from one to ten. Only a relationship with Jesus can truly make that grow.

NOVEMBER 3
Straight Talk from Paul

I want you to be free from the concerns of this life. An unmarried man can spend his time doing the Lord's work and thinking how to please him. But a married man has to think about his earthly responsibilities and how to please his wife. His interests are divided. In the same way, a woman who is no longer married or has never been married can be devoted to the Lord and holy in body and in spirit. But a married woman has to think about her earthly responsibilities and how to please her husband. I am saying this for your benefit, not to place restrictions on you. I want you to do whatever will help you serve the Lord best, with as few distractions as possible. 1 CORINTHIANS 7:32-35

Paul said people shouldn't get married. Essentially, that is not a true statement, though for centuries it has been purported as truth. This letter to the Corinthians, and chapter 7 in particular, details Paul's response to earlier letters he received from the church. Some at Corinth were teaching that sex was a wicked practice, even within the confines of marriage. Using Paul's single status and his vigorous defense of sexual purity, they set Paul up as the poster child for a "No Sex" campaign. Paul is reasoning his way out of such a position in this letter.

His reasoning initially reads as if Paul is saying it is best to not marry. Paul presents the argument of spiritual focus—not sexual abstinence—as a good reason to be single. If men and women do not marry, they are free from the duties that go along with running a household and can instead focus on God's work. Paul is big on moderation in all things, though. In the end he says, "Do whichever works for you. Maybe you're more distracted by being single! Just be sure you're married if you need the physical intimacy" (see verses 35-37).

What we don't see clearly in Paul's words are his assumptions about the timing of Jesus' return. Paul's discourse throughout his letters makes it clear that he was expecting a speedy return on Jesus' part. *Sure, there's nothing wrong with marriage*, he reasoned. *But why would people want to focus all of their attentions on something so all-consuming when Jesus will be back before we know it?* Jesus meant what he said when he proclaimed, "No one knows the day or hour" (Matthew 24:36; Mark 13:32) . . . not even the super-apostle Paul! At the same time, perhaps Paul's words can encourage you in this: both marriage and non-marriage are good and profitable for a person, so don't be anxious about either!

 **STEP** Choose to be free to chase Jesus. What is God asking you to do to focus on him? Ask him.

New Beginnings

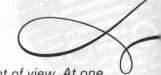

We have stopped evaluating others from a human point of view. At one time we thought of Christ merely from a human point of view. How differently we know him now! This means that anyone who belongs to Christ has become a new person. The old life is gone; a new life has begun! 2 CORINTHIANS 5:16-17

I often counsel young women who have sexual experience in their past. My heart was completely broken for a young girl who had recently gotten engaged and had confided in her new fiancé that she was not a virgin. Previous to knowing the Lord, she had lived as if she had not. (Imagine that!) Brace yourself for the young man's response: he told her that he needed to ask for advice from men in his life because he wasn't sure he could be with someone who had a past!

Of course we want to believe that true love waits. And it often does. It always should. But many get to the age where they are ready to be married and cry, "I wish I would have waited." Because now wedding plans are being discussed, and one fiancé is struggling with a past the other is bringing into the marriage bed.

Can I point out that we all have a past? It may be one of being angry, struggling with an eating disorder, participating in recreational drug use, cheating on homework, lying . . . but didn't Jesus come to set the captives free? What we have done in the past has wounded us, but Jesus came to bind up those wounds and to proclaim liberation. *Who was he?* This should not be the focus as you look at a guy you care for. *Who is he?* is the question of the hour. I wish every girl would ask this question. It would not only help us find the new creation in Christ, but also to recognize if the old creation is still running the show!

Marriage is a picture of Jesus and his church. As such, his will is that you bring as little baggage into that honeymoon suite as possible. Consider Paul's instruction, though, that we stop judging by human standards (where a person has been and what he or she has done) and begin evaluating where that person is *now* and how Christ has changed him or her. Jesus says if we remain in him, we bear fruit (see John 15:5) . . . but this is after he picked us up from the burn pile and grafted us onto that vine! Find a guy who is firmly attached to the vine, and you won't have to worry so much about where he's been.

 Ask God if there are any planks in your eye needing removal today (see Matthew 7:3-5, NIV).
DG

The Marriage Ring . . .
Or Is It a Boxing Ring?

[Josiah] did what was pleasing in the LORD's sight and followed the example of his ancestor David. 2 KINGS 22:2

My brothers and I watched my parents separate twice during our growing-up years. Ours was not a loud family. If I'm mad at you, I'm more likely to hide in a closet and make you wonder where I am for hours than I am to mince words with you. (Or at least that was the immature me!) I was once furious with my brother for helping my cousin beat me in a game of checkers. I ran about a mile to our neighborhood pharmacy. There I spent hours reading magazines and giggling at the thought of my family frantically looking for me. It never occurred to me that was what was truly happening, or how close they came to calling the police. I got grounded.

My dad was like me. When things were tense for him, he would simply stay away. He spent hours at his dental office, late into the night doing lab work. If anyone dared to complain he was gone a lot, he could point to the need to financially provide for the family. Marriages don't do well when deprived of time together. Mom didn't like it, and Dad got grounded too.

My mom and dad worked out their issues like champs. I know they both wished all of their fifty-five years together had been like the last five, which were beautiful. Marriage may be something that scares you because of what you've witnessed.

Today's verse is profound. You see, 99 percent of the time, a king was "like his father before him" (a phrase seen in the Old Testament frequently). This led to a lot of evil in the land. But Josiah, as noted in today's verse, did what was right even though his father had done evil. He chose to set his eyes on David as his example rather than his father.

We don't have to fear marriage as a battleground, even if that is what we have witnessed. There's hope to turn family history around. Though the norm is to follow in our parents' footsteps, Jesus is in the business of rewriting history. His precepts are true, and when followed, they bring blessings and peace. Chains of the past will be broken and marriages set free.

Whether your parents have a great marriage or not, select a couple outside your home who has a marriage like the one you'd like to have one day. Watch them! SW

Doesn't Marriage Mean He'll Be the Boss of Me?

Submit to one another out of reverence for Christ. For wives, this means submit to your husbands as to the Lord. For a husband is the head of his wife as Christ is the head of the church. EPHESIANS 5:21-23

At twenty-four I had no business counseling Cam (not her real name), who was older than me, through her marriage problems. I had been married all of six months, and my man was an absolute gem. Sure he left his socks on the floor wherever he had happened to remove them, but even then I knew I was in good shape if that was my biggest issue. And I knew it wasn't right that Cam's husband was *demanding* she had to submit to his authority at all times.

Technically he was correct. In the body of Christ we are to submit to one another (which literally means to voluntarily cooperate with another person). It is a mutual agreement to do life with one another, and every Christian is under the mandate to live in this way. Cam's husband was demanding "my way or the highway" . . . which is not the same thing at all.

He was also technically correct about the issue of the man's headship, but "headship" doesn't mean "boss of." It means "source of." Jesus is the head of the church . . . its source. From the head originates sense and propriety for the rest of the body, and while it would be a terrible misrepresentation to say we girls don't possess reason, God set up a certain order in the world after the fall of humankind. Man is responsible and accountable for his family, not in a position of power and authority over his wife. Cam's husband wanted to arm wrestle her emotionally at every turn. By the time she and I sat down to talk, Cam felt utterly demeaned and discounted.

What's that mean for you now? If you are dating, you should want to please your boyfriend, *as he should want to please you*. You should both find yourselves trying new things, new foods, new styles, and new hobbies . . . all because it's important to the other person. You should find yourselves laying down preferences for the other's sake and bragging about the other's accomplishments. Anything else may not look so much like Jesus and his precious bride, the church. And if you can't do it now, it won't change when you're married!

 Ask a woman you admire what it means to submit to her husband.
SW

How Old Do I Have to Be to Get Married?

It's better to stay unmarried, just as I am. But if they can't control themselves, they should go ahead and marry. It's better to marry than to burn with lust. 1 CORINTHIANS 7:8-9

There are two camps when it comes to the age-of-marriage debate. One camp espouses early marriages, but unless we go as far back as medieval times, early marriages were typically political in nature and among the upper classes. Still, this camp believes an early marriage staves off bad decisions made from youthful passion.

By the eighteenth century average ages for matrimony had crept into the midtwenties. In the "other" camp many believe a certain level of maturity should be achieved before a walk down the aisle. This camp may argue marriages between older persons have a higher success rate, *but they don't*. In fact, guys who marry in their late teens have a lower divorce rate than guys who marry in their twenties.

We have seen both types of marriages succeed, and we have seen both types fail; therefore, we don't think it's wise to camp on this debate at all. The thing is, many people are like a bull in a china shop, carelessly plowing through relationship after relationship and jumping into the first wedding band offered. There is a lesson to be learned from the pearl hunters of old. Pearls qualifying as precious gemstones most often are found in the wild . . . but they are maddeningly rare. Before pearl farms, hundreds of oysters had to be opened before even one pearl might be found. Are you waiting for a pearl? Or are you running off to date night with every oyster who asks you?

Paul is not saying, "Hey, if you have sexual urges, it's time to tie the knot." He was speaking here to people who believed spiritual gain was to be found in denying the flesh. God wants our obedience, not our sacrifices (see 1 Samuel 15:22). You may be ready to marry a sweetheart at eighteen. That is between you, your parents, and God. You may be called by circumstances to wait longer. We have many single friends in their thirties who are *longing* for a partner to run to the finish line with. We are proud of their committed wait, and we know when they do finally start their new lives with someone, that someone will be receiving a great gift.

 **Action STEP**   How will you know when to marry? Commit your answer to God.

Anybody Out There?

"I know the plans I have for you," says the LORD. "They are plans for good and not for disaster, to give you a future and a hope." JEREMIAH 29:11

One of the greatest fears we encounter as girls is never finding a life partner. What if there is someone for everyone out there . . . except for me? What if I never marry? What if I'm the old maid? Should I just trust that the first guy who comes along is the one for me? Does God have one person picked out for everyone?

Author J. R. R. Tolkien said every marriage is a "mistake" if we have to base it on the thoroughness of our search for a partner. Someone "better" could likely be found given enough time. But something mystical happens when the two become one flesh. The one we are with indeed becomes our soul mate.

Biblically, there is only one spouse addressed for us, and that is Jesus. God created us to be in a relationship with him. He is our beloved, and his grace is sufficient each day for both the loneliest and the most well-connected person. So what's the deal with this male/female attraction? Well, it's pretty necessary for the continuation of life, for one thing. But the beauty of when a man and a woman find each other and marry is that it's a picture of the relationship God purposes to have with us. One groom (Jesus) and one bride (his church) kept completely and zealously pure for one another.

The only "soul mate" we are intended to have in this life is God. Recognizing this truth weeds out a lot of the shaky theology found in the questions above, or at least helps us recognize they are the wrong questions to begin with. God's intention for our lives is pure good. If we remain single, he is enough. If we marry and lose our spouse only to marry again . . . God is enough. If we make a bad choice and our hearts are broken . . . he is enough, for he was meant, from the beginning, to be our first love.

Commit your future fully to Jesus in prayer. Don't be afraid of a good wrestling match! Talk it out until his promise for a hope and a future seems certain.

Divorce Is So Yesterday

Jesus responded, "[Moses] wrote this commandment only as a concession to your hard hearts. But 'God made them male and female' from the beginning of creation. 'This explains why a man leaves his father and mother and is joined to his wife, and the two are united into one.' Since they are no longer two but one, let no one split apart what God has joined together." MARK 10:5-9

Back in the Old Testament days, Israelite men could be terribly hard hearted. At the time, some men were so determined to get out of their marriages they actually *killed* their wives to do so. In an effort to save lives, an exasperated Moses gave divorce as a way out to those who were hardened.

In Mark 10, we see Jesus coming up with something brand new. "What do *you* want to encourage?" Jesus is asking. "Divorce? That's so old covenant. I am doing a new thing." He says it's not good to separate what God has put together. Do you believe Jesus is doing a new thing in marriages in the church today? We do. Here's some evidence.

The University of Chicago conducted a survey in 2011 and found while 50 percent of "nonreligious" marriages end in divorce, 42 percent of Christian marriages do too. Researchers from the University of Connecticut and the University of Virginia were not ready to accept those findings. Redefining "Christian" as those who attend church, share their faith, and accept the Bible as inerrant, they say Christians are *much* less likely to divorce than people who do not attend church. In other words, the divorce rate of the "churched Christians" is more like 15 percent. There is a difference.

Now, that doesn't make it easier if you're part of that 15 percent who has felt the pain of divorce. If your parents are divorced, we cannot change that, but we can encourage you for your future marriage by suggesting this: maybe only guys who are active in church should be on your potential date list.

Action **STEP**   Do something to encourage the marriage of a couple you know from the church. Write them a letter of encouragement. Give them a free night of babysitting so they can go out on a date. Tell them you are going to pray for them every day for a month.

Wuv, Twue Wuv

I am my lover's, and he claims me as his own. Come, my love, let us go out to the fields and spend the night among the wildflowers. Let us get up early and go to the vineyards to see if the grapevines have budded, if the blossoms have opened, and if the pomegranates have bloomed. There I will give you my love. SONG OF SONGS 7:10-12

Those are some steamy love words from Solomon. They may be easy to swallow if you are one who has been steeped in romance novels or movies, eager to find your own "Farm Boy" (remember *The Princess Bride*?) who can be revived from "mostly dead" by the mere thought of a lifetime spent with you. Or maybe you are among the more jaded, wondering if true love even exists. (You may be considering settling as Buttercup almost did for "wuv, twue wuv" with a guy she didn't even *like*.)

As great as romantic movies are, the picture they paint of "falling" in love is both dangerous and unrealistic. Here, then, is a list of realistic rules from a couple of happily married girls:

- One: Do not make warm fuzzies the number one indicator light on your dashboard of love. When we are crushing on a guy, our brains literally work overtime to convince us the emotions we are experiencing are the real and final deal. It's not all pussycats and rainbows, this love thing. The rain is going to fall, and the wind is going to howl . . . even in the midst of true love.
- Two: Avoid the term "falling in love." If you really fall in, you can really fall back out. When we fall, it's not planned. That's why falls are typically called accidents. Love is a decision we make, and the wedding vows paint a decent picture of the requirements of love: in sickness and in health, for richer and for poorer, till *death* parts us.
- Three: No thrill rides. Done correctly, feelings richer and deeper than can ever be imagined emerge from the ashes of a slow-cooked love. It is not a zero-to-sixty-in-three-seconds thrill ride.

 **Action STEP** Don't even think about loving a guy until you and Jesus are seriously in love! If you're already in a relationship, would you be willing to take a step back, slow down, and work on the Jesus part first?

Try Some Kindness

Do not judge others, and you will not be judged. Do not condemn others, or it will all come back against you. Forgive others, and you will be forgiven. Give, and you will receive. Your gift will return to you in full—pressed down, shaken together to make room for more, running over, and poured into your lap. The amount you give will determine the amount you get back. LUKE 6:37-38

Chad Eastham, researcher on all things teen and a keynote speaker for the Revolve Tour, says guys like girls who are kind and intelligent. He's quick to admit it sometimes looks like guys like other things—beauty, an attitude, a perfect body—but when it comes time to slip a ring on the finger, he's not the only one who says men deserve more credit than they are given.

In 1997 librarian Marylaine Block observed the results of an NBC survey on television: What do men look for in a woman? The results were categorized in a fashion she thought offensive to men. Just about 48 percent of the men said they want beauty. Thirty-six percent said intelligence, and 16 percent wanted a combination of the two. Block figured there was no way men could be so emotionally narrow so she decided to conduct her own survey. She was able to get detailed answers from fifty-six of her male friends. As expected, her friends reported a wide variety of attractors, but there were a few things every guy mentioned without fail.

Only one thing was mentioned by all fifty-six guys: they *all* said the girl must be kind. I have witnessed some heart-wrenching unkindness between opposite genders. Name-calling, put-downs, nasty looks, coldness to touch—I have seen more than I would want to. One day I informed a girl whom I know well that an old boyfriend of hers had experienced a personal revival. I was shocked to see her revulsion. "I don't really care what happens to him," she said, turning a cold shoulder to me as if I embodied this guy she hated so much. I couldn't help but think of this spiritual principle from Luke 6. Kindness can't be faked. We love or we don't. But when it is employed with 100 percent honesty, the odds are in favor of the kindhearted. It works with kittens and puppies. And it works in the deepest of human relationships: what you give out is what you get back.

 Kindness can stop the hand of the oppressor, turn away wrath, and win favor. It is part of the fabric of God's very character. Be kind to all you meet today! SW

It's Not Good to Be Alone

The LORD God said, "It is not good for the man to be alone. I will make a helper who is just right for him." . . . While the man slept, the LORD God took out one of the man's ribs and closed up the opening.
GENESIS 2:18, 21

A few years ago, I worked with Nancy Leigh DeMoss to bring *Lies Young Women Believe* into print. As a part of our preparation, we sent blogger and author Erin Davis on a journey to interface with teens across the nation to find out just what they are struggling with in terms of lies. One of the most heartbreaking lies we identified in our tour of America was "having a career outside the home is more fulfilling than being 'just' a wife and mom." The young women we talked to said things like "It has become uncool to want a husband and a family" and "For me the whole family idea is kind of overrated." We live in a world where women have the freedom to have careers, but they are fearful of feeling undervalued if they do anything but have a career!

Mind if I turn the tables on this? I interviewed my son and his best friend about this. They said that they felt sorry for women because the world was telling them they didn't have the freedom to act like they might love being wives and moms. Then they pointed out that a guy who acted like his career was more important than a relationship with a woman would be considered a jerk! How true! We have eaten a feminist lie, and it has not empowered us but has taken away our freedom to enjoy the idea of having an amazing relationship with one man one day. God created woman because it wasn't good for man to be alone. In most cases, it's not good for us to be alone either.

Have you believed a lie that marriage is a second-rate position? What do you think God would have you do with that?

Visit liesyoungwomenbelieve.com today, and join in the conversation with hundreds of other teen girls who want to live in truth!
DG

Whose Side Should I Take?

"Honor your father and mother." EPHESIANS 6:2

At the end of her parents' big, long divorce Jena came to me with a big question. Her dad had been unfaithful and done some really strange things to hurt her mom. Her mom had been coldhearted and controlling for a very long time. She couldn't tell whose fault it was, but she was pretty sure that in this case it took two to tango! But the court was asking her to decide who to live with, and it made her feel like she'd be taking sides. She wanted to know whose side she should take.

Neither. The Bible says to honor your father and mother. Period. It doesn't say to honor them if they aren't divorced, have never fought, and don't have any faults. Divorce isn't easy, and hopefully you've been able to weather it or help a friend weather it without feeling like you needed to take sides.

Here are a few tips to help you walk in honor.

Don't take sides. This means you spend time with each parent as much as is possible and that you don't say anything negative about one parent to another. Speak in honor, and your heart will follow.

Avoid role reversal. Many times after divorce, a parent (or both) will experience deep depression. They don't function at their best. They are mourning something once (or in some cases, still) very dear to them. Give them some time, but don't try to be the parent. Back off. Let them lead. Honor!

Talk to someone outside the family who also loves both your mom and your dad. You'll need to have someone you can trust with your inner conflicts. Find a neutral friend of your family or your pastor's wife to talk with when it becomes hard to avoid taking sides or if you have a sad mom or dad on your hands. A trusted family friend will help you make good choices when it gets hard.

Tell your parents how you feel. It's not good to keep your feelings stuck inside. This is hard for everyone, and your parents can most likely handle what's going on inside of you better if you tell them. (Reading minds is rarely effective.)

Pray often. God is walking through this with you. He sees you. And he feels your hurt. Talk to him about it.

 Tell your mom or dad how you are feeling about their relationship today no matter if they are divorced or doing great.

DG

What Exactly Is a Vow?

Most of all, my brothers and sisters, never take an oath, by heaven or earth or anything else. Just say a simple yes or no, so that you will not sin and be condemned. JAMES 5:12

Can anything really match the beauty of traditional vows?

I, (name), take you, (name), to be my (wife/husband), to have and to hold from this day forward, for better or for worse, for richer, for poorer, in sickness and in health, to love and to cherish; from this day forward until death do us part.

I have witnessed many marriages in my short time on earth. And I have seen some of those same unions end. They all said the same things, that they would forsake all others, and there were promises made about both health *and* bad times. But then discouragement and disillusionment entered in . . . and it really wasn't for better or for worse after all.

Vows are about what we will do unconditionally, yet most people make them with caveats, or provisions, in mind. *I'll do all these things as long as my needs are being met. But when I'm not getting what I think I should get . . . attention, education, a certain salary, an agreeable place to live . . . it's my prerogative to get out.* I'll bet Robertson McQuilkin's wife was glad he didn't see it that way.

McQuilkin was only fifty-seven when his wife was diagnosed with progressive Alzheimer's disease. Many of his well-meaning friends suggested he put her in an institution. She deteriorated to the degree she could no longer speak in sentences and would even confuse a simple yes for a no, but McQuilkin remembered the vows he had made. He took an early retirement, resigning as president of Columbia International University, and remained by her side until she passed away.*

We live in a culture that does not honor faithfulness or truth; God tells us for this reason we should be quite hesitant to take a vow. Why perjure ourselves? Just say yes or no, the Bible says, and then live by it. Don't make promises that depend on other people's behaviors or circumstances. Only promise what *you* will do.

 **Action STEP**   Practice saying only yes or no.

---

*You can read McQuilkin's story at http://www.christianitytoday.com/ct/2004/februaryweb-only /2-9-11.0.html?start=5.

NOVEMBER 15
Four Key Ingredients

Love is patient and kind. Love is not jealous or boastful or proud or rude. It does not demand its own way. It is not irritable, and it keeps no record of being wronged. It does not rejoice about injustice but rejoices whenever the truth wins out. Love never gives up, never loses faith, is always hopeful, and endures through every circumstance.
1 CORINTHIANS 13:4-7

We didn't really know each other. From the time I first met my husband to the day we walked down the aisle, less than a year had passed. I admit that's not an ideal timeline. It's really fast, but we did better than Jonathan's grandparents. They met on Good Friday and married on Easter! The good news is that they stayed married until death separated them. Jonathan and I plan to do the same, and though we didn't know each other the way we thought we did on August 19, 1989, there was one thing we agreed on. We were never going to say "the *D* word," even in jest.

Relationship experts say if two people can agree on four things—kids, money, faith, and in-laws—they are more likely to have a long, happy marriage. The number one detractor in marriages today is finances, namely large chasms of debt dug out by years of not discussing finances. When it comes to kids, there is more to discuss than whether or not to have them: How will you raise them? Discipline them? School them? How many? As for in-laws, you don't marry just one person; you become a full-fledged member of a second family. That second family, if radically different from your own, has the potential to wreak all kinds of havoc in the life of your marriage.

First Corinthians 13 is often read as a picture of perfect love. It does not speak to "agreement" as much as the ability of each person to yield to the other. Do you know how long you would have to wait to find a guy who literally agreed with you 100 percent? It's only after you've spent about a year in marriage that you uncover what your spouse really thinks about these things. Agreeing is born out of yielding.

Love bends to the will of the other and is ruled by kindness rather than power. Love favors the other person, wanting the other to succeed. It doesn't mock, tease, or wound. It keeps order and does not invite drama. Love invites agreement, not because it makes two people think alike, but because it makes two people favor each other.

 *Action* **STEP** Ask a couple you respect what they think the top four ingredients of a successful marriage are.

NOVEMBER 16
Kids Are Hard Work

Children are a gift from the LORD; they are a reward from him. Children born to a young man are like arrows in a warrior's hands. How joyful is the man whose quiver is full of them! He will not be put to shame when he confronts his accusers at the city gates. PSALM 127:3-5

The London Press once reported that Prime Minister Cameron and his wife left their little girl behind at a pub. A lot of pubs in England are arranged to have a large garden in the back where kids run free and play while adults spend hours visiting with friends and getting caught up on life. The family had arrived in two cars, and each parent thought the little girl was with the other, when in fact she was in the garden. As public figures the couple took a beating over their "parenting skills."

We don't judge them. Parenting is full of insanity, and parenting *you* has been no different! But let's get one thing straight: kids are a blessing. If a child (that would be you) has been given to a family, that child is intended to be a blessing from the Father. You are a gift *given* by almighty God himself. I know this to be truth, as I was not able to conceive. I did ask God for children, and I did not care where they came from . . . he surprised us with two fully grown but still "forming" teenage girls. They are my answers to prayer, yes, *given* by almighty God himself.

The psalmist compares children (again, that's you) to arrows. Arrows are weapons! Odd, right, that you would be called an instrument of war or hunting or self-defense? Yet this is what you become as your parents age. Children come to the family when the parents are strong and in their youth; as the parents age, the children are now able to provide for and defend the parents. It's a beautiful song and dance . . . starring you! You've been a lot of work, but you're worth it!

 *Action* **STEP** Reminisce with your mom or dad about a time when you were hard work. Enjoy a good laugh over it. SW

Anything but Babysitting, Please!

Children are a gift from the LORD; they are a reward from him.
PSALM 127:3

It was the mother of all temper tantrums. As a general rule I didn't take on too many babysitting assignments in my teens, but how do you say no when your brother is in the hospital with a shattered leg and someone needs to stay with his daughter, my niece? I was on toddler duty, like it or not.

Cassie was about two years old. As cute as she was, she was equally stubborn, and she had the lungs to back her up. She didn't want to go to bed. I did. And a battle ensued. At some point I called my mom and asked what to do. "Just let her cry it out," Mom said. So I covered my ears with a pillow and fell asleep with the little fire alarm blaring on the floor beside me. I woke several hours later to Cassie restored to all of her preciousness, arms and legs tangled around my torso, sleeping like an angel.

It's funny, neither Dannah nor I liked to babysit. But both of us really have loved being mothers. Whether or not you like babysitting, hanging around with the little cousins at family dinners, or helping out in the nursery is irrelevant in terms of enjoying motherhood one day. Don't be too hard on yourself if you don't like babysitting. You aren't really supposed to want a baby . . . yet.

But of greater concern is the feminist-planted notion that having babies is a second-class position to being what some contemporary writers have called "fremales," the women who are free from husband and children to do anything they want. If that's your attitude, you might want to study what God says instead of what the thinkers of this world say. He says that children are a gift. And a reward. A reward is something given in recognition for service and effort. It's not that we can't enjoy a good career. Work all you want, but when it's time to stop, maybe you could consider a baby the great reward!

 Go ahead! Babysit for someone today. For free!
SW

It's Not about You

Don't be selfish; don't try to impress others. Be humble, thinking of others as better than yourselves. Don't look out only for your own interests, but take an interest in others, too. PHILIPPIANS 2:3-4

There is actually a blog for people who do not want to become parents. It says our culture has become "child-centric" and calls people back to a healthier egocentric existence. What? Are you kidding? We hope you hear the foolishness in that statement. The website actually has a "Top 100 Reasons Not to Have Kids" list which contains more self-indulgence than we have seen in a long time. Among other ridiculous claims on this list are statements that childless people have happier marriages, suffer less depression, and are able to be great aunts and uncles because they have not been jaded by their own kids. Wow!

Did you know that the Bible actually says that in the last days people will be so caught up in themselves that they will be "without family love"? Paul writes in 2 Timothy 3:2-3, "People will be lovers of themselves . . . without love" (NIV). The Greek word for love is *astorgos*, which means "family love." We live in a day and age where the love of self is growing and the love of family is diminishing. Is it the last days? No one will ever know. But we can know that God does not like the current mentality that children and families are an imposition on self.

It's not about you!

Your life was meant to be shared with and for God. That means you'll live a chaotic, messy life going through the ups and downs of others. God calls you to be humble and consider others better than yourself. One thing is for certain: if you aren't living that way now, it will be very hard to embrace giving up yourself for a family one day. When it comes to the way you care about and for your friends, are you more egocentric, or do you put them first?

 Talk to a girlfriend today about the pressure to be a woman who doesn't want to have kids. Does she feel it? Do you?

You're Just like Your Mother!

Pay careful attention to your own work, for then you will get the satisfaction of a job well done, and you won't need to compare yourself to anyone else. For we are each responsible for our own conduct. GALATIANS 6:4-5

Rudyard Kipling's Mowgli of *The Jungle Book* is a great example of how we grow up to imitate those who nurture us. Even though Mowgli is a human child, he grows up with a pack of wolves that love and care for him. He becomes like them. He hunts like them. Plays like them. We become like those who raise us.

This is good news for some of us. You may hope to imitate your parents, and rightfully so. Remember the blessing of such an upbringing, but remember, too, that you must run your own race. *Imitate* is an action verb, so you must actually *do* the good you saw your parents doing. You don't get their gold medals on the awards platform—they do. Fortunately, they've trained you to win your own awards.

Some of us, however, do not have admirable examples. There is good news in this as well. (Even fictional Mowgli found that he wasn't exactly like his parents. For one, he had the masterful ability to pluck painful thorns from the paws of his brothers.) You have innate gifts in you planted by God, and no one can take that away. No matter who has raised you, you are his!

Do you need a good real-life example? Well, Nelson Mandela might be just what you are looking for. Not only is he one of current history's greatest advocates of peace and human value, but he also exemplifies a man who grew to do things differently than his father. His father was a polygamist, having four wives at one time. Nelson went on to love deeply his first wife, who was killed in a car crash. Though he had two other wives in his decades of living, he was married to them at separate times. He's not perfect. But he's doing it differently (and better) than his dear old dad.

You are not your parents, for good or for bad. Fear that "I may become just like them" or "I could never live up to their example" is just that—fear. And perfect love drives out all fear (see 1 John 4:18). If God's Word is reliable, then you've got this one. Do not be afraid.

 Treat your mom, dad, or both to a special treat today.

Finding Mr. Right

"Haven't you read the Scriptures?" Jesus replied. "They record that from the beginning 'God made them male and female.' And he said, 'This explains why a man leaves his father and mother and is joined to his wife, and the two are united into one.' Since they are no longer two but one, let no one split apart what God has joined together." MATTHEW 19:4-6

Graciela Asturias may have gotten one of the most unique marriage proposals ever. To celebrate her twenty-seventh birthday, her boyfriend Alex bought her a ticket on a specially designed Boeing 727 that creates the experience of microgravity during four 5-minute plunges—going straight up and down between twenty-four thousand and thirty-five thousand feet. (Can you say pass me the barf bag?) While Alex and Graciela were floating in the cabin, Alex asked her to marry him. Don't worry. The ring didn't float away while at zero G. The couple was happily engaged!

Today's Bible passage was an earth-shattering challenge when issued. Back in the day men were imbued with all the privileges. Women and children were mere property. Nonetheless, Jesus called strong, manly men to a place of tenderness and oneness with their wives and children. Jesus was not only rebuking divorce, he was also speaking against the overall idea of treating women like property. Where do you go to find a guy tender enough to rock a crying baby, change a dirty diaper, and tell everyone he knows it's the best thing he's ever done? (And one that knocks your socks off with a great proposal, zero G or not?) Do those guys even exist today?

We know a lot of them. But they are a bit busy these days. You won't find them out hunting for girls, so if *you* are out hunting . . . you may be meeting the wrong guys. These guys are family loyalists. They are serving their communities and churches, and they are probably in a sport or something like music or theater that takes up even more of their time. The best way for you to find him is to get so wrapped up in God that he has to chase God to find *you*. Of course that makes it sound so simple, and it's not, but there are good guys—good husband and dad material—out there. Be patient. They are truly worth the wait!

 **Action STEP** Ask a trusted older and wiser friend to help you make a list of key characteristics found in a good husband and father.

NOVEMBER 21
Adoption Stories

You have not received a spirit that makes you fearful slaves. Instead, you received God's Spirit when he adopted you as his own children. Now we call him, "Abba, Father." For his Spirit joins with our spirit to affirm that we are God's children. ROMANS 8:15-16

Jonathan and I have two daughters today because Dannah's beloved fell off a Jet Ski and broke his pelvis. (No kidding!) My band was playing at a summer camp in New Jersey, and Bob and Dannah were the camp speakers. One of the Jet Skis Bob brought along broke down and had to be left behind. When Bob returned to get the repaired watercraft, he had an accident, making it immediately apparent he would not be able to do an upcoming event in California. *Could we go in his place?* California is tough, but someone had to go.

Two months later I sat in an auditorium chair listening to Dannah teach like a Jedi master (only better and with much clearer skin) when a girl tapped me on the shoulder. There was a girl crying in the bathroom. Could I go talk with her? And that's where I met my oldest daughter, Rachael, wrestling with a painful past and an uncertain future. We offered a home, and she and her sister Marie bravely accepted. Just like that, the homeless and the barren were both brought into family. It hasn't been easy, and it's never been perfect, but God's goodness is evident in this. You are an adopted child as well.

Sin alienated all of humanity from God, and his Word says that by the time Christ died for us, we were not only out of the family, but enemies. We may come to Jesus in bondage, as enemies, but by the time he is through with us, those chains are gone, and he sends us on to the Father as God's own daughters.

God wants a big family. Separated from his kids by sin and disobedience, he made a way through Jesus to again add children to his household. He adopts and adopts and adopts. I pray one day you would do the same. If only those who are unable to conceive adopt, we will not be able to place the world's 200 million orphans in loving homes. The problem is epidemic, but our own Father has set the pace for us to follow!

Action **STEP** Visit websites, such as holtinternational.org, to catch up on the orphan crisis in the world today.
SW

What If . . .

My dear children, I am writing this to you so that you will not sin. But if anyone does sin, we have an advocate who pleads our case before the Father. He is Jesus Christ, the one who is truly righteous. He himself is the sacrifice that atones for our sins—and not only our sins but the sins of all the world. 1 JOHN 2:1-2

I cannot answer for what made me childless, but after two years using no contraception, Jonathan and I became suspicious . . . maybe we couldn't do this baby-making thing. We were both tested and came out "normal" . . . still no babies. We chose to forgo expensive tests and procedures, believing God would give us children in his own manner and in his own time. We didn't even pursue adoption. But look what God did! At just the right time, we were given two beautiful teenage girls.

Parenting is scary. Even though people affirm us all the time with, "You're such great parents," it feels like a farce every time. Parenting is a long road of "what ifs" . . . What if I'm a terrible parent? What if I can't afford this? What if my kid is hurt, gets sick, or hurts someone else? What if she is bullied? What if I'm the subject of many hours of therapy somewhere down the road? These aren't terrible questions. After all, who else is as well acquainted with our personal frailties as we are? I am a sinner. Can a sinner possibly parent well?

You will mess up whether you parent or not. God's Word is such a great treatise on right living. Follow it to the letter, and you will be not only the perfect child of God, but also the perfect parent. But if . . . just if . . . you should happen to slip (and if perhaps your parents have slipped a bit), you have the perfect attorney in your corner. John uses the word for a lawyer, *parakletos*, to describe Jesus here. Jesus speaks on our behalf to a Father eager to erase our guilt and set our relationship with him to right again.

It is the perfect gift of grace. Parents, however, aren't perfect. They are doing the most difficult job imaginable with, to be honest, a limited set of natural abilities. Should you choose to take on such a task, limited, too, in your flesh, do not be afraid. You are represented by the attorney with the best record of not only acquittal but also rehabilitation in the history of criminal behavior . . . ever.

 Ask a parent or mentor to pray for you as a potential future parent.
SW

Would It Be Good to Be Rich?

Sell your possessions and give to those in need. This will store up treasure for you in heaven! And the purses of heaven never get old or develop holes. Your treasure will be safe; no thief can steal it and no moth can destroy it. LUKE 12:33

The wealthy are entitled to *give* their children up to $13,000 per year tax free. This can legally come from both parents, so it is possible to receive $26,000 each year. If a gift tax form is filed with the IRS, the wealthy can give a one-time gift of up to $5 million tax free. I actually have friends who do this! They give their kids $500 a week in allowance! While you may be salivating at the thought of being cared for by copious amounts of money you did nothing to earn, please consider this to be the financial equivalent . . . of being punked.

A tragic number of young people getting "rich" in this manner soon go broke. (Certainly you've heard of those rare lottery winners, who just a few years down the road are worse off than before because they've spent all of their winnings!) Although they're accustomed to never hearing the word *no*, life inevitably rears its ugly head and utters that word for the first time. Those who have never learned to work, who have felt entitled to good fortune, are unprepared to face what comes next.

If your parents have the ability to be generous with you, be thankful. (An appropriate time of year to consider it, don't you think?) It's a gift, not an obligation. If there is *any* inheritance earmarked for you, your job is to be filled with awe at such generosity. It is their prerogative to give to you, not your entitlement to receive.

In the meantime, consider your own responsibility. Hard work always puts food in storehouses. The Bible says so. When we give, we are blessed. The Bible says so. If we save up more than we need, moths come in and destroy our excess, and thieves come in to steal. The Bible says so.

We hope you haven't been punked. We hope you know what it is to earn a little, save a little, give a little, and be content with a little. This is moth-proof, theft-proof living!

 How can you express thankfulness to your parents for how they provide for you? Take some time to do whatever comes to mind.

What's the Right Way to Worship?

Praise him with a clash of cymbals; praise him with loud clanging cymbals. Let everything that breathes sing praises to the LORD! Praise the LORD! PSALM 150:5-6

We see nearly every type of worship represented in Scripture—it's like a worship bazaar in those pages.

Are hymns too traditional? No way! Colossians 3:16 says we are to "sing psalms and *hymns* and spiritual songs to God with thankful hearts" (emphasis added). Paul wasn't talking about three specific types of songs here, but about the tendency of the Holy Spirit to move in a variety of ways.

Is rock music too contemporary? Psalm 150 just may be the musician's psalm. It lists horns, lyre and harp, tambourine, dancing, strings, flutes, cymbals, and singing. Of course it doesn't mention rock music—rock wasn't invented for another 2,500 years. But the word *praise* occurs in little Psalm 150 thirteen times. It was a psalm traditionally used in raucous celebrations during festival times, indicating the usefulness of many kinds of songs in worship.

And what is the proper position during worship? Should we stand, sit, kneel, lie down, or raise our hands? All are mentioned specifically in God's Word. None are right or wrong. Though more public displays of worship such as the raising of hands may feel awkward at first, some of its origins are pretty cool. One image for the raising of hands is that of remembering our position as God's child. A child will raise her arms in asking her daddy, her abba, to hold her.

Raising hands is also a way to hold up our "standard" in battle. The standard is an army's banner, identifying just whom the army belongs to. When Joshua fought the Amalekites, Moses held his hands up to God (sometimes with the help of two other men) for an entire day. As long as Moses' hands were raised, Joshua was winning (see Exodus 17:8-16). We raise our hands to indicate the battle is God's and he is victorious.

 Worship is really one way to say thank you to a God who created and loves you. Be involved in worship this week during this thankful season. Do not merely observe. Sing, dance, praise, raise holy hands.

Do Guys Struggle with Beauty?

People are like grass; their beauty is like a flower in the field. The grass withers and the flower fades. But the word of the Lord remains forever.
1 PETER 1:24-25

Let's see . . . we didn't bother to ask our husbands this question. Seemed a little weird. Plus, we've seen them preen in front of a mirror. Guys are more concerned with virility, though. Are they strong? Can they provide? They like the idea of women admiring them and men being envious of their prowess.

What would it do to a boy's view of his "beauty," then, to be born with no arms or legs? This is precisely the story of Nick Vujicic. Photographs show an adorable little blond guy bravely adjusting to every hurdle life can throw his way, but Nick says an epic battle raged inside. He knew he was a sinner in need of God's grace, but he threw down the gauntlet with God. "I won't let you in my heart until you tell me why," he said. "Why did you take away from me what everyone else has?"

One day Nick read the story of a man more disabled than himself, and it clicked. In a video interview he says, "There's no point being whole on the outside if you're broken on the inside. I needed to know the truth of who I am, why I'm here, and where I'm going when I'm not here. And I haven't found that truth anywhere else but in Jesus Christ. I am not a man without arms and legs. I am a child of God." The miracle of Nick's obedience to his King has seen over two hundred thousand people around the world surrender at the throne of God.

Wow. I wonder what lies we've been believing about our eyebrows, the flab under our arms, or our unstoppable bootie that could possibly be greater to overcome than the lies Nick has stared down. You can watch his video testimony. He's a handsome guy. But truth is not about beauty or arms and legs . . . you cannot watch his story and believe otherwise.

Peter says our physical beauty and prowess both will fade and wither. It's not uncommon to hear, "She was a beautiful woman once." It happens to everyone blessed enough to grow old. But God's Word remains forever. That's why Nick asked the right questions. And it's where he found the right answer.

Action **STEP** Spend time today thanking God for any obstacle he has put in your way, especially if it has to do with beauty or your body, and ask him to use it like he has Nick's!

What's between the Dashes?

None of us can hold back our spirit from departing. None of us has the power to prevent the day of our death. There is no escaping that obligation, that dark battle. ECCLESIASTES 8:8

This is going to sound like science fiction, but we promise you it is real—there is an emerging "science" that aims to give the dying a second chance somewhere down the road. Cryonics is a process by which the diseased body is injected with chemicals to stop molecular degeneration, then frozen and stored in a deep freeze in the hopes that one day science will be able to bring the body back to life and cure whatever disease did the patient in. Some cryogenic patients, not wanting to be reunited with an aging body, have only their heads cryogenically preserved. We kid you not.

Solomon did not validate the ideals of cryonics. He said no one can hold back death at its appointed time. A king would not have the power to do so. The greatest doctors cannot stop death; the strongest armies are powerless against it. Get the picture? Yet with our Prince of Peace there is nothing to fear. He has defeated death—the resurrection hoped for by those cryogenically frozen is *exactly* what Jesus will cause to happen for those who are found hidden by faith in him!

This world, the time we spend in the dash between our birth year and the time of our death, is far more frightening than death. Author Randy Alcorn says this world is the closest many of us will ever have to come to the gates of hell. C. S. Lewis wrote, "Has this world been so kind to you that you should leave with regret? There are better things ahead than any we leave behind."

Bronnie Ware is a nurse who devoted several years to caring for dying patients. She interviewed each and wrote a book, *The Top Five Regrets of the Dying.* Paraphrased, here they are:

- I should have been more diligent in chasing my dreams.
- I worked when I should have been with my family.
- I wish I had shared my feelings more openly.
- I didn't keep in touch with good friends.
- Happiness was a choice, and I missed it.

 See if there are any regrets you already have that can be put to rest forever today.

What Should I Do with Nightmares?

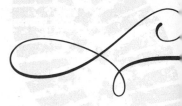

When a strong man like Satan is fully armed and guards his palace, his possessions are safe—until someone even stronger attacks and overpowers him, strips him of his weapons, and carries off his belongings. LUKE 11:21-22

I needed a strong man, though not in the boy/girl sense. I was just a little girl, and I was having nightmares. In my dream I would slip into the closet underneath our stairway—the big one where we kept our vacuum cleaners and suitcases—during a game of hide-and-seek. In the darkness I would become aware of someone else's presence in the space with me . . . and then . . . the laugh. It was corny and no doubt inspired by the Wicked Witch of the West, but it was paralyzing when I was ten years old. I tried to run but could get no feet—no traction.

When I was older and married, a long spate of nightmares terrified me even more. I would dream I was at my husband's wedding. He was marrying someone other than myself, and no matter what I tried, I could not change the situation. I woke up crying night after night, so relieved to find Jonathan sleeping beside me. Those were terrible, terrible dreams.

What should we do with nightmares? This is the stuff of the gospel! The good news is that Jesus is the provision all the world has been waiting for and longing after, bearing up under the suffering of living nightmares until the stronger man can arrive and drive out the one who terrorizes. Jesus is the one who is greater than the strongman.

When Jesus answers our prayers, he gives evidence of the strongman's eviction. This is not a war in which the results are yet to be determined. Jesus wins. It's already done. There remains no need then to suffer under the strongman's power. In both nightmare cases when I prayed God's Word . . . the dreams immediately ceased.

> "It is about the greatness of God, not the significance of man. God made man small and the universe big to say something about himself."
> JOHN PIPER, *Don't Waste Your Life*

Action STEP Use Scripture to pray, for yourself and others, that bad dreams would be evicted! In fact . . . God's power is evidenced when we pray his Word in *every* situation!
SW

NOVEMBER 28

Why Am I Here?

Now get to your feet! For I have appeared to you to appoint you as my servant and witness. You are to tell the world what you have seen and what I will show you in the future. ACTS 26:16

There's an old story about the role purpose plays in our lives. The story is of a research group that hires people to come work construction for ten dollars an hour. First thing in the morning the crew reporting for work begins digging holes, all of the same dimension. After lunch the crew is told to fill the holes back in. They are paid in cash at the end of the day and invited to come back for double pay the next day. Only half return. Why? We want to know we have purpose. At some point, even money cannot assuage the fear that we are wasting our lives away.

How nice would it be to have the advantage Paul had of Jesus flat out appearing and announcing his plans. Granted, Paul had to be blinded for this to occur, but the blindness was temporary! (See Acts 9:3-18.) Or the advantage Susan Stafford had to speak to Jesus from the confines of her jail cell. Jesus told her straight up he was about to rescue her, but she was to immediately leave her life of prostitution. She never looked back.

It just doesn't happen that way for most of us. In fact, you may be struggling today with the question of exactly why you are on this earth. Keep struggling if that is the case, for you have landed on one of life's most important questions. I was required to read a book by Auschwitz survivor Viktor Frankl (*Man's Search for Meaning*) my freshman year of college. The book chronicles Frankl's observations from a Nazi death camp as to why some people survived the camps and others gave in to the seemingly inevitable. Frankl decided it came down to one thing—purpose. Those who could hold on to memories of family and a sense of belonging while trusting a greater purpose still awaited them somehow survived the horrors of the camp. Frankl did not allow himself to be a victim but continued to assume he was a victor. The difference is enormous.

 **Action STEP** Sometime in the next week watch the old black-and-white Christmas movie *It's a Wonderful Life* with some friends. Purpose is summed up so beautifully in this story.
SW

What's inside Me?

A tree is identified by its fruit. If a tree is good, its fruit will be good. If a tree is bad, its fruit will be bad. You brood of snakes! How could evil men like you speak what is good and right? For whatever is in your heart determines what you say. MATTHEW 12:33-34

From the outside it looked great. The stainless steel had recently been polished. No pictures were hanging on the front of our Frigidaire; that's not HGTV enough for my design-conscious husband. Opening it up was another story. My guy doesn't cook, and after three weeks on the road ministering to teens like you, "stuff" was growing in there. No, you can't always tell what's going on just by looking at the outside. Sometimes you have to take a look—and a whiff—inside.

You and I are not like a refrigerator with a nice hard casing that keeps in all the bad smells. You and I are soft and pliable—jars of clay, the Bible says in 2 Corinthians 4:7. Whatever is on the inside somehow manages to seep to the outside. Jesus said we are like trees that can be named (identified) by our fruit.

Jesus was addressing the Pharisees, but just in case you and I have pharisaical tendencies, let's take notes! The Pharisees were religious leaders who took care to obey the Law to the nth degree. No stone was left unturned by these men. If they were high-end models today, they would be the ones starving themselves to the point of zero percent body fat. They would be the ones wearing the hottest designers, the ones expecting paparazzi to fall all over them on the red carpet. Image was everything.

But inside, the Pharisees were not quite as holy. They were like my refrigerator—a lot of things were rotting in there. They were the next top model, so catty toward the other girls. They might be the mean girl or the queen bee. Their thoughts toward others were so careless and biting they had failed to recognize something. That rotten, bitter feeling inside was not their disgust for other, lesser people after all. It was the rotting of their own souls rising up like bile in their mouths.

Being beautiful on the outside isn't everything, is it? In fact, when we smell something rotten coming from the inside, it's probably a good idea to put the beauty brushes down until the stench is removed.

 **STEP** Identify the smelliest thing in your heart's fridge. How can you remove it?

SW

Joy to the World

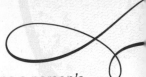

A cheerful heart is good medicine, but a broken spirit saps a person's strength. PROVERBS 17:22

"Joy is the serious business of heaven," C. S. Lewis said in his book *Letters to Malcolm.* He wasn't kidding. There was something significant in both a physical and a spiritual sense in God's mind when he created this little thing we do called smiling.

God made it easy for us to smile. A slight smile can be created by as few as six facial muscles. In contrast, it takes nearly *all* of a person's facial muscles to create a frown. (For the record, there are at least forty-three facial muscles.) Maybe that's why we complain so much . . . it's easier than frowning!

A smile is part of a universal, nonverbal communication system. No matter where you are in the world, a smile is received and understood to mean both happiness and acceptance. It's hard to fake smiles. When not genuine, the forehead and the corners of the eyes fail to wrinkle. In a study, people who looked at photos of smiling faces consistently rated the smiling faces more attractive than the faces of people not smiling. Smiling makes you pretty.

People who smile are healthier than people who are unhappy. A smile is legitimately an immune system booster. Smiles also reduce blood pressure as the brain releases endorphins and serotonin. It's the all-natural high!

Finally, you are not the only one who benefits from a smile. A smile is imitative behavior. All emotions are technically "contagious," meaning we will mimic, even subconsciously or minimally, the emotions we witness or perceive from others. This is why a highly negative person is toxic in a group.

You can *give* the world joy. Then again, you can be a giver of bitterness or hostility. One thing most of us on this celestial ball would probably agree to is the sentiment that we need more joy. Joy to the world, right? 'Tis the season!

 Give smiles away for free today. Make them intentional, but make them real.

The Gift of Unity

How wonderful and pleasant it is when brothers live together in harmony! For harmony is as precious as the anointing oil that was poured over Aaron's head. . . . Harmony is as refreshing as the dew from Mount Hermon that falls on the mountains of Zion. And there the LORD has pronounced his blessing, even life everlasting. PSALM 133:1-3

People are awesome! God's creativity knew no bounds when he fashioned the variety of physical traits, senses of humor, artistic bents. . . . God created something *good* when he came up with humanity.

People are also insanely frustrating! It's like the old song by the band Genesis: "I could say day, you'd say night. Tell me it's black when I know that it's white." I'm the same way, and so are you. We base whatever is normal on our own experiences or opinions. And oh, do we ever get offended easily! It's a wonder we ever find occasion for unity.

One of the most beautiful expressions of unity in the church is found in music. Yet as a drummer, I find myself at times the center of the contemporary versus traditional worship music controversy! I grew up in a liturgical church with no "modern" instrumentation. When my husband and I first led worship in Pennsylvania years ago, we introduced percussion one element at a time. For a while I was actually playing congas, bongos, a snare drum, and a few cymbals. Interestingly, as I made concessions meant to bring unity to the church, I became less certain that modern worship was the *only* culturally relevant approach. Seeking unity softened my heart . . . and made me a better drummer to boot!

Today as we lead contemporary services, I see elements of liturgy present still. Our worship songs tell stories, confess Jesus as Lord, offer repentant hearts before God's throne, and celebrate him with abandon. All of this we do as *one*, just as when I was young we would recite a psalm of praise as one. Worship music is a beautiful display of and participation in unity for the body. God says unity is the most precious offering of worship his children can offer up to him. God really doesn't want us to be like Israel of old, dividing into twelve tribes of warring jealousies, favored sons thrown under the bus by jealous brothers. The church has a new command. Come together. Surrender your right to be right. Then watch his blessings flow.

 Have you had to be right about an issue in the church? Today, lay down your rights to be right.
SW

DECEMBER 2

Being My Sister's Keeper

The LORD asked Cain, "Where is your brother? Where is Abel?" "I don't know," Cain responded. "Am I my brother's guardian?" GENESIS 4:9

Honestly? The answer to Cain's question is yes. His brother's spiritual outcome is not necessarily something he would be judged for, but at the same time, he had a responsibility. What was Cain really saying? Maybe he was insinuating his brother was God's concern, not his own. "I thought *you* were his keeper, God. What's wrong—did you lose him?" Cain's impudence is amazing here. What a dork!

But, really, don't we do the same jerky thing when we refuse to do whatever is necessary for our sisters in Christ? You have responsibility if you see your Christian sister making a mistake, doing something bad, needing a hand, walking into danger . . . you need to be there.

What if you gave someone this gift—to be her guardian? You could adopt John Ortberg's five rules for friendships that matter:

You can ask each other anything. No exceptions.
You must answer with truth. No lies.
If you don't answer, you have to explain why.
Nothing said to each other will ever be shared with others.
We don't get to judge each other, only guide with truth.*

Think about the kinds of things you could ask each other with these rules. What would it be like to ask and answer questions like the following and never be offended?

Am I a hypocrite?
Do you see me disobeying God in anything?
Am I a complainer?
Do you see Jesus in me?

One of the greatest gifts you can give to your best friend(s) is that of agreeing to be real. What an honorable job! If you're up for the taking, I think you'll find this gift to be an incredible ride!

 **Action STEP**   With whom might you be able to have a friendship contract like this?

---

*Adapted from John Ortberg, "Higher Stakes Friendship" *Leadership Journal*, February 6, 2012, http://www.christianitytoday.com/le/2012/february-online-only/higherstakes.html?start=1.

DECEMBER 3
Integrity? What's That?

Be careful to live properly among your unbelieving neighbors. Then even if they accuse you of doing wrong, they will see your honorable behavior, and they will give honor to God when he judges the world. 1 PETER 2:12

Peyton Manning was quarterback of the Indianapolis Colts for fourteen years when they decided to let their franchised (lifelong) quarterback go. This guy has an endless list of credentials—name an award, and he has won it; I think maybe he should be proudest of the award from *Sports Illustrated* columnist Rick Reilly. Reilly wrote Manning a published thank-you letter expressing thanks for fourteen years in which Manning "didn't sext anything, wreck anything, or deck anyone."

Someone also made a website where people like you and me could write about personal encounters with Manning. There aren't any bad reports. If people blogged about encounters with me over the past fourteen years, my record would pale in comparison. And columnist Reilly's concluding words? "That's grace. You had it in the huddle and you had it in the pocket and you had it at the end. So thank you, Peyton Manning. And bravo. You wore the horseshoe, but it was us who got lucky."

It would appear from today's passage that Peter would like each of us to have such a letter written on our behalf. He says we are to avoid behaviors native to our sin nature (like deceit, hypocrisy, jealousy, and unkind speech), but he never suggests we remove ourselves from this world. Instead he says we should stay in plain view, being certain the good things we do are seen—integrity. He encourages us to pursue a good reputation even among pagans—integrity.

Integrity is on a short leash in the church these days. Only one-quarter of Americans report Christianity as having an influence on their lives even though 80 percent claim to be believers in God. How do we bring integrity back? We each, one believer at a time, must embrace

- a life of discipline, by training our eyes to focus on the prize;
- a life of obedience, knowing that it's a choice in the end; and
- a life of observed behavior, by letting others grade us regularly.

Let's face it. We are not born with integrity. We train for it.

 Action **STEP** Write the three keys to integrity on an index card and use them as a bookmark for the next month.
SW

Where Your Heart Is

The Lord says, "These people say they are mine. They honor me with their lips, but their hearts are far from me. And their worship of me is nothing but man-made rules learned by rote." ISAIAH 29:13

We really enjoyed a movie called *The Invention of Lying.* Have you seen it? It centers on a man's humdrum life in a world where no one ever tells a lie. Brutal honesty is the name of the game. In a moment of desperation, the man invents lying. Because no one has ever lied before, he discovers he can get whatever he wants since his lies are still understood to be truth. Even if he changes the facts over and over again, no one questions his inconsistency.

He is in love with a girl. She has truthfully told him he is not handsome enough. His genes will not create beautiful babies. Finally, she asks if there is a chance their children could look only like her . . . and he knows he can lie. She will believe him. Because he loves her, he tells the truth. Their children would be a perfect mix of the beautiful girl and the short, fat guy with a snub nose.

The movie is clever. Real lies are not. Lies break hearts. In today's verse, the problem is that Israel kept telling God through religious services and rituals that she belonged to him. She made promises and offered sacrifices . . . and it just made him want to vomit. Her praise and worship came, as theologian Matthew Henry said, "from the teeth outward."

You and I are like God when it comes to love. I don't want false shows of affection, and I doubt you do either. The adverb *far* in Isaiah 29 is *rachaq.* Adverbs answer the question "where?" and positionally, Israel was very, very far removed from God in her heart.

The guy in *The Invention of Lying* gets the girl. She realizes he has made a choice to tell the truth. He has given her his true heart, even though the words are not flowery and beautiful. This is a gift we can give to God as well—a heart that matches our words.

 Draw God a picture and title it *Here is where you are. Here is where my heart is.*

Put a Cork in It

If you claim to be religious but don't control your tongue, you are fooling yourself, and your religion is worthless. JAMES 1:26

This morning my husband went to play tennis and left me home writing. I love to write and am immensely humbled and honored that God is allowing me to do this for a living, but . . . (Yes, here's the qualifying "but," which erases everything good I may have said leading up to that one little word.)

But . . . I love to play tennis, too, so I was pouting a little, and I sent him this text message when he hadn't come home for three hours: "Where are you? Don't worry about me, I'm safe and warm, sitting around and getting flabby."

And like the words after "but," sarcastic remarks are typically followed by the qualifier, "I was just kidding," which is only partially true. Most sarcasm has a bit of truth to it; the remark itself is like taking a little nugget of negative truth and wrapping it in a funny coat. People laugh when we make sarcastic remarks . . . but those remarks hit their target nonetheless. The problem with sarcasm is that it originates in our own insecurities, meaning we use it to cut others down to our own size.

James uses an equestrian term, *chalinagogon*, here to discuss the tongue. The reins of a horse bridle are connected to a metal bar in the horse's mouth. When pressure is applied to the reins, the horse responds to the corresponding pressure in its mouth. In this manner even the smallest person can control a massive beast. Sound like your tongue? A massive beast with a mind of its own? James makes it clear the tongue produces words and attitudes that align with our hearts. Want to know what someone's heart looks like? Listen for a while, and you should have a pretty good picture.

Your siblings, your friends, your parents, your teachers . . . even your enemies . . . do not need any additional assistance in being cut down to size. This world is providing plenty of that Kool-Aid. We have the chance to provide instead a safe place and a cool, refreshing drink from streams that give life. Can your tongue be tamed?

 Say one authentic, encouraging thing to everyone you talk to today.

DECEMBER 6
Gifts to Give Yourself

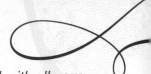

The man answered, "'You must love the LORD your God with all your heart, all your soul, all your strength, and all your mind.' And, 'Love your neighbor as yourself.'" LUKE 10:27

One of the most honest confessions we've heard about this verse came from a senior in high school. His class had been challenged to step it up in leadership. A "family" meeting was called and the entire school sat in a circle . . . looking at one another . . . until finally, this young man broke the silence. "I think the reason we have been called here is because we aren't loving each other the way the Bible says to. We're supposed to love each other the way we love ourselves. I don't know about you guys, but I happen to love myself . . . a lot. I really love me." He said more, but the point he made was already a good one. We're told to love others like we love ourselves and to put others' needs above our own (see Philippians 2:1-4). Elsewhere, God tells men to love their wives as they love their own bodies . . . again, we kind of like ourselves (see Ephesians 5:28).

That being said, there are a few things it's good to "give" yourself every day. It starts with time spent with God and with family. Get some of each every day. Ten or fifteen minutes spent with people who know you and love you best will go a long way. To know you are loved at home *and* by the King of the universe? Priceless.

Give yourself treats and rewards. Treats are those things you can look forward to each day like your morning cup of coffee or the twenty-minute cat-nap after school each day. Rewards are things set aside for a job well done such as meeting goals or completing tasks. Not only will treats and rewards (in moderation) spur you on to a life of thanksgiving, but they will also refresh your body so you can get out there and pour yourself out. It's an awesome circle, because when you refresh others, your spirit then becomes refreshed! (See Proverbs 11:25.)

Finally, give yourself time to unplug from everything, and get some time to yourself in nature. Take a beloved dog with you . . . they are perfect companions. No need for an action step today. Just put these things in practice! Oh, and temper the treats and rewards so you have time for the others!

DECEMBER 7

Just Care

I am giving you a new commandment: Love each other. Just as I have loved you, you should love each other. Your love for one another will prove to the world that you are my disciples. JOHN 13:34-35

We've heard it a hundred times. Be a good Samaritan. But few people sustain caring for as long a time period as the Good Samaritan—or Dean Germeyer—did.

Dean Germeyer has his own consulting group in Chicago and lives on the fifty-fifth floor of a condo just off Michigan Avenue. That's the big bucks area of town. One day Germeyer suddenly found himself befriending a frightened older lady on a flight home—she'd already missed one flight, and it was looking like she may not make her connection in Chicago. Germeyer himself ran her wheelchair through O'Hare when they landed, but they had missed her flight. The lady behind the airline counter smiled and gave the elderly traveler a voucher for a discounted hotel room.

Germeyer would have none of that. "She's somebody's grandma," he told *ABC World News,* just one of the media outlets that carried this "Good Samaritan" story. He loaded her in his own car, took her home where his wife had a nice meal waiting, put her up in a luxury hotel, and hired a personal car to take her to the airport the next morning.

Germeyer has been interviewed for news shows, has received a slew of "thank you" e-mails from all over the country, and now he's in a devotional for teen girls. I hope this is more than fifteen minutes of fame, because this is a great story. Someone cared! Someone went out of his way to be sure a frightened elderly traveler did not have to be afraid or alone. It didn't cost him much money—under $250, he said. It took only a portion of one night of his forty-three years of life.

John writes in 1 John 3:17, "If someone has enough money to live well and sees a brother or sister in need but shows no compassion—how can God's love be in that person?" Caring means going out of your way, walking the extra mile, giving someone the shirt off your back, and all of those other awesome clichés. It is, in the case of Jesus' followers, proof positive that we belong to him.

 **Action STEP** Find a way to care for another person in a sustained manner this week, investing a little time or money, going a little out of your way, and maybe even involving a third party who is able to help you.

DECEMBER 8
Less Truly Is More

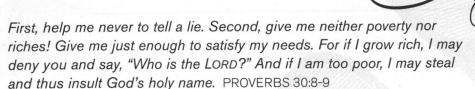

First, help me never to tell a lie. Second, give me neither poverty nor riches! Give me just enough to satisfy my needs. For if I grow rich, I may deny you and say, "Who is the LORD?" And if I am too poor, I may steal and thus insult God's holy name. PROVERBS 30:8-9

I love movies. But two hours seems an unbearably long time to sit still. The other day I actually got the whole family to sit still for *The Mighty Macs*, the story of coach Cathy Rush who led tiny Immaculata College to national championships three years in a row, including her inaugural year! There are plenty of good themes in this surprisingly good (low on the cheese factor) movie, but one scene in particular stuck with me.

Coach Rush is begging the Mother Superior for more money for the team. They are playing in ancient skirted uniforms; they have no warm-ups, no travel budget, no matching shoes; and they have to play home games at a local high school gym. This is in 1971, not the dark ages. The Mother Superior says she would be delighted to help and asks Rush to follow her. She leads the coach through a destitute hospital to a row of dorm rooms in the back. Throwing open the door of her own "home," the boss-lady nun says, "Anything I have is yours. Take whatever you need." The room contains a neatly made bed, one table, and a lamp. Point well made.

Somewhere along the line we have bought the lie that stuff will make us happy. Think of all the things you "just had to get" at Christmastime last year, now broken or forgotten, buried in a closet. Proverbs 30 has an interesting take on both having too much and having too little. Those who have too much forget they are dependent on God. And, since we can't take our possessions with us when we leave this world, we will be separated from our stuff—with no notice (because we do not know the day or hour when we will die).

How foolish to establish our worth based on how good our clothing, cars, or laptops are. No one would argue that a new shiny toy doesn't bring happiness in the beginning. It does. So does acquiring money. But they aren't lasting joys.

 Ask your family to consider a scaled-down Christmas this year. Sit down together to determine what that might look like for your family.
SW

Thank You, Thank You, Thank You

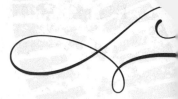

Always be joyful. Never stop praying. Be thankful in all circumstances, for this is God's will for you who belong to Christ Jesus.
1 THESSALONIANS 5:16-18

What is Thanksgiving to you? As kids we remember Thanksgiving being this incredible chance to hang out with the cousins, playing and eating once-a-year delicacies until it was finally time to fall exhausted into bed.

Christmas had a different feel and a different focus. It wasn't the play, the food, the aunts and uncles' good-natured teasing—"So, do you have a boyfriend?" The focus was this living thing in the corner of the room. Presents spilled from underneath its branches, each one picked up and shaken at least five times before the magic hour arrived. So very often, these gifts were obligatory purchases, so we'd get some cheesy twenty-dollar item that we never used from an aunt who was exhausted by the volume of twenty-dollar gifts she had to buy for an entire family of nieces and nephews. Does this sound familiar? How spoiled we can be!

One of the greatest internal struggles created by the holiday season centers around this issue of *getting*. It's hard to achieve a spirit of thanksgiving when we are drowning in good "things" and at the same time tragically aware of just how little they satisfy. Why is it so important we give thanks to God anyhow? Does he not see that this year we've been abused, lied about, bullied, and left with very few true friends? On top of that, he knows we have blown it in just about every way possible, right?

In the middle of our circumstances, God walks with us. Maybe it's not the circumstances we're supposed to say thanks for, but the fact he's here. We can complain about what we've been through, but certainly not about him, his loyalty, his affection, and his compassion. The world has taught us to look through the filter of our circumstances, but the world is pitifully blind. What if we filter our view instead through that of Jesus wanting to live in and through us? Could I experience true gratitude in knowing that the God of the universe is in this thing with me up to his neck . . . and he loves me?

 *Action* **STEP** Say thank you at least ten times today. Get in the habit of gratitude.

DECEMBER 10
What We Really Want

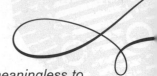

Those who love money will never have enough. How meaningless to think that wealth brings true happiness! The more you have, the more people come to help you spend it. So what good is wealth—except perhaps to watch it slip through your fingers! ECCLESIASTES 5:10-11

What do kids really want for Christmas? We don't know about you, but for us the magic of presents under the Christmas tree didn't last forever. When we were young, it was a highlight of the year for the Sears Christmas catalog to arrive in the mail, and we'd sit down with siblings, immediately marking page after page of toys we'd like Santa to deliver. By our tween years, we had all begun to notice all of those well-wrapped overindulgences were losing their charm. We found ourselves being warmed instead by a family movie night or a loud, competitive family game played out in front of a roaring fire. Hanging out with our cousins became much more anticipated than unwrapping gifts. We began wishing it could last longer, these times of family togetherness, and when our moms and dads had to shuffle back to work, the piles of still untouched gifts didn't take away the sting of a lonely day.

Almost half of British kids consulted told the *Daily Mail* in 2011 that they would rather be given time with their parents than a sack full of presents. Know what else kids say they want? Tradition!* Quick . . . what is your favorite family Christmas tradition? Close your eyes and imagine it right now, and see if a smile doesn't overtake your face. Traditions give us a sense of belonging to our tribe . . . our family. No matter how things change from year to year, we love the security of knowing that at Christmastime we (there's the belonging) always (there's the security) do (insert your family tradition).

Don't get me wrong. Kids want things. Adults want things. But things don't fulfill. Money and wealth and cool tech gadgets are not fulfilling. They are nice, they come in handy, and they provide opportunity. Check out what else Solomon said they are good for—they entice other people to come in and "help" us use up our good fortune. No, you cannot hang on to wealth and "stuff," and you wouldn't want to if you could. Family and tradition . . . now that's a different story!

 Ask your parents how your favorite Christmas family tradition was started.

*http://www.dailymail.co.uk/news/article-2073417/Women-fuss-Christmas-say-men—think-theyd-better.html#

DECEMBER 11

Buy Nothing Christmas

The crowds asked, "What should we do?" John replied, "If you have two shirts, give one to the poor. If you have food, share it with those who are hungry." LUKE 3:10-11

Not long ago my brothers and I were looking through some old family photos and found a plethora of Christmas photos featuring . . . a plethora of wrapped gifts. Seriously, it's a wonder one of us wasn't buried under an avalanche of "giftitude"! I wonder if such a holiday tragedy is on record anywhere.

My parents overdid Christmas. They enjoyed it—we were giddy with the sight of full stockings and the mountain of gifts under the tree—but it all seems like overkill now. I'm not saying my parents did anything wrong. They wanted to give us more than they had as kids, and they felt blessed to be able to do so. Each generation does some reflecting, I suppose; as you reflect on the eve of your own adulthood, what do you think is an appropriate plan for gift giving at Christmastime?

There's a trend sweeping the nation—it's been dubbed "Buy Nothing Christmas." The web page currently has sixty-three ideas for alternative ways to celebrate Christmas without losing an arm and a leg (financially speaking) in the process. This is the kind of idea always generated by one member of the family; sometimes it takes a little longer to get others to buy in. The general theme of the site seems to echo John the Baptist's instructions to three groups of people in Luke 3:10-14—all three groups were encouraged to live their lives on the principles of sharing with those who do not have enough and of not taking advantage of others.

What does it mean to be in a right relationship with God? John and the prophets have told us that repentance is evidenced in the way we treat other people. When we care only for ourselves, for what we have and what we can get, we are not in right relationship with God. John highlights the idea of giving not by saying we should give more money, but he says we should hold loosely even the things we possess. In other words, if someone needs a shirt . . . take one out of your closet, out of your suitcase, or even off your back.

 Check out the "Buy Nothing Christmas" page on Facebook, and discuss with friends and family anything on there you or they would like to try out. SW

DECEMBER 12
Stuff That Lasts

As surely as I live, says the Sovereign LORD, Sodom and her daughters were never as wicked as you and your daughters. Sodom's sins were pride, gluttony, and laziness, while the poor and needy suffered outside her door. EZEKIEL 16:48-49

What a whirlwind trip. I woke up one morning in July thinking I was on a travel hiatus until late August only to find I had been invited on a last minute two-day visit to Haiti. You don't get offered a free trip to Haiti and say, "No, thank you." I wanted to check it out for myself.

The best part of the trip was meeting the little girl I sponsor through Holt International. Noelly shyly met me inside the gate of her small, clean home and took me to her front porch, where the family spends most of their time. Noelly's grandmother has been blind for five years. She was lying on the porch suffering with a bad infection in her big toe. It may not seem like a big thing, but with no clean water and considering this family's destitution, that toe infection could have been the thing to take Grandma's life. The family had had nothing to eat for three days. They were taking in warm water with salt to stave off hunger pangs. We were able to give them a month's worth of food and a few small toys for the girls, as well as lollipops—even Grandma was lying on the porch sucking on a strawberry lolly when we left. It was like Christmas.

Only it wasn't. There is no end in sight for this family's poverty, and I know the occasional gifts I send won't change this family's life any more than the pile of gifts you will unwrap on Christmas morning will change your life. Gifts are nice, aren't they? But they don't last. Stuff does little to make our lives better—in fact, the Bible is clear that things clutter our lives and cause us to forget God.

This is why God says it's better to give than receive. Sure, Noelly liked her toys a little, but what really made her eyes light up was food, a hug from a new friend, and the fact we took time to be with her. Her mom asked only one question as I left. "Will you be back?" With all my heart, I hope the answer is yes.

 Check out your local news today. Who is suffering just outside your doorstep?

DECEMBER 13

An Experiment in Clutter

Everything else is worthless when compared with the infinite value of knowing Christ Jesus my Lord. For his sake I have discarded everything else, counting it all as garbage, so that I could gain Christ. PHILIPPIANS 3:8

On a scale of one to ten, how difficult are these items for you to throw away?

- Stuffed animals from childhood? _____
- Souvenirs picked up on vacations? _____
- Old youth group and camp shirts? _____
- Photographs of places and people you no longer remember? _____

It's tough to part with things of sentimental value, but in the words of the immortal playwrights . . . *You Can't Take It with You*!

I was on the beach in Haiti when a man came along selling souvenirs. If you've ever been to a non-Western country, you learned quickly what the words "hard sell" mean. These guys don't take no for an answer. (Once when I was in Egypt, a man picked me up, put me on his camel, and then demanded money to help me down. It doesn't help to insist it wasn't your idea. They have learned just enough English to get you up there, but not enough to argue with you!) My instinct was to pick up a little something that said Haiti on it, but then I started thinking *why*? I'm on a quest to be satisfied with less and to buy less . . . why clutter up my house with one more thing? I've learned something about my reminders from other trips—I have warm memories when I see them, but I notice them only once every five years.

What if you went through your room? Could you pare down what you have, using a litmus test of how often you look at it, hold it, show it off, or appreciate it? Could you ask for and buy Christmas gifts using the same test? Paul wanted to be sure he valued only one thing—that relationship with Jesus. It's funny we would use such a weak word as "worthless" in translation when Paul uses a rather offensive Greek word (*skybala*) bordering on "poop" as its meaning. He used to value his position and his goodness, much as we might value possessions. But it's all waste compared to knowing Jesus. Sometimes it just takes us a while to realize it.

 *Action* **STEP**   Try paring down the room with the test above. How did it go?
SW

Shrewd Celebrations

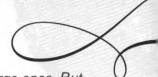

If you are faithful in little things, you will be faithful in large ones. But if you are dishonest in little things, you won't be honest with greater responsibilities. And if you are untrustworthy about worldly wealth, who will trust you with the true riches of heaven? LUKE 16:10-11

Okay, this is an idea for Christmas that is really "out there," but I'm going to pay homage here to my pragmatic youngest daughter (her sister would call her stingy). I've heard Marie—a regular all-nighter on Black Friday—say for three years running now, "We should open Christmas gifts *after* Christmas. We'd spend a guaranteed 70 percent less."

I think Marie is onto something for several reasons. First of all, knowing Marie, I also know her motivations. They are not, "This way we could get more stuff." Marie has taught me to love "stuff" less. She is satisfied with little and always has been. She is also satisfied with spending little, and this is likely very good money management. Money is a tool . . . useful in good hands and dangerous in the hands of a fool. Good or harm can be wrought with the use of the same dollar, which is why money itself is amoral. It's neither good nor bad. But the possession of it is a sacred trust. While money is entrusted to individuals, God doesn't intend the majority of it to be used for personal gain or consumption. That's why in the parables the servants who did nothing with the money entrusted to them were called wicked, and the responsibility was removed (see, for example, Matthew 25:14-29). If I spend less on Christmas, it doesn't mean I have more to tuck away in the bank. It means I have more to give.

Marie is also right because more Americans identify Christmas as a time to be with family than a time to remember Jesus' birth . . . and this is backward. I'm not on a crusade to banish shopping mall Santa or boycott "Grandma Got Run Over by a Reindeer." But Jesus is our everything. He is real, and he is eternal. Apart from him we can do nothing. And we definitely pay more homage to the make-believe chubby bunny in the red suit than we do to the one who sacrificed his very inheritance that you and I might simply have one. Maybe putting a few days between the real and the make-believe would do us some good? It's something to think about anyhow.

Share this devotion with Mom and Dad. What do they think?

SW

Trouble Brewing

"Don't be afraid, Mary," the angel told her, *"for you have found favor with God! You will conceive and give birth to a son, and you will name him Jesus. He will be very great and will be called the Son of the Most High. The Lord God will give him the throne of his ancestor David. And he will reign over Israel forever; his Kingdom will never end!"* LUKE 1:30-33

Wait, I'm pregnant? Before I'm married?

I wonder if Mary had ever pondered such a thing. Her parents had arranged a *nice* marriage for her with a nice man, but before the arranged time of the wedding a horrible truth was made known. The "virgin" was with child. Now, I have no qualms about the authority of God's Word. Mary, it has been made clear, was with child because of God's work through his Spirit, not through natural means involving Joseph. Mary was a virgin indeed. But there was no room in the consciousness of these simple, hardworking people for such a fantastic story. Mary must have been looked upon as a girl who had committed a terrible indiscretion. Joseph's future was in danger of being compromised as well. This was the original *16 and Pregnant* plot!

Matthew 1 says that Joseph was a good man. He did not want Mary to suffer any more than he wanted to bear the brunt of so much humiliation, so he decided to divorce her (end the engagement) quietly. God intervened by letting Mary and Joseph have a peek at his plans, but consider this . . . he probably didn't make that same visitation to everyone else in town. The couple were going to be social pariahs and that was that. Perhaps it helped to know Mary would give birth to the Son of God . . . perhaps it only complicated matters. How do you discipline the Son of God? Teach him? Mold him? Joseph and Mary surely knew now more than ever how very simple they were.

This is the family into which our Savior was born. Two frightened people, not even yet married, faced the future given them not by choice, but by prophecy.

 Wow. Take a few minutes to journal what your thoughts might be if you were in Mary's shoes.

DECEMBER 16

No Room in the Inn?

She gave birth to her first child, a son. She wrapped him snugly in strips of cloth and laid him in a manger, because there was no lodging available for them. LUKE 2:7

What would happen if you got pregnant in high school? Well, you know, your parents would have to help to answer that question. We think they'd probably love you right through the mess. There's an unwritten promise that parents make when they adopt or give birth. They are in through thick and thin! God has made a similar promise to us.

No one made Mary and Joseph such a promise, and they hadn't even made a mess! They were walking entirely in God's will. Gossip is not a new phenomenon—can you imagine the whispers and stares as Mary and Joseph made their way toward Bethlehem to register for the census? It would be a relief to get away for a few months.

Bethlehem was a small town. When we hear the word *inn*, we typically think of a building with a lot of rooms and a pool our parents won't let us swim in for fear of bacterial infections. No such concept existed in the Middle East. But hospitality was a necessity for desert travelers; many homes contained an "upper room" so the weary could grab some rest while their pack animals were turned loose to feed.

It is unclear in the Bible whether this unoffered spare room belonged to a family member or to a stranger, but either way the results are sad and astonishing. This girl is about to give birth to a baby, and not one person can make room for a proper birthplace. No one clears out another guest so that Mary can give birth in privacy. Not one family member steps forward and offers lodging or assistance. (Maybe they'd heard the rumors!)

Consider the power of God in this. You cannot squelch his purposes. Even though the baby was born into abject poverty and disregarded even by Joseph's relatives in Bethlehem, it wasn't long before wise men from the East came to seek him out, to pay homage, and to bring gifts appropriate for a King.

 **Action STEP** Read Luke 1 and 2 and reflect on the historical images of Jesus' birth. Do you have a guest room for this poor, humble family in your heart this Christmas?

Honoring the King

When they saw the star, they were filled with joy! They entered the house and saw the child with his mother, Mary, and they bowed down and worshiped him. MATTHEW 2:10-11

They say that once you win an Olympic gold medal, your life changes forever. Suddenly you are vaulted (a great pun if you're a gymnast) to megastar status. It has to be mind boggling.

Jesus deserved the same treatment at his birth. Here are some things the prophet Isaiah said about his qualifications:

- "The Lord himself will give you a sign: The virgin will be with child and will give birth to a son, and will call him Immanuel." (7:14, NIV)
- "He will be called: Wonderful Counselor, Mighty God, Everlasting Father, Prince of Peace." (9:6)
- "I will give him a portion among the great, and he will divide the spoils with the strong, because he poured out his life unto death, and was numbered with the transgressors." (53:12, NIV)

Yep, Jesus should have been a rock star from the start, yet his early days were somewhat quiet, normal, and inconspicuous . . . if it weren't for the visit from three guys from the East.

We sing "We Three Kings," but a better translation for these gents (likely many more than three) is wise men. These men were probably Persian and had long ago been entrusted prophetically by Daniel to watch for a messianic event heralded by a great star. They were not necessarily God followers . . . yet. But then they worshiped with the gifts they had been inspired to bring.

With gold they worshiped him as king. Frankincense set him apart as a priest. And myrrh? This was an embalming oil, signifying his atoning death for your sin and mine. Legend says these men returned home not only God followers, but ambassadors and priests for the God they had now seen and believed. Their first job was complete—waiting and watching for that star. Their second job was just beginning—bringing the good news of a Savior, who was Christ the Lord.

 *Action* **STEP**

ACTION STEP 1: Select a gift for Christ as Lord. What can you daily give to worship him?

ACTION STEP 2: (Be sure to "like" Dannah Gresh on Facebook today. It's her birthday!)

The End of Silence

Suddenly, an angel of the Lord appeared among them, and the radiance of the Lord's glory surrounded them. They were terrified, but the angel reassured them. "Don't be afraid!" he said. "I bring you good news that will bring great joy to all people. The Savior—yes, the Messiah, the Lord—has been born today in Bethlehem, the city of David! And you will recognize him by this sign: You will find a baby wrapped snugly in strips of cloth, lying in a manger." LUKE 2:9-12

Don't you just hate it when a new friend (especially when it's a guy) says she (or he) will call you or text you and then . . . nothing. Nada. Zip. Silence. Or how about when you and a friend get into a spat, but kind of make up? At least, you think you have and she says she'll Skype you. But never does. Excruciating, right?

God was once silent for *four hundred years*, setting up a favorite moment of the Christmas story! When Malachi wrote the last words of a message from God, it was the end of Act I. There was no king on the throne in Jerusalem (it was captive to the Persian Empire), but there were priests on duty, all descendants of Aaron as God had commanded. The people were oppressed but united.

You know how when you go to a play there is often a big scene change between Act I and Act II? God did the same here. The curtain reopens in the New Testament to a king on the throne who is a descendant of Esau (Herod) and priests in the Temple who do not even know their lineage. Rome ruled the world, including Herod's "kingdom"; all of Israel was fractured.

These words of the angels to the shepherds in the fields were the beginning of Act II. The scene had been changed in the darkness, and now the lights were up again! Can you imagine hearing God speak after four hundred years of silence? Perhaps these shepherds had heard stories of a God who spoke to his people, but they had never seen it for themselves. No wonder they trembled!

Do you think God is working in your world today? The wars and "rumors of wars" (Matthew 24:6; Mark 13:7) . . . do you think he is busy getting the scenery changed for Act III? We do. When God is "silent," he is never truly silent. Get ready for Act III, friend. It's the final curtain.

Action **STEP** Read the news or watch a broadcast tonight. Ask God to give you peace, knowing he is readying this world for the final curtain.

Wanted: Dead or Alive!

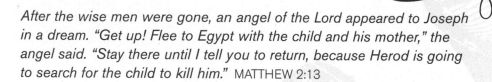

After the wise men were gone, an angel of the Lord appeared to Joseph in a dream. "Get up! Flee to Egypt with the child and his mother," the angel said. "Stay there until I tell you to return, because Herod is going to search for the child to kill him." MATTHEW 2:13

I was shot at not long ago. Well, it wasn't really *me* the shooters were going after, but the effect was the same. Some men on a motorcycle had committed an armed robbery on the street just outside my car in Haiti. The next thing I knew, two guys from a gas station were shooting at the robbers three feet away from my car window . . . and the guys on the bike were shooting back! Aaagh! I hit the floor of the car.

While I wasn't the target, I still felt attacked. Jesus was the target of many attacks, even at his birth. The throne in Jerusalem was occupied by an impostor named Herod. Herod was pro-Rome, and as such he was able to buy, cheat, and bribe his way onto the throne of Israel. Herod was not, as required by God's law, from the lineage of David. Prophecies about a Messiah terrified him, as he misunderstood Jesus' Kingdom to be an earthly one. It was in his heart even before Jesus' birth to take out anyone who threatened his throne.

Herod wasn't the only one unhappy about Jesus' birth. All of Jerusalem was concerned. They wanted no king but Herod, who allowed them to pursue the desires of their flesh with little consequence. Though they were under the oppressive thumb of Roman rule and were not truly independent, they were at least left to pursue their own devices without interference. A new king, even one who had come to set them free, could seriously disrupt things.

Many people hesitate to receive Jesus for the same reasons today. There is a throne room in our hearts, and a throne that never sits vacant. Someone always is ruling. It's either us, a paralyzing fear, someone we have let rule our emotions through idolatry, or it is the King of kings himself. Like Herod, many seek to keep him from his place on that throne. But unlike Israel, you and I have a choice. We *can* invite Jesus to reign.

 Does Jesus sit on the throne in your heart? Ask him to do so, carefully deposing everything else that has ever reigned there.
SW

DECEMBER 20
Defying Science

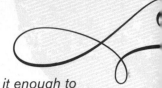

Isaiah said, "Listen well, you royal family of David! Isn't it enough to exhaust human patience? Must you exhaust the patience of my God as well? All right then, the Lord himself will give you the sign. Look! The virgin will conceive a child! She will give birth to a son and will call him Immanuel (which means 'God is with us')." ISAIAH 7:13-14

What a bunch of hoopla swarms around the Virgin Birth! Larry King is regarded as the greatest television interviewer of all time. Asked whom he would most like to interview, he said Jesus. What would he most like to ask Jesus? "Were you really born to a virgin?" King said that answer would define all of history for him.

King is right. So much of both history and the future hang in the balance of that answer. Who is Jesus? Is he a misunderstood man, perhaps one of the best and most influential ever to live? Or is he God?

Apparently atheist Richard Dawkins also understands the importance of the issue. He has dubbed virgin births, and all other miracles, violators of the principles of science. Thank you, Mr. Dawkins. This is the precise point. Miracles are that which only God can produce. Even though God had said the Messiah must come through David's lineage, man was unable to produce a line of kings morally healthy enough to naturally fulfill this prophetic word. King after king did what was evil in God's eyes. God had to supersede David's lineage to do what man was unable to do—produce a King with the credentials (perfection) to pay for our sins.

Miracles defy science because science, to be measured and proven, involves repeated observations. The Virgin Birth happened only once, thus it is outside the confines of science. How has Christmas become so devoid of this truth? Mary became pregnant having performed absolutely no act of sexual intimacy! While the more commercial aspects of Jesus' birth (the manger and the wise men) make for a great Hallmark movie, we have to ask if perhaps we have lost our wonderment that God not only chose to become one of us, but he chose to start in the same manner. An embryo nourished in the womb, finally turning upside down in the birth canal, and attached to Mary by a cord that Joseph likely cut with shaking hands. Immanuel. God is *with* us!

 This Christmas we are fighting to get the wonder back. Will you join us?

DECEMBER 21
A Pagan Celebration

Some think one day is more holy than another day, while others think every day is alike. You should each be fully convinced that whichever day you choose is acceptable. ROMANS 14:5

Christmas has its critics. Of course you know we don't celebrate on the actual date of Jesus' birth. He was born in January . . . or April. One tradition says April Fools' Day started for "fools" who insisted Jesus was born April 1. Who knows? We don't, and perhaps that is just the point. Humans get so hung up on dates and traditions and festivals. If we knew the actual day, there would no doubt be a sect of people worshiping the date itself, completely missing the point.

The early church didn't celebrate the birth of Christ. But back in AD 336 the Roman Empire had its first Christian ruler, Constantine. He wanted to "Christianize" the empire from top to bottom, so he declared an already pagan holiday, the Feast of Saturn, to be Jesus' birthday. We've adopted most of the feast's practices, including time off from work, the singing of songs, and the giving of gifts.

Almost every element of our current practices is adapted from pagan traditions! From Santa entering the home via chimney, to the Yule log, to the Christmas tree, pagan practices can be credited for our current behavior. Is Christmas, then, a pagan celebration? That is up to you and me.

As much as we've encountered the "Merry Christmas" versus "Happy Holidays" debate in recent years, Christmas is still an excellent opportunity for us to lift Jesus up publicly at a time when hearts are more open than any other time of the year. People are acutely aware of God's presence during the month of December as those who have wandered during the year sense a call to return to the church and to set things right in their lives. The fact that some attend church only a couple of times a year and fall off their New Year's resolutions like a tyke coming off the training wheels should not deter us.

In effect, what has happened is this: people in pagan cultures have heard the Good News and redirected their traditions to point toward Jesus. Maybe we should stop defaming this and do the same with our lives!

 Lead a family discussion. How do we point others to Jesus during the Christmas season?

Why So Sad?

Why am I discouraged? Why is my heart so sad? I will put my hope in God! I will praise him again—my Savior and my God! PSALM 42:5-6

Enough of sugarplum fairies and adorable North Pole elves! Let's talk about the rougher edges of Christmas: depression. I have had my fair share of struggling with depression. Once to the point of needing medical intervention. If you struggle, I can identify. Most often depression is triggered by something— exhaustion from overworking yourself, the loss of someone you love, a life-changing move, or a financial crisis. There's usually a reason for it. Christmas is the most difficult time of the year for millions of Americans. Reports of depression during the holidays, in fact, spike as much as 45 percent on a yearly basis! That's a lot of heaviness floating around in the eggnog. I think it's because all that happiness around us can be extra annoying if we have reason to be sad.

Notice in verse 5 above that the psalmist is asking a rhetorical question ("Why am I so sad?"). He does not bother to answer himself, possibly due to the burden such an answer would be. It's not a good place to dwell. Instead the psalmist moves on to what he can control. He can praise God. If depression is the sickness (and it is, in a very real measure), then praising God is the medicine.

We don't want to make light of depression. It is a serious struggle for many, and even warranted at times. My mom is still missing my dad like crazy two years after he has gone to be with Jesus. She has moments of depression. But God would not promise a way out if such a way did not exist. To give him praise, he says, delivers us from a heaviness that would otherwise sink us.

Think of the last time you were sick. As you began to take medication, it's likely you did not notice a change with the first pill. But over time, did you notice a lifting of symptoms? The aches began to lessen. Strength returned. Sleep came more easily. It is the same with praise, if only we will have the faith to swallow such a prescription.

 If you are experiencing an unusual heaviness, focus daily on praise. Help others you know to do the same. (If this heaviness has lasted a long time and has you thinking about hurting yourself, tell someone immediately. As in, right now!)
DG

DECEMBER 23
A Warrior's Perspective

I knew you before I formed you in your mother's womb. Before you were born I set you apart. JEREMIAH 1:5

Gianna Jessen was hated from the moment she was conceived. True, there is a lot of Scripture that contradicts such a statement. But early in life Gianna received some strong signals from those around her that she was not wanted.

Gianna survived a saline abortion during her birth mother's third trimester of pregnancy, arriving in the world at just over two pounds. She was not expected to live. Her first seven months of life were spent with a foster family who refused to nurture her. Instead, they kept her isolated in a back bedroom.

Gianna's next foster parent was told that baby Gianna would never move. But she did. Her foster parent was told Gianna would never hold up her own head. But she did. She was told Gianna would never crawl. But she did. And now Gianna walks with no braces or walker. She travels the world telling people about the only thing that matters to her, which is Jesus. She has run two marathons. She has a killer good voice. And here's how Gianna explains her survival. . . .

"They just didn't know who they were trying to kill," she says.

Like Jeremiah, Gianna has possessed a God-ordained purpose from the moment she was conceived. Her mother's hatred (she has contacted Gianna and still has no affection for her) could not thwart God's purpose. Gianna's struggle with cerebral palsy could not thwart God's purpose. Loneliness, longing, and years of patronizing comments have not been able to destroy God's purpose in this warrior's heart. She speaks with greater clarity and a fiercer faith with each passing year.

How about you? Do you know the fierce protective love of your heavenly Father? Do you know that as he knit you together, his work was not haphazard? Can you believe he sees you, enthralled by the wonder of what he created in you? Are you willing to trust his protection, even when it looks like hardship? And as you clear your throat, can you imagine that maybe, just maybe, you, too, are alive by and for divine appointment?

 Bow before the King of kings and wait. Now write down what you heard him say to you, about you, and on your behalf. When this world comes at you, do they have any idea who they are messing with? This is a warrior's perspective.

Evangelism 101 . . .
Find Your Style

Jesus came and told his disciples, "I have been given all authority in heaven and on earth. Therefore, go and make disciples of all the nations, baptizing them in the name of the Father and the Son and the Holy Spirit. Teach these new disciples to obey all the commands I have given you. And be sure of this: I am with you always, even to the end of the age."
MATTHEW 28:18-20

A lot of people are talking about Jesus today. It's Christmas Eve, and even those who don't usually attend church may take a stab at it tonight. (Though, surprisingly or not, it's the second-highest church attendance day, with Easter coming in first.) Why not take this opportunity to share your faith?

Not everyone has the wiring of a street preacher, so please don't process the great commission as, "Oh great, I have to go stand on a street corner and wave my Bible at passersby." Then again, maybe you have been wired to do just that.

You may be confrontational, like Peter. Peter cut off the ear of the soldier trying to arrest Jesus. Yet he was the same in the Temple courts, winning thousands as he challenged, "You, with the help of wicked men, put [Jesus] to death by nailing him to the cross" (Acts 2:23, NIV). That's pretty direct! But people repented.

Maybe you are intellectual like Paul. Paul was able at the drop of a hat to turn biblical truths into modern-day parables appealing to poets, philosophers, and scholars. He reasoned with people right up to the door of belief.

A lot of people lean toward a testimonial approach—many who were healed by Jesus ran home and brought people to see the man who had just rescued them. After Jesus rose from the dead, he appeared to hundreds, giving them quite the mind-blowing story to tell!

Relational evangelism is almost equivalent to hanging out. Matthew would first earn the trust of sinners and tax collectors, then invite them to discuss the Scriptures. Perhaps you are a great influencer and can get people to attend church and concerts with you. Or maybe you are a servant, causing people to ask, "Why do you do the nice things you do?"

 You've got time today. It's a do-anything-you-want kind of day. Find an "Evangelism Style Assessment" online and determine which style is yours. How can you use your unique wiring to answer Jesus' command?

A Spoken Testimony

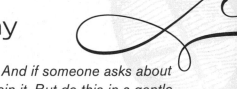

You must worship Christ as Lord of your life. And if someone asks about your Christian hope, always be ready to explain it. But do this in a gentle and respectful way. Keep your conscience clear. Then if people speak against you, they will be ashamed when they see what a good life you live because you belong to Christ. 1 PETER 3:15-16

Merry Christmas!

The night that Jesus was born, the angels announced his arrival. Shepherds went to see him as a result. Sometimes we just have to speak about him to get people to come. About 78 percent of Christians cite a personal relationship or friendship as the reason they became a follower of Jesus. Compare that to the 6 percent who cite conversion via a pastor or 5 percent via Sunday school. Even allowing for margin of error, we can see our public lives pack a wallop.

So . . . that being said . . . do you ever need to speak up? All signs, again, point to yes. Otherwise Peter would not have said we should be ready to explain our hope at a moment's notice.

Many people hope it will be enough to live out a strong and silent testimony, and most days that probably is enough. But works can be done by anyone, and sometimes they speak to nothing more than the goodness of the human spirit. The spoken word of your testimony can only be done through the power of the Holy Spirit, and it points directly to God's glory. The truth is, lifestyle evangelism and a spoken testimony work together as a symphony! When one is lived and the other is shared, a work of art emerges that causes something to stir in the hearts of all who see and hear it.

What is your story? Half of your symphony is composed as you live your life before the eyes of your neighbors, family, and friends. They *are* watching. But that's only half of the story. What will you say when you are asked to explain all they have seen?

It doesn't matter if your story is wild or tame; it's a story needing to be told in order for your symphony to be complete. Somewhere out there is a friend or neighbor-to-be who is going to need to be swept away by the song of your life. That's pretty amazing, isn't it?

 Celebrate Christ's birth today by writing out the story of learning to follow Jesus. Keep it simple, and don't worry if it's short. It's your song.

What Exactly Is It That Jesus Did?

By his death, Jesus opened a new and life-giving way through the curtain into the Most Holy Place. And since we have a great High Priest who rules over God's house, let us go right into the presence of God with sincere hearts fully trusting him. For our guilty consciences have been sprinkled with Christ's blood to make us clean, and our bodies have been washed with pure water. HEBREWS 10:20-22

Steph decided not to date until she was out of high school. She just wanted to focus on Jesus for four years. Wes agreed to wait for her. But through it all, he bought her gifts and wrote her cards as if they were dating, waiting until the day he could share them with her. After Steph's high school graduation, Wes presented her with a trunk full of the gifts and cards that had amassed. Wow.

As we were preparing to write these devotions, Steph sent a list of things she wished she had known in high school; we were surprised to learn that she—a girl who had lived so counterculturally in an effort to be in relationship with Jesus—had struggled with understanding what Jesus had done for her.

We all fail now and then, and this is where bondage often sets in. *How can God forgive when I mess up over and over again?* Even in the Old Testament, God made a way for sins to be forgiven. If his people presented their best sacrifice, he would forgive the sins of the previous year (see Hebrews 9). God invited only one man into his presence—the high priest. And this he did only once a year—the Day of Atonement. A thick, heavy veil separated the room where God met the priest from the rest of the Tabernacle. But that wasn't all the veil separated. It separated people from God.

When Jesus died, there was a great earthquake. That veil, now in the Temple, was torn in two and crumpled to the floor. Jesus' body, too, was torn to shed his blood for the removal of our sins. His life became a permanent sacrifice, not one having to be made yearly. The atoning blood is no longer sprinkled on an altar, but on our consciences, so we can come to him with boldness. How can I walk in freedom even in moments of failure? God has made a clear way to come into his presence. He has set us free! And whomever the Son sets free . . . is free indeed (see John 8:36)!

 Go right into the Holy of Holies, and lay down your guilt once and for all! Stay until you know God welcomes you, has cleansed you, and has freed you!

When People Don't Agree

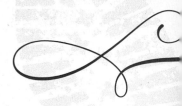

Let all who are spiritually mature agree on these things. If you disagree on some point, I believe God will make it plain to you. PHILIPPIANS 3:15-16

No two people will agree on matters of belief 100 percent of the time. You can be as gentle as a newborn kitten and still find yourself on the back side of an argument. What to do?

As Paul addresses the church here, he talks about two kinds of maturity. Just a few verses prior to today's passage, he says he has not yet achieved perfection (verse 12). Paul didn't think he would be perfect on earth. He is simply saying he has not yet received the fullness of his salvation—*after* he dies, he will be raised again completely restored in Christ. This is the thing Paul insists we agree upon. As you share your faith, this is the key:

> All have sinned and fallen short of God's standards. (See Romans 3:23.)
> The wages (consequence) of sin is death. (See Romans 6:23.)
> While we were still sinners, Jesus died for us. (See Romans 5:8.)
> Three days later he defeated the grave and rose again. (See Romans 1:4.)
> If you agree Jesus is Lord and believe God raised him from the dead, you
>   will be saved. (See Romans 10:9.)

If people disagree with you on these points, we can then say with confidence that they are not (yet) Christ followers. There are plenty of other issues though. What movies are inappropriate? Do you go to heaven if you've committed suicide? Should we have non-Christian friends? What exactly is a swear word? Paul has a lot to say to the church about righteous living; here he gives a helpful basic summary that speaks to a second kind of maturity. He says if we are ready to run the race, having trained well, then we can pick up some clarity on these other issues on the run.

Paul is personally steadfast on issues of righteous living. He does not engage long term with the church on these secondary issues, and he cautions elsewhere not to get into useless arguments. Arguing is not evangelism. Be clear on what righteous living looks like. Be ready to talk about it and model it. But focus on the gospel. Live and let learn in all other areas.

 *Action* **STEP** Look up and memorize the verses from Romans listed above. Don't argue righteousness with anyone who doesn't understand these basics first.

DECEMBER 28
How Not to Hate

How can they call on him to save them unless they believe in him? And how can they believe in him if they have never heard about him? And how can they hear about him unless someone tells them? And how will anyone go and tell them without being sent? That is why the Scriptures say, "How beautiful are the feet of messengers who bring good news!"
ROMANS 10:14-15

I know a few amazing illusionists who are believers. I once spent a day with Living Illusions. Kristen does amazing escape acts from underneath beds of nails or from the inside of a water torture cell, and Kevin's eye for the theatrical has earned the duo spots on the Discovery Channel and at the Olympics.

Many of you will remember Brock Gill from recent Winter Jam tours. Brock is not only a great illusionist with an impressive résumé, but he goes well out of his way to be sure his fans are cared for. Not many celebs will do that.

Then there's Penn & Teller. No, I don't know P&T, but Penn has something in common with the others. As die hard as Living Illusions and Brock Gill are about their faith, Penn Jillette is equally passionate about his belief that there *is no* God. He defines himself as "beyond atheist." I believe Penn Jillette, a brilliant man, is in a world of trouble. I also believe he would thank me for saying so.

A few years back Penn was offered the gift of a Bible from a man in the audience. What followed was a thoughtful response by Penn on YouTube that ended up being one of the best treatises on evangelism ever. "If you believe that there's a heaven and hell and people could be going to hell, or not getting eternal life or whatever, and you think that it's not really worth telling them this because that would make it socially awkward . . . how much do you have to hate somebody to not proselytize? How much do you have to hate somebody to believe that everlasting life is possible and not tell them that?"

What you have to share is the best news possible. Even Penn recognized that the man gave him a Bible out of one motive—love. He loved him enough to risk rejection. Even this hardened atheist regarded the man's feet as beautiful, for he had brought a message of grace rather than condemnation. How are your feet looking these days?

 **Action STEP**   Give a gift today along with a little note expressing God's love. Give this gift to a nonbeliever, and do this because you know your *news* is *good*.
SW

DECEMBER 29

It's Us versus Them . . . Isn't It?

When I first came to you, dear brothers and sisters, I didn't use lofty words and impressive wisdom to tell you God's secret plan. For I decided that while I was with you I would forget everything except Jesus Christ, the one who was crucified. I came to you in weakness—timid and trembling. 1 CORINTHIANS 2:1-3

Here's an interesting question: Is your life influenced primarily by Christian culture, or by Jesus? Many people seem to have forgotten the latter option exists.

Author Donald Miller tells the story in his book *Searching for God Knows What* of the time he "shared the gospel" with a group of Christian college students. Warning them in advance he would leave out one important element, their job was to identify the missing piece. He went on to talk about sin, the curse of death, the promises of righteous living, the unmatched splendor of heaven, and the importance of repentance. Not one student could tell him what he had omitted . . . though he steeped his presentation in Christian culture, not once had Miller mentioned the name of Jesus.

How then do *we* share the gospel with *them* . . . whoever *they* may be? Carl Medearis (*Speaking of Jesus: The Art of Not-Evangelism*) says an "us versus them" mentality does not align with Scripture. Jesus never drew polarizing lines with the crowds who came to him. The New Testament is a story of walls coming down. There is no Greek or Jew . . . there is only Jesus. There are no slaves or free men . . . there is only Jesus. There is no male or female . . . there is only Jesus (see Galatians 3:28).

Why does this matter? We cannot carry out the command to love our neighbors if we are continually choosing sides. Those who are not like us do not need to be remade in our image. They need to know Jesus. That Egyptian kid who is a Muslim—he is my neighbor. That Indian girl who grew up Hindu—she is my neighbor. Medearis believes Christians should stop "evangelizing," which puts the responsibility (and credit) on us, but he doesn't believe we should stop telling people about Jesus, an act allowing Jesus alone to run the show.

 Talk about Jesus . . . a lot. But don't do this expecting any returns. Do it because you love Jesus. Let him draw people to himself. That's his job.

The Problem with Disconnect

[Jesus] told them, "Go into all the world and preach the Good News to everyone. Anyone who believes and is baptized will be saved. But anyone who refuses to believe will be condemned." MARK 16:15-16

It's interesting to imagine various things in Scripture as they *could* relate to technology today.

Revelation says when Jesus returns, "every eye will see him" (Revelation 1:7, NIV). We have no problem conceding that nothing is too difficult for God. My grandma, however, believed this verse possibly alluded to live satellite feeds. Imagine Jesus' return on FOX's live satellite feed. Interesting.

John describes the locusts of the fifth plague looking "like horses prepared for battle" (Revelation 9:7). Their wings sound "like the thundering of many horses and chariots rushing into battle" (Revelation 9:9, NIV). Many have hypothesized these locusts could be military aircraft.

It's never been easier than today to obey Jesus' command to "go into all the world." Social networking sites and smartphones put us in instantaneous communication with all seven continents—it truly is the World Wide Web. Discussions about faith-related issues have increased with social networking, yet according to The Barna Group, only 7 percent of Americans report any change in spiritual status over the past five years. We are talking more about Jesus, but it's having little to no impact.

As much as we talk or tweet about Jesus, we need to remember we fight a barrage of bad news items on those Internet feeds. There is sexual abuse in the church. Hate speech toward homosexuals claims to be reflective of God's heart. People see and hear and read . . . and say, "No, thank you. Not if that's Jesus." You and I know Jesus—the real Jesus—but sometimes even we forget he isn't an American, he's not of an economic class, he doesn't affiliate with any political party, and his ways are not our ways. Somehow we need to understand him in the same way we hope to present him, and it may begin with admitting we haven't arrived yet. The Good News remains the same! Keep talking! Keep tweeting! But by all means, keep getting to know Jesus.

 Don't rely on the Internet as your lifeline. Hold a real Bible in your hands, and interact with real people face-to-face. Our Facebook one-liners just aren't cutting it! SW

DECEMBER 31

There's the Gospel . . . And Then There's Everything Else

God loved the world so much that he gave his one and only Son, so that everyone who believes in him will not perish but have eternal life. JOHN 3:16

Without mentioning specifics, I recently caught an interesting comment in the heat of one of our nation's largest faith controversies. A news crew was interviewing a man who had spent the day defending religious freedom, including a stint holding some picket signs. "Oh yeah," the man smiled into the camera. "I've been cussed at, called names, even flipped the bird. But that comes with the territory when you are defending the gospel."

I caught two flaws in the man's statement. The first comes at the end of his comment. Jesus' commission was to make disciples (*mathēteusate*). This is a long-term command involving a progressive learning of God's Word. Jesus also said we were to baptize new believers and teach them to obey; nowhere does he commission us to *defend* the gospel. In 1 Peter 3:15, Peter writes about making a "defense" (*apologia*) for the tenets of faith. Since the apologia was a Greek system of argumentation that included formal speeches, it is not wise to equate quippy statements on poster board with the kind of reasoning Peter speaks of. This is why Peter's words are better translated, "If someone asks about your Christian hope, always be ready to explain it."

Second, the man on the news said his defense was of the gospel. Here we must be very careful . . . the gospel is a message of Good News. Now I'm *totally* into holiness, just ask my kids. It's kind of my soapbox. But even I know the gospel is the good news of salvation by faith and not by works! Even I know the Son of Man didn't come into the world to condemn it but to save it. This man was standing up for a matter of holiness . . . not to be confused with the gospel. This guy sought to condemn a behavior; the *gospel* (Jesus) came to set man free from such behavior. There is a difference.

Here's the crazy thing . . . I didn't disagree with the man on the news. I disagreed that his actions were defending the gospel. It doesn't get much plainer than John 3:16. This is the Good News. Stick to this when you share your faith, and you will bear fruit.

 Happy New Year! Start the year well by memorizing John 3:16-18.
SW

Topical Index

To learn about more
great books and live events
by Dannah Gresh
and Suzy Weibel
go to *purefreedom.org*

PURE FREEDOM

Dannah Gresh's home for connecting moms and daughters